By the same author

Cicely Saunders – The Founder of the Modern Hospice Movement
Changing the Face of Death
The Gardeners
The World Walks By (with Sue Masham)
Teresa of Avila
The Road to Canterbury – A Modern Pilgrimage

Tutu

Archbishop without Frontiers

Shirley du Boulay

Hodder & Stoughton
LONDON SYDNEY AUCKLAND

Copyright © 1988 by Shirley du Boulay

First published in Great Britain in 1988. This edition 1996.

The right of Shirley du Boulay to be identified as the
Author of the Work has been asserted by her in accordance
with the Copyright, Designs and Patents Act 1988.

10 9 8 7 6 5 4 3 2 1

British Library Cataloguing in Publication Data
A record for this book is available from the British Library

ISBN 0 340 64274 2

Typeset by Hewer Text Composition Services, Edinburgh
Printed and bound in Great Britain by
Cox & Wyman Ltd, Reading, Berks

Hodder and Stoughton Ltd
A division of Hodder Headline PLC
338 Euston Road
London NW1 3BH

To all who seek peace and justice
in South Africa

Contents

Acknowledgments 8
Map of South Africa 10
Hail Stick of Redemption 12
Prologue 15
1 'Hertzog is my shepherd' 19
2 Forbidden pastures 31
3 Growing into priesthood 43
4 No passbook required 55
5 An oasis in the Eastern Cape 67
6 Out of South Africa 79
7 Dean of Johannesburg 92
8 The mountain kingdom 106
9 The Church wakes up 120
10 A parish without frontiers 128
11 The hottest ecclesiastical seat 142
12 Crying in the wilderness 155
13 David and Goliath 169
14 Voice of the voiceless 182
15 A kind of sacrament 198
16 'Everybody's Bishop' 208
17 'Tutu can't swim' 229
18 Archbishop of Cape Town 245
Epilogue 259
Postlude 268
Curriculum Vitae 271
Notes 279
Select bibliography 287
Index 289

Acknowledgments

I would like to thank all those whose help made this book possible, especially: Malcolm and Helene Alexander, Bishop Timothy Bavin, The Rev. Dr Allan Boesak, Professor David Bosch, The Rev. Brian Brown, Canon and Mrs Ronald Brownrigg, Bishop Duncan Buchanan, Canon M. and Dr E. Carmichael, William Carmichael, The Rev. Charles Cartwright, The Rev. Michael Cassidy, Brother Charles CR, The Rev. Frank Chikane, The Rev. Richard Coggins, Margaret Comber, Martin Conway, Michael Corke, Gregory E. Craig, Margaret Davies, Christopher Doherty, Sheena Duncan, Brother Edward SSF, Jose Emery, The Rev. Christopher Evans, The Rev. Dr Sydney Evans, John Ewington, The Rev. James Fenhagen, Frank Ferrari, The Rev. Bill Fosbrook, Kevin Garcia, Brother Geoffrey SSF, Tim and Sarah Goad, Rev. Simon Gqubule, Professor John de Gruchy, Bishop Richard Harries, Mr and Mrs Havemeyer, Moira Henderson, Dr William Howard, Archbishop Trevor Huddleston CR, Anne Hughes, Archbishop Denis Hurley, The Rev. Jesse Jackson, Lady Johnston, Vernon E. Jordan, Helen Joseph, Sister Josephine SPB, Mother Julian SPB, Sydney Kentridge, Martin Kenyon, B. M. Khaketla, The Very Rev. E. L. King, Dean of Cape Town, Anne Kingsley, Father Kingston CR, Dr Wolfram Kistner, J. L. R. Kotsokoane, Arthur Krim, Christa Kuljian, Melanie Lambert, Ian Linden, Rev. Gerrie Lubbe, Ruth Lundie, Canon Norman Luyt, Caroline Macomber, Father Sipho Masemola, Sophie Mazibuko, Professor J. M. Mohapeloa, Father Zakes Mohutsioa, Justice Moloto, Murphy Morobe, Stanley Motjuwadi, Dr Ntatho Motlana, Sally Motlana, Shirley Moulder, Mr and Mrs Mqotsi, Dr Margaret Nash, The Rev. Dr C. F. Beyers Naudé, Bishop Donald Nestor, Bishop Simeon Nkoane CR, Archdeacon David Nkwe, Canon Paul Oestreicher, Godfrey Pitje, The Rev. Barney Pityana, Bernice Powell, Dr Mamphela Ramphele, Bridget Rees, Dr and Mrs Rockwell, Dr Robert Runcie, Archbishop of Canterbury, Archbishop Philip Russell, Marjorie Sandle, Judith Scott, Father Sebidi, Father Sekgaphane, Thembi Sekgaphane, Joe Seremane, Professor Gabriel Setiloane, Joe Sibiya, Dr Michael Sovern, Bishop J. S. Spong, Father Tom Stanton CR, The Rev. Peter Storey, Barry Streek, Father Aelred Stubbs CR, Helen Suzman MP, Bishop John Taylor, Bishop Selby Taylor, Daphne Terry, Leah Tutu, Professor Charles Villa-Vicencio, Bishop John Walker, Mrs Betty Ward, Father Dale White, Canon Boyd Williams, Professor Francis Wilson, Dr Tim Wilson, The British Council of Churches, The Catholic Institute for International Relations, The South African Council of Churches,

Acknowledgments

Manuscripts and Archives Department – University of Cape Town Libraries.

I must single out Elizabeth Storey, for typing many of the interviews and for her support, Dan Vaughan, who read the entire manuscript and made valuable suggestions but who bears no responsibility for any errors remaining, to my editor Louise Tulip, and my husband John, whose encouragement sustained me through thick and thin.

Also thanks for hospitality to Dr and Mrs Rockwell, the Sisters of St Benedict's, Margaret Davies, Megan and Doug Walker, and Shirley Moulder.

There are others who, because of the political situation in South Africa, cannot be named.

Lastly, I must thank Archbishop Tutu for allowing me to write about him and for refusing to be canonised.

S. du B.

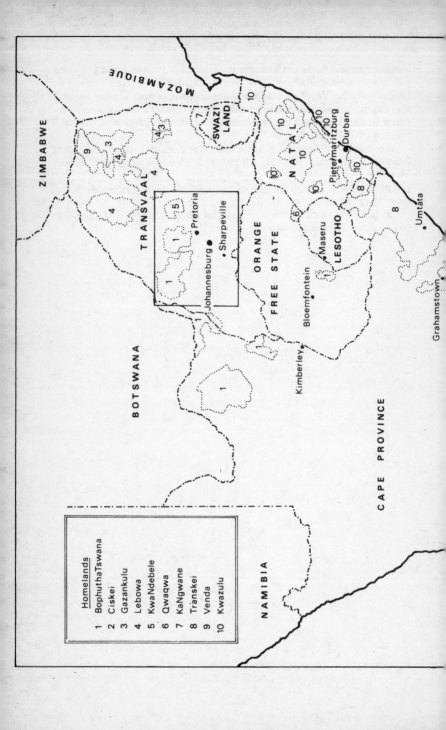

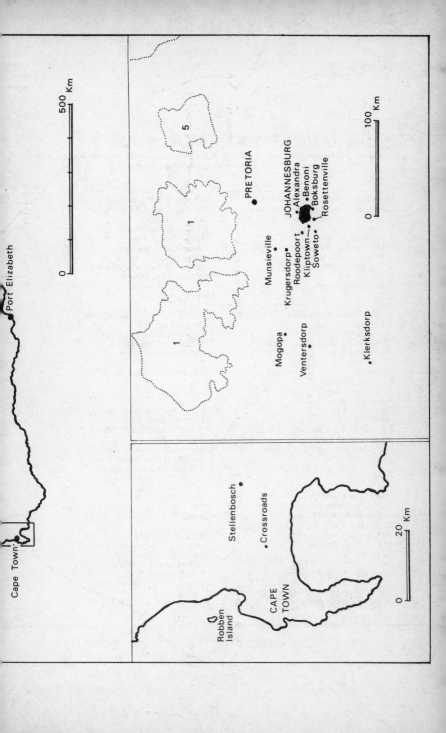

Cape Town

Port Elizabeth

500 Km

PRETORIA

5

1

1

Munsieville

Krugersdorp
Roodepoort
Kliptown
Soweto

JOHANNESBURG
Alexandra
Benoni
Boksburg
Rosettenville

Mogopa
Ventersdorp

Klerksdorp

100 Km

Stellenbosch
Crossroads

Robben
Island

CAPE
TOWN

20 Km

HAIL STICK OF REDEMPTION

(A praise-song in the traditional mould, composed by Mzilikazi-ka-Khumalo and Temba Msimang and sung at Desmond Tutu's enthronement as Archbishop of Cape Town.)

Sing, here comes the misimbithi stick
Sing, here comes the redemption stick
Which grew from barren soil
Grow, Mpilo kaTutu
It was weak as it grew
It kept bending as it grew
Here is the misimbithi stick
Which sprang from barren soil
Grow, Mpilo kaTutu
It was weak as it grew
Sing

PRAISE: The msimbithi plant
Which grew and shone
And attracted scholars
They say what kind of plant is this
Which attracts while on barren land?
They rush to the Anglicans
Saying this comes from fertile soil
Soil from the mission
At home in Sofaya [Sophiatown]
It shone at Christ the King
And it bore fruit
All my life
I'd never seen a msimbithi bear fruit
It was the fruit of the saviour
I had never seen a msimbithi plant
Bear spiritual fruit

CHOIR: Sing

PRAISE: The msimbithi stick
Plucked by Trevor Huddleston
One of the Anglican bishops
He plucked it, and smoothed it
He plucked it, and sharpened it
And made it a weapon
To protect the believers

PRAISE (by a few men): Go on!

POET: The stick hits fighting veterans
By hitting those in power

Who say it will hit its own people
Because they are the wrongdoers
But a black skin
Doesn't mean darkness
And a white skin
Doesn't mean brightness
This stick hits those who rule it
And leaves those who are ruled
Because it hits those in power

CHOIR: Sing

POET: Even overseas in England
They saw the stick
They were drawn by its sharpness
They started fishing for it
They fished for it by air
It crossed the seas on the air
When it came, they anointed it

CHOIR: Sing

POET: Even overseas in America
They clap hands for it
Its weight was felt at Harvard
And all of Boston agreed
Norway also felt its weight
And gave it Nobel honours
This man rates with Luthuli
Among black heroes
He rates with King
Among black heroes

CHOIR: Sing

POET: Hail spiritual stick
Your people congratulate you
Hail stick of protection
Today you protect everyone
A black man you protect
And a white man you protect

ULULATION: li-li-li-li-li-iiiiiiiiiii

Hail Stick of Redemption

POET: The stick for feeling water
Crossed the Johannesburg stream
Today it has crossed the sea
To pave the way in Cape Town
At the top of the believers
Go on mysterious stick
Collect your sheep and lead them
These sheep were given to you
They were given to you by blacks
They were given to you by whites
They were given to you by ancestors
They were given to you by those above
Let the sheep graze
Take them from the kraals of oppression
Take them from the kraals of darkness
And lead them to green pastures
Lead them to pastures of freedom
Lead them to spiritual pastures
Where they'll feed
with no consideration of colour
Then the msimbithi stick
Will become the stick of redemption

CHOIR: Sing, here is the msimbithi stick
Sing the song of redemption
HalalaHalalaHalalaHalalaHalala

Prologue

It is October 18th, 1984. While in America Bishop Desmond Tutu has learnt that he has been awarded the Nobel Peace Prize. He flies back to Johannesburg to be with his family, friends and colleagues. The mood is jubilant. People of all races sing, dance, laugh, cry and embrace one another in joy. The Bishop stands and leads them in an African hymn; then he speaks. He is, he says, merely 'a little focus' of the stalwarts of the struggle for freedom. He thanks God for those who have gone into exile, those who have been banned or detained without trial, those who have died. This award is for them and for all the people who suffer daily under apartheid:

> This award is for you – Mothers, who sit near railway stations trying to eke out an existence, selling potatoes, selling meali, selling pigs' trotters.
>
> This award is for you – Fathers, sitting in a single-sex hostel, separated from your children for eleven months of the year.
>
> This award is for you – Mothers in the squatter camps, whose shelters are destroyed callously every day and who have to sit on soaking mattresses in the winter rain, holding whimpering babies and whose crime in this country is that you want to be with your husbands.
>
> This award is for you – three and a half million of our people who have been uprooted and dumped as if they were rubbish. The world says we recognise you, we recognise that you are people who love peace.
>
> This award is for you – dear children, who despite receiving a poisonous gruel, designed to make you believe that you are inferior, have said 'there is something that God put into us which will not be manipulated by man, which tells us that we are your children.' This award is for you – and I am proud to accept it on your behalf as you spurn a travesty of an education.
>
> This award is for you, who down the ages have said we seek to change this evil system peacefully. The world recognises that we are agents of peace, of reconciliation, of love, of justice, of caring, of compassion. I have the great honour of receiving this award on your behalf. It is our prize. It is not Desmond Tutu's prize. The world recognises that and thank God that our God is God. Thank God that our God is in charge.

With these words, Desmond Tutu is, as always, identifying himself firmly with the oppressed people of South Africa, the 'non-whites', for years victims of a regime which has legislated the subservience of the many to the few, a people whose peaceful resistance has been continually countered by yet more repression, for the most part a people who, astonishingly, remain loving in a world of hate and fear. In accepting this award, he has stepped decisively on to the world stage – a black South African, a Christian, a reconciler, a fearless critic of apartheid, who has become a spokesman for his people, a voice of the voiceless.

Desmond Tutu's rise from his birth and childhood in the barren black townships of the Transvaal to international spokesman for his countrymen and holder of the highest Anglican office in South Africa, Archbishop of Cape Town, was against all the odds. In any success story there is an element of luck and Tutu constantly admits his debt to the people he was fortunate enough to meet, but it takes more than luck and kindness to turn a small black boy into an Archbishop. The road from township to Bishop's Palace is paved by more than good intentions.

The extraordinary attempts to discredit him made by the South African Broadcasting Corporation, much of the white press and even the government itself, have made it hard to know the man himself, difficult to discern the true from the false. Many of the judgments made of him are based on ignorance and misinformation. Is he pastor or self-publicist, churchman or politician, reconciler or rabble-rouser, peace-maker or agitator?

He is a man of many layers; his small frame embraces many contradictory tensions. He has a deep need to be loved, yet he inspires as much hate as any man could tolerate. Very much his own man, he is also a man of the people, all too familiar with the humiliation of living in an apartheid society and still as at home with the youth of Soweto as with the dignitaries with whom he now associates. His desire for peace is matched by such indignation at the injustice of apartheid that his remarks – outspoken, articulate, witty, courageous and sometimes naïve in their spontaneity – fuel flames of outrage. Though he was slow to take an active part in the maze of South African politics, since becoming Dean of Johannesburg in 1975 he has shown, in both words and deeds, that religion and politics cannot be separated. If his attempts to stand above division and to reconcile opposing parties have left him isolated and subject to criticism from all sides, so too has it given him a freedom to speak what he feels is God's will. For above all he is a man with a deep spiritual life, whose conviction stems from long hours of prayer and meditation.

Though he now has the ear of Presidents and Prime Ministers, though he is so well-known a symbol of his country that a New York cab-driver talking to a journalist on his way to South Africa simply reacted by saying 'Ah yes – Tutu', he is a son of the soil of Africa and it is in the dusty ghettos of Johannesburg that his story must begin.

I

'Hertzog is my shepherd'

Black children born into the South Africa of the thirties did not think it strange that they lived in corrugated-iron shacks while whites sunned themselves in the pleasant gardens of rich homes; they did not wonder why there were places they could not go, even seats on which they could not sit; they were humiliated, but not surprised, when their middle-aged parents were addressed as 'Boy' and 'Girl'; they took it for granted that they walked on dirt tracks in unlit streets, that there was no sewage or electricity, that they were lucky if they were not hungry. That was how God had made the world – there were the 'haves' and the 'have-nots', and whether you were one or the other was determined by the colour of your skin.

Racial discrimination had not yet been fully enshrined into the apartheid laws, so life for blacks then was marginally more tolerable than it was to become. That whites were superior to blacks was, however, quite simply an accepted fact of life. Whites assumed that they should rule, that they should enjoy the riches of the land and that the blacks were there to serve their white masters and then become invisible as quickly as possible.

In 1925 the Prime Minister, General Hertzog, made a speech in the Orange Free State outlining his political programme. Segregation, he said, would protect 'civilised labour' – that is, white and 'coloured' (mixed race) – from 'uncivilised labour', the cheap labour of blacks. He proceeded to implement these ideas in a series of laws which became known as the 'Hertzog Bills'; their effect was encapsulated in a parody of the 23rd Psalm by an African poet:[1]

> Hertzog is my shepherd; I am in want.
> He maketh me to lie down on park benches,
> He leadeth me beside still factories,
> He arouseth my doubt of his intention.
> He leadeth me in the path of destruction for his Party's sake.
> Yea, I walk in the valley of the shadow of destruction
> And I fear evil, for thou art with me.
> The Politicians and the Profiteers, they frighten me;
> Thou preparest a reduction in my salary before me

In the Presence of mine enemies.
Thou anointest mine income with taxes,
My expense runneth over.
Surely unemployment and poverty will follow me
All the days of this Administration,
And I shall dwell in a mortgaged house for ever.

It was into this world that, on October 7th, 1931, Desmond Mpilo
Tutu was born. His father, Zachariah, had profited from a Mission
School education and was at the time Headmaster of the Methodist
Primary School in Klerksdorp, a small town in the Western Transvaal.
Many people remember Zachariah as a tall, thin, gaunt man – proud
and impressive, very concerned that his children should be healthy
and properly educated; a few knew that he sometimes drank too much
and would then treat his wife in a way that deeply upset the young
Desmond. Aletha Matlhare was a domestic servant, only educated to
primary school level and a gentle woman who had a deep and lasting
effect on Desmond. She became known as 'Komotso', 'the comforter
of the afflicted', as she always took the side of whoever she felt was
being worsted in an argument, whether they were right or wrong.
Their children were all given both European and African names, a
common practice in those days when the influence of the missions
was still strong, the European name being a concession to their
Christian background. The eldest was Sylvia Funeka, then there was
another girl who died young, Desmond Mpilo was next and finally
Gloria Lindiwe, the youngest.

Zachariah was a Fingo, one of the Xhosa tribes from the Eastern
Cape, Aletha a Motswana and Aletha's mother, Kuku, a Mosotho. So
from an early age Desmond and his sisters spoke Xhosa, Tswana and
Sotho. Were they, then, Xhosa or Motswana? Like many urban blacks
they did not know or very much mind, though sometimes Zachariah
would tease Aletha for being a Motswana. It is the Nationalist government who tried (and still tries) to force ethnicity upon the blacks;
tribal origin was not interesting or important to the Tutus; certainly
it was not considered a divisive matter. They were *Africans*, more
precisely *South Africans*, and that was where their national pride lay.

But being black in South Africa is no way to be confident of your
identity. One of the worst things about racial discrimination is that,
as Desmond Tutu was to say years later,[2]

> You are brainwashed into an acquiescence in your oppression and
> exploitation. You come to believe what others have determined about
> you, filling you with self-disgust, self-contempt and self-hatred, accept-
> ing a negative self-image ... and you need a lot of grace to have that

demon of self-hatred exorcised, when you accept that only white races really matter and you allow the white person to set your standards and provide your role models.

These black boys, shunted off to live in dusty ghettos, rejoiced in anything which affirmed their humanity, which proved that blacks can succeed. So it is not hard to share Desmond's delight when one day he picked up a tattered copy of the American magazine *Ebony* and read about the exploits of an American black, Jackie Robinson, who had broken into major league baseball. Desmond 'didn't know baseball from pingpong' but he vividly remembers his pride in this fellow black's achievement:[3]

> I grew inches that day and I puffed out my chest, even though I was alone lolling against a wall, as I drank in what was like nectar from the Gods – this account of how my soul brothers and sisters were making it against untold odds those many thousands of miles across the seas . . . They were black like me, like us and here they were achieving against tremendous odds.

So he and his friends were agog to learn of the victories of Jesse Owens at the 1936 Olympics – victories which took place before the eyes of no less a racist than Adolf Hitler himself; they listened with wildly beating hearts to the music of Nat King Cole, Louis Armstrong, Fats Waller and Marion Anderson; they were dazzled by the dancing of the Mills Brothers and intoxicated by the zoot-suits introduced into the black townships by the all-black musical *Stormy Weather*.[4]

> I don't suppose one made the connection explicitly, but deep down in our psyches the gnawing self-doubt, the self-hatred, that insidious poison was being drained out of our systems and we were being prepared to accept the exhilarating obligations of being free responsible persons.

When Desmond was about eight years old, Zachariah was transferred to Ventersdorp, to a school of Africans, so-called 'coloureds' and Indians, who lived in town in the white areas. Desmond was a pupil there, and this mixture (later to be lost in favour of segregation not only between black and white, but between all the different racial groups) did not seem strange to him or his friends: 'Nobody then thought it was a potent or explosive mixture, nor curious that Indians should live cheek by jowl with whites. The heavens did not seem to have fallen in.'[5] Nevertheless, here Desmond met racial discrimination. The black community spoke Setswana and Afrikaans, so he learned the language hated by blacks as 'the language of the oppressor' and was able to understand the white boys taunting him as he cycled into town to buy his father a newspaper. They jeered '*Pik*' as he passed, to which he, thinking they were referring to the garden implement would, when at a safe distance, retort with schoolboy humour, '*Jou graaf*' (You're a spade). Only later did he realise that they were deriding him for being 'Pitch black'.

Looking back from the 1980s, when relations between black and white had deteriorated even further, Tutu finds it incredible that he was able to spread his copy of the *Star* or the *Rand Daily Mail* on the pavement and kneel to read it. 'Nobody walked over the pavement or jostled me.'[6] He recalls too, that whereas today most black soldiers are thought to be traitors to the liberation struggle, during the Second World War they were regarded as heroes by their fellow blacks. It was a matter of great pride if someone in the family wore a uniform; indeed his own uncle was a sergeant in the Union Defence Force. Like small boys anywhere, he and his friends enjoyed playing soldiers and would rush to the side of the road to wave ecstatically to the troops going 'up North'. They did not know that many Afrikaners were opposed to South Africans joining the war effort; they did not mind that black soldiers were not trusted with guns, but faced the might of Rommel's Afrika Corps armed only with assegais.

What Desmond did mind was seeing his father humiliated. Sometimes when walking together they would be stopped and Zachariah would be asked to produce his 'passbook', that divisive and hated document which every 'non-white' was forced to carry and to produce on demand. If they could not, they faced heavy fines, imprisonment, being sent to badly paid work, or forcible removal to one of the poverty stricken 'tribal areas' officially reserved for blacks. The passbook (which with typical humour the blacks called the '*Dompas*' – the 'Stupid pass') was the key to racial segregation and economic exploitation; it controlled every movement black people made outside the reserves or the locations. It was the badge of division as surely as was the Star of David the Jews had to wear in Nazi Germany.

As he saw more of the white areas, Desmond came across other things he could not understand. He was used to the children from the black locations scavenging for food, but sometimes he would go to town during school hours and see black children picking out fresh fruit and sandwiches from the dustbins of the white schools. The white children, it turned out, had more than they needed and preferred the lunches their mothers had prepared for them to the school meals provided by the government. Despite the desperate need of the black children, there was no school-feeding for them; it had been stopped by Dr Verwoerd because the government decided that since they could not feed all black children they would feed none at all.

Occasionally, too, Desmond wondered at some of the things they were taught at school. Certainly the students were not at all politicised. In fact, Desmond feels they were thoroughly unsophisticated and naïve, hardly questioning what appeared to be the divine ordering of their segregated society. But even they were disturbed by one of their history textbooks, written by a Methodist missionary:[7]

> We found it distinctly odd that in virtually every encounter between the black Xhosa and the white settlers, Mr Whitehead invariably described the Xhosas as those who *stole* the settlers' cattle and of the settlers he would write that the settlers *captured* the cattle from the Xhosa. We did not press the point at all, or hardly at all, in class discussion; but when we were outside we would mutter that it was very funny. It certainly seemed to be stretching coincidence to breaking point. We often remarked that after all, these farmers had no cattle when they landed in South Africa, and all the cattle had to be procured from the indigenous peoples.

For the most part, Desmond was fortunate in his early contacts with whites. There was, for instance, the Greek who ran the only café in town and who always gave him sweets; but he was to make more significant friendships in his early teens, when Zachariah's job took him to another town in the Western Transvaal, Roodepoort.

Roodepoort location was a slum area, the houses separated by dirty, dusty lanes and the air filled with the stench of overflowing night soil buckets. Here Desmond's mother worked at Ezenzeleni Blind School, the first school for black blind people, which had been founded by the Reverend Arthur Blaxall and his wife. Forty-five years later Arthur Blaxall still remembers a man called Radcliffe, blind, deaf and dumb, whom Mrs Blaxall, entering with incredible patience into his dark, silent world, taught to be more independent than anyone would have thought possible. Through her Radcliffe learnt to read and write English in Braille, to 'listen' to speech and music by placing his fingers where he could sense the vibrations, even to walk from his hostel to the Blaxalls' home. Young as he was, Desmond was deeply moved by her dedication; when she was an old lady he wrote to her:[8]

> I can still see Radcliffe, who was born blind, deaf and dumb, standing by the piano with a pipe in his mouth, stamping away with his foot to the rhythm that was coming from the piano. Or even seeing him dancing with you at some of the socials that we used to have. Or enjoying the music of a guitar and knowing that it had taken you many, many, many months of patient teaching to get him out of himself so that he could 'hear' the rhythm that went through the pulsations that went through

his fingers. And that you had helped him to become human whereas in normal African circumstances with that degree of handicap he would have been reduced to a twilight existence.

Mrs Blaxall had not only given meaning to Radcliffe's life, she had done something to ease the resentment black people felt for whites. Desmond's letter ends:

> We cannot compute your influence. Knowing you has made it virtually impossible, I think, for people to be embittered because of how they were treated in this country, because they would recall how you had treated them as if they were what they knew themselves to be, human beings made in the image of God. And so your contribution to this country is immeasurable. And thank you very much, Nomsa ['Mother of people'].

More significant still was a meeting that has become part of South African folk history. One day, in the early 1940s, Desmond was with his mother at Ezenzeleni when a white man wearing a cassock and a huge black hat passed them. As he passed, he raised his hat to Mrs Tutu in greeting. Desmond was overwhelmed. He simply couldn't believe it – a white man raising his hat to a simple black labouring woman. The white man was Bishop Trevor Huddleston, then a parish priest in the black Johannesburg location Sophiatown, who was to make such a massive contribution to the struggle for justice in South Africa.

In 1943, when Desmond was twelve, the Tutus moved yet again, this time to Munsieville, the black location in Krugersdorp. It was as sordid and run-down as most of the locations, its houses row upon row of identical boxes, but it had a certain vitality, was smaller than many of the townships, and people were fond of it. Being one of the original locations – black people had been living there since 1910 – it was nearer to the white areas than those built later, when black areas were designed to be out of sight of white eyes, so the Tutus led a less segregated life geographically and there was at least some relationship between blacks and whites.

The five of them lived in a typically crowded house. They had three rooms – Desmond's bedroom doubled as a sitting room and a dining room – there was no electricity, no sewage, and the dirt street in front of the house had rocky outcrops. Desmond's younger sister lives there now and it is still, forty years later, in the same deplorable condition. But they did have running water and a bathroom and Aletha was a skilful housewife; visitors remember it as a very sweet home, where they always received a warm welcome. In true African style, the Tutus shared what they had. Zachariah would always notice if one of his pupils was late for school because he had so far to walk and would take him in to live with his family; many boys were rescued by the Tutus in this way.

Though the Tutus were better off than most, times were often hard. Desmond used to go to the white suburbs to collect and return laundry for his mother to wash; she would be paid two shillings, a princely sum, which went a long way in those days. Indeed, during the school holidays, when Zachariah was not working, it had to cover all their needs. They usually spent Christmas holidays with Aletha's mother Kuku, in Boksburg, where Zachariah would work in a bottle store as a delivery boy. Kuku was still taking in washing and the children would wait for her to return with the bread she had saved from the lunch her white 'madam' had given her. Sometimes there would be marmalade as well, but this strange jam, both sweet and bitter, was not popular.

Desmond remembers his childhood as quite a happy time. He was loved – and probably rather spoilt – by his sisters and, though there was no money to spare, fun was derived from very simple things. Nobody had toys, but when the house was being cleaned they would put all the chairs on to the stoep and soon they would become a train; they would make cars out of odd pieces of wire and play football with an old tennis ball. To earn a bit of pocket money Desmond would walk three miles to the market with his friend Joe Sibiya; they would bring back bags of oranges and sell them at a small profit. Later he sold peanuts at suburban railway stations and caddied at the Killarney golf course in Johannesburg. There was one occasion when another close friend, Stanley Motjuwadi (who later became editor of the African magazine *Drum*) found him 'bawling in the clutches of a towering cop who had mistaken him for a waif';[9] but for the most part he enjoyed these early money-making adventures and was quite a good businessman. He also joined the scouts, once walking nearly eight miles from Munsieville to Stirkfontein and earning both his 'Tenderfoot' and 'Second Class' badges; he was even awarded a Proficiency Badge in cooking.

One morning in 1945 a scrawny, spindly legged Desmond, wearing shorts but no shoes, reported for his first day at Western High, the government secondary school in the old Western Native Township, near Sophiatown. Black children had to go to different areas for different levels of education; at the time Western High was the only High School on the entire West Rand, serving several townships. It was a large school and pretty rough. There were about sixty pupils to a class and not enough desks to go round; in fact, for the first six months the younger children had to write on their laps or kneeling on the floor. However, under the headship of Mr Madibane, the doyen of black educationalists and a great Anglican churchman, it had become famous, turning out many black leaders and becoming known as 'Madibane High'.

Classes lasted from 8.30 a.m. until 5 p.m. Being a school for blacks, there were no school meals, but the children were given sixpence by their parents with which to find their own lunch and tea. Stanley and Desmond used to go to the soda fountain in Main Street, Sophiatown, and buy roasted peanuts, a slice of bread covered with fish crumbs and a glass of flavoured water. That cost them threepence, a 'tickey'; the other tickey went on a 'fat cake', which resembles a doughnut and which Desmond still enjoys, for the afternoon break.

Like any township urchin (as Desmond refers to himself in those days), the acquisition and spending of pocket money was a continuing challenge in their life of poverty. Stanley and Desmond used to travel the fifteen miles to school together on the train, where they became famous as card sharps. As Stanley explains:[10]

> We would take on workers commuting with us and never lost. A deft scratching of the heart was a hint to Des to call hearts. A scooping with the open hand was spades, and three outstretched fingers meant clubs. According to strict ethics this was cheating, but deprived boys have to survive, was our logic then. The workers we were fleecing did not seem to mind it. In fact they admired Des' prowess and nicknamed him 'Professor'.

Once a month, when Desmond's father gave him some money, they bought themselves a pack of fifty cigarettes, which soon disappeared. It was Desmond who discovered that by buying tobacco and papers and making '*zolls*', they could smoke for the whole month.

Desmond was hard-working and bright, but he was not good at arithmetic, in fact failing arithmetic nearly prevented him passing Standard Six and qualifying for his first-year Junior Certificate. However, 'The Shark', as Mr Madibane was known to his pupils, did not live up to his nickname and allowed Desmond to move up. His trust was justified, for in the first half-yearly exams Desmond came top, on aggregate, of all 250 pupils in Form 1. In the next form there were desks, but Desmond, Stanley and another boy all had to share a desk meant for two. Desmond, being left-handed, somehow managed to sit crab-like, occupying three-quarters of the space and squeezing the other two to the end. This led to endless fights between the two friends and to Stanley dubbing him a 'selfish southpaw'.

That Desmond was unusually intelligent was willingly accepted by his contemporaries. Joe Sibiya recalls the speed of his thought: 'He was streets ahead of me. We would read something together and he would apply it in all sorts of ways. I couldn't follow him. I hobbled along, it was so strenuous trying to keep up with him.' Joe was also impressed at the way he would take nothing for granted: 'Let's read this verse,' he would say, 'and see what it really means.' His photographic memory enabled him to answer a classmate's question with 'Your answer is on page 179 of Duggan, three lines from the top of the page.'[11] And already his sense of humour was evident. For instance he was once asked by the zoology master for a definition of heredity. 'It is when your son looks like your neighbour or your best friend,' he retorted.[12] On another occasion he delighted a physical training instructor, more remarkable for his bulk than his brains, by telling him about what he called 'Einstein's Law of Common Sense' – that when a body is immersed in liquid it experiences an apparent loss of weight.

Though in many ways Desmond was an ordinary, if exceptionally gifted, township boy – 'no angel' according to Stanley, and not above taunting white officials on the trains – he was already showing impressive moral courage. Joe Sibiya remembers him as 'a very honest guy who used to put us to shame. For instance if we went off to rob a peach tree he wouldn't come.' He was slow to anger, would not harbour grudges and would rather discuss than engage in fisticuffs. He has inherited his mother's gentle, caring temperament and would have nothing to do with anything that hurt others; when his friends joked and laughed at one another Desmond would say they should laugh *with* them, not *at* them. It has been suggested that his unwillingness to take part in the fights that were an inevitable part of township life could have been because he was physically frail – his grandmother gave him the name 'Mpilo', meaning life, as he was not a strong baby – but from the impression he made on his contemporaries it is hard to believe that, had he been the toughest boy in class, he would ever have been an aggressive child.

When Desmond was fourteen – though according to Father Huddleston he was so small he looked about twelve – his studies were interrupted for nearly two years by a serious illness. At the time he was staying at a new hostel run by the Fathers of the Community of the Resurrection in Sophiatown, as commuting from Munsieville was proving too expensive. (Even finding the fare home for weekends was often difficult; when there was no cash for him, he would walk into town and collect the two shillings his mother earned from her white 'madam'.) He hadn't been eating well, but that had not seemed particularly unusual, as the students in the hostel prepared their own food, tending to live on a diet of fish and chips and bread. However, one day Desmond was driving through Sophiatown with one of the Fathers, when he had a very bad headache and needed to sit by the window to breathe. He was taken to Rietfontein Hospital, where tuberculosis was diagnosed. He was there for twenty months, receiving the treatment usually given in those days, pneumothorax. At regular intervals air was introduced into the pleural cavity in the chest, allowing the lung to collapse; Desmond describes it as rather like immobilising a broken arm by putting it in plaster. At the same time he was given a new drug, PAS, which killed off the tubercular organisms.

It was an unpleasant treatment and Rietfontein Hospital, a state-run TB sanatorium, was a depressing place, full of burnt-out cases of TB and syphilis, but for Desmond this illness turned out to be a cloud with several silver linings.

First, it was in hospital that his lifelong friendship with Father Huddleston developed. Every week, for all those eighty odd weeks, he would visit Desmond, not in any official capacity – he was not the hospital chaplain – but because they took such pleasure in each other's company. Father Huddleston found Desmond quite exceptionally bright, interested in everything and a marvellously optimistic patient. He in turn was the greatest single influence in the life of the young Desmond, who still wonders at Father Huddleston's pastoral care and love: 'Who was I? – just another black boy – that he should visit me.'

Though he was a cheerful patient, never sliding into depression, the one thing that really distressed Desmond was the fear that he might drop behind at school; it was a particularly bad time for him, as he was due to take his first public exam, the Junior Certificate. He was always anxious to know what he was missing, so Father Huddleston brought books – *Treasure Island*, *Oliver Twist*, whatever they were currently reading in class and more besides – while Stanley, apart from keeping him abreast with what was happening in the world of sport, would bring his school notes. Zachariah had always encouraged Desmond to read and he had a huge collection of comics – *Superman*, *Batman*, whatever he could get hold of – which were the rather surprising source of his love of English. In hospital he had time to read prodigiously, so far from falling behind, though admittedly he missed his Junior Certificate, Desmond became the best-read pupil at the school.

It was in hospital, too, that Desmond's Christianity became firmly embedded. The Tutus were a devout Christian family, more concerned with the essential message than with any particular denomination. Zachariah's father had been a minister of the Ethiopian Church of South Africa, Desmond was baptised a Methodist, while they were living at Ventersdorp they followed Sylvia's lead into the African Methodist Episcopal Church, then finally, in 1943, they all became

Anglicans. He even had a spell with an Independent African Church, as a relative of his father's was a minister of an obscure sect. Desmond used to carry the banner round Roodepoort location singing *'Simon Peter, Ndicedise'* – 'Simon Peter, help me', becoming known by the location children as 'Simon Peter's son'. His ecumenism started early.

In hospital everything seemed to come together. The devout background was there, the long weeks lying still gave time for reflection and Father Huddleston acted as the catalyst. Desmond did not then understand the white priest's political views, but was convinced that everything he did stemmed from his prayers and his faith:[13]

> He was full of laughter and caring. He made you feel special. He was a wonderful man (he is a wonderful man), a white man who made you feel you mattered. And he was so genuine, caring passionately about his parishioners in Sophiatown. His white cassock became grubby quickly as he walked around its streets, because he attracted children so naturally and they all wanted to grab him crying all the while, 'Hello Fada, hello Fada'. At one time his office would be filled with urchins playing marbles on the floor and the very next moment it held some very important personage, an ambassador or an influential businessman.

So in hospital he made a great friend, he laid the foundation on which his wide-ranging knowledge was to be built and he found a faith which quite surprised him by its intensity. He remembers on one occasion when he was very ill, haemorrhaging badly and coughing up a lot of blood, being overcome by a profound sense of calm and saying to God, 'Well, if I have to die – okay.' His Christianity had moved from outward observance to the depths of his soul.

When he left hospital he began the disciplined spiritual life that was to intensify as the years went by. He made his 'first really good confession' to Father Huddleston in the Church of Christ the King in Sophiatown; he became a server at his parish church of St Paul's in Munsieville – later training other boys to be servers; he would often, to the surprise of his friends, slip quietly off to church and pray for an hour at a time.

If Father Huddleston was the greatest single influence in Desmond's life, there were many others and he never tires of acknowledging his debt to them. While the Tutus were attending the African Methodist Episcopal Church, Desmond was very impressed by Pastor Makhene, a very gentle man with a quiet authority that nobody ever thought to challenge. Desmond, aged about eight at the time, felt very flattered that he was allowed to play with the Makhene teenage children and loved being in their calm, peaceful home. Then there was Father Sekgaphane, an African priest who, after a long and serious interview, admitted the Tutus to the Anglican Church. He never scolded the boys, he too was a gentle man – Desmond is always impressed by gentleness – and the boys sometimes accompanied him to 'outstations'. 'At the end of the service people would be dancing attendance on him, ushering him into a private room to eat the special meals they had prepared and leaving us nonentities outside. But he would never sit down to eat until he was sure that we had been fed.'[14] That simple action left an indelible impression on at least one of the boys. 'Maybe at the back of my mind I was saying "I'd like to be like him".'

At Ventersdorp there were the Blaxalls, whose names, says Desmond, 'should be inscribed in letters of gold when a proper history of South Africa is written'[15] and Ezekiel Mphahlele, who was to become a well-known writer and a Professor at the University of the Witwatersrand. He was then a clerk and driver to Arthur Blaxall, quietly studying for a degree in his spare time and becoming the first person of any race to obtain an MA in English with distinction at UNISA, the University of South Africa. Desmond feels that Mphahlele too probably owes much to the Blaxalls. Ezekiel encouraged the children to read, telling them 'to make a book your friend'; he also encouraged Desmond in physical activities. He had taken up running and physical training to overcome a physical ailment and Desmond, admiring his grit and determination, used to join him on long runs. In order to give Desmond more confidence to face up to the township bullies, Ezekiel also taught Desmond boxing.

When Desmond came out of hospital he was for a while isolated in his parents' bedroom and his friends had to talk to him through the window – Joe Sibiya was mystified at Aletha's wrath when she once found them sharing an orange. But eventually, apart from an atrophied right hand, he seemed to return to normal health. Certainly he had plenty of energy and would join in anything that was going. 'Find children playing ball – he'd join them. Find children playing hide and seek – he'd be there,' recalls Sally Motlana, to whom he was like a brother. He loved everybody, even the thugs, the '*tsotsis*'; the younger boys, no doubt sensing this, would 'follow him round like little puppies'. His leadership qualities were beginning to show.

Back at school he was very put out to find he had fallen behind Stanley. Again 'The Shark' had pity on him and allowed him to join the 'Matric' class; again he was justified as Desmond continued to come top of his class. At the end of 1950, once more commuting from Munsieville and studying long hours after dark by candlelight, he passed the Joint Matriculation Board of the University of South Africa; his subjects were English, Afrikaans, Mathematics, Zoology, History and Zulu. His schooldays were over. Now he had to decide what to do.

2

Forbidden pastures

While Desmond was in his last two years at school the political face of South Africa was changing; life for the blacks was to become worse, far worse.

In 1948, at a time when racial segregation was being challenged by the United Nations and in America the black voice was beginning to be heard, in South Africa the National Party won the General Election by promising apartheid to the white electorate. Apartheid, the Afrikaans word for 'apartness', was explicitly designed to preserve white supremacy or *baaskap* (boss-ship) by separating blacks from whites in every sphere of life. It aimed to produce a black community with no rights, no political power, no defence; it extinguished any possibility of black majority rule. The white government was mortally afraid of African unity and, taking refuge in the policy of 'divide and rule', they sought to keep the huge majority of Africans, estimated at the time at 8½ million (not to mention 1 million 'coloureds' and ½ million Indians), under the control of about 2½ million whites.[1]

The apartheid system gave the existing racial segregation the support and protection of the law, backed up by police powers of imprisonment and arrest. The first legislation to be drafted was the Prohibition of Mixed Marriages Act. Marriage between white and black had been banned since 1923; this was now extended to include marriage between whites and 'coloureds' or Indians. A year later the Immorality Act was passed, making illegal any form of sexual contact between whites and 'non-whites'.

Though these laws led to countless individual tragedies – there were over 10,000 convictions under the Immorality Act before it was repealed in 1986 – their national significance was slight in comparison with another piece of legislation passed in 1950, the Population Registration Act, in which every individual South African was classified by race – white, 'coloured', Indian or Native, as the majority community was called at the time. (At various times the black population have been referred to as Kaffirs, a word which means 'heathen', though many were in fact Christians; Natives, a claim the whites were anxious to disprove; and Bantu, an African word for people. The renaming of the Department of Bantu Affairs as the Department of Plural Affairs opened the door to endless ridicule from blacks. Desmond still jokes that presumably a black from the country is 'a rural Plural' and there was even a suggestion that a primitive drawing might be 'a rural Plural's mural'. Except when deliberately insulted, they are now generally referred to as blacks, and are content to be so-called.)

Whites, despite consisting of a mixed bag of Dutch, English, Portuguese, French, Germans, Greeks and others, were regarded as one unit, as were Indians; but Africans were split into linguistically based 'national units', regardless of whether they even knew the language of the group into which they were put. This cold-blooded division of people was carried out with far less feeling than the botanist Linnaeus showed for the classification of plants. Skin colour in South Africa varies from the richest black to 'European' white, with an infinity of shades in between. Nor can a definition always be confirmed by lips and hair; appearance alone was often not enough to determine ethnicity. Instructions as to where to look for the signs that would denote a particular race (fingernails, the whites of the eye) were issued to clerks in the government departments responsible and in cases of doubt crude tests were devised. Perhaps the most laughable and the most humiliating was 'the pencil in the hair' test. If the pencil stayed firmly in the tight curls, then the verdict was 'African'; if it fell through straighter locks, then it was 'coloured'. So families could be divided, sometimes with brothers and sisters being given different groupings, on the strength of the gravitational weight of a pencil.

Parliament was busy in 1950. In that same year it also passed the Group Areas Act, known by some as the Ghetto Act, by Prime Minister Dr Malan as 'The Kernel of Apartheid'. This Act created the machinery whereby racial segregation could be not only legally perpetuated, but extended. Every section of the population, as classified in the Population Registration Act, was allocated separate residential and trading areas. Traditional property rights were disregarded and commercial life was disrupted as thousands of blacks, 'coloureds' and Indians were uprooted; every 'non-white' was haunted with anxiety as they waited to hear if they would be moved, when it would happen and where they would be sent. This legislation was necessary, according to the Minister of the Interior, so that there should be the least possible contact between the various communities. It was, he was convinced, in the interests of the material, cultural and spiritual development of all races that the white man and Western civilisation should be supreme.

The African, says the policy of apartheid, must not be a burden to the white man; he is only allowed into the 'white' areas to work. So the system of 'reserves' became, in the Bantu Authorities Act of 1951, the basis of the bantustans – the 'homelands' or 'reserves'. There are ten bantustans, some, like Bophuthatswana, consisting of several different geographical areas separated by corridors of choice land allocated to whites. Here, in what Tutu calls 'these dumping grounds', irrespective of where they were born or spent their lives, is where blacks officially belong, where their only political rights are exercised and where they return if they fall sick, become redundant or grow old. The black community was being, in effect, retribalised under the aegis of the white rulers. An African writer compared this compartmentalisation to some racial Messiah let loose in London, 'shuffling the population according to their original tribal or clan groupings, putting English, Welsh, Irish, Scots, Jews into separate locations. Then further dividing the men of Sussex, Wessex and so on – or your Macdonalds, Mactavishes or Mac-what-nots . . .'[2]

It was in any case hardly a fair division of a vast, beautiful and rich country. The Africans, comprising about 73 per cent of the population, were allotted 13 per cent of the land; it was for the most part the poorest land, with no major towns or cities and generally lacking the natural resources with which South Africa is so abundantly blessed. There was hardly any work to be had in the homelands, but the inhabitants of the bantustans provided cheap labour for the mines, the white farms and industry. Often black people had (and still have) to travel miles every day, leaving home as early as 4 a.m. and returning late at night. They were, as this African writer clearly thought, being treated like animals:[3]

> Like game reserves, the Homelands have always been regarded as places where the African could be seen in his 'natural, unspoilt surroundings'. Like game reserves, 'strangers' may not be admitted without a permit and residents may not leave the reserve without a permit. Animals in game reserves cannot make decisions for themselves as they do not have the power of rational thinking. In the African reserves decisions about development are taken by the white government and their officials. All animals belong to a game reserve and the fact that they are sometimes brought out of the reserve for entertainment and other uses will never change their status. When the animals are no longer of use to humans outside the game reserve they have to be sent back to it – by force.

So how, in the increasingly restricted life of the 1950s, was Tutu going to earn his living? He was exceptionally intelligent, reasonably ambitious and one of the ½ per cent of black Africans who had qualified for university entrance by passing the examination of the

Joint Matriculation Board of the University of South Africa; it was natural that he should aspire to one of the top professions open to him. The peak of black aspirations at the time was to become a medical doctor, exemplified in Tutu's youth by Dr Xuma, who lived in Sophiatown and had been President of the African National Congress (ANC) while Tutu was an impressionable schoolboy. Dr Xuma was admired to the point of envy. He had a qualification no one could deny, he had studied in America, England and Europe and he could earn quite a respectable salary. With this example and with his own recent experience of illness, Tutu's first ambition was to become a doctor and to do research into TB. He gained a place at the Witwatersrand Medical School, but he could not get a bursary. There was no other source of finance, so that avenue was closed before he had even taken the first steps down it. He decided to follow in his father's footsteps and become a teacher, so in 1951 he went to the new government college outside Pretoria, the Bantu Normal College, to study for a Teacher's Diploma.

It was one of the first Bantu Education institutions, all the lecturers being appointed by the Nationalist government. The standard of teaching was quite good, but it was impossible to escape the persistent reminders of racial segregation. The students even had to live in rondavels – small round thatched huts – so that they should 'develop along their own lines'; conventional rectangular buildings were, as Desmond recalled years later, 'somehow harmful to our Bantu psyches'.[4] They endured endless insults, especially as the college was in white Pretoria. Stanley Motjuwadi, who went on to train as a teacher with Tutu, recalls how he was once going through a park when he saw some white boys sitting on the grass and realised he would have to pass them. Instinctively he scented trouble and was prepared to sprint off. As he neared the group one of them stood up and threw a stone at him, so he started running. A second stone was on its way when the white boy's friend stopped him. Was there, perhaps, a civilised white boy in the park? There was not. As Stanley ran, he heard the boy say, in Afrikaans, 'What the hell, why do you dirty that stone?' Another incident shows black wit in the face of white boorishness. A friend of Tutu's was walking along Paul Kruger Street, the main street in Pretoria, when he saw three burly Afrikaners coming towards him. 'I don't give way to monkeys,' said one of them, pushing his way through. The black boy let him pass, bowing gracefully and saying, 'I usually do.'

Racial prejudice even found its way into the classroom. There was a biology lecturer who showed the students a specimen of human skin under a microscope. One of the boys enquired about the spots he could see on the enlarged fragment. 'Never mind about them,' he was told, 'the skin comes from a native I killed in the bush. I tried to wash it off in acid, but it wouldn't go white.' Another occasion Desmond remembers was during the oral examination for his Finals, when the examiner pointed to some ink that had been spilled on a desk and said scornfully, '*Kaffirwerk*'.

The students do not seem to have minded this loutish behaviour too much – they were used to it, brought up to it, they had never known anything else. But Tutu's tolerance was stretched when a black priest, Canon John Tsebe, was at the receiving end of this sort of treatment. It was at a meeting of the college debating society at which Tutu, as chairman of the society, had invited Father Trevor Huddleston to speak. After the address – on the relevance of religion to the problems of everyday life – the Afrikaner Principal, a member of the Dutch Reformed Church (DRC), asked Father Huddleston to his house for a cup of tea. Huddleston's request that he might bring an African priest with him was greeted with embarrassed silence and the three men walked across the veld to the Principal's house, where Father Huddleston was entertained in the sitting room, while Canon Tsebe was shown into the office. Huddleston recalls: 'We all had tea – was it from the same pot? – and were treated courteously, but separately. Only the light of the moon and the sounds of the veld we shared as South Africans that night.'[5]

Tutu, like most of his friends and contemporaries, was not politicised and did not think in terms of boycotts or strikes, or even of peaceful demonstrations, but he was deeply aware of the unjust society in which they lived. Iron was beginning to enter the souls of these black students. When they listened to the news and heard that, for instance, a white had been killed in a car accident, the whole place would erupt as they cheered and shouted 'One oppressor less'. Desmond remembers even then feeling that this degree of bitterness, in people who were going to become teachers and mould the minds of children, was very frightening.

In 1954 Tutu passed the Transvaal Bantu Teacher's Diploma and taught for a year at his old school, Madibane High, living with his parents and commuting from Krugersdorp, as in his High School days. He used the time on the train to mark students' essays, leaving the evenings free to study for a postal degree. The following year, he obtained his BA from the University of South Africa; his subjects were Zulu, Sociology, English, History of Education, Biology and History.

Again he was fortunate in the people he met – maybe something in him drew these people to him. He was helped in his studies by one of the great South Africans who were active in the non-violent protest campaigns of the 1950s – Robert Mangaliso Sobukwe. Sobukwe, who a few years later was to become the first President of the Pan-Africanist Congress (PAC) and whose declared aim was government 'of the African, by the African, for the African', was the first major political figure that Desmond came to know personally. Sobukwe was someone to whom students often turned and though Tutu did not join in his political activities, the qualities he admired in 'The Prof', as Sobukwe was known at the University of the Witwatersrand, give a clue as to the way he himself was developing:[6]

> He had an outstanding intellect and yet walked with the humblest, who felt at home in his company. He was too great to have a base or mean thought, and so quite amazingly he was untouched by bitterness, despite the unjust and cruel experiences he underwent for what he believed with all the fibre of his being. Even his most determined opponents had to admit that his was an attractive and magnetic personality. All who met him fell under the spell of his irresistible smile and charm. Even the Security Police ate out of his hand. They could not help it. He had the gentleness of a dove and yet he had the unshaken firmness of the person of principle.

On July 2nd, 1955, Desmond Tutu, with a year's teaching experience and a BA behind him, was married. His bride was Leah Shenxane, who had been one of his father's brightest pupils. She lived with one of her elder brothers in a rented backyard in Munsieville, while their mother worked as a domestic servant in Springs. Leah was a close friend of Desmond's younger sister Gloria, so she had known the Tutu family for years and was frequently in and out of their home. As a giggling, noisy primary schoolgirl she had made no impression on the studious Desmond. 'He was a stuck-up Headmaster's son. All I could say to him was "Hi". I never got to talking to him as he was always hoity-toity, reading. I liked him the first time I saw him, but he was too stuck-up to notice.' By the time she was at teacher training college, a beautiful as well as a highly intelligent girl, he did, with Gloria's encouragement, notice her. It was not long before he asked her to marry him.

Despite the richness of their married life, despite over thirty years' close and happy reliance on this strong woman, it was not inevitable that Desmond should marry. The manner of his proposal shows that already he was drawn to a religious way of life. He made it clear to Leah that if she rejected him he would not ask anyone else; it was not a threat, he assured her, but he had been seriously contemplating joining the Community of the Resurrection (CR). He was to become even more deeply indebted to this admirable group of men, but already their influence, in particular that of Father Huddleston, was making an indelible mark on him.

However, any vocation he might have had was not put to the test; Leah accepted and they began to plan their wedding. Despite their poverty, African love of ritual and ceremony ensured that somehow it would be a great occasion. Desmond could not afford a new suit, so his sister Sylvia promised to buy him one; she was to bring it on the day of the wedding and there were some anxious moments when the celebrations were about to begin and there was no Sylvia, no wedding suit. She arrived with minutes to spare, to the relief of everyone, especially the best man, Stanley Motjuwadi, who having no suit of his own, was wearing Desmond's (which was too large, so had to have the sleeves tucked in) and would, presumably, have had to return it to the groom. African and European customs combined, with Leah in a white dress, bridesmaids, cars and a reception in the community hall together with the ritual slaughtering of beasts, without which no African ceremony would be complete.

After their marriage, Desmond changed jobs as well as status, and began teaching at Munsieville High School, newly built next to the Anglican school where his father was still Headmaster. There are many who remember being taught at primary level by the father, at High School by the son.

Teaching conditions at Munsieville High School were not easy. There were often as many as 60 to a class, with an age range from 14 to 27. This long span was because people would attend school for a year or two, then go out to work for a few years to earn some money – perhaps to support younger members of their families, perhaps to pay their own fees as there was no free education – then return to complete their education.

To say Tutu was a popular and successful teacher would be an understatement – he was a sensation. He was inspiring, even when teaching mathematics, a subject at which he had not himself excelled; he could keep order; he was loved; he fired his pupils with a new vision of life.

Three languages were used at Munsieville High School: English, Afrikaans and the appropriate mother tongue. Language has always been an emotive issue in South Africa. The pupils resented Afrikaans, the language of the oppressor; they even disliked their mother tongue, Xhosa, Tswana or Sotho, as Bantu education sought to force it on them, thereby excluding them from the mainstream of South African life; English was favoured, as on the whole the black students related better to the English, perceiving them as more liberal, more under-standing, more subtle. But Tutu transcended these attitudes. For him language was a means of communication, a tool. If you have a number of tools at your disposal, why deprive yourself? He taught without prejudice, trying to encourage his pupils to use any language imagin-atively and well. His Xhosa-speaking pupils were 'raving mad' over his classes, he even succeeded in arousing interest in Afrikaans classes, and his teaching of English remains to this day a bright memory in his pupils of thirty years ago.

Joe Seremane was one such pupil. As a student he won prizes in a student publication called *Young Opinion*, primarily for English-speaking students; once, talking about Charles Dickens, he so im-pressed a woman in charge of a book exhibition in Johannesburg that she called the white students together to listen to him. He still feels indebted to Tutu's inspiration:

> The dream I have is that when I retire I want to sit down and write. He planted in me that desire. I found through his teaching that it is through writing that you can make a contribution towards improving the lot of humanity. I owe that dream to Desmond, who fired me. People often say 'Oh Joe, you write so well' and I always respond 'It's not me, it's Desmond who taught me all those things.'

It was his ability to arouse interest that enabled Tutu to keep order. Where other teachers used a system of repetition and the rod, having to force the students to work, Tutu encouraged and inspired, so that they would work willingly and on their own. He never used corporal punishment or needed to. Though well aware of truancy and tricks and able to deal with them, when the boys teased and distracted the girls Tutu had only to say, 'Talk to them, tell them to go away, tell them we are working.'

An incident that took place when Tutu was teaching at Munsieville High School shows that he already possessed the courage that was to be tested so often in later life. Munsieville was a rough area, the gangsters tougher than anywhere else on the Reef, even in those days carrying guns. One day a group of them came to the school looking for girls. There was panic. The Headmaster hid in his office, the teachers locked the classroom doors and in Tutu's class the girls were crying, the boys rushing to secure their doors. Paying no attention to their cries of 'Don't go out, they'll kill you', Tutu threw open the door and confronted the gangsters, who were as surprised as the students were frightened. For a while he talked to them, eventually managing to take the gun. Soon the terrified pupils heard the sound of laughter as their teacher sent the gangsters packing.

He was more like a friend than a teacher to many of the pupils, who would often read in their spare time and discuss the books with him. Their affection was shown in their manner of address. His colourful rendering of *The Three Musketeers* of Dumas led to the nickname 'D'Artagnan'; he introduced them to the French Revolution with an insight that earned him the title 'Monsieur'; others, knowing that his pet name at home was 'Boy', called him *'Braboy'* – lovable boy, charming boy.

Like all good teachers, his influence went beyond the subjects that he taught; for instance in discussing Christopher Marlowe's *Faust*, he would reflect on the nature of ambition. Joe Seremane still remembers the soft, chilling tones of Tutu delivering Marlowe's lines when Faustus realises the commitment he has made – that he has given up his soul:

> Ah, Faustus, now hast thou but one bare hour to live,
> And then thou must be damned perpetually;
> Stand still you ever-moving spheres of heaven,
> That time may cease, and midnight never come . . .
> O lente, lente currite noctis equi:
> The stars stand still, time runs, the clock will strike,
> The devil will come, and Faustus must be damned.

The dramatic rendering and the quality of the thought that accompanied his teaching of the play had a permanent effect on Joe's attitude to ambition: 'Through that type of presentation he was telling us we should be masters of our aspirations and ambitions. Don't sell your soul for anything. Every time you have an ambition you've got to reflect seriously and see what the implications are for you and for society as a whole. You must not be self-centred.'

Tutu the teacher could control because he could inspire, he could pass on his vision of life because he was loved and respected. The total man was emerging in all his richness.

Desmond Tutu had barely begun teaching when the government struck again: On March 31st, 1955, the Bantu Education Act was implemented. It was the most deliberately vicious of all the legislation of the 1950s, seeking, as it did, to ensure that black people remained for ever in a position of servitude. The declared aim of the Act was to produce Africans who would aspire to nothing higher than 'certain forms of labour'.

That the Nationalist Government found such an Act necessary was a back-handed tribute to the mission schools. It is easy to criticise the missions as being an arm of Western imperialism, to claim that they invaded African soil armed with a Bible in one hand and a gun in the other; probably it has more truth than many Christians would wish to recognise. However, there is no doubting the contribution they made in the field of education.

It was the missions who started educating Africans in the 1850s. They erected the buildings, paid the teachers and supervised the running of the schools. After three-quarters of a century the State gave small Grants-in-Aid, inevitably tied to corresponding State control, but as late as 1945, when Tutu was a fourteen-year-old schoolboy, there were only 230 government schools against 4,360 mission schools. Even so, it was not enough, and the Africans struggled to contribute to their children's education themselves. Father Huddleston remembers how:[7]

> Empty garages, disused church halls, the backyards of private houses became private schools . . . Many times I have gone round to the school in Tucker Street, an old, crumbling red-brick chapel; its windows broken, its wooden floor curving and cracking under the weight of children sitting there, a hundred, two hundred perhaps, their slates in their hands, no desks, no benches, no blackboards, no books . . . Just the teacher sitting at a rickety wooden table, trying to hold their attention . . . 'Say after me . . . C A T . . . say it . . .'

The Africans' avidity for education is boundless, not least because, in the words of Chief Albert Luthuli, 'The riches of the land and the material opulence of the city are not for Africans. All the more, then, did we regard education as a thirsty wayfarer yearns for a water-hole.'[8]

But at least, under the mission schools, there were some Africans who were receiving a reasonable education. For the lucky ones, there were high standards and a broad range of subjects, corresponding to the British syllabus; the two cultures met and married, each enriching the other. Occasionally people claimed that schools like Edendale and St Peter's, Rosettenville, produced 'Black Englishmen' – claims that angered Chief Albert Luthuli: 'I am aware of a profound gratitude for what I have learned. I remain an African. I think as an African, I speak as an African, I act as an African, and as an African I worship the God whose children we all are. I do not see why it should be otherwise.'[9]

The government, however, did think it should be otherwise. Seeing black Africans becoming educated, realising just how able they were, that there was no reason, intellectually, why they should not occupy the highest positions, was not at all what it intended. Educated Africans might spread liberal ideas, they could even threaten white domination.

Politicians wanting to manipulate the social order must deal with the system and content of education.

The Bantu Education Act was based on the findings of the Eiselen Commission of 1949. Its lengthy report included research into the relative brainpower of Africans and Europeans and concluded that the African child differed from the European so slightly, both physically and psychologically, that there was no reason why they should not profit from a similar education. Despite these findings, the government devised a system of 'Bantu Education' which was to be taken away from the Department of Education and put under the Department of Native Affairs, whose Minister was, at the time, Dr Verwoerd. Soon South Africa would be able to boast of having the only educational system in the world deliberately designed to render its pupils unable to participate in the running of their country.

The Nationalists felt no shame in what they were doing; speakers debating the issue in Parliament as early as 1945 rivalled one another in their mutual assurances. J. N. le Roux asserted: 'We should not give the Natives an academic education, as some people are prone to do. If we do this we shall later be burdened with a number of academically trained Europeans and non-Europeans, and who is going to do the manual work in the country?'[10] 'The Natives should learn to be good natives as tribal natives and should not be imitators of the white man,' cried C. R. Swart.[11] Another speaker, Captain Strydom, was adamant that the African must not be allowed to develop, particularly in education: 'We say the African must live in his hut and we must live in the house. He must remain separate and in his place.'[12] When the Bill was eventually tabled in 1953, most fervent of all was Dr Verwoerd, himself a product of German universities and a Nazi sympathiser:[13]

> My department's policy is that Bantu education should stand with both its feet in the reserves. What is the use of teaching the Bantu child mathematics when it cannot use it in practice? . . . It is of no avail to him to receive a training which has as its aim absorption in the European community. Until now he has been subject to a school system which drew him away from his own community and misled him by showing him the green pastures of European society in which he is not allowed to graze.

The whole basis of apartheid was exposed as he said: 'I just want to remind honourable members that if the Native in South Africa today is being taught to expect that he will live his adult life under a policy of equal rights, he is making a big mistake.'

Gone were the days when blacks could hope to receive the same education as whites. Now they were to be fed what Tutu accurately calls 'a thin gruel'. Apart from studying their mother tongues, gaining a rudimentary knowledge of Afrikaans and English and long hours devoted to religious activities, there was little intellectual sustenance. The three Rs gave way to manual, even menial, work: 'Broom, pick and shovel are the tools he must be familiar with. It sometimes happens that children spend as much as a whole week in the brickyard making bricks for school buildings. Or they have to stop school work to go road-making.'[14] Heavy penalties were imposed on anyone teaching without the Minister's permission. A retired African teacher gathered some children together, partly to keep them off the streets; he was found teaching them under the trees, arrested and fined £75.

The old textbooks were banished, to be replaced by hastily written books considered suitable for Bantu schools; teachers were retrained, deprived of professional status and owned, body and soul, by the Department of Native Affairs. Their morale was lowered by deplorable service conditions, loss of security of tenure and low pay. The salaries which European teachers enjoyed were considered in no way a fit or permissible criterion for paying Bantu teachers, who were, in effect, forced to become collaborators in apartheid.

It is not hard to imagine the effect these changes had on Desmond Tutu. He who wanted his pupils to become free, independent adults, able to think for themselves, was being told deliberately to limit their knowledge. Years later he addressed the students of the University of the Witwatersrand on freedom and education. With an exuberant string of metaphors he accused the educational system of teaching people what to think rather than how to think: 'It is designed to produce docile unquestioning creatures who could not say "boo" to a goose. They are taught that the best way to survive is by toeing the line, not rocking the boat and keeping in with the herd – totally at variance with the ideals of true liberalism (which, do note, is close to liberation).'[15] His anger mounted as he decried a system of education that stuffed people with 'predigested "facts" and readymade, shop-soiled, flyblown hackneyed responses'. Good education, for Tutu, is meant to make people realise their full potential, become more fully human. There is no reason to believe he did not think in the same way in 1955; how could he be party to this new dispensation?

It was a hard decision. He had only just qualified as a teacher, he had no other job to go to. He loved the children, he loved teaching and he excelled at it. The Act was implemented first at the junior level, so he stayed for three years to follow through the children he had started to teach, and then he left.

3

Growing into priesthood

The anguishing decision to leave the work he so enjoyed caused Desmond Tutu to ask himself some very radical questions about what he should do with his life. During his time at Munsieville High School he thought long and hard and made his decision: he offered himself to the Bishop of Johannesburg to train for the priesthood and was accepted.

He had no illusions about his vocation, freely admitting he 'didn't have very high, noble, reasons for going to theological college'. There was, however, a sound basis for his choice. He was a deeply committed Christian, actively involved in the life of the Church. In 1955, along with his old scoutmaster Zakes Mohutsioa, he had been admitted as a sub-Deacon at Krugersdorp, so he was regularly administering the chalice during Holy Communion, reading the Epistle, even conducting Matins; he had for a while been choirmaster. He had fallen under the spell of people like Father Sekgaphane, Pastor Makhene and Father Trevor Huddleston, whose influence had inspired him to consider following in their footsteps. In any case, he needed a job, one which gave some direction to his life. But these various pulls do not amount to the mysterious magnetism of a vocation; it is quite probable that had it not been for the Bantu Education Act, he might have lived out his life as a brilliant, but relatively obscure, teacher.

It cannot have been an easy decision. Desmond Tutu knew his abilities – how could he not? – and the ministry was, in those days, a less significant job than teaching for an ambitious black person. Black priests were respected by their own community, but they occupied a lowly place in white eyes – remember Canon John Tsebe, who was not allowed to drink tea in the white man's sitting room. They were, according to another friend of Tutu's, Godfrey Pitje, 'doomed to be shepherded and controlled by white priests, able only to eat the crumbs from their tables'. Though the gap was narrowing, there had been a gross disparity between the stipends of black and white priests; nor could black priests realistically aspire to high positions on the clerical ladder – the first black Bishop, Alpheus Zulu, was not consecrated until 1960. On a personal level, Tutu's father was deeply depressed that this gifted young man, whom he had educated to university degree standard and had hoped might become headmaster of a High School, should make a move that was, at least in his eyes, a step down the professional ladder. Even some of Desmond's friends disapproved. Joe Seremane, who was in prison on Robben Island for political offences at the time, remembers how he and his companions, many of whom were Christians, were devastated at the news that their brilliant teacher was becoming a priest – from their experience of the way he taught, they had been expecting him 'to produce many Einsteins'. In any case, they felt cheated by the Church, whose part in the struggle for liberation had disappointed them. 'What a waste,' they said, 'a wonderful brain like that going into the Church.'

Nor were candidates for ordination going to be free of apartheid; the government was tightening its grip even on the churches. The year that Desmond was accepted for training saw Dr Verwoerd's announcement of the Native Laws Amendment Bill, with its infamous Clause 29(c), known as 'the church clause', stipulating that no church in the 'white' areas could admit an African without the permission of the Minister of Native Affairs. Though defiance and protest from the churches caused this Bill to be amended and to have little effect, its very existence reveals that the Church, enjoined by Christ to teach all nations, could be threatened by racist legislation. The religious climate was one that saw individual churches observing their own forms of racism, for instance providing a special bench at the back of churches for blacks to occupy and preventing them making their Communion until the end, when all the whites in the congregation had been up to the altar. Might their black lips sully the cup?

However, Tutu's mind was made up – he later referred to 'God grabbing me by the scruff of my neck' – and in 1958, when he left Munsieville High School, he went to St Peter's, Rosettenville, the theological college run by the Fathers of the Community of the Resurrection. St Peter's College had grown from being a school for catechists and interpreters in the first decade of the century, to becoming a college for training Africans to the ordained ministry. In comparison to English theological colleges the standard had not been high, but by 1958 the Principal was Father Godfrey Pawson, honoured by his fellow monks as the most outstanding lecturer in their Community at the time. He was very much an English priest, a profoundly orthodox Anglo-Catholic. Though he was too old to empathise very well with the Africans and though many of them found him a formidable figure, under his leadership St Peter's reached new heights.

Desmond, not easily frightened of anyone, was well able to profit from his teaching.

There were two courses open to the students: the Certificate of Theology, examined internally, and the Licentiate of Theology, which fell under the auspices of the Church of the Province of South Africa. Desmond was one of only two students in his year who were doing the L.Th., which was considerably the higher of the two courses – the equivalent of the general ordination examination in the United Kingdom. The syllabus covered Old and New Testament studies, Church History, Doctrine, Greek, Morals, Ascetics and Worship.

Not many blacks offering themselves for ordination training were graduates. Desmond Tutu was unique in both having a degree and four years' teaching experience. He was a star from the moment he arrived at the college; the only student who came near him was Laurence Zulu, who was to become Bishop of Zululand. Father Aelred Stubbs, who succeeded Father Pawson as Principal and was in charge of St Peter's for Desmond's last two terms, remembers him well: 'My view of Desmond intellectually is that essentially he's an assimilator, rather than an original mind. He was very quick, very bright. He was also very acceptable from an English point of view, because of this great gift of assimilation, more than any other African I've known.' He was so quick, so advanced, that he found the lectures slow and dull, and Father Pawson would give him private tuition. He excelled in tests, his name usually coming top, with marks in the 80s and 90s. He did so brilliantly in the first part of his exams (his results surpassed those of any of the white students at St Paul's in Grahamstown) that he was expected to get a *summa cum laude* in his finals. So he did, in a tragi-comic way. The registrar for the examinations managed to lose all the students' exam papers. Father Stubbs was particularly upset for Desmond, who had been doing so well, and he insisted that his papers should be marked at the level of his previous exams. Such was the confidence of his teachers that he was given the benefit of the doubt and awarded his L.Th., with two distinctions.

His contemporaries were surprised to find him humble, more concerned to encourage them in their studies than to relish his own success. He would be embarrassed when he was congratulated on his high marks and would refer to his private tuition in a self-mocking way, saying that 'only educated people have extra tutorials'. Father Stubbs thought it 'greatly to his credit that he didn't become an intolerable little prig, which could easily have happened'. Though there were some who were jealous of him, a few who did not like his manner and called him 'a strutter' and one or two among the staff who felt he was too ready to accept gifts from liberal whites anxious to help the students, he was popular. Sipho Masemola, now a priest in the East Rand, delighted in his jocular, gregarious personality, 'bubbling with love for people'. David Nkwe, now an Archdeacon in the diocese of Johannesburg, remembers him 'oozing love, laughter and caring'.

It is impossible to exaggerate the importance of the Community of the Resurrection in Tutu's spiritual development – he regards his debt to them as incalculable. It is they who, in his words, 'enabled me to see very clearly something that I hope has stayed with me – the centrality of the spiritual.'[1] Every day there was compulsory meditation before breakfast, followed by Matins and Mass. There were frequent retreats and devotional addresses. He was continually impressed at the amount of time these men devoted to prayer; apart from the round of monastic hours, there was always someone on his knees in the Fathers' chapel. They taught by example rather than by precept; whole generations of black students were impressed at the way their spiritual life was demonstrated in their total identification with the oppressed and suffering – when the residents of Sophiatown were forcibly removed, they were there, when there were problems in the schools, it was they who would be speaking with the voice of sanity. Through their influence, Tutu's spirituality became rooted in the ordinary, the everyday, the down-to-earth:[2]

> It is from these remarkable men that I have learned that it is impossible for religion to be sealed off in a watertight compartment that has no connection with the hurly burly business of ordinary daily living, that our encounter with God in prayer, meditation, the sacraments and bible study is authenticated and expressed in our dealings with our neighbour, whose keeper we must be willy nilly.

His absorption of an incarnational spirituality, that sees God in everything and everyone, continues to constrain him not only to do whatever he can to help people in trouble, but to love his fellow man, whether or not that love is returned or even welcomed.

It was through the years at St Peter's that the Eucharist, prayer, meditation and retreats became so integral a part of Desmond's life. He used often to be found praying in the chapel at 5.30 in the morning and the habit of prayer has never left him. 'If I do not spend a reasonable amount of time in meditation early in the morning, then I feel a physical discomfort – it is worse than having forgotten to brush my teeth! . . . I would be completely rudderless and lost if I did not have these times with God.'[3]

Again there were individuals whose influence was to stay with him, again it was gentleness and selflessness that most impressed him. Father Timothy Stanton, a shy and reserved man who in his late sixties went to prison for six months rather than testify in a trial for subversion involving two Afrikaner students, is still his Father Confessor and spiritual director: 'He is quite undoubtedly a holy man, truly saintly. I remember how I was amazed that he, the Vice-Principal, and a white man to boot, would join us black students in doing some of the most menial chores in college.'[4]

In his third year Desmond was made senior student. It was the custom for the senior student to be appointed by the Fathers, though he had to represent the students – an absurd position that no one could accomplish very satisfactorily. David Nkwe, who was in his first year while Desmond held the office, was very impressed at the way he made all the first year students feel important, no one was allowed to feel insignificant. Most of them saw him as someone with a bright future; some saw him as a future lecturer, who might one day be Principal of the college, one or two claim to have seen him as a future Bishop, but they all remember him as someone who was already taking the lead. For instance in the way he encouraged the students to realise that a senior student must have their confidence and not merely be imposed on them by the Fathers; in turn he persuaded the Fathers that the college could be more democratically run. His role as a reconciler was beginning.

By 1960, when he had passed his L.Th. and was ordained Deacon, Tutu had discovered his vocation as a priest and his gift for reconciliation was emerging. However, he still did not think politically. He was not unusual. Black people in those days put up with conditions which twenty-five years later would be considered quite unthinkable. Like many of his contemporaries Desmond simply did not consider standing up to the government or becoming involved in organising resistance. But there were those who did; in fact looking back at the 1950s is to look back on a decade of protest.

It was in 1952, with the Defiance Campaign, that black South African protest first hit the world's headlines. The previous year had seen black freedom abused and eroded by more and more legislation against them and at their annual meeting in December the African National Congress, who had been trying to represent the interests of African, 'coloured' and Indian people since 1912, passed a resolution that the government should be asked to repeal 'six unjust laws'. If they did not, the ANC, together with the South African Indian Council, would organise a campaign of peaceful resistance. Anthony Sampson, then editor of the African magazine *Drum*, attended the meeting and heard 300 people sing the hymn that had become the Congress anthem, '*Nkosi Sikele' iAfrika*'.[5]

> I watched the faces of the crowd, transformed by passion. A delicate little clergyman with a tiny goatee beard, straining his thin throat with singing; a ragged old man swinging his arms to the rhythm, gazing rapturously at the rafters; a bulging woman shouting the song with indignation in every syllable. I noticed, to my surprise, a meek-looking messenger who delivered packages to *Drum* singing earnestly among the crowd. He came up to me afterwards. 'Please, baas, don't tell my baas that you saw me here . . .'

At the end of the anthem Dr Moroka, then President of Congress, raised his hand in the ANC salute, calling *Mayibuye*; the crowd shouted back *Africa*. ('Come back, Africa' – the traditional ANC slogan. It refers to the old days of freedom before the white man came.)

The government's response was that it had no intention of repealing the laws, which in any case were protective, not degrading; it would quell any disturbances and deal with the leaders.

Mass protests – 'a warm-up' according to Chief Albert Luthuli, then President of the Natal Congress – were organised on April 6th, a date chosen with grim humour. It was the tercentenary of Jan van Riebeeck's arrival in the Cape;[6] a day when whites would celebrate 300 years of 'progress', while blacks could only look back on 300 years of exploitation. There were gatherings all over the country: in Cape Town, Pretoria, Port Elizabeth, East London and Durban. Crowds of up to 10,000 demonstrated their support, while in Johannesburg Dr Moroka called for 'a solemn oath that we will muster all our forces of mind, body and soul to see that this state of affairs, these crushing conditions under which we live, shall not continue any longer'.[7]

The campaign proper was launched on June 26th, known as Freedom Day since 1950, when demonstrations and strikes in opposition to the Suppression of Communism Act were held on that date. It spread like wildfire through the country and continued for months as volunteers deliberately defied the apartheid laws, intending to be arrested and to put such strain on the prisons and law courts that the system would break down:[8]

> The first day set the pattern for the campaign. In the next five months, eight thousand people went to jail for one to three weeks. They marched into locations, walked out after curfew, travelled in European railway coaches, entered stations by European entrances. Everywhere they marched quietly and did what they were told, singing hymns with their

thumbs up. They always informed the police beforehand, to make sure they would be arrested.

A new spirit was emerging as people learned to act politically – the country would never be quite the same again.

But that is to speak with hindsight. On Desmond and his fellow students, engrossed in their studies at the teacher-training course in Pretoria, the Defiance Campaign made little impact. There was the odd person who would raise his fist in the ANC salute during the singing of the National Anthem, they would read about people being arrested, but somehow it did not seem their business. Desmond admits that 'You would think "How wonderful", but you didn't think that this called on you to be particularly involved.'

By 1955, when the Freedom Charter was written, Desmond was, through Father Huddleston's involvement, a little closer to events, but he was still fairly remote. He was coping with the implementation of the Bantu Education Act and his decisions consequent on that; he was married a week after the Charter was proclaimed – there was plenty to occupy his attention. 'You just said, "Well, there's another landmark in our people's march to freedom", but you didn't think that there was any significant part for you to play.'

The Freedom Charter must be one of the most democratic documents ever written. A leaflet in several languages was sent out by the multi-racial National Action Council of the Congress of the People. In a poetic style, reminiscent of the Lebanese mystic Kahlil Gibran, it addressed farmers, miners, factory workers, teachers, housewives and mothers. Each group of people was separately invoked:

WE CALL THE PEOPLE OF SOUTH AFRICA BLACK AND WHITE
LET US SPEAK TOGETHER OF FREEDOM!
We call the teachers, students and the preachers.
Let us speak of the light that comes from learning,
and the ways we are kept in darkness.
Let us speak of great services we can render,
and of narrow ways that are open to us.
Let us speak of laws, and governments, and rights.
LET US SPEAK OF FREEDOM.

The responses flooded in, sometimes drafted formally, sometimes scrawled on odd bits of paper. Their demands were discussed and drafted into a Charter at a meeting on the weekend of June 25th/26th; the site chosen was a football ground in Kliptown, near Johannesburg, where 3,000 delegates packed the enclosure, while another 2,000 watched from outside. By the Sunday evening the leaders were able to read the Preamble and the ten points that make up the Charter. As each section was read it was acclaimed by a show of hands and shouts of *Africa*. The ten sections are headed:

THE PEOPLE SHALL GOVERN.
ALL NATIONAL GROUPS SHALL HAVE EQUAL RIGHTS.
THE PEOPLE SHALL SHARE IN THE COUNTRY'S WEALTH.
THE LAND SHALL BE SHARED AMONG THOSE WHO WORK IN IT.
ALL SHALL BE EQUAL BEFORE THE LAW.
ALL SHALL ENJOY EQUAL HUMAN RIGHTS.
THERE SHALL BE WORK AND SECURITY.
THE DOORS OF LEARNING AND CULTURE SHALL BE OPENED.
THERE SHALL BE HOUSES, SECURITY AND COMFORT.
THERE SHALL BE PEACE AND FRIENDSHIP.

It ends, 'These freedoms we shall fight for, side by side, throughout our lives, until we have won our liberty.'

Hardly a revolutionary document – in fact it has been criticised for its declaration that 'South Africa belongs to all who live in it, *black and white*'. Nevertheless, as the great campaigner Helen Joseph gave her speech on houses, security and comfort, the police arrived, bearing a warrant to investigate for high treason. Until darkness fell, they searched the delegates and seized thousands of copies of the Charter. They were wasting their time; an idea cannot be destroyed. Over thirty years later the Freedom Charter lives in the hearts and minds of millions of black people in South Africa and Kliptown football stadium is revered as holy ground.

As the Congress Movement grew stronger and more unified, so it posed a greater threat to the government. At sunrise on December 5th, 1956, eighteen months after that great day at Kliptown, 156 leaders of the Movement were arrested and charged with high treason, a charge which carried the death penalty. The 'Treason Trials' dragged on for four long years, ending with the acquittal of all the defendants.

The young ordinands at St Peter's, Rosettenville, have one very special memory of the Treason Trialists. During the second year of the trial, charges were dropped against sixty-one of the accused. Two of the released men, Chief Albert Luthuli and Professor Z. K. Matthews (known as 'The Chief' and 'The Prof'), came over to the priory and met some of the students, who were becoming increasingly concerned about the fate of their country. David Nkwe was impressed by the way Tutu reacted to the visit of these two great statesmen, one a future Nobel Prize-winner, the other head of Fort Hare University until he was forced to leave. Tutu spoke for all when he said 'we need a dozen such people to demonstrate to our country that blacks are human beings'.

While Tutu was in his last year at St Peter's, South Africa hit the world's headlines again in one of the blackest days of its history – March 21st, 1960.

During the 1950s a few African countries had gained independence and 1960 saw no fewer than seventeen other States throw off the shackles of colonial rule: early in 1960 the British Prime Minister, Harold Macmillan, warned the South African government of the strength of African nationalism in his famous 'winds of change' speech. The spirit of freedom was in the air. The South African resistance movements, encouraged by the examples of their neighbours in the north, decided once again to voice their protest in organised, peaceful defiance. The ANC intended to hold demonstrations against the pass laws throughout the country on March 31st. In a clearly competitive move the recently formed Pan-Africanist Congress (the 'Africanist' element who had left the ANC, wanting government 'of the African, by the African, for the African' rather than believing, with the ANC, that South Africa belonged to both black and white) decided to launch its own campaign ten days earlier. The people were to leave their passes at home, assemble outside police stations and demand to be arrested.

Early in the morning of March 21st the PAC leaders surrendered themselves at Orlando police station. As the day drew on, people began to gather round the country; in Sharpeville the crowd swelled to some 10,000. They had been led to believe that a statement would be made announcing changes in the pass laws and they waited quietly. Suddenly, without any order being given, the police panicked and opened fire. Seven hundred shots were fired into the crowd: 180 people were wounded, 69 killed, many shot in the back as they turned to run away. At Langa township, 1,000 miles away, 2 were killed and 49 injured in a similar situation. That night the crowds went berserk, burning Bantu education schools and public buildings.

The ANC called for a national day of mourning, which was to take the form of a stay-at-home strike on March 28th, the day of the funerals. On the same day the government announced that both the ANC and the PAC were banned. Two days later a country-wide 'state of emergency' was declared.

News of the massacre flashed round the world. Like many others, Tutu heard of it on the radio. 'We were just stunned, we really were. You were benumbed and you didn't, you didn't quite believe. Again there wasn't a great deal that you could do. There you were feeling angry, impotent and not knowing what there was for us to do.' He felt great pride in the Bishop of Johannesburg, Ambrose Reeves, who became a thorn in the flesh of the authorities by drawing attention to the shame of Sharpeville. When the state of emergency was declared Bishop Reeves, fearing arrest, fled to Swaziland. On his return he was greeted by a protective demonstration of students of St Peter's, who felt the clear support of his flock would make it harder for the government to take action against him. Their gesture must have touched him, but did not affect the authorities. For a few days he stayed at St Benedict's House, the convent next to St Peter's, shadowed by a police car. The students were mystified by the comings and goings of the police car, shattered when their Bishop was eventually deported. They were seeing the brutality of the government from a new perspective.

Some people wonder at Tutu's lack of involvement in the political protest of this period – indeed he has been known to question it himself – but he does not feel there is much to be gained from self-recrimination; in any case it was only the minority who were politically active. His first concern was to learn to be a good priest. In December 1960 he was ordained Deacon in St Mary's Cathedral, Johannesburg, and took up his first curacy at St Alban's Church in Benoni location.

Here his Rector was Canon Mokoatla, a powerful and strict character, an impressive preacher – one of the old-style African priests. Godfrey Pitje didn't feel he treated Desmond very well: 'He was a typical black Englishman, exuding confidence. He seemed to be saying "I have arrived where I am by dint of hard work and effort. These young fellows will never get to the same position".' He tended to treat his new curate like a small boy, who should do menial tasks like washing his car; nor did he help to find reasonable accommodation for Desmond and Leah and the three children that had by now been born to them.

The Tutus' first two children, Trevor (after Father Trevor Huddleston) Thamsanqua and Thandeka Theresa, were born while Tutu was still teaching. The birth of his first child was, for the proud father, 'A very definitive kind of experience. I had a thing in the back of my mind about the perpetuation of my name. Having a son as firstborn says you have arrived, you have made it.' It was not only a proud moment, it was a humbling one. 'You have a little sense of what it must mean to be God. Here you and your wife are and this precious thing has come about through your creative attributes. You have a kind of religious experience when you see your child for the first time.'[9]

Unfortunately, while they were at St Peter's, which in those days was run rather like a monastic institution, he and Leah had not been able to live together and Leah had been so lonely without him that Desmond's mother had looked after the children during the day so that she could start training as a nurse. At Benoni the family, with the birth of Nontomdi Naomi in 1960 now five in number, could at least be together, but in conditions barely acceptable for animals. They were housed in a garage, one room serving as the main bedroom, the children's bedroom, the sitting room and dining room; they used the small second room as a kitchen. Father Stubbs says the Tutu family were living in the worst conditions, without exception, which he had seen any African priest endure. The garage was next to a stable, so in summer it was infested with flies; in winter it was cold, very cold – hardly suitable conditions for someone who was still under the shadow of TB. To the surprise of those who felt Tutu had materialistic ambitions, he never complained. In fact, he did not react in any way, accepting it as part of his vocation to the life of a priest. Canon Mokoatla, typical of the old guard, saw nothing wrong at all. 'These young men need to be put through it,' was his attitude, so, for Tutu's first year as Deacon, the garage was their home.

At the end of 1961, now thirty years old, Tutu was ordained priest. His ordination was not the joyous event it might have been. Bishop Reeves, who should have officiated, had already been deported, while the attitude of Canon Mokoatla left much to be desired. He made himself responsible for Desmond, but completely disregarded Leah and the children. Had it not been for Godfrey Pitje, who brought them to the ceremony, they might not have been present. Godfrey remembers how painful this was for him, seeing them so excluded, let alone for Leah.

Soon after he became a priest Tutu was moved to Thokoza, to a new church in a recently built township – a result of the Group Areas Act. Strictly speaking, he was not yet ready for a church of his own, but here, though he was responsible to the Rector at Natalspruit, he was effectively priest-in-charge and had a fairly free hand. He was also given better accommodation – a four-roomed municipal house. It was a matchbox, with few facilities, but an improvement on a garage.

In these first two years in the ministry Tutu acquired valuable experience. Despite the way Canon Mokoatla treated his curate, Tutu respected and admired him. He is, in fact, greatly indebted to the old priest, for it was through him that Desmond acquired the rudiments of preaching. He learned to take preaching seriously, he learned how powerful a good sermon can be. The foundations of his oratorical style were laid at Benoni.

He also discovered the privilege of priesthood. 'There is the joy of being welcomed into a home as you go round visiting the parishioners. And people share some of their deepest secrets with you; that always leaves me feeling very humble.'[10] His easy, loving way with people endeared him to the parishioners, who were so fond of him that it has even been suggested that Canon Mokoatla was a bit jealous. Tutu, in turn, was deeply impressed by the people he met,[11]

> staggered at the strength of their attachment to Our Lord and amazed by the strange kind of joy they have in the midst of their poverty and suffering. They sometimes brought tears to my eyes. I was infinitely more well off than they were, but when I was grousing they were able to thank God for something good that had happened to them.

Years later Desmond spoke of pastoral visiting to a group of Deacons about to be ordained as priests:[12]

> You can sit all day in your house and not visit your people, not take communion to the sick, to the aged, and nobody will usually complain to you, but your church will grow emptier. You can't love people and not visit them. You can't love them unless you know them, and you can't know them unless you visit them regularly. A good shepherd knows his sheep by name.

Tutu was becoming a pastor, the best sort of pastor who cares, really cares, about his parishioners. Already he felt keen pleasure in visiting their homes, in taking Holy Communion to the sick and the dying. He remembers pain and guilt at the memory of a sick woman who died without a visit from him; he knew he should have called on her and had not.

If initially his vocation had not been overwhelmingly strong, there was no doubting it now.

4

No passbook required

While Tutu was still a curate in Benoni he became the subject of a long correspondence between Father Stubbs and the Reverend Sydney Evans, the Dean of King's College in the University of London. Father Stubbs was becoming increasingly aware of the need for St Peter's to have an African member of staff who could hold his own academically; he was sure that the most suitable man known to him was Desmond Tutu. It was unusual to send someone overseas so soon after his ordination – normally the young priests would serve three years in their first curacy – but Tutu was an older man who had already held a responsible job as a teacher. Father Stubbs was keen that his star pupil should come over to England to read for a degree in theology, then, when he returned to South Africa, that he should join the staff of St Peter's.

Between them, Father Stubbs and Dean Evans made the practical arrangements. In order to sit for a degree at the University of London a 'Statement of Eligibility' was necessary; papers had to be submitted to show the candidate's attainments up to that point. In the case of students from the United Kingdom this is routine, but the papers of overseas students are scrutinised rather more closely. However, soon a delighted Tutu was able to tell the Dean that he had this essential piece of paper, though 'his bank balance was nil'.[1] Money was found from several different sources, including the diocese of Johannesburg and the Community of the Resurrection; he was also given bursaries by King's College and awarded a scholarship by the World Council of Churches' Theological Education Fund. South African politics made this a delicate matter: Tutu advised the Dean that it should be referred to as a 'Church Bursary', as anything to do with the WCC, given its support of revolutionary movements, would be 'hardly acceptable to our government'.[2] Eventually the path was clear; on September 14th, 1962, Tutu arrived in England.

For a while, living in lodgings without his family, he was lonely and homesick, but after a couple of months one of the college tutors found him a curate's flat at St Alban's Church in Golders Green. Desmond wrote ecstatically to the Dean: 'Father Trueman has brought off a coup! The flat is a pleasant modern one with two bedrooms, a bathroom, a kitchenette, a larder, a living room-cum-dining room and a study.' He could have it rent-free in exchange for 'a modest amount of Sunday duty'.[3] Soon Leah arrived with the two older children, Trevor and Theresa, for the moment leaving the youngest, Naomi, with Desmond's mother in Johannesburg. 'It was obviously quite another world to which we had been transported. For one thing we had splendid accommodation in salubrious quarters. There was a park, a ubiquitous and pleasant feature of London, just round the corner from our flat, with penned animals, a further delight to our children.'[4]

It is hard for those who have not been the victims of an oppressive regime to appreciate quite the revelation that living in England was for the Tutus; racism in the United Kingdom is not in the same league as in South Africa. The Tutus hardly realised themselves how conditioned they had become by living under apartheid:[5]

> You didn't know that gnawing away at you was this worm which was sowing a horrible kind of self-doubt in you. You wondered when they called you non-this, non-the-other – you are a non-European coming from non-Europe – whether in fact they weren't perhaps right . . . The most horrible aspect of apartheid, a blasphemous aspect, is it can make a child of God doubt that they are a child of God, when you ask yourself in the middle of the night 'God, am I your step-child?'

So imagine the delight with which they experienced the extraordinary novelty of walking freely, without having to look nervously for signs saying whether or not they were permitted to be where they were; the surprise in seeing mixed couples walking hand-in-hand – for a long time Desmond instinctively worried that their arrest could be imminent; the joy with which they put away their passbooks. 'To be able to just walk around and use any exit, I mean it's almost ineffable. It's difficult to express the sense of exhilaration, of liberation, of being made to feel human.'[6] Desmond and Leah would walk in Trafalgar Square, late at night or in the early hours of the morning, just to savour the freedom of knowing they would not be accosted by a policeman asking for a piece of paper, knowing they would not be told there was a curfew and that black people should not be there. They sometimes asked for directions, even knowing perfectly well where they were going, simply for the pleasure of being addressed courteously by a white unarmed policeman. Once Tutu was waiting in a bank, due to be served next, when a white man rushed past him in a great hurry and tried to jump the queue. 'As a well-behaved Bantu, I was ready to let this happen when the lady bank clerk told him firmly but politely that *I* was next. You could have knocked me down with a feather.'[7] He went back later to thank her and tell her she was now his 'pin-up'. He was even more impressed when she told him she would have done it for anybody.

A familiar tradition of English life, wonderfully pleasing to Tutu, was Speakers' Corner. There he witnessed people 'sometimes spewing forth the most outlandish sentiments' in the presence of a policeman, there not to silence the oratory but to protect freedom of speech. Similarly he was amazed, after the bland lies broadcast by the South African Broadcasting Corporation, to hear the irreverence and abrasiveness with which politicians were interviewed on television; impressed that the Prime Minister, when responding to the weekly challenge of 'Question Time' in Parliament, was treated with such scant respect. There was, he thought, 'a proper iconoclasm about. Sacred cows were for the slaughter. It was exhilarating.'[8]

Overseas students do not necessarily find life in the United Kingdom easy, but Tutu was one of the lucky ones, his passage smoothed by the small but highly developed network of the Community of the Resurrection. It was through Father Stubbs that he was greeted at Heathrow Airport by the writer Nicholas Mosley, through him too that he met Martin Kenyon, who was to become a lifelong friend of the whole Tutu family.

Martin Kenyon, a man of many friends and at the time an energetic bachelor, introduced Desmond to aspects of British life that elude many native-born Britons. Within weeks of his arrival he took him to the Travellers' Club in Pall Mall, where Tutu, in a manner not typical of London clubs in the early 1960s, was warmly welcomed and addressed by the porter as 'Sir'. After the treatment he was accustomed to receiving in his own country, this reception must have been a gratifying experience; his most vivid memory of the occasion, however, is eating grouse and picking the shot out of his teeth. With Martin he indulged his passion for cricket at no less a mecca than Lord's, where they sat in the stand reserved for friends of MCC members. They went together to a residential conference on 'Nationalism, Neutralism and Neo-colonialism', where Tutu was one of the tutors; the speakers included the President of the African National Congress, Oliver Tambo, exiled since 1960 from South Africa and Tutu's old hero, Bishop Ambrose Reeves. A free afternoon was spent visiting Haddon Hall, home of the Duke of Rutland; on another Tutu played in that traditional cricketing event 'England v. the World'. One summer holiday they all went to stay in a cottage next to Martin Kenyon's parents in Lydbury North, a remote Shropshire village on the Welsh borders, where the Tutus' black skins were as much a novelty to the villagers as the young calves were to the Tutu children.

People are often amazed by Tutu's lack of bitterness, and he is quite ready to admit how much this is due to his time in England. He is quite certain that had they not had this experience they could have had enormous chips on their shoulders.[9]

> Now, because we have met white people and suddenly seem to have made a tremendous scientific discovery, that actually white people aren't so bad, we have been able to go back to South Africa, and even when we have encountered horribleness we have known that no, you can't have stereotypes, because that's exactly what they have been doing to us. That they are ordinary human beings, some of them good human beings and some bad human beings. And so we can walk tall.

So, too, his delight in the academic education spilled over. After the stultifying restrictions of education for blacks in South Africa, he marvelled at the 'bewildering array of options', delighted in the lack of dogmatism, typified by the lecturer who invariably used the phrase 'It is not unreasonable to suppose . . .', and was overcome by sitting at the feet of people who were, at least in his discipline, household names. 'Mind boggling! Well, I couldn't contain myself. And here they were, I mean you could really touch them!'[10]

He had indeed been well guided. King's is a fully constituted college of the University of London, taking London degrees. Though in the early 1960s it was less radical, less critical, less exciting than it was to become towards the end of the decade, it had a sound academic reputation and was the one college in London that specialised in teaching theology both to those who went on for a fourth-year ordination course, and those who, like Tutu, were already ordained. Being a multi-faculty college where students had contact with other disciplines, it was more alive to the outside world than many universities, becoming a magnet for overseas students and boasting teaching staff of the calibre of Professor Ulrich Simon and Professor Geoffrey Parrinder. Not least, it was ahead of many universities in its disregard of colour.

The college had experienced the embarrassment of overseas students coming half across the world only to find they were unable to settle in England, could not stand the climate or, most humiliating, could not cope with the academic standards. Tutu gave the lie to anyone who thought, as some still did, that blacks were of a lower intellectual calibre; his tutors still remember him as a pleasure to teach. The Dean found him 'A joy to have around. He was so vivid, pulsating with life.' Richard Coggins, for a while his tutor in Old Testament studies, experienced him as 'hungry and thirsty for knowledge and well able to absorb and digest it'. He threw himself into the life, determined, as Canon Ronald Brownrigg said, 'to be baked on both sides academically'. He did so well in the Preliminary exams at the end of his first year that the College authorities decided he should change from the ordinary Pass course to the far tougher Honours course, which included Hebrew and the History and Philosophy of Religion.

Liberation theology was not yet a force in the Christian Church; the Jesus of the theological colleges of the early 1960s was no social revolutionary. Tutu was being trained as a traditional Anglican theologian, in a settled atmosphere which gave no hint of the tests to which his thinking was to be put. It did, however, give him a background of knowledge and insight against which his personal faith and inner commitment deepened. It formed the sound hull of a ship which was going to take the buffeting of violent storms.

When it came to the Final BD examinations there were high hopes that he would get a First. He found it an exhausting ordeal and was not pleased with his own performance, but happily his fears were misplaced; he did so well that he was viva'ed for a First. It was the only year that the University Examiners for the BD had vivas and, surprisingly for someone so articulate, Tutu failed on this oral examination. He was, however, awarded a good Second.

It was the custom for graduates who were about to be awarded their degrees to be wined and dined by the Principal or the Dean. In 1965 it was the Dean who took the chair, so it was for him to select one of the students to reply to the toast. He chose Tutu and never forgot his words:

> It was the most moving thing. Desmond said something like this: 'When I was in Africa I thought that perhaps I was no less important than anyone else, though I didn't have any reason to believe this might be true, until I came to England, to King's, where I was treated like everyone else. And this was the turning point. So my gratitude to England and my gratitude to King's is that I have discovered who I am.'

The next day Tutu went to the Royal Albert Hall, a spectacular event attended by hundreds of people, where he was awarded his degree by the Chancellor of the University, the Queen Mother.

Though the intention had been that when he graduated Tutu should return to St Peter's to teach, Father Stubbs, hearing how well he had done, was willing to adjust his plans in order to give Tutu the opportunity of doing a postgraduate course. The tutors were enthusiastic; so was Tutu, in a way which shows how he was beginning to see his future role in South Africa. He wrote to the Dean:[11]

> I would, I think, want to have a shot at it. In a sense it is part of the struggle for our liberation. Please, I hope it does not sound big-headed or, worse, downright silly. But if I go back home as highly qualified as you can make me, the more ridiculous our Government's policy will appear to be to earnest and intelligent people. Away from home we do unfortunately bear the burden of representing our people, who are judged by our achievements or lack of them. I hope this does not sound like something out of Hyde Park Corner.

Previously it had been considered impossible to complete a Master's degree in theology in less than two years, but in 1965 a new higher degree was introduced, taking only one year. So, with the blessing of his tutors and a good Upper Second degree, Tutu was in a position to enrol for the course – the only remaining hurdle was financial.

Tutu, it has to be said, was not good with money. He has been accused of irresponsibility and extravagance, but the truth lies more in a kind of innocence. He had not been brought up with the idea of money as a familiar commodity. If South African blacks had money, they spent it, for the simple reason that they needed something. There was no question of saving – with scarcely enough to go round, the matter did not arise. Couple that background with Tutu's spontaneous, generous personality, add a wife and four children (Mpho, the youngest, was born in England in 1963), and the accusation has to be modified.

The Dean and Father Stubbs, who between them looked after the Tutus like a couple of caring uncles, took endless pains on their behalf, not least in seeing they had enough to live on, and Tutu was appreciative and grateful. On one occasion he had overspent and, in accepting a rebuke from the Dean, wrote back. 'I cannot explain how this happens, for I assure you I am not extravagant. You have been so generous to us. I have done nothing but get and get. I have not given at all.'[12] In his own way, he *would* give, and they knew it.

Eventually his various grants and scholarships were extended, leaving only the question of what subject he should take. At first Father Stubbs favoured Old Testament, but the Dean, doubting whether he had done enough Hebrew, suggested New Testament. In the end Desmond decided for himself. New Testament would be 'full of theological nit-picking', he told one of his tutors; the growing religious force in Africa, the one he needed to know more about, was Islam. It was a theme that had woven itself into his academic life since, as an ordinand, he had entered for the 'Archbishop's Essay Prize', whose subject had to be either Islam or Calvin. The prize had been instituted by Archbishop Joost de Blank, who was appalled at the ignorance of the Anglican clergy in the areas of Calvinism, crucial to an understanding of the Dutch Reformed Church, and Islam, a strong influence in the Western Cape and a growing force throughout Africa. Professor Monica Wilson, who was one of the examiners, found that St Peter's students were by far the best. Best of all was Tutu, who wrote on Islam and won the prize. Now this would be the subject of his Master's degree.

Alongside Desmond's social and academic life in London were his duties as a curate. In Golders Green he had his first experience of ministering to a white congregation, where – not quite knowing what to expect – he discovered his parishioners were ordinary human beings, with the strengths and weaknesses, resentments and triumphs, joys, foibles, sins and sorrows of any other group of people. That this was something of a revelation, surprising him enough for him to recall his reaction in a public statement years later, speaks yet again of the iniquity of apartheid, which leads its victims to believe that human emotions vary with skin colour. Though the churchmanship at St Alban's was a little low for Tutu, and despite the verger, who lived in the flat below the Tutus, protesting that the children made too much noise, both parishioners and curate were content. Even the cold – it snowed from their arrival on Boxing Day until well into February – did not reach them. They felt 'wonderfully insulated' by the warmth of the parishioners and of the priest, the late John Halsey and his wife. Soon the tiny flat became open house to the entire parish. Anyone with worries or problems or just wanting a bit of company was assured of a welcome.

After nearly three years in Golders Green, Tutu wrote to the Dean of King's College, saying he would welcome a change to a parish in a less well-to-do part of London. Wishes can be granted in strange ways: he was moved; but not to a working-class parish, not to another part of London, but to a village in Surrey's 'Gin and Jaguar' belt – Bletchingley. The Tutus were to be thrown into English life in all its variety.

In those days Bletchingley was a mixed parish. There was a council estate, built in the 1940s, but with several aristocratic families of the 'landed gentry', a peer of the realm, a chairman of Lloyds, a number of farmers and farmworkers, some of whom had lived in the village for generations, the tone was almost feudal. This encounter with the British class system was not at all what Tutu had in mind. 'The inhabitants of Bletchingley were divided as with a knife into those who lived on the housing estate and the landed and monied gentry who had the proper accents and had gone to the right public schools and to Oxford and Cambridge.'[13] Nor was a black South African curate quite what the Anglicans of the village had expected – it was rare to see a black skin at all in Bletchingley, least of all in the pulpit. Yet this surprising partnership was to be a resounding success.

That it was such a success was due as much to the parishioners as to Tutu. Though outwardly Bletchingley was a prototype commuter village of the 1960s, once inside the perfectly restored old cottages with their manicured gardens, the manorial houses and the fine old church with its Norman tower, a very different picture emerged. According to Canon Ronald Brownrigg, who was Rector during Desmond's time, this was due to half a dozen people who, by virtue of the way they lived, became leaders of the community. The church was so strong that Sunday, Holy Week and religious festivals were dedicated solely to religious activities – nothing else happened in the village. The spirit was such that the entire village had clubbed together to pay for an Arab ordinand to be trained in Bangalore; there was nothing unusual in finding the floor of the local geriatric asylum being cleaned by a lady of title. The churchmanship was high, which appealed to Desmond, who wrote approvingly to the Dean of King's College about his first impressions: 'The Parish is Catholic with regular confessions and Reservation and a general Intercession book that appears to be used quite conscientiously by the parishioners.'[14]

Outstanding amongst these local leaders was Uvedale Lambert, Guardian of the Shrine at Walsingham, Sheriff of Surrey, Master of Foxhounds and a member of the old Church Assembly before the Synod came into being. He was a successful gentleman farmer, a devout Christian, a brilliant theologian and a member of the Fraternity of the Community of the Resurrection, the lay wing of the order. His home, South Park, a manor house with its own chapel, was for many years a sort of spiritual salon, where twice a year he and his American wife, Melanie, would give 'Holy Parties'.

Never did the spiritual and the secular meet more graciously than at South Park. On arrival the 'retreatant' (if that is the word) would be greeted with an excellently mixed dry Martini, he would be fed on delicious food and could wander round the lovely house and gardens. Yet these weekends, known by some as 'Gin and God' parties, were predominantly serious, with regular prayer and worship and at least seven teaching sessions, taken by members of the Community of the Resurrection like Father Raynes, for whom South Park was almost a second home.

Martin Kenyon was a member of this circle, and one day he

happened to mention to Uvedale Lambert that he was trying to find a curacy for an exceptional black South African who was studying for his Master's degree in theology at King's College. 'I think,' ruminated Lambert, 'that Bletchingley is ready for an overseas curate.' And so it was; the acceptable face of paternalism brought Tutu to Bletchingley.

Uvedale Lambert was right; the parishioners responded enthusiastically to the idea. One August Sunday, at the eight o'clock service, the Rector put up a list in the church detailing the various things the Tutus would need – beds, chairs, cutlery, linen – and asking for those willing and able to give anything to sign against the appropriate item. By the end of the ten o'clock service the list was full and within twenty-four hours the cottage, loaned to the Tutus by a cousin of the Lamberts until the curate's house was vacant, was furnished. Early the next week Uvedale Lambert and the Rector went up to Golders Green in one of the farm Land-Rovers and brought Desmond and Leah, Trevor, Theresa, Naomi and Mpho, to their new home.

People still living in Bletchingley admit that initially there was, at least in some quarters, 'a certain reserve'; but it was soon overcome. John Ewington, the organist for many years, says 'Desmond just won them over as he wins everybody over, not only by his example – he was obviously a very prayerful man – but also by his great sense of humour. He's always laughing, this most infectious laugh.' His jokes, which he is not too proud to repeat, are ingenuous and do not translate easily to the page. Though he is a talented mimic – he and his great friend Walter Makhulu[15] could make their audience helpless with laughter as they imitated the South African police at a road block – his humour has none of the cool acerbity that makes for real wit. Teasing and jocularity are, in him, more a way of expressing the richness of his emotions; they show a desire to share and communicate, a spilling over of goodwill. He relishes jokes about his colour, responding to compliments with 'One of the great advantages of a black skin is that when you blush nobody notices', he is amused by the thought of being 'tickled pink' and was delighted that when he preached from the high pulpit, which is backed by a dark Jacobean screen, all the congregation could see of him were his teeth and the whites of his eyes. His friendship with Uvedale Lambert blossomed from the moment when they were moving his luggage and Uvedale, knowing Desmond had had TB, tried to save him from lifting heavy things. 'What's the matter, Uvedale,' Tutu said, 'don't you like to see me working like a nigger?'

The village were soon accustomed to seeing their new curate roaring round on his Vespa, often with one or two children aboard, or meeting him in the local fish and chip shop, buying the family's supper. People would drop in to the Clerk's House, a charming old cottage in the main street, to chat to Leah as she scrubbed the kitchen floor and snatch a word with Desmond as he took a break from studying for his Master's degree.

As the local people came to know the family, their instinctive kindness towards a newcomer became more specific, more focused; Bletchingley generosity towards the family, especially the children, was impressive. As the only black children in the village, they got more than their share of attention; all four were, in any case, alert, amusing and bright. (When Naomi joined the rest of the family in 1963, flying over with the Bishop of Pretoria, she had delighted the passengers by spending most of the flight dancing 'the twist' – the current rage – up and down the aisle.) A friend of Melanie Lambert's, whose kitchen window was by the bus stop, was amused to hear Trevor disciplining the other local children, as they arrived, helter-skelter and often late, to catch the school bus. 'This will not do,' he said, 'the way we meet this bus. We must do it in a much more orderly fashion. Now let's line up as each person arrives and we'll walk with dignity into the bus.' So from that moment, a punctual row of children walked in perfect order on to their bus.

Several people began to feel that Trevor needed more stimulation than he could have in the village school, so they clubbed together to send him to Hawthorn's, a private school, where he was one of the top three students the whole time he was there. It was a 'Tory blue' private school, turning Trevor temporarily into a rabid royalist; he and his friends wept when the Labour Party won the 1966 Election. Such is the power of conditioning.

The village gave most bounteously to the Tutus: when he went back to South Africa they put their hands in their pockets again to buy him a car; later, when he was in Lesotho, some of them gave him a horse. There are those – not, it should be said, from Bletchingley – who feel that Tutu accepts too readily, but this criticism shows a failure to understand African generosity. What Africans have, they share – ask anyone who has had the privilege of being entertained in an African home. The Tutus were moved and grateful, their gratitude was unbounded, but they did not find it odd; it was exactly what they would have done themselves. In any case, as Melanie Lambert says, however much they received materially, they gave more, far more: 'They were full of such love and such humour and joy, joy, triumphant joy.'

What then, did Tutu give to Bletchingley? While the abiding memory of him is his capacity for love and joy, he also, not surprisingly, woke them to the realities of life in South Africa. Bletchingley was not an active village politically; the generosity of its inhabitants was not motivated by any strong feelings about social injustice, it was more a combination of kind hearts and collective white guilt. Sarah and Tim Goad, who lived in the next village and knew Tutu well, say that, but for him, nobody would have thought much about South Africa. 'If pressed, the people of Bletchingley would hedge their bets on South Africa. Desmond pricked our consciences. Our view of South Africa now is 99 per cent Desmond.' He could, and did, tell them just what life was like for blacks in South Africa. John Ewington is not alone in feeling he cannot believe everything he reads in the newspapers:

> It is not until someone like Desmond, whom you know and trust implicitly, gives you a first hand account, that you know what it's like. That it is horrifying and that it's a police state. He told us how the police can knock at the door and take away the husband or the wife, and if a neighbour doesn't happen to see, that person has just gone and you have no idea where they've gone, they just disappear.

In a very small way Tutu had begun to speak for his people.

This awakening of white consciences was incidental, peripheral to his work as a curate – politics seldom came into his sermons. He and the Rector, Ronald Brownrigg, made a good team, sharing their duties, even sharing their days off. Since his time at Benoni Tutu has kept regular 'quiet days' and he would insist that once a month they went out of the parish, took a room in a local convent, and spent a day sleeping, eating, praying and reading. He was happy, too, with the ecumenical tradition that the Rector was establishing. The parish had strong links with the Roman Catholics and the Methodists; all three denominations used the Anglican church, with its better facilities, they all contributed to the parish magazine, joined forces on many committees, even sometimes prepared mixed couples for marriage together.

Tutu was not afraid to speak out. There were at St Mary the Virgin, as at many Anglican churches, two strains of churchmanship, whose wishes were met by slightly different services, one at eight o'clock, the other at ten. Tutu thought it scandalous that the parish should be separated for Holy Communion, and he said so. On another occasion he gave a talk in which he defended two people who were not popular in the village, vigorously reprimanding his audience for their behaviour. As a pastor, too, he trod where others might fear to go. A parishioner once went to church in a state of such anger with a neighbour that she did not feel able to make her Communion. She was no sooner home than the telephone rang. It was Tutu, asking her what the trouble was and did she want to see him.

However well Tutu fitted in to the Surrey scene – and he was as at home at South Park as in his garage in Benoni – he was an African, expressing himself with typical African warmth and a spontaneous lack of inhibition which, at first, came as a shock to the reticent English. In worship he would give himself totally, indifferent to whether the congregation approved or even noticed. When conducting the Veneration of the Cross on Good Friday he did not follow English custom and kneel, with head touching the ground. As he reached the Cross he would kick off his shoes and lie on his face in total prostration, flat on the floor with arms extended. After the Midnight Mass at Christmas, he was once seen dancing in the starlight, quite alone: he was just dancing round the churchyard with the joy of Christmas. How enriched Western Christianity could be by more such encounters.

The parishioners cannot speak too warmly of Tutu. 'Bletchingley fell in love with the Tutus,' says one. 'He just loved everybody; you can't help responding to that,' says another. A third, when they left, said, 'Everyone loved them so much it was an agony.' Twenty years later, when, as Bishop of Johannesburg, he returned to preach, he told the congregation how back in South Africa, surrounded by hate, the memory of their love had protected him 'like a ring of fire'. The press, expecting a political sermon but disappointed, were there in force, astounded at the way 'the parishioners of Bletchingley treated Desmond as one of their own. Time and again, arms clothed in Harris tweed enveloped him while women in quilted green anoraks smothered him with kisses.'[16]

When Desmond had obtained his Master's degree and the family prepared to leave, the whole village, including those who were not church-goers, turned out for the farewell party. The Tutus were presented with a large cheque and their luggage grew more and more unmanageable as everyone gave them presents; there were even four specially made vestments. By the end of the party everyone was in tears. Some of those tears were shed by people who understood something of the South Africa to which the Tutus were returning.

5

An oasis in the Eastern Cape

It was indeed hard for the Tutus once again to become second-class citizens. They had known what to expect, but found that no preparation could reconcile them to their racially divided country. Soon after they returned to South Africa Desmond wrote to Martin Kenyon:[1]

> I don't want to sound melodramatic, but it is extremely difficult being back here, having to ask permission from various white officials to visit my parents! Having to carry my heavy passbook and look out for entrances meant especially for us . . . It is as well that Our Lord expects us not to like but to love our enemies and neighbours. It will be extremely difficult to love the white man as it is. Awful sentiment isn't it?

It is easy to take Desmond's lack of bitterness for granted, to forget that it is something for which he has had to struggle, that he prays constantly for the strength to win this struggle, even pleading for help from friends. He wrote, again to Martin Kenyon, 'Pray for us that we may not succumb to the temptation to hate and become bitter.'[2] That his prayers have been answered is due to good fortune as well as good nature; as he was fortunate in his inter-racial contacts in England, so he was to find himself, in his first post as a qualified theologian in South Africa, in a non-racial, non-denominational institution that was determined to create a harmonious environment, as far as possible disregarding the government's petty restrictions. After only a few weeks in Johannesburg the Tutus moved down to the small town of Alice, in the Eastern Cape, where Tutu had been appointed a lecturer at St Peter's College, since 1961 part of the Federal Theological Seminary, known in South Africa as Fedsem.

St Peter's enforced trek from Rosettenville to Alice was caused by various manifestations of apartheid as, by 1960, the Anglicans, the Methodists, the Congregationalists and the Presbyterians all needed new premises for training 'non-European' candidates for the ordained ministry. The influence of the Christian missionaries may have been ambiguous – the missions have, after all, been dubbed 'the soft edge of imperialism' – but there has never been any doubting their dimension of real concern; they did, for the most part, strive for a non-racial society. That was something the Nationalist government could not tolerate. One by one, it picked them off.

The Congregationalists had been part of Adams College, one of the oldest and most famous institutions for African education in South Africa, whose illustrious sons included Chief Albert Luthuli; the College refused to register under the Bantu Education Act and was forced to close in 1956. The Methodists and Presbyterians had trained at the equally famous Fort Hare University since 1921. As part of its scheme to tribalise the universities, the government took over Fort Hare, reserving it for Xhosas only. Most of the lecturers, including Professor Z. K. Matthews, the African Vice-Principal, resigned in protest and two more denominations lost their theological base. The Anglicans at Rosettenville had been living for years under the Damoclean sword of the Urban Areas Act; it had been increasingly difficult to get permits for Africans not resident in Johannesburg to study there. Finally it became impossible and they too were homeless.

Out of the evil that, in a nominally Christian country, had deprived Christians of their theological training, came good; the Theological Education Fund, prospecting for sites for the four denominations, suggested that they should come together in a Federal Seminary. Relationships between the Churches were not close, so a commission was set up to investigate the viability of the idea. Eventually, agreement was reached, but the level of trust was so low that it was decided that each Church should remain autonomous within the union. The Bishops then decided that the Community of the Resurrection should be invited to run the Anglican department; they accepted and the name of St Peter's was retained.

After more deliberation, and much searching, a site was chosen at Alice, near Port Elizabeth. It was close to both Lovedale College and Fort Hare University, which before government intervention had earned formidable academic reputations and between them produced leaders like Nelson Mandela, Robert Sobukwe, James Moroka, Oliver Tambo, Steve Biko and Gatsha Buthelezi. St Peter's may in one sense have been moving from the sophisticated life of the city to a sleepy village, but it was making its home in an area with its roots deep in the Xhosa tradition as well as in a British colonial past, finding itself in the political heartland of African resistance.

The seminary was, in its proximity to Fort Hare, next to a political minefield. It should have been natural for the seminary and the university to work together, but Fort Hare, now run by the Bantu Education Department, was in a state of deep despair. In any case, how could a seminary devoted to educating and freeing South Africans collaborate with an institution run by a government dedicated to keeping them in a state of servitude? The question of their academic relationship was the cause of a long and bitter battle, with feelings so passionate that the seminary was brought to the verge of disintegration, but eventually a compromise was reached. The four denominations made independent decisions, the Anglicans agreeing, whenever possible, to make the possession of a non-theological degree the basis of entry into the seminary. Thus St Peter's made some use of Fort Hare without any sacrifice of autonomy or integrity.

The move from Johannesburg had taken place in the early 1960s, so when Tutu, trained at St Peter's, Rosettenville, arrived at St Peter's, Alice, the seminary had been in its new home for nearly four years. The four constituent colleges – Methodist, Congregationalist, Presbyterian and Anglican – retained their independence by living in separate colleges with their own Principal, their own staff, their own refectories, while worshipping together in the assembly hall at least once a week, sharing a central administrative block, the library – considered to be one of the best theological libraries in South Africa, if not the whole of Africa – and later, as they grew more confident in their ecumenical stance, the lectures. Each Principal took it in turn to be President for a two-year period and the students, together with those from St Paul's, Grahamstown and St Bede's, Umtata, took the same examinations, the Associate of the Federation of Theological Seminaries. The partnership was, eventually, a success. Church unity is crucially important in South Africa, with its numerous Independent Churches (formerly known as 'Separatist Churches'), and the creation and the forging into a unity of the four distinct traditions comprising the seminary was, according to Father Aelred Stubbs, the President from 1965 till 1967, the most significant ecumenical achievement in South Africa in the 1960s.

Particularly significant was the utter refusal of anyone at the seminary, staff or student, to bow to the pressures of a racial society – Alice stood proudly as an oasis in the desert of apartheid. Visitors arrived to feel they were in another land, where black and white could be together without causing any trouble and where, as one of them said, 'Even the air was different'. Simon Gqubule, the only other black on the staff in Tutu's time, points out a subtle but important indication of the depth of their non-racialism. 'As a community we paid no attention to colour. It was not something we did consciously, we *unconsciously* paid no attention to it.' The various permits necessary for Africans, 'coloureds', Indians and whites to live together had been obtained; the restrictions of 'petty apartheid', decreeing where men of different skin colour should sleep, eat and wash, were quite simply ignored. So, for instance, Father Stubbs and his Vice-Principal,

Father Mark Tweedy, had rooms in the same block as the students, who themselves mixed with total freedom, all sharing the bathroom, the showers, the lavatory – living, in short, as students anywhere. They somehow got away with it, though their activities were probably known to the Special Branch.

This non-racial climate was, of course, balm to the souls of the Tutus. Leah wrote: 'The Seminary is a marvellous place. The friendliness and cooperation is such that you would have to travel the far corners of the Republic and still be lucky if you found anything like it . . . What happens outside the Seminary is unprintable.'[3] Desmond found it 'exhilarating and great fun being here. We are so far getting on like a house on fire with the CR.'[4] Mpho, the only one of the children not at boarding school, was, at four years old and more fluent in English than Xhosa, slightly confused, telling someone she was 'a non-white European'. They were thrilled with the house, an L-shaped bungalow furnished for them by the CR Fathers, and filled it with people; the Tutus, in turn, were a roaring success. Canon Michael Carmichael, then Principal of St Bede's Theological College in Umtata, remembers the Tutus 'taking everyone by storm, throwing their immense friendliness and warmth around'; Elizabeth Crace, visiting them one Christmas, carried away a lasting impression:

> South Africa to me means singing and dancing and fun and happiness, not poverty and problems – that is what we are all missing when we think of South Africa. Africans have this marvellous capacity for happiness which we poor Europeans don't have to anything like the same extent and the Tutus are the best exponents of it. We all love talking about Desmond – even thinking about him is good, he gives you such hope.

Tutu came like a breath of fresh air to the students. As well as being a lecturer at the seminary, he was Anglican Chaplain to Fort Hare. The students, who found the university a claustrophobic place, full of rules and regulations, would take refuge in the friendliness of the seminary; particularly they felt at ease with the Tutus, flocking to their Sunday 'Coffee Evenings'. Tutu took an active part in the various plays and revues put on by Ruth Lundie, who taught English at the seminary. They would do sketches in which colour roles were reversed, yellow make-up put on black skins, black on white. On one occasion a Presbyterian minister who had agreed to sing 'Glasgow Belongs To Me', was overcome by scruples (the last line, 'When I am tight on a Saturday night', was too much for him) and withdrew. Tutu, dressed in kilt and sporran and entered as 'Father Desmond MacTutu', took his place, rendering the songs with 'great shrieks and howls' in an atrociously ham Glasgow accent.

Tutu was one of six lecturers, teaching mainly Doctrine and Greek. Surprisingly, in view of his academic record, he found the work very testing and wrote humbly: 'I am of course up to my neck in work, having to organise my little knowledge into notes that are readily assimilable.'[5] Leah went further: 'I can't say he is enjoying it, he is still trying to find his feet. He is so lacking in self-confidence that I said to him, in anger, that it would take him a century to find them.'[6]

He was, in fact, considered the most highly qualified black Anglican theologian in the country, better qualified, as Father Stubbs willingly admits, than either he or Father Mark Tweedy. Perhaps this was part of the problem. Tutu was already all too aware of his responsibility as a representative of black education and now the CR Fathers, previously his teachers and mentors, were his colleagues. But if he found it all a bit daunting, he did not show it and everyone believed the confident façade, one of the lecturers saying, 'he was, as you would expect, confident, but he was never aggressive in a nasty way'. Nor did the students have any inkling of the truth; Zakes Mohutsioa, his former scoutmaster, now at Fedsem as a mature student, found him 'Impressive, thorough, very fine, very strict'. Hardly a tribute to a nervous teacher.

Tutu was not going to be party to any teaching that made life easier for blacks because they were blacks. He had himself experienced the oppressive mental bondage under which blacks laboured, continually told they were not as intellectual as whites, suffering under the paternalistic assumption that blacks could not hope to equal whites in civilisation, though 'one day perhaps . . . in a thousand years . . .' He fought against any insularity, black or white, for example in his insistence that his students should read and understand the works of theologians like Paul Tillich and Karl Barth. They may have had little or no preparation for such work, there may even have been a feeling among the white staff that this was a little more than should be expected, but he refused to compromise or accept any difference in standards. Never can Tillich or Barth have been so popular as at Alice, where they were symbols of intellectual equality.

Alongside his duties as a lecturer, Tutu was also continuing his private studies in Islam, which, after taking his Master's degree at King's College, he had studied further during two months in the Holy Land on his way back from England to South Africa. At Alice he started to work for a doctorate with the University of South Africa; his thesis, combining his interests in Islam and the Old Testament, being on Moses and the Koran. Father Stubbs did his best to arrange his teaching schedule in such a way that he had time to study and Brother Charles, who had tutored him in Islam at Rosettenville, remembers him lying ill in bed romping through a paperback Arabic grammar as if it were a novel. Though Tutu did not complete the thesis, this does not lessen the respect in which he is held academically. In fact Father Stubbs suggests that

> He had the kind of academic excellence that made it a perfectly reasonable thing to do and I don't doubt that if other things of an ecclesiastical political nature had not intervened, he would have gone ahead and got it – he's certainly got the ability. It's one of the reasons one never minds Desmond getting all these Honorary Doctorates, because he could have become a Doctor in his own right if he hadn't been called to a more active part as a leader.

This leadership role was one into which Tutu grew slowly, almost unwillingly. His rise is reminiscent of Shakespeare's 'Some are born great, some achieve greatness, some have greatness thrust upon them'.[7] Desmond's achievements belong to the third of those categories, though greatness was not so much thrust upon him as emerging, with a remorseless inevitability, from his religious beliefs. His political role is inextricably entwined with his calling as a pastor.

It was at Alice that he first began to experience politics and religion as being indivisible. Since the days of his first curacy at Benoni, Tutu had been first and foremost a pastor, feeling that this was where his vocation lay. Though he enjoyed his teaching work at the seminary, he knew that ultimately what he said was less important than what he was, the values for which he stood: 'It was more exciting to see the students grow in their relationship to our Lord Jesus Christ than it was to see them acquire some of the academic and technical things which I taught. In fact it was, and still is, tremendously thrilling to see people grow in spiritual stature.'[8] It was largely as a pastor, specifically in his job as Chaplain to Fort Hare University, that he earned the love and respect of the students, perhaps by caring spiritual counselling, loving concern over personal problems or as a sometimes humorous reconciler. (He once diffused a potentially explosive situation when one of the Methodist students objected to invoking the name of the Virgin Mary – a tactless remark in this non-denominational setting. The ensuing silence was broken by a laugh from Tutu: 'You've done away with the whole theory of intercession!')

His pastoral care could also take the form of standing up for justice. He continuously affirmed the students' dignity as human beings, he wanted them to understand that they had a *right* to share the good things of the world; the message was not new, but Tutu's ability to put it across was impressive. And the context was one of an oppression and injustice harsh even by South African standards.

The early 1960s had been a low point in black African resistance. After the Sharpeville Massacre the government banned both the African National Congress and the Pan-Africanist Congress, with penalties of up to ten years' imprisonment for anyone found to be furthering their aims; legislation grew increasingly repressive, detention without trial was given the spurious dignity of law and horrifying reports emerged about the conditions under which blacks were imprisoned, the torture they endured at the hands of the security police. After nearly fifty years with a policy of non-violence, the ANC, operating underground under the leadership of Nelson Mandela, formed an armed wing, Umkhonto we Sizwe (The Spear of the Nation), which, based in a house in a northern Johannesburg suburb called Rivonia, was to carry on the struggle in a new way, sabotaging installations and offices, but expressly not injuring or killing people. The Pan-Africanist Congress, not content with these limited targets, formed its own armed resistance wing, *Poqo* (meaning 'pure', 'standing alone'). The main national liberation movements had consistently refused to use any form of violence, but, as Umkhonto's manifesto points out, 'The time comes in the life of any nation when there remain only two choices: submit or fight. That time has now come in South Africa. We shall not submit and we have no choice but to hit back with all means within our power in defence of our people, our future and our freedom.'⁹ Predictably the security police unleashed their power. Poqo was broken, in August 1962 Nelson Mandela was arrested, the following July the Rivonia headquarters were raided and most of the remaining leaders arrested. The subsequent 'Rivonia Trial' led to their imprisonment for life.

During these bleak years Tutu was in England. 'In one sense he didn't miss much,' says Father Stubbs, 'but in another he missed going through that experience of deep darkness, a deep kind of death in a way.' Tutu was, however, to be involved in the next stage of African resistance.

The late 1960s were a time of seething unrest in the Eastern Cape. Many of the students had brothers, fathers or uncles imprisoned on Robben Island, banned, gone into exile; there was the constant fear of informers. From this cauldron a new response to white oppression was beginning to emerge – black consciousness.

The Black Consciousness Movement started in 1968 at a conference of the University Christian Movement at Stutterheim, a white area not far from Alice. It was a multi-racial conference and most of the whites were in sympathy with black aspirations; nevertheless the black students were becoming more and more frustrated by their inability to have a voice in formulating policy.

There were at the time only three black universities in South Africa, as against nine white, so the blacks were outnumbered. Further, the leadership positions were being taken by whites, who, with the advantages of better school education and wider reading, were more articulate, more confident. Perhaps most crucially, the whites, not sharing the same problems as the black students, could not enter completely into the black predicament. For instance, while they were legally free to be present at the conference without special permission, the blacks had to apply for permits to be in a white area. Because of the stance they took against apartheid, the black students did not see why they needed permission to be anywhere in South Africa; they refused to apply, thereby risking arrest. They found the white response to this sort of situation naïve. The whites might, for instance, suggest that they should all lie in front of the vans when the police came to round up those blacks without permits, but the oppressed and per-secuted students knew all too well what the result of that would be. The whites would simply be removed, possibly reprimanded; the blacks would be arrested and would spend the conference in the police cells.

These differences – of numbers, education and legal status – led to the black students pulling out of the main conference and discussing their problems in their own caucus. They decided their needs were not being met in a multi-racial organisation and that the whites could never have a real appreciation of their problems; it was time they formed their own organisation. The aspirations of the blacks should be met by the blacks alone. Hence SASO, the South African Students Organisation, first of the Black Consciousness groupings, was born.

Steve Biko, the first President of SASO and known as 'The Father of Black Consciousness', defined this new ideology, whose emphasis was on the inner attitude of the black man to himself:[10]

> All in all the black man has become a shell, a shadow of a man, completely defeated, drowning in his own misery, a slave, an ox bearing the yoke of oppression with sheepish timidity. This is the first truth, bitter as it may seem, that we have to acknowledge before we can start on any programme designed to change the status quo. It becomes more necessary to see the truth as it is if you realise that the only vehicle for change are these people who have lost their personality. The first step therefore is to make the black man come to himself; to pump back life into his empty shell; to infuse him with pride and dignity, to remind him of his complicity in the crime of allowing himself to be misused

and therefore letting evil reign supreme in the country of his birth. This
is what we mean by an inward-looking process. This is the definition
of 'Black Consciousness'.

How then, did Tutu respond? Broadly he was, of course, in total
sympathy with the aims of these radical young students. They were,
after all, affirming the dignity of the black man in their way, just as
he was in his. But there were differences. The students felt that Tutu's
assumptions about the future of South Africa were too optimistic, they
found his views too moderate, lacking the sense of urgency which
coursed through their veins. After four years in England his attitude
was so essentially non-racial that he was in a sense *above* race. While
he longed for co-operation, sharing and harmony between black and
white, while he wanted to call upon the white students and radicalise
them, Black Consciousness was saying otherwise. In the words of
Justice Moloto, a student at Fort Hare at the time, 'It was important
for the black man to withdraw from the white man, consolidate himself,
to learn leadership skills and only come back and meet the white man
on an equal footing. And we must, therefore, come together and work
out our strategies in such a way that when we do go out we are not
going back to the white man cap-in-hand.' Despite this difference in
stance, the students respected Tutu deeply, appreciating that he was
operating first and foremost as a Christian priest and that, on the staff
of a non-racial seminary and Chaplain to a backward, government-
controlled university, he was in a very difficult position.

But if he was not as radical as the students, he was not afraid to
stand up and be counted. For instance he refused to meet Sir Alec
and Lady Douglas-Home when they visited the seminary to meet the
staff. 'I stayed away because although the Homes are themselves
probably attractive people, we thought the Conservatives had behaved
abominably over issues which touched our hearts most nearly.'[11] He
frequently spoke up, often in a way which has remained in the minds
of those who heard him.

Barney Pityana, a student at Fort Hare and very active politically,
remembers an occasion in 1967. The setting was the conference of
the Anglican Students Federation at Michaelhouse in Natal, the
subject under discussion was Bishop Crowther, the Bishop of Kimberley and an outspoken critic of apartheid – was the government right
to deport him? Some of the white delegates, mostly from Stellenbosch
and Cape Town Universities, spoke up on the side of the government,
saying the Bishop's behaviour was 'unpatriotic and unSouth African'
and that he deserved to be sent packing. As he listened, Barney's rage
mounted at the white students' assumption that everyone shared their

views on what was and was not patriotic; he weighed in, trying to overturn the motion. To his pleasant surprise Tutu, who, as a university chaplain, was present, supported Barney with a powerful speech in defence of all critics of apartheid. The respect in which he was held ensured that he was listened to with rapt attention – though it did not, of course, affect the fate of Bishop Crowther, who was soon on his way back to the USA.

Tutu would also make his views known from the pulpit. He used regularly to take his turn preaching in 'the travesty next door',[12] Fort Hare University, his congregation often the whole university, not just the Anglicans. One such occasion was in 1968, soon after that dreadful August night when Soviet troops marched into Czechoslovakia. Tutu spoke about human rights, comparing the position of the black South Africans under apartheid with the Czechs, trampled by the Russians. Afterwards the university buzzed with excitement, the students, knowing the mentality of the authorities all too well, fearing he would never be invited to preach at the university again. He was not.

These were two of many occasions which were, in a sense, paving the way to an experience which was to bring Tutu face-to-face with the savagery of apartheid and its perpetrators in a way he had not previously witnessed – the Fort Hare strike.

It was after the August vacation in 1968, the year when students all over Europe and America were making their voices heard. There was no formal student representation at Fort Hare, as that would be to condone the government-run university, with all that it implied; nevertheless there had been a series of strikes, as the students called for an end to racist education, demanded more competent academic staff or protested, for instance, at the presence on campus of the Deputy Minister of Bantu Education. A climax was reached when a new Rector, J. J. de Wet, was appointed and a group of active Christians, including Barney Pityana and Justice Moloto, asked to see him. They wanted 'to persuade him to treat them as responsible human beings, not as a lower form of human life'.[13] The Rector, far from listening to them, demanded that the graffiti and slogans should be removed and that they should put a stop to the insubordination reigning on campus; if this was not done, disciplinary action would follow. The group, seeing this as victimisation, refused to accept the mantle of formal leadership he was trying to throw on their shoulders, arguing that on these matters he should address the whole student body. The students backed this demand, the Rector insisted he would only talk to a small group: it looked as if stalemate had been reached. Eventually the students agreed to elect a delegation, at which point the Rector refused to see them.

At this the whole campus erupted into protest; 500 of the 550 students sat, defiantly but quite peacefully, on the lawn in front of the administration buildings. This continued for several days; demonstration simply took the place of work as, in an orderly and well-disciplined way, they clocked in, broke for lunch, sat it out for the rest of the day. Then one day, at eleven o'clock, there was an announcement on the loudspeaker that all the students were going to be expelled; they were to be off the campus by two o'clock. Nobody moved. At precisely two o'clock all hell was let loose as police screamed on to the campus in armoured cars, complete with dogs and guns and tear-gas. Before they knew what was happening, the petrified students were surrounded at gun point, wondering what was going to happen to them. Soon, with the indomitable spirit of black South Africans, they started singing freedom songs, while a small crowd gathered, helplessly watching. Nobody was allowed out, nor was anyone allowed through to talk to them – until that is, Tutu came over from the seminary. The police tried to prevent him, but he simply said, 'Don't stop me, because if you are arresting the students you can count me, as their Chaplain, with them,' and elbowed his way through. For the rest of the day, as they were herded off to their rooms to pack their bags and put on to buses to take them to the railway station, he stayed with them, offering encouragement and support.

Tutu's total identification with their cause impressed the students deeply. He was, according to Justice Moloto, 'as visible by his presence as other people, the white lecturers from Fort Hare for instance, were by their absence. He has always been a leading light in the black man's struggle, whether in a very small way on a university campus or at national level.' For Barney Pityana, this incident actually changed his life: 'It was a deeply moving experience. The students flocked round him in relief and excitement, asking for his blessing. I knew then what I wanted to do. That was the first real experience of my feeling of what it means to be a priest. And I thought there was something in it for me.'

It changed Tutu too. 'I never felt so desolated,' he said years later. 'I was angry with God. I couldn't understand how he could let all that happen to those students.' He was, says Father Stubbs, 'completely bouleversed, bewildered, by the experience – he hadn't realised just how savagely the students could be dealt with by the authorities.' The next day, celebrating Mass in St Peter's Chapel, he completely broke down. Elizabeth Crace was there: 'I remember so well in this lovely Chapel with its grey stone floor, kneeling at the Communion rail while Desmond came with the chalice and the tears pouring down his face and splashing on the grey floor. I remember thinking they looked like black tears, because they left these black marks on the grey floor.'

Tutu may have initially had reservations about the thinking that was to become the Black Consciousness Movement, but he never failed to listen to the students, talk and argue with them, and to show solidarity with them. By the end of his time at Fedsem he had come to identify with them very strongly.

It was a rich time, those two years in Alice. Tutu was bursting to communicate and he did so; he had opportunities to fulfil his deep need of a pastoral role; he entered the political arena in a new and more intense way. He also took part in the Churches' struggle to articulate the Christian response to apartheid by taking part in various commissions and sitting on committees of theological education. He could have stayed at Alice; he was in fact earmarked as a future Principal of the seminary and was already due to be Vice-Principal in January 1970. However, with mixed feelings, he decided to accept an invitation to be a lecturer in the University of Botswana, Lesotho and Swaziland, based at Roma in Lesotho. So once again he was to be away from the action in South Africa.

6

Out of South Africa

In moving from Alice to Roma Tutu was making the first of a series of difficult decisions: over the next ten years he was to change his job five times. Was he ambitious, restless, uncertain of exactly what he should be doing with his life? Was it that his gifts led to a constant stream of tempting offers which, with his inborn desire to please, he found hard to refuse? Was he, as one of his colleagues has suggested, 'in a hurry'? Though all these ingredients may well have been present, in every decision the mix was different. There was only one constant, that was his wish to do what he understood to be God's will; for that understanding he has, in every case, prayed long and hard.

The later decisions were to become more complex, more agonising; in 1969, when he was invited to Roma, the issues were relatively straightforward. Personal ambition was not the obvious motive – indeed there were those on the seminary staff who thought that to give up the opportunity to be Principal of the biggest theological college in South Africa was plain foolish – but it played its part: 'I enjoyed teaching and this was an opportunity to work in an institute of higher learning. Also teaching at a university had kudos and it was good for your CV.' The higher salary was welcome to a father of a growing family, and, further, having experienced life outside South Africa, the opportunity of a good job in a society free of apartheid was tempting. But his decision to accept a lectureship at Roma revolved less around his own wishes than the needs of his family, in particular the education of his four children. He had always been determined that they should not be educated under Bantu Education and at Roma the educational opportunities would be better.

Tutu is a loving and concerned father; his regular Christmas letters, circulated to an ever-growing group of friends around the world, are full of the hopes and achievements of his family. Though he has been criticised for sending his children overseas for their education – 'It's all very well for him,' poorer South Africans sometimes say, 'what about our children?' – he has refused to be moved. It is a very human response; most people wish to give their children the best they can and at the time there were no private schools in South Africa that would take black children. Neither were the Tutus unique; black South Africans who could manage to have their children educated overseas have been doing so since Professor Jabavu, the first South African graduate and a father figure of African education, qualified in London over fifty years ago.

While the Tutus were at Alice the three older children were at fee-paying schools in Swaziland: Trevor at Waterford, the famous multi-racial school in Mbabane, Theresa and Naomi at St Michael's, a convent school in Manzini, where they were soon to be joined by Mpho. Though Desmond and Leah's friends have made generous contributions towards the children's education (Trevor's fees were paid in full by Tutu's old parish of Bletchingley), and while the children were bright, much of their fees being covered by scholarships, there were still expenses which the Tutus often had difficulty in meeting. Even ferrying the children to and from school was, with six trips of over 800 miles every year, a substantial cost in petrol alone; living at Roma would halve the travelling distance. An even greater advantage was that the two younger children, Naomi and Mpho, could be educated at the primary school on the university campus, where there were special allowances for the children of staff.

Roma gets its name from a Roman Catholic Mission established there in 1862, though the university only dates from 1945. It began very humbly when four Roman Catholic priest-lecturers, with strictly limited resources, began teaching five students in a converted primary school, later to be extended with the help of the Paramount Chief of Basutoland and named Pius XII College. It was soon taken over by a religious order and by the early 1960s there were 175 students, accommodation for about twenty members of staff, a modern science block and the beginnings of a university campus. They were, however, having financial problems; worse, there were difficulties with the 'special relationship' they had entered into with the University of South Africa. It was becoming clear that the college could not continue to function in its existing form. At about the same time the governments of what were then the High Commission Territories of Basutoland, Bechuanaland Protectorate and Swaziland were exploring the possibilities of providing more higher education for their nationals. Could a partnership be arranged? Eventually it was agreed that an independent, secular university, serving principally the three countries of Bechuanaland, Basutoland and Swaziland, should be founded by taking over the grounds and buildings of Pius XII College.

On October 9th, 1964, the university was formally inaugurated as an autonomous institution, granting its own certificates, diplomas and degrees. By 1970, when Tutu started work, the three countries had been granted independence and the university had correspondingly changed its name to the University of Botswana, Lesotho and Swaziland. Though there were no racial or religious barriers to admission, the 400 students included only a few whites, mostly the children of members of staff. The only racial conflict on the campus concerned staffing – should they all be African or should whites be appointed? The majority feeling was that lecturers from the three countries the university was founded to serve were preferred over other Africans; whites, for the most part, accepted that they were only there for as long as they were needed.

Tutu had been to Lesotho on holiday, when he had climbed a mountain in his walking shoes and, according to Ruth Lundie, one of his companions, 'quite fallen in love with the place'. Lesotho, 'The Kingdom in the Sky', is a mountainous region surrounded on all sides by the Republic of South Africa, the only country in the world whose entire area is more than 1,000 metres above sea level. Bushman paintings, cannibal caves and fossil footprints of five-toed dinosaurs 180 million years old are reminders of old Africa, long before the white man came. Even today there is a timeless quality about the blanket-wrapped people riding the famous Basotho ponies – often the most reliable form of transport – across the spectacular mountains. Not least, it is out of South Africa, out of reach of apartheid.

It is not, however, free of political strife, nor was it free of South African interference. Lesotho politics were dominated by religion, with the government mainly Roman Catholic, the opposition mainly Protestant – a situation Tutu referred to as 'an Ulster in reverse'.[1] White South Africa backed the ruling Basuto National Party, a preference which was felt in the university by the constant fear of informers. The government was suspicious of a federal university; it liked to know what was going on, was always on the watch for 'subversives'.

In January 1970, soon after Desmond arrived, the Basuto National Party committed the ultimate sin in a democracy – it interfered with the elections. Half-way through the count it realised it was losing, so, with fewer than ten of the sixty seats unannounced, it accused the Opposition of thuggery and chicanery, stopped the elections and declared a State of Emergency. Under Chief Leabua Jonathan the Basuto National Government, initially anxious to keep on good terms with South Africa to whom it was an economic hostage, ruled until the coup of 1986 (brought off with the connivance and assistance of that same fickle South African government) removed it from office.

By the time he came to Roma Tutu was known to the ever-vigilant South African authorities, already unpopular with them and regarded as a potential subversive, though he was in no way actively involved in politics. He was working hard teaching theology to the degree-course students; he was still studying for his doctoral thesis on Moses and the Koran; as always he was fulfilling his pastoral role, both officially, as the Anglican Chaplain, and simply by being himself. And his desire to do something about the injustice in his country was beginning to find expression in his growing involvement with black theology.

The term 'Black Theology' reached South Africa around 1970. It originated in America, where it was largely a theological response to black power; in South Africa it is intimately related to black consciousness.

A major trend in modern theology claims that theology is not formed in a vacuum: it is a response to circumstances, it speaks from a specific situation. Black theology (which is liberation theology in South Africa) emerges from the pain of suffering and oppression; it is not occasioned by abstract problems of human suffering, it tries to meet the anguish and the questions of a specific people who suffer hunger, poverty, humiliation and fear at the hands of other human beings, whose lives are governed by literally hundreds of oppressive laws, whose rights and privileges are determined not by the fact of their humanity, but by their pigmentation – a people who had come to question their own identity. To conquer the humiliating self-doubt of the black man living under apartheid and to assert the value of every human being is something for which Tutu never ceases to strive:[2]

> Have you seen a symphony orchestra? They are all dolled up and beautiful, with their magnificent instruments, cellos, violins, etc. Sometimes, dolled up as the rest, there is a chap at the back carrying a triangle. Now and again the conductor will point to him and he will play 'ting'. That might seem so insignificant, but in the conception of the composer something irreplaceable would be lost to the total beauty of the symphony if that 'ting' did not happen. In the praise ascending to God's throne something totally irreplaceable of your unique way of loving God would be missing. We are each, says Jesus, of unique and inestimable value.

As God chose to come to earth as a man, not as a spirit or as an animal, then men are temples of the Holy Spirit. We must not only accept and affirm one another, but honour one another, because 'We are God-carriers and ought to genuflect to one another as we do to the reserved sacrament in the tabernacle'.[3] So to accord people different treatment by virtue of their race is as silly as to imagine a university where qualifications for entry 'were to be determined by whether one had a large nose or not, and if you did not possess such a proboscis then you had to obtain special permission to enter this institution of higher learning reserved only for those with large noses.'[4]

Tutu espoused the cause of black theology instantly and enthusiastically. Though his opposition to apartheid stems from a simple awareness of the dignity of man, he could not but be attracted by the opportunity of giving his instincts theological backing. Much of his time, both while he was at Roma and later, was spent going to black theology conferences, writing papers, giving talks. The violation of the humanity of the black man was, he wrote in one such paper, the reason for the emergence of black theology:[5]

> Black theology has occurred mainly in South Africa, where blacks have had their noses rubbed in the dust by white racism, depersonalising them to the extent that they have – blasphemy of blasphemies – come to doubt the reality of their own personhood and humanity. They have come to believe that the denigration of their humanity by those who oppress them is the truth about themselves ... Liberation theology becomes part of a people's struggle for liberation; it tries to help victims of oppression to assert their humanity and so look the other chap in the eye and speak face to face without shuffling their feet and apologising for their black existence.

In writing that, Tutu could have been writing from the point of view of black consciousness: humanity stands central. The black man is important and he is important for what he *is*, not for what he does. It is a hair's breadth from a religious approach. Though there were many Christians behind the emergence of black consciousness, they did not have to concern themselves with theological issues; black theology, its theological counterpart, obviously does. It needs to justify the ways of God to Man, to seek to understand the exploitation of man by man. When every day the black man sees the ladder of privilege, with the exploiter on the top rung, the exploited on the bottom, he must ask 'Whose side is God on?' He must question whether Jesus was necessarily the Jew of history or the white man of Western Christianity. Why should he not have been black?

Black theology has little difficulty in arguing that the God of the Bible is on the side of the oppressed. Tutu's thinking on the subject of liberation as a theme of the Old Testament is one of his major contributions to understanding a black view of theology. He rejoices that the first book of Genesis – 'a magnificent hymn to creation, a paean of praise to God the Creator'[6] – should have been written at a tragic time in Jewish history, when the Israelites were exiled in Babylon, surrounded by strange gods, depressed and dejected. (Might one compare their response to the gallant spirit of the black South Africans, singing freedom songs when confronted by bullets, tear-gas and arrest?) In his own forthright style, Tutu explores the parallels between his fellow blacks and the rabble of Israelite slaves, working as builders for their taskmasters, chastised when they could not make bricks without straw. He points out that though the Israelites suffered for long years, though they must have thought that God did not care, even that he did not exist, history shows that eventually they were set free, that they did reach the promised land:[7]

> This God did not just talk – he acted. He showed himself to be a doing God. Perhaps we might add another point about God – He takes sides. He is not a neutral God. He took the side of the slaves, the oppressed, the victims. He is still the same even today, he sides with the poor, the hungry, the oppressed, the victims of injustice.

But though the Bible affirms that God is always on the side of the downtrodden, it is not because they are better or more deserving than their oppressors, but simply because they are oppressed, because that is the kind of God he is. 'So to the anguished cry, "God, on whose side are you?" we say emphatically, God is on your side, not as some jingoistic national deity who says "my people right or wrong," but as one who saves and yet ultimately judges those whom he saves.'[8]

God's compassion does not mean he ceases to judge, so Tutu warns that liberation is challenging, costly, demands a high sense of responsibility. He argues that the spirit of the Israelites was broken: they had been dehumanised by their bondage, acquired a slave mentality:[9]

> We know just what this sense of inferiority can do to people. We develop a self-hatred and despise one another as a result. And we treat one another as scum. Have you seen how we drive in town and how we drive in Soweto? In Soweto we stop our cars anywhere because we despise one another and treat one another as of little worth.

There is little use in casting off one form of oppression, only to put on the almost equally oppressive garments of bitterness and division.

The Jesus of the New Testament explicitly came to the poor, the broken-hearted, 'to preach deliverance to the captives, to set at liberty them that are bruised'.[10] There is no question whose side he is on. When Tutu writes on liberation in the New Testament he is most concerned with personal liberation, freedom from sin, sickness and hunger. 'People are set free *from* bondage to the world, the Devil and sin, in order to be free *for* God, and to be fully human because Christ came that they might have life in its abundant fullness.'[11] His constant plea is for a South Africa liberated from oppression and injustice so that it may be filled with reconciliation, caring and compassion.

Though books on black theology frequently include a chapter by Desmond Tutu and though he is one of its most eloquent and persuasive communicators, he is not a black theologian in the technical sense; he has not read, reflected or wrestled with the issues in sufficient depth – even if he felt the inclination he has not had the time. His thinking is expressed more in sermons, devotional talks and addresses than in serious theological writing. (Though it should be said that many theologians, like the distinguished Professor John de Gruchy, have no doubt he could make an important contribution – there is no question as to his theological ability.) Desmond Tutu's involvement with black theology is a natural consequence of his faith; it is part, not the whole, of his theological pilgrimage.

Tutu's theology is deeply incarnational, rooted in the fact that, in Jesus, God has entered fully into the human situation. (It is significant that he is very drawn to William Temple's statement that Christianity is the most materialistic of all religions.) 'The God whom we worship is wonderfully transcendent – St John in his Gospel sums it up by saying "God is Spirit". Yet when this God wanted to intervene decisively in the affairs of Man, he did not come as a spiritual being. He did not come as an angel. No, he came as a human being.'[12] While the centrality of the spiritual is never in question, the encounter with God forces Tutu to seek a spirituality relevant to his time and his situation. 'He is the transcendent one who fills us with awe – the *mysterium tremendum et fascinans.* But He does not allow those who worship Him to remain in an exclusive spiritual ghetto. Our encounter with Him launches us into the world, to work together with this God for the establishment of his kingdom.'[13]

So there can be no separation of the spiritual and the material, the religious and the political. There can be no 'pie in the sky when you die', no dodging the social responsibility the Christian shoulders when he is baptised. Tutu's involvement in black theology confirmed his growing instinct that, in South Africa, Christians must proclaim the injustice of apartheid and God's firm stand with the oppressed:[14]

> Liberation theology challenges churches everywhere to be true to their calling to exercise a prophetic ministry in speaking up for the dumb, the voiceless, for those too weak to speak up for themselves, to oppose oppression, injustice, corruption, and evil wherever these may be found. This could be a call to martyrdom, but if God is for us who can be against us?

In August 1971, after only eighteen months at Roma, temptation was once again put in Tutu's path. He was asked by Dr Walter Cason, the acting Director of the Theological Education Fund, to allow his name to be shortlisted for the post of Associate Director responsible for Africa. It was an attractive offer. The job was challenging and reasonably well-paid; he would be contributing to the very organisation which had made it possible for him to go to King's College; the idea of moving back to England, where the TEF was based, appealed to the rest of the family, not least because the children would once again have the educational advantages of the United Kingdom.

The Dean of King's College, whose name Tutu had given as a referee, wrote enthusiastically to the Director, Dr Shoki Coe. His opinion was that Desmond Tutu would be 'a fine worker in the field' and that both domestically and academically he felt it would be a wise appointment. But he did have reservations:[15]

> I have no hesitation at all in strongly recommending you to consider him as a candidate for this vacancy, though it is with the greatest regret that I do so because I have always hoped that Desmond would become a theological teaching power in South Africa, and bringing him to Europe seems almost to be undermining his influence there.

Further, he wondered just what his old pupil's motivation was in considering the post. Was there some element of social advancement? Was he considering the post primarily for the sake of his children?

Tutu was, however, offered the job and he accepted, reasoning on the same pragmatic lines as he had two years earlier: it was a wonderful opportunity, both for him and his family. 'I wouldn't want to make out I was idealistic or anything of that sort. I'm just trying to do what I can.' So in January 1972, on a bitter winter's day, all six Tutus arrived in England, tired and cold, to be met at Heathrow by Tutu's new secretary, Betty Ward, and her husband, together with Jim Bergquist, who was already working with the TEF. They all drove to a furnished house in South-East London, where the Tutus were to stay until they moved to a permanent home in Grove Park. The assumption was that after some sixteen hours' travel they would spend the day settling in; but, far from attending to his creature comforts, Tutu insisted on going straight away to the office in Bromley to meet his new colleagues.

The Theological Education Fund was founded to improve theological education in the third world. It was started in 1960 by Charles Ransom, an Irish Methodist missionary who had worked in India, where he had been appalled at the inefficiency of a system in which the denominations operated separately, so from the beginning the whole thrust was ecumenical. The aim was to help the churches of Africa, Asia and Latin America – the 'younger churches' as they were then called – to be free from dependence on Western missionary societies; the intention was to train indigenous teachers for the theological seminaries, indigenous pastors to lead the congregations. $4 million was provided by John D. Rockefeller Jr and eight American missionary societies, this money to be spent over five years, a period which became known as the 'First Mandate'.

It was an *ad hoc* organisation, only continuing if the mandate was renewed and financial support was available. The success of the first mandate led to a second and a third, and it was at the start of this third mandate that Tutu arrived to take up his post. The policy by then was that senior staff should come not from the West, but from the areas for which they were responsible. Thus the Taiwanese Director, Dr Shoki Coe, dealt with North-East Asia, supported by four Associate Directors: Aharon Sapsezian from Brazil was responsible for Latin America, Ivy Chou from Malaysia for South-East Asia, Jim Bergquist from the USA for the Pacific, with Africa under the aegis of Desmond Tutu.

Though Tutu was by then forty-one, he had never worked in an office before and, to start with, he had little idea what was expected of him. His job description was necessarily vague, involving 'working from this office, collaborating with our international team of directors and the TEF Committee, corresponding with theological colleges and others in Africa engaged in various forms of theological education, and spending quite a large part of the year travelling in order to visit these people.'[16]

Travel was indeed an important part of the work. Each Director would visit his area, possibly making as many as five trips a year. He would find out the needs of the theological colleges and encourage them to formulate projects that might be funded by the TEF; he would then suggest how the grants should be given to whom. The climax to the year's work came at the Annual General Meeting every July, when for a week the Directors would present their cases before the international committee and justify their requests – like Cabinet Ministers before a budget, each wanting the largest share of the financial cake.

For Tutu this side of the work was both difficult and exasperating. He would return from his trips to Africa bubbling over with excitement, determined to do something for everyone he had seen. He sometimes became so over-emotional that it was hard for him to be specific and business-like; he could barely control his understandable wish that as much as possible should be given to the people he was trying to help. He enjoyed spending, he longed especially to help Africa – so much that at first he seemed to find it hard to understand that, despite the huge budget, money was a limited commodity. It was an experience that, with his gift of assimilation, was to stand him in good stead. During his time at the TEF he learnt to manage money, he learnt to negotiate and he became an impressive administrator. Father Aelred Stubbs, who was present at the 1973 AGM, was amazed at the mastery with which the man he had first known as a young ordinand handled the situation. At about the same time he read a paper at a conference in Johannesburg on 'Theological Education by Extension': the extent to which he had developed and grown made a tremendous impact on people, some of whom had not heard him speak since he was a curate in Benoni.

In spending nearly half the year travelling to the Third World, he was seeing and experiencing more than most people do in a lifetime. He saw the violence and repression of Amin's Uganda, he was in Ethiopia just before the overthrow of Emperor Haile Selassie, he witnessed the terrible aftermath of the Biafran war. There was some-times personal danger – he was detained in Kampala airport by Amin's security police, who held up the plane and went through his papers, somehow missing a report highly critical of the regime. At Salisbury airport he was searched by Ian Smith's security men, who found a draft of a paper he was writing on black theology. 'That's not theology,' they screamed at him. 'That's politics.' But they let him through.

He felt continually blessed by being a member of the Christian Church, delighting in experiences of fellowship – particularly by the way he was accepted into people's homes, even when he could not speak their language. 'The fact that we were Christians was enough to pull us towards each other and bind us together.'[17] On one occasion he was at a packed church service in Zaire, where most of the congregation were black but whose language he did not understand. He considered it a profound parable of what it means to belong to the body of Christ when he found himself next to a white missionary, an American Baptist, who acted as his interpreter.

During the first two years of the Third Mandate the Theological Education Fund dealt only with the most necessary projects, as it was deliberately taking time to reflect on and analyse the current situation in the Third World Churches. A key concept to emerge from this period was 'contextualisation', a term that was to become important in South African thinking with the formation, in 1981, of the Institute for Contextual Theology.

The term had been created in the Presbyterian Church in Taiwan. It means all that is implied in indigenisation, yet it seeks to press further. While indigenisation involves responding to Christianity in terms of the local traditional culture, contextualisation also embraces secular conditions, technology and, most particularly, the struggle for human justice. So in contextual Christianity the Church seeks to tie economic and socio-political change to its indigenous cultural roots. This thinking must appeal to anyone working for change in South Africa and Tutu was proud to have been associated with the early development of the concept.

There had been some concern as to whether a South African black would be acceptable to blacks in other parts of Africa. Given the suspicion surrounding blacks in official positions in South Africa, would they fear he was collaborating with the government? However, Tutu's engaging personality ensured that this hurdle was soon cleared. The doubt was rather whether his outspoken contributions to conferences would lead to his not being allowed back into his own country. Indeed at one stage there were rumours that agents provocateurs were being sent from South Africa; their brief – to incriminate him by tripping him into treasonable statements.

His colleagues found that, despite his ebullient nature, he could be moody if he was worried or angry. He has, to an impressive degree, stood above racial bitterness, but in the early 1970s he still carried the scars of living in an apartheid society; people found they had to be careful what they said, or rather how they expressed it. For instance he could be upset by the assumptions behind some phrases in the English language. English people do not think what they are saying when they use phrases like 'as black as sin'; they do not wonder at the way the term 'black magic' involves the devil, while 'white magic' is sorcery in which the devil is not invoked. Tutu could be hurt, sometimes with every justification; once he came into the office speechless with fury after someone had said, 'You bastard, get back to Uganda'. But he could also be quite simply touchy; nor did he bother to conceal his feelings. He was, for example, hurt and insulted for a very long time by an absent-minded member of the office who did not hear his 'Good Morning' greeting and failed to respond.

Once they had become accustomed to his combination of ebullience and sensitivity, his colleagues found him delightful company. For his part, he revelled in the lively mixture of nationalities, each person having his or her own distinctive idiosyncrasies and differing ideology. They were indeed a colourful group, who between them had seen much of the world's tragedies. Dr Coe had been banished from Taiwan, Ivy Chou, a cousin of the then Prime Minister Chou En-lai, though now Malaysian had been born in mainland China, Aharon Sapsezian was a Brazilian national of Armenian extraction and Jim Bergquist, the only Caucasian, was a North American Lutheran. Their ideological differences became the springboard for discussions that were noisy, friendly and sometimes constructive. They would, for instance, argue about the term 'the Third World', by then in general use, in relation to their own backgrounds. Desmond Tutu and Dr Coe claimed that their countries still had colonial status, that they were second-class citizens in their own countries, that in fact they did not, as Aharon Sapsezian claimed, come from the Third World at all, but the Fourth. These conversations, especially this first real encounter with Latin American liberation theology, were another milestone in the development of Tutu's political awareness.

Life in England was, for the Tutus, 'an almost paradisial existence'.[18] Tutu's horror of Bantu Education knows no bounds, so it is easy to imagine his delight in knowing that Trevor was attending Colfe's, a grammar school founded, ironically, in 1652, the very year when the feet of permanent white settlers first trod on South African soil. Theresa and Naomi went to Ravensbourne School for Girls in Bromley and Mpho to the local primary school. The Tutus were buying their own house, Desmond and Leah had the vote – Leah was so delighted at being canvassed by rival political parties that she used to promise her vote to every supplicant. Most important of all, they came to enjoy being what they are, black South Africans.[19]

> We learned to grow in self-confidence and self-acceptance, not needing to apologise for our blackness, indeed to take pride in that which it had seemed wise to God to create us. We did not always articulate this as black consciousness (though such it was). What we learned and were exhilarated by was the new knowledge that we should have a proper pride in ourselves and realise that we could be best only at who we had been created to be and not in striving fruitlessly at being someone else.

Never happy without a pastoral role, Tutu was licensed as an Honorary Curate at St Augustine's, Bromley; whenever he could, he would preach or celebrate the Eucharist. He made a deep impression on the parishioners and their Vicar, Charles Cartwright:[20]

> His message was of the love of God for all his children whatever and wherever they were. And it was God's love that shone from Desmond himself. We all felt – yes really felt – the love of God when Desmond was with us. The other commanding mark of his presence was joy. Whenever he came, to a Eucharist, to a meeting, to a party, to a meal –

the whole company bubbled over with the sheer joy of being together with him. It was always as though the very place was lit up by his presence and permeated by his infectious laughter.

This joy, felt by countless people who have been close to him, is the fruit of a life constantly fed by the richness of his spiritual life. Prayer, regular attendance at the Eucharist, meditation, retreats and the reading of devotional books are an essential part of every day of his life, no matter what the demands may be upon his time. He would urge his colleagues at the Theological Education Fund to make space for this spiritual nourishment. He appreciated the opportunities provided in the timetable for regular worship and prayer, but found it insufficient. He questioned whether the community was a supporting, prayerful fellowship; whether it set a good example; to what extent the Eucharist was the centre and powerhouse of the life of the college.[21]

> Because, as you know, for Christians God the Holy Spirit works through what we call the covenanted and uncovenanted means of grace, the sacraments being the former and other devotional means – meditation, prayer, retreats, Bible and devotional reading – being the latter. And there is no other way available to us to cultivate a real and deeply personal relationship with God our great lover in whose presence we want to luxuriate, falling into ever greater and deeper silence, the silence of love, the stillness of adoration and contemplation – the sort of stillness which is so eloquent when it happens between two who are in love.

Theological education was one of Tutu's great interests. He was doing well at the Theological Education Fund, there was even talk of him becoming the next Director. But once again he was to be swept on by the ineluctable tide of his advancement.

7

Dean of Johannesburg

In 1974 Leslie Stradling, for many years Bishop of Johannesburg,
retired, so the search was on for his successor. Many people were
realising that it was time the Church had another African Diocesan
Bishop – the only one at the time was Bishop Alpheus Zulu, who was
forced by white prejudice to wait long years for his bishopric. Father
Aelred Stubbs and Father Leo Rakale, a much respected black priest,
led a powerful lobby for Tutu, who was thought to be the only African
competent to be a Diocesan Bishop, as opposed to a Suffragan or
Assistant. Though he had spent so much time out of the country, he
was well remembered from his time as a priest in the diocese. More
recently he had impressed those who had met him when he had visited
Africa on behalf of the Theological Education Fund. Indeed Father
Stubbs was so keen that Tutu should become Bishop of Johannesburg
that he decided not to accept nomination himself.

The Elective Assembly, consisting of about 150 clergy and laity, sat
all day without reaching a conclusion. The proceedings of an elective
assembly are confidential, but it is widely reported that Tutu's share
of the vote increased steadily, indeed that he finally came within
nineteen votes of being elected. However, when after six inconclusive
ballots it was clear that an impasse had been reached, a group of
whites lobbied the Dean, Timothy Bavin, feeling that he would be
acceptable to a wide cross-section of people: the Dean, who had in
the earlier ballots consistently voted for Tutu, eventually accepted
nomination, 'With some confidence, because I didn't think there was
the slightest likelihood of my being more than an ingredient in
the pot'. His modesty was, however, misplaced. Despite continued
pressure from the Tutu lobby, before the day was out Dean Bavin
had been elected Bishop. As soon as he was consecrated he invited
Tutu to become his Dean – an arrangement which even Tutu's
supporters consider with hindsight to have been more appropriate
than, at that stage, his election as Bishop of Johannesburg.

The Tutu family were thrown into turmoil. Leah quite simply did
not want to go; she was very happy in England, where they had their
own house, their own friends. The three girls were living at home and

going to good schools. Trevor had just started a degree course in Zoology at Imperial College, London, and came home frequently. Returning to South Africa, once again to be enslaved under apartheid, would change all this.

For Tutu it was more complex. While from the personal and domestic point of view he was in total agreement with his wife – after all, he had said he found life in England 'a paradisial existence' – he needed to discover God's will for him, then to find the courage to do it. His instinct was to go on retreat, to have a few days to pray and reflect on this decision; in fact his duties and his inclination coincided, for he was booked to take a retreat in Woking.

It was a traumatic decision. Not only was there his own wish to stay in England and avoid disrupting his family, but he would have to break his contract with the Theological Education Fund, which still had three years to run. On the other hand he was under great pressure to accept. For instance, Canon Carmichael, who had been asked by Father Leo Rakale to use his powers of persuasion, wrote him a long letter, pointing out that the situation in South Africa was one that needed an articulate black person in a position of leadership, someone who could express to the Church and to white society just how the blacks felt. No doubt Tutu also remembered a conversation in Zambia the previous year, when several black colleagues attending the All Africa Conference of Churches Consultation had urged him to come home: his response, that he would come back when there were signs that conditions were changing, was met with 'There won't be change, until people like you come back and fight for it'. Even Dr Coe, who might have been expected to encourage him to complete his time with the TEF, took the longer view, saying, 'Either you go back now or you never go back', and promising to try to persuade Leah that the right decision would be for them to go back so that her husband could make his contribution to their country's struggle.

However much Tutu values advice from his friends, it is, in the end, the voice of God to which he listens. Few of the retreatants realised that during those few days in Woking he was himself at a watershed, agonising, though twelve years later they all remember noticing a special quality of inspiration and dynamism about him during those few days. Frankie Brownrigg, though she did not at the time appreciate the personal implications, was deeply moved at the way he talked about the courage needed to take a leap in the dark – 'the capacity to jump with confidence into the everlasting arms in the darkness of God'. In the course of the retreat he made his decision. Despite his enjoyment of life in England, despite the wishes of his wife, despite his contract and the annoyance that would be felt by some of his colleagues at the TEF, though with the support of his children – something their grateful father still remembers appreciatively – he would go back to South Africa as the first black Dean of Johannesburg and Rector of the St Mary's Cathedral Parish.

He was welcomed home with joy. For the first time in the history of the Anglican Church in South Africa a black man was to occupy high office in the large, wealthy and vibrant diocese of Johannesburg; better still, he was no token black, but someone eminently qualified to hold the position. He would be able to demonstrate that a black man is not inferior to anyone. The black community, especially the clergy, were ecstatic – vindicated, optimistic, injected with a new confidence. In Archdeacon Nkwe's words:

> In most cases in South Africa, when a black person in a position of authority succeeded it was thought 'He's an exception'; if he failed people said 'What did you expect?' In Desmond Tutu we were assured that history was being made by a black person becoming Dean of Johannesburg and demonstrating to all and sundry that God does not only choose white people to become Deans.

Those who knew Tutu were confident, too, that he would not allow racialism in reverse, but would show that the Church is above race.

There was barely standing room at his Installation, an ecumenical occasion witnessed by 3,000 people of all races, including most of South Africa's church leaders and Archbishop Sirkassian of the Armenian Orthodox Church, a member of the World Council of Churches who was representing the Theological Education Fund. At the end of the service the new Dean astonished everyone by his confidence, as he stood at the west door being hugged and kissed, even – unbelievably in the Johannesburg of the 1970s – by white women. A new era had, undoubtedly, begun.

The arrival of a black Dean was front-page news in many of the South African papers, itself a comment on the crazy society apartheid creates. One of the consequences of his appointment that drew considerable attention was the question of where the Tutus should live. As all the previous Deans had been white, the deanery was in a white suburb, the affluent area of Houghton. Despite the Group Areas Act, in which residential areas are determined by race, the Tutus were invited to move into the official residence, but they adamantly refused to become 'honorary whites', electing instead to share the conditions of their fellow blacks by living in Soweto. After owning his own house in a pleasant leafy suburb of London, Tutu was even more conscious than most black people of the poverty, dreariness and inadequacy of the conditions under which they were expected to live. One of his letters to England was written in St Mary's Cathedral, as he sat in the confessional 'waiting for "customers"'.[1]

> Large crowds are scurrying home past the Cathedral on their way to the main Johannesburg railway station; they seem like so many ants. In the morning it is the same story only the traffic is in the opposite direction. Because Blacks live more than 12 miles away, mainly in the twin city of Soweto (abbreviation for *So*uth *We*stern *To*wnships) with nearly a million black inhabitants. They start from home in the dark and return when the street lights (where they have them) are on. They hardly see their children except over the weekend and their transport is woefully inadequate, with dangerously overcrowded trams and buses.

It should be added that black South Africans are daily reminded of how they *could* live – if they were white. Daily they see the cars speed along fast, wide motorways, taking their owners the short distance to rich residential areas with smart houses, usually with their own swimming pools; they know that there the air is clear, the streets lit and the gardens bright with flowers. Daily, as they enter Soweto, which in 1975 still had no electricity, they pass the huge generator which feeds only the white areas; they return to unmade-up roads, dark streets, small back yards and the murky atmosphere which rises from several thousand coal stoves. There is a swimming pool – one, built at Father Huddleston's initiative and shared by 1 million people.

Having decided to live in Soweto, the Tutus had to be 'influxed' into Johannesburg, as apartheid declares that no black can live in the city without special permission from the authorities. If some people were disappointed that Tutu missed an opportunity to crack the Group Areas Act by living in Houghton, many more were delighted at this symbolic gesture of identification with his people. Neither Desmond nor Leah was, however, content to be housed in one of the monotonous boxes that are considered adequate for black people, so they spent some time and money improving it – an activity indulged in by people the world over, but the object of criticism when done by a black South African clergyman.

Outside St Mary's Cathedral there is a large notice, proclaiming in four languages (English, Afrikaans, Zulu and Sotho) that the church is open to all races. Of the five priests on Dean Tutu's staff, two others were black, three were white; the choir, servers' guild and team of sacristans were racially mixed, as were the congregation, the majority of whom, attracted by the multi-racial mix, came from outside the parish. For Tutu, who remembered when black people had to sit on a bench at the back of the church, not coming up to the Communion rail until after the whites, this was a microcosm of the South Africa that *could* be:[2]

> As I have knelt in the Dean's stall at the superb 9.30 High Mass, with incense, bells and everything, watching a multi-racial crowd file up to the altar rails to be communicated, the one bread and the one cup given by a mixed team of clergy and lay ministers, with a multi-racial choir, servers and sidesmen – all this in apartheid-mad South Africa – then tears sometimes streamed down my cheeks, tears of joy that it could be that indeed Jesus Christ had broken down the wall of partition and here were the first fruits of the eschatological community right in front of my eyes.

Yet despite the initial welcome, despite the extent to which black and white were integrated (previous Deans included people like Gonville ffrench-Beytagh, whose courageous non-racial stand had led to his being accused of treason), some of the congregation left, finding that taking non-racialism from a white mouth was one thing, somehow they could not tolerate it from a black. Though Tutu could take comfort from those, both black and white, who began to attend the cathedral precisely because they *wanted* the ministry of a black person, the defections were deeply hurtful to someone as sensitive as he, especially after the enthusiasm and love he had experienced at Bletchingley. The more so as some claimed to be put off even more by his manner than by his colour.

Wherever Desmond Tutu goes he makes his mark; it was not long before St Mary's Cathedral felt the impact of his personality. In worship, for instance. When he arrived St Mary's was still using the 1662 version of the Communion Service and was quite content with it; within weeks he introduced the new 'Liturgy '75'. He encouraged his congregation, many of them self-conscious Europeans, to move about the church, insisted on including the Kiss of Peace, and – horror of horrors – even wanted them to hug and kiss one another.

Half the congregation were up in arms, feeling he was riding roughshod over their feelings, that he was being too authoritarian. Even those broadly in sympathy with him felt that allowing the organist to speak against the new liturgy at the start of the service at which it was introduced was hardly giving the opposition sufficient voice. Surely, especially in such a conservative parish as St Mary's, a former teacher should realise the importance of preparation, should give some teaching of the theological significance of what they were doing?

He brought a liberal, world-wide perspective, allowing members of the congregation to put on experimental services, appealing to many by being in favour of the ordination of women and by making a point of using non-sexist language, always changing 'men' to 'people' – at the time one of the few priests in the country consistently to show this particular sensitivity. Intercessions had previously been concerned primarily with South Africa; Dean Tutu's prayers regularly embraced the whole world.

There were those who were pleased that complacency was being shown the door, excited by his ideas, stimulated by the larger horizons. Others, however, found it all a bit much. One honest parishioner complained ruefully, 'He was so enthusiastic and one doesn't always feel like being enthusiastic.' Bishop Bavin generously admits that the Dean sometimes ruffled his feathers; he found him 'very disturbing and challenging', not least because he was so often right. For instance Tutu was not content with the perfunctory five minutes prayer at the beginning of a staff meeting. Why could they not have a Eucharist, followed by a period of silence? And if that took forty minutes instead of five, what was wrong with that? He was concerned too, if they seemed to be speeding through an agenda too smoothly, lest efficiency meant glossing over pastoral problems.

The parish was going through a bad time financially and some provident members of the parish council dreaded finance meetings under Dean Tutu, never being quite sure 'what madcap scheme he would come up with next'. They were worried by the ease with which he spent money and disturbed by some of his impulsive ideas. For instance he was keen to link Soweto formally with the cathedral. While people from the townships had always been free to come, he wanted to ensure they received a warm welcome. He suggested that the cathedral should send a bus round Soweto to bring worshippers to St Mary's. He saw it as a way of saving them the long and awkward journey; the parish council was not only horrified at the expense but saw it as stealing sheep from other priests' pastures.

Expectations had been polarised, some people hoping Dean Tutu would be like Dean ffrench-Beytagh, some hoping he would be more conservative. So, too, were the reactions. For every person who found him irritating, scores felt, with Helen Joseph, 'He was a man of God. He really manages to bring God close to you.' For everyone who criticised his extravagance, several rejoiced in the activity he stimulated. But his greatest contribution as Dean was the confidence he gave to black members of the congregation, the way he involved them in the running of the cathedral. It was no longer the white man's church; for the first time black Christians had a sense of being at the heart of things. Bishop Bavin feels Tutu prepared the way for his successors by proving that if one is black one is not incompetent or insensitive. 'I think Desmond actually helped to give the cleaner or the cook, those who hadn't the education or the sophistication of the white members of the congregation, a sense of having a part to play in the councils of the cathedral and therefore being able to look fellow cathedral members in the eye – not to be cringing. The black members increasingly became not simply on the receiving end of decisions but part of making them.'

This was what Desmond Tutu passionately wanted to do – to affirm the black man's dignity; it was indeed one of the reasons why he had agreed to return to South Africa. He wanted to make his own contribution to the liberation struggle, to tell black people that they did not have to apologise for who they were, 'that they were of infinite value because they were created in the image of God'.[3] What amazed him was to discover that it was whites, more than blacks, who needed to hear the message, 'that they must not behave like bullies, who know that they are hollow inside and must have people take notice of them by throwing their weight around or by amassing material possessions, as if *that* was who they were'.[4]

Reconciliation is in every part of a man or it is nowhere; Dean Tutu showed himself as a reconciler in every dimension of his life – including humour. He could joke, for instance, about white fears of black retaliation. In 1975 there was still total apartheid on the beaches and Tutu would say 'The whites think the black people want to drive them into the sea. What they forget is, with apartheid on the beaches – we can't even *get* to the sea.' He could reduce people to helpless laughter by demonstrating his first principle of reconciliation. Soon after he became Dean, Helen Joseph remembers him at a party. He found the highest chair in the room, climbed on to it and stood as tall as his small frame allowed:

> If I am standing up here (voice high as he stretches even further upwards) and the fellow I am speaking to is down there on the ground (crouched low and pointing downwards) I cannot speak to him about reconciliation. I must pick him up by the shoulders and stand him on his feet. When we are face to face – *then* I'll talk to him about reconciliation.

In sermons, addresses, at conferences and in articles, he put his case. Reconciliation is only possible between equals. If society is ordered in such a way that one section of the community is denied its humanity, with all its obligations and responsibilities, then the other side is also enslaved – whites cannot be truly free until blacks are free. 'The freedom of the white man is bound up with that of the black man. So long as the black man is dehumanised and unfree, so long too will the white man remain dehumanised and unfree because he will be plagued by fear and anxiety.'[5] In a situation of injustice and oppression it is impossible to say that God does not take sides, or to speak about forgiveness without asking for repentance from the perpetrators of injustice. Small wonder if words like forgiveness and reconciliation tend to be dismissed, regarded by the oppressed as acquiescence in their oppression:[6]

> It is forgotten that reconciliation is no easy option, nor does it rule out confrontation. After all, it did cost God the death of His Son to effect reconciliation; the cross of Jesus was to expose the sinfulness of sin when he took on the powers of evil and routed them comprehensively. No, just as there can be no cheap grace, so there can be no cheap reconciliation, because we cannot cry, 'peace, peace' where there is no peace.

In taking this stance, in insisting that the problem belongs as much to the oppressor as to the oppressed and placing himself firmly in the role of a reconciler, he was taking the first step along the political tightrope on which he was to balance for the rest of his public life. And if it was a balance that sometimes, from the outside, might look slightly precarious, it is in reality a poise very firmly held, infused with an inner confidence, a 'centredness' that can only belong to someone deeply rooted in something beyond the changing world of outer events.

Tutu himself finds it hard to chart his political development: he is a man of instinct rather than analysis. But there are a few milestones which mark his journey from detached student to international spokesman. Though at the time of Sharpeville he felt helpless, when he was at King's College he was realising that any contribution he might make to South Africa's struggle for liberation would be strengthened if he could sharpen his intellectual tools to their keenest edge. The traumatic Fort Hare strike was the catalyst for a deeper emotional involvement; intellectual backing came from his involvement with black theology and his encounter with Latin American liberation theology at the TEF. By the time he became Dean of Johannesburg he knew that politics and theology, especially in South Africa, could not be separated. Further, he was aware that he had been given 'the privilege of a platform' and that now, thanks largely to his time at the TEF, he had 'a proper sense of self-confidence'. At last he had been remorselessly drawn into the political arena: from this time there was to be no question as to his involvement, only how his part could best be played.

Whether or not the Church should be involved in politics is a question that has been debated since the Prophet Amos urged the importance of social justice to the Israelites over 2,000 years ago. There are firmly held convictions on both sides of the argument.

Those who believe that the Church should concern itself exclusively with the things of the spirit, that religion is a private matter between man and his Creator, argue that the business of religion is to prepare its followers for eternal life. If this earthly preparation involves suffering, then that is part of God's plan and it is our duty to bear it with patience; in any case society will always contain injustice, it is only individuals who may, by the Grace of God, be converted. Nor, the argument might continue, is there anything intrinsically wrong with hierarchical systems; the master–servant relationship is an extension of divine lordship; after all the Bible itself says there must be hewers of wood and drawers of water. The Church's duty is to advocate peace and unity in the social system in which it finds itself; if in doing this it casts a blind eye to injustice – well, it is not its business anyway.

On the other side of the argument are those who insist on God's power to transform human life. It is therefore the Church's job to act as God's agent in improving the quality of life on earth. This work must be done through the structures of society; if these structures militate against justice, then they must be changed. It follows that the Church must be involved in that fight for change. Further, that the Church has a responsibility to 'remind the state that justice is the only basis for true order, and that the state exists for the good of *all* people under its authority'.[7]

When Desmond Tutu became Dean of Johannesburg he was, considering his forty-four years and his South African background, less politically aware than one might have expected. His contribution to the liberation of his people had been in becoming a good priest; he had, in any case, spent nine of his adult years out of the country. Now he was in a key position in the most politically aware city of South Africa. He lost no time in becoming involved in the struggle in all its dimensions.

Father Aelred Stubbs, while admiring the strength of Tutu's Christian faith and witness, felt strongly that now that his old pupil was in a leadership position he should be more in touch with the current political climate. He encouraged him to go and see a group of young activists centred round the Black Consciousness leader Steve Biko, including a remarkable young doctor, Mamphela Ramphele. With an eagerness and humility that impressed Father Stubbs, Tutu took up the suggestion, and though unfortunately Steve Biko was in detention at the time of his visit, he spent a couple of days with the group. Dr Ramphele realised that when Tutu left the country it was at a time when black people were trying to show that they too were human beings by *doing* things. Now, in the 1970s, the mood had changed. 'We are people because we are people, not because we are just as good as the Western cultured people, not because we can do just as well in this field or in that field. We also are people and now we are actually going to determine the pace of change.'

It was not difficult for Tutu to appreciate the new South African reality. Meeting Steve Biko's group, talking to respected leaders of the Soweto community like Dr Motlana and Tom Manthata, above all living in Soweto, where every day he was in touch with the people, sharing their lives, he soon filled in any gaps in his understanding caused by his time abroad.

Tutu did not find it hard to justify his stance theologically. Since his student days he had been studying the Scriptures, looking for what they had to say about liberation:[8]

> Do they say God is concerned only about individual salvation and has no interest in the redemption of the socio-political and economic matrix in which individuals live? Does it say the world is religiously and ethically neutral and of no consequence to salvation and the final consummation of all things, that what happens in the market place, in the courtroom, or in Parliament is of no particular religious significance, and all that matters to God is what is confined to the sacred sphere of the ecclesiastical? Does it say God is in fact not really interested too much in what happens from Monday to Friday but only in that which happens on Sunday, and that He does not much care about the plight of the hungry, the dispossessed, the voiceless, the powerless ones – that He does not take sides? When two persons are engaged in a conflict and one of them is considerably stronger than the other, to be neutral is not just and fair and impartisan because to be neutral is in fact to side with the powerful.

After five years out of South Africa he was shocked at the increasing tension he found in the black community, especially among the young; he was filled with a sense of foreboding and alarm. He warned a local synod that the Church must concern itself, immediately, with the needs of the youth: 'We are creating a monster for ourselves which we won't be able to handle unless we address the needs of the youth here and now.' In a letter to his English friends he wrote that[9]

> change, real change, must happen quickly if it is going to be peaceful. I am worried that many whites don't want to know just how deeply hurt and disillusioned blacks are; and change may come too late for it to be significant and peaceful. The Church must be prophetic, speaking hope and judgement and love and reconciliation and repentance.

Those who did not take him seriously were soon to regret it.

Again and again he appealed to people's humanity. In January 1976, in an address to one of the regional groups of the South African Institute of Race Relations, he pleaded with his audience to come out of their fool's paradise and listen to one another; to face reality and resist the temptation to say only what people wanted to hear. He reminded his audience that whites are human beings: 'They laugh, they love, they cuddle babies, they weep, they eat, they sleep – they are human. But if they are human, why, oh why can't they see that we laugh too, we love too, we weep too, we cuddle babies too, we eat, we sleep – why can't they see that it is impossible for things to go on like this?'[10]

But he found grounds for hope. He wondered – as does anyone who knows them – at black people's capacity to forgive, admitting that the seeds of bitterness and hatred are sown early in a black person's life, yet, after all he has endured at the hands of whites, he is still ready to extend the hand of friendship. He found hope in the Black Consciousness Movement, that was giving blacks a sense of their own worth. Hope that the Afrikaner, who had braved dangers in the pursuit of his own freedom, would understand that others shared this need. He had hope of the English, because they come from a tradition that affirms human freedom; hope because of the many in the white community who stood up for justice. Ultimately, he had hope because 'This is God's world and he is in charge. We were all created by the same God, redeemed by the same Jesus Christ and are sanctified by the same Holy Spirit. We belong together. The survival of the white man depends on the survival of the black man and vice versa, and this includes so-called Coloured people and Indians.'[11]

There might be time for peaceful change, but the whites must listen, they must act before it was too late. 'Do you refuse to hear our anguished cries? . . . How loud and how long do we have to shout for you to hear?'[12] He warned that the people were desperate and would resort to desperate measures.

Desmond Tutu is a man of action, his theology needed to be incarnated. What he should do came to him a few weeks later, during a three-day clergy retreat in Johannesburg; on May 6th, 1976, in his first public political initiative, he sent an open letter to the Prime Minister, John Vorster.

It is a remarkable letter, heartfelt yet statesmanlike, direct yet never failing to be tactful and courteous, eloquent, informed and precise in its suggestions. He writes as the Anglican Dean of Johannesburg and spokesman for his people; he is writing to the highest political figure in the land, but he appeals to him first in the context of their shared humanity:[13]

> I am writing to you, Sir, as one who is passionately devoted to a happy and stable family life as the indispensable foundation of a sound and healthy society. You have flung out your arms to embrace and hug your children and your grandchildren, to smother them with your kisses, you have loved, you have wept, you have watched by the bed of a sick one whom you loved, you have watched by the deathbed of a beloved relative, you have been a proud father at the wedding of your children, you have shed tears by the graveside of one for whom your heart has been broken.

Tutu also appealed to the Prime Minister as an Afrikaner, whose forebears had known the humiliation of being a subject people, who knew that 'absolutely nothing will stop a people from attaining their freedom to be a people who can hold their heads high, whose dignity to be human persons is respected, who can assume the responsibilities and obligations that are necessary concomitants of the freedom they yearn for with all their being.'[14] He pointed out that blacks could not attain this freedom in the 'homelands', because they felt they had contributed to the prosperity of an undivided South Africa. In any case they could not understand why whites, comprised of Greeks, Italians, Portuguese, Afrikaners, French, Germans and English, should be said to form one nation, while blacks, most of whom are much closer to one another ethnically, are said to form several and split up accordingly. He did not make any accusations concerning the 'divide and rule' thinking which he knew very well lay behind the development of the 'homelands', but simply pleaded that everyone, black and white, should be fellow South Africans.

He went on to admit that he had seen little evidence of the move against discrimination based on race which had been announced by 'Pik' Botha, who was at the time the Ambassador to the United Nations – he was not impressed by cosmetic changes such as the removal of signs from park benches. Though he gave the Prime Minister credit for his efforts to promote détente and dialogue, it had to be qualified approval:[15]

> In these efforts many of us here wanted to support you eagerly, but we feel we cannot in honesty do this, when external détente is not paralleled by equally vigorous efforts at internal détente. Blacks are grateful for all that has been done for them, but now they claim *an inalienable right to do things for themselves*, in co-operation with their fellow South Africans of all races.

With great restraint and politeness, Tutu objected to the power given to the army and the security police without making them accountable to the courts; he appealed for the detainees – that they should be released or punished if found guilty of indictable offences; he reminded the Prime Minister that freedom is indivisible and that the whites would not be free until the whole community was free; most crucially, he warned that there was a limit to the blatant injustice and suffering that a people can take. 'I have a growing and nightmarish fear that unless something drastic is done very soon then bloodshed and violence are going to happen in South Africa almost inevitably.'[16]

The letter suggests three ways in which the government could demonstrate that it was sincere in saying it wanted peaceful change. First it must accept the urban black as a permanent inhabitant of 'white' South Africa, with consequent freehold rights – he would then have a stake in the land and would not easily join any who wished to destroy his country. Second, it must repeal the pass laws. Third, it must call a National Convention, made up of leaders recognised as such by the community.

Three weeks later, at the beginning of June, the Prime Minister answered, questioning Dean Tutu's motives in writing and suggesting he was merely trying to put out political propaganda. When the Dean asked for permission to publish the reply he received a curt rejection.

Tutu's nightmare was to become reality, sooner and more tragically than even he had feared. On June 16th, 15,000 children from Soweto organised themselves into a mass protest, objecting to separate Bantu education and in particular to the use of Afrikaans, the language of the hated oppressor, as a medium of instruction. Singing, they marched from school to school, determined but peaceful, armed only with their placards; they were met with police gunfire. Hector Peterson, just twelve years old, was the first of over 600 people to die in the next few weeks, most of them schoolchildren and students.

At the time Tutu was Vicar-General, as Bishop Bavin was overseas, and he was in the cathedral when someone telephoned to say they were shooting children in Soweto. His horrified, disbelieving enquiries to the authorities were met with assurances that everything was under control and that the brigadier to whom he eventually spoke was not going to answer questions from anyone. The Dean replied that he was not anyone, he was Vicar-General of the diocese and he was very concerned and wanted to know what had happened – at which the brigadier hung up on him.

Tutu spent most of the day in Soweto, talking to children and parents, trying not to show anger, trying less successfully to conceal his tears. It was a day of such pain and trauma that he remembers very little, but he does recall the next Sunday saying to his largely white congregation, 'We have been really shattered by the deafening silence from the white community. You will say, what could you do? And all I would say to you is, what would you have done had they been white children? And that is all we would have wanted you to have done.'

As trouble flared all over the country and the toll of deaths and injuries mounted, Tutu was suffering a particular personal anguish. Earlier in the year, even before he wrote to John Vorster, he had agreed to become Bishop of Lesotho. With the anger and frustration in the townships reaching fever pitch he had, once again, to leave the country.

8

The mountain kingdom

Despite the fact that those who work for the Church are not supposed to show ambition and are in fact criticised if they aspire to its highest offices, Desmond Tutu has never denied that he was ambitious. Nevertheless, the invitation to allow his name to go forward for election to the bishopric of Lesotho threw him into a turmoil of indecision and anguish.

It was too soon. He had only been Dean for a few months, he was barely settling down, beginning to feel accepted, growing to love the people of St Mary's. 'It had seemed to be work that God wanted me to do. I thought that I had turned the corner in terms of hostility. I mean people began to think that perhaps I *might* be a Pastor.'

It was too soon and he decided to refuse. But he was put under tremendous pressure to accept, in fact he was quite literally pursued. The diocese of Lesotho even went to the unusual lengths of sending a delegation to Soweto; they were waiting as he left a meeting at the church of Regina Mundi and came home with him, using all their powers of persuasion to urge him to change his mind. They argued that he was the only man available and that he must stand.

He asked advice from Leah, from the parish council, from friends and colleagues. Leah, only just coming to terms with leaving England, was almost indifferent to being uprooted yet again. With a commendable lack of self-interest, she pointed out that when the delegates had made such an effort it would look very arrogant if he disregarded their pleas. The parish council, on the other hand, urged him not to consider it. They did not all see eye to eye with him, but they did not want yet another change. The last few years had been very traumatic, with a long interregnum after Dean ffrench-Beytagh's trial and deportation, then the swift elevation of Timothy Bavin after only eighteen months as Dean. They needed some stability and felt that his duty lay with them. On the other hand, there were those who felt that as leadership in the Anglican Church is vested in the bench of Bishops, the sooner Dean Tutu joined them, the sooner he would be able to play his part as a leader. The argument closest to Tutu's heart came from Phillip Russell, at the time Bishop of Natal. If God is active in an elective assembly, he reasoned, then it is wrong to refuse to stand because if it was not God's will that he should be Bishop of Lesotho then he would not be elected anyway. Yet the pendulum of indecision swung again as Father Aelred Stubbs advised him very strongly against accepting nomination – he had not been Dean for long enough.

There were a few people in the parish who felt that in even considering nomination their Dean was guilty of culpable ambition; there were even suggestions that he was using his position in Johannesburg as a stepping stone to higher things. However Bishop Bavin, who knew him better than most, is confident that Tutu was not thinking about himself or what the move would mean for him; he believes that his concern was for the people he would be leaving and the people to whom he would be going. There is no doubt that for Tutu it was sheer agony. 'There have been very few occasions when I have felt so torn apart. Which way should I go? What is God's will for me?'[1]

On the day of the elective assembly Tutu was in Pietermaritzburg, attending a meeting of the Federal Theological Seminary Council.[2] He was lunching with the Principal, rejoicing that the election must be over and that as he had heard nothing they must have chosen someone else, when he was called to the telephone. He had been elected Bishop of Lesotho. His reaction, 'Oh *no*', cannot have been very encouraging to the bearer of the news. As if in a nightmare, he went home to Leah and wept; he felt God was being unfair to demand this of him. He had wanted to be a Bishop, but never less so than at the time of his election.

On July 11th, 1976, Desmond Tutu was consecrated Bishop of Lesotho in St Mary's Cathedral, Johannesburg, where less than a year before he had been installed Dean. The next month, in a snow-covered Maseru, he was enthroned at St James's Cathedral. The eager crowds, delighted to have won the Tutu tug-of-war, packed the cathedral to overflowing, many grateful to listen to the service on loudspeakers and catch the smallest glimpse of the proceedings. Among the first to embrace the new Bishop were King Moshoeshoe II, Queen Mamohato and the Prime Minister Chief Leabua Jonathan.

It was only three weeks after the Soweto riots and by then Tutu's distress at leaving Johannesburg was even more intense. It was agonising for him to leave then, when there was so much to do in his own country; there was also the fear – justified by the remarks of a few of the enemies he was beginning to acquire – that people would say that he was running away. However, Tutu is a resilient man, who throws himself wholeheartedly into whatever he is doing. The sadness of leaving South Africa was never completely assuaged, but once the anguish of indecision and the immediate pain of parting were behind him he found a deep satisfaction in being a Bishop. It suited him on many levels, from the superficial to the profound. At one end of the scale was his delight in ritual and ceremony with its attendant pageantry and dress – a pleasure he shares with many Africans; he admitted to an English friend that he still enjoys seeing himself in photographs, 'especially if I'm coped and mitred'. But the real significance was that he had become 'pastor of pastors'.

From the very beginning he made it clear how he wanted to be regarded; at his enthronement sermon he appealed to the diocese to call him 'Father' or 'Bishop', not 'My Lord', saying, 'I want to be your father in God, not an ecclesiastical bureaucrat.' He knew that there were those who would enjoy addressing a fellow black with due formality and might feel disappointed that their first black diocesan Bishop should refuse to be thus honoured, but he knew who his model should be. 'The pattern of my lordship was determined by our Lord himself and it is spelt out in terms of one who tied a towel round his waist to wash the disciples' feet.'[3]

In this sermon he also asked that callers should use the front door of the Bishop's House. This might seem an odd request – surely the front door is the one visitors normally use? In fact Bishop Tutu was showing great sensitivity to the Basotho.[4]

> When most of your diocese are simple country folk, who are very humble, it is so easy for the Bishop to be seen to accept the sophisticated and the educated and the high and the mighty through the front door and that these good people, the people of the land, are made to go to the back like servants in South Africa.[5]

He went further; if anyone came to the back door, he promised that his wife would greet them with a bucket of cold water.

Tutu had seen too much of separation, of people being compartmentalised, divided and deprived of dignity, so he was careful about giving too much time to the social duties that fall to a Bishop's lot and can set him apart from his people. He was living in Maseru, the capital of the kingdom and the headquarters of all its official bodies like the Diplomatic Corps; he was a personal friend of the King and Queen. (He once had to stay at a party at the Palace until 3 a.m.; the King was enjoying his company so much that he was refused permission to go home at a time more suitable for a busy Bishop.) The Tutus could easily have been caught up in a round of cocktail parties and official functions, but both he and Leah tried to restrict themselves to the minimum. He also relinquished the chairmanship of many diocesan committees, retaining this role only with the least developed school that he felt most needed his attention.

By freeing himself as much as possible from bureaucracy and the peripheral concerns that can consume the time of people in senior positions, he was trying to give himself space for real involvement at a pastoral level. He wanted the Bishop's presence to be a familiar event, not a rare occurrence; to be seen as a shepherd of his people, not a purple-clad bureaucrat. In order to keep in touch with as many people as possible he celebrated the Eucharist at different churches in Maseru each day of the week; once a month he went with one of the Cathedral staff to take communion to the sick and elderly; occasionally – usually at Christmas – he went to the Central Prison in Maseru.

Visiting the country districts was more complicated. The twenty-three parishes, some with as many as twenty 'outstations', were spread over an area about the size of Belgium, and while by African standards the diocese was not geographically or numerically large, the mountain-ous nature of the region – the Maluti Mountains occupied three-quarters of the country – meant that communication presented a very real problem. There were few roads or telephones and the main method of transport was on horseback; travellers could meet thunder-storms or find themselves on a road made impassable by erosion or, in winter, by snow. Even under good conditions it could take days, walking and riding, to cross one parish. So conducting two confir-mation services, for instance, could take a Bishop three days. He would probably go by air into the country, spend a couple of hours riding to a remote village on horseback, then spend a night in a hut and conduct a confirmation service the next morning. Several hours' riding would bring him to his next destination, where he would hold a second service and ride to the nearest airstrip, where there would almost certainly be a long wait before he could catch a flight back to Maseru.

The essentially urban Bishop Tutu was not at all accustomed to this sort of thing, but he took to it with good humour, trekking for as long as eight hours on horseback, collapsing exhausted into bed and tackling another five hours the next day. He complained wistfully, 'I did not know the ground was so far. There was no rapport between me and the horse – when I go up, he goes down with rather unpleasant consequences for certain unmentionable parts of my anatomy.'[6] How-ever, he was exhilarated the first time he persuaded his mount to gallop.

He would use the long journeys on horseback as a chance to get to know the priest who was travelling with him. Though he was criticised for being out of the country too much (largely honouring previous commitments), his pastoral concern for his priests was very real. It was in Lesotho that he began a practice he was to continue all his life. He put details of his staff – a Suffragan Bishop, a Dean and about forty priests – in his intercession book, noting their birthdays, wedding anniversaries, the names of wives and children and any particular problems in their personal or professional lives. Every day he prayed for each one by name. 'Like the high priest of Israel, I saw my Pectoral Cross in a sense as being like the breastplate with the 12 precious stones reminding me that I had to be carrying specially the clergy in my heart regularly.'[7]

Donald Nestor, then a priest in the diocese, now Suffragan Bishop of Lesotho, was one man who deeply valued Bishop Tutu's personal concern:

> He trusted me in my work and upheld and encouraged me. He knew me as a person quite deeply and wanted to build me up. He would give pertinent spiritual advice, not necessarily when asked. He could penetrate to what was essential about me and tell me things about myself which other people had not seen – for instance he would tell me not to apologise so much. He could see where I would be most useful and was concerned for me to grow.

In a surprisingly short time, Tutu managed to meet most of his parishioners, even the most far-flung. For them his visits would be a great event, eagerly awaited, joyously celebrated. He would be met by a posse of horsemen wearing their colourful Basotho hats, the church would be crowded with people, many of whom had walked for miles, and the service – in Sotho and English – with the speeches, meals and festivities, could last as long as five hours. He loved it. He revelled in the warmth, generosity and love of the Basotho:[8]

> When I arrived as their Bishop, the people said *ke ntate*, this is our father. And they really meant it. That was something that shattered me. It was not just a convention or a polite title; they believed I was their father in God, that was what I was challenged to become. Every time it happened I was filled with awe and a great sense of responsibility as well as joy.

This sense of responsibility came as something of a shock; he discovered not only the loneliness of high office, but the problem of power. Though he tried very hard to exercise a participatory ministry, he could not escape the Church's hierarchical element. All the various committees and bodies in a diocese are advisory to the Bishop and every decision is ultimately his; in diocesan synods a Bishop can ignore all the advice he is given and veto their decisions. He found that he was quite unprepared for the exercise of this power; the only way he could learn to handle the demon was to draw on his experience as a pastor and a priest.

Ultimately he was convinced that the only thing that really mattered was love – both people and clergy must know that they are loved. At his consecration a Bishop is given a ring, symbolic of the sense in which he is married to his diocese; this is something very real to Bishop Tutu. When his great friend Walter Makhulu became Bishop of Botswana Tutu wrote him a long and moving letter, sharing the joy and the pain of being a Christian Bishop:[9]

> You will look splendid in cope and mitre. But I know too, that many times you will weep tears because God has given you the gift of tears. You will weep tears of joy; you will weep tears at being overwhelmed by God's grace; you will weep tears at the love of God's people because Walter, all they want is that you should love them. And then you can do virtually anything with them. They will eat out of your hand. You can scold them. You can be strict. And they will know when you love them. You can never bluff love.

As South Africa was part of the British Empire for 100 years, there is a very real sense in which all South Africans, from far-right Afrikaner to far-left black radical, feel comfortable with British culture. Tutu, like all educated South Africans of his generation a product of the British mission schools, is at home in any culture: it is easy to forget that he is first and foremost an African, with his roots firmly in South African soil. He can straddle cultures so comfortably that his old scoutmaster Zakes Mohutsioa can say 'when he's among Europeans he's a European, when he's among Africans he's an African'.

During his time as Bishop of Lesotho he was more regularly and more predominantly close to African thinking than, as his life became more and more cosmopolitan, he was ever to be again. There were people in Lesotho untouched by Christianity, who held to their old beliefs, giving great significance to dreams, making sacrifices to their ancestors. There were still witch doctors, who were recognised by the government and had their own association. At the extreme, one of the problems that the clergy had to tackle was the question of initiation schools to prepare teenagers for manhood and womanhood. Though attempts had been made to stop these customs since the time of King Moshoeshoe I, they were still held in secret, sometimes leading to people being ritually killed so that their organs could be used for medicine. It was the Bishop who had to conduct acts of exorcism after these practices had taken place.

Some people who only know Tutu superficially feel he has lost contact with his African roots – for instance, when he was at the seminary in Alice he was criticised for bringing up his children in too Western a way, particularly for sending them to multi-racial schools. However, people close to him, like Barney Pityana, appreciate that he is deeply African, from his ability to speak several African languages – Zulu, Sotho, Tswana, Xhosa – to his taste for ting and tripe,[10] the instinctive way he moves round the altar in a slow, dancing rhythm, and his enjoyment of African hymns and festivals.

Most profoundly, most pertinently, is the extent to which his spirituality is African. The African theologian Professor Gabriel Setiloane suggests that when Tutu is speaking at his best it is the African in him who is speaking, because he is filled with that mysterious quality known as '*ubuntu*'. *Ubuntu* is often translated as humanity, but it is deeper than humaneness, deeper than generosity of spirit or understanding; it is the very essence of that mysterious quality which makes a person a person in African understanding. The worst thing that can be said about anyone is that he has not got *ubuntu* – he is not a person.

This quality of *ubuntu* is the springboard of Tutu's thinking; it is deep in his being, it shines from him, irradiating his words and actions. He is fond of quoting a Xhosa saying that penetrates to the heart of African thinking: 'A person is a person through other persons.' Though he himself is very punctual, he feels the world could learn something from that aspect of Africa which can infuriate Europeans – 'African time'. He claims that behind this concept lies the conviction that people are more important than punctuality. Being in tune with the rhythm of the universe and with life – which includes the ancestors and those not yet born as well as those living in the world at any particular moment – is of greater value than rigid adherence to the clock. Related to this idea is the way he frequently refers to himself as 'we'; he points out that when a Xhosa is asked how he is and says 'We are well', he is not using the 'royal we', he is reflecting his membership of the family of mankind.

He sometimes illustrates the interdependence of people with a parable:[11]

> Light bulb used to shine and glow wonderfully. Everybody was attracted to brilliant light bulb until light bulb grew with pride and arrogance. He thought his brilliance was self-generated. He disdained the flexes hidden away in the ceiling which connected him to the dynamo, the source of

his energy. Then one day someone unscrewed light bulb from the socket and laid him on the table. Try as he would, light bulb just remained black and cold and people passed him by without paying him the slightest attention.

Africans have always been a deeply religious people, with a world view, Tutu argues, more consistent with that of the Bible than the world view emanating from the West. This essential difference between black and white attitudes can rarely have been better put than by Nelson Mandela:[12]

> In South Africa, the conflict has emerged as one of race on the one side and one of ideals on the other. The White man regards the Universe as a gigantic machine hurtling through space and time to its final destruction: individuals in it are but tiny organisms with private lives that lead to private deaths: personal power, success and fame are the absolute measure of values; the things to live for. This outlook on life divides the Universe into a host of individual little entities which cannot help being in constant conflict thereby hastening the approach of the hour of their final destruction.
>
> The African, on his side, regards the Universe as one composite whole; an organic entity, progressively driving towards greater harmony and unity whose individual parts exist merely as interdependent aspects of one whole realising their fullest life in the corporate life where communal contentment is the absolute measure of values. His philosophy of life strives towards unity and aggregation; towards greater social responsibility.

Christianity in South Africa cannot but be associated with the white missionaries, who brought their culture as well as their religion. Consequently, there has been a movement to develop an indigenous African theology. African theology is an attempt to relate African culture and spirituality to Christian faith and is sometimes seen in opposition to black theology, a theology of political protest. The theologian John Mbiti, who sees a clear distinction between the two, writes that African theology 'grows out of our joy and experience of the Christian faith, whereas black theology emerges from the pain of oppression'.[13] However, in an article published just before he came to Lesotho, Tutu, who is an exponent of both theologies, prefers to emphasise the similarities between the two. He writes movingly about the unity between black people, whether they have crossed the Atlantic or remained in the continent of their ancestors:[14]

> All of us are bound to Mother Africa by invisible but tenacious bonds. She has nurtured the deepest things in us blacks. All of us have roots

that go deep in the warm soil of Africa; so that no matter how long and traumatic our separation from our ancestral home has been, there are things we are often unable to articulate, but which we feel in our very bones, things which make us ... different from others who have not suckled the breasts of our mother, Africa. Don't most of us, for instance, find the classical arguments for the existence of God just an interesting cerebral game because Africa taught us long ago that life without belief in a supreme being was just too absurd to contemplate? And don't most of us thrill as we approach the awesomeness of the transcendent when many other of our contemporaries find even the word God an embarrassment? How do you explain our shared sense of the corporateness of life, of our rejection of hellenistic dichotomies in our insistence that life, material and spiritual, secular and sacred, that it is all of a piece?

He goes on to claim that there cannot be one, universal theology; that theology can only be relevant if it has 'the humility to accept the scandal of its particularity as well as its transience'. Both African and black theology have arisen as reactions against a situation in which black humanity has been defined in the terms of the white man; in which 'to be really human he had to see himself and be seen as a chocolate coloured white man'. They both assert that if the Incarnation is taken seriously, then Christianity for the African must be incarnated in Africa, speaking to the African from an African context. Both repudiate the tacit claims of the supremacy of Western values.

Yet he admits there are also differences. He is critical of African theology for failing to produce a sufficiently sharp cutting edge or to address contemporary problems satisfactorily; he believes it can learn from the more abrasive black theology. Blacks must stop testing their theology against the value systems of the West and develop their own insights. 'It is only when African theology is true to itself that it will go on to speak relevantly to the contemporary African – surely its primary task – and also, incidentally, make its valuable contribution to the rich Christian heritage which belongs to all of us.'

Immersed as he was in fulfilling his episcopal duties, Bishop Tutu, by now part of the political scene, did not evade the further responsibilities this laid on him. He found no difficulty in accepting that the Church had a role as watchdog, that it should keep abreast of what was happening in government. In fact in his first sermon in Maseru he pointed out that the South African government was always looking for examples of mismanagement in countries run by Africans; that South Africa was watching Lesotho, so Lesotho must set an example. Unfortunately Lesotho was not setting a good example and Tutu did not take kindly to the unelected government, still in power as a result of the 1970 coup. The Anglican, Catholic and Lesotho Evangelical Churches worked not only for reconciliation between themselves, but between the government and the opposition. Bishop Tutu, a driving force in ecumenical relations, did not hesitate to criticise the government, or, with other church leaders, to issue statements about 'the sad state of affairs in Lesotho, warning against infringement of the standards set by the Gospel of Jesus Christ, for injustice is injustice whoever it is who perpetrates it'.[15] While his courage was applauded by people like the ecumenical Christian Council of Lesotho, the government, not surprisingly, resented it bitterly. They must have been fearful of his influence, because they not only attacked him through the Press, but the Minister of Information even went to the lengths of organising a campaign against him.

As far as South Africa was concerned Tutu could not do much more than keep in touch with events, but it is a measure of the respect in which he was now held in his own country that in September 1977, when Steve Biko was buried in Kingwilliamstown, it was Tutu who was invited to give the funeral oration.

Steve Biko is honoured not only as the founder of the South African Students Organisation and Black People's Convention, not only as a student leader and political activist, but as a thinker whose views have made an ineradicable mark wherever human rights are taken seriously. 'Selfless revolutionary', a phrase he used of others, has been applied to him. The question has even been raised as to whether he should be regarded as a Christian martyr. His arrest, detention and brutal death at the hands of the South African security police was one of the most violent acts of a violent regime. The shock waves reverberated far beyond South Africa; the free world was outraged that a young man of such noble ideals should no longer be able to play his part in creating the free South Africa for which he had given so much – indeed for which he died.

Biko was only thirty when he was killed, so one can only guess how he would have developed, but during his lifetime there was a difference not so much in content as in emphasis, between his thinking and Bishop Tutu's. Both shared the common ideals of trying to give the black man back the dignity of which apartheid had tried to rob him, both were adamant that they were fighting for the liberation not only of the oppressed but also of the oppressor. However, Biko was not only more overtly political, but also more single-mindedly dedicated to the uplifting of the African spirit, while Tutu aspires to a climate where the colour of the skin is irrelevant. So successful has black consciousness been that there are many who claim that it has done its work and that had Biko still been alive he would have by now moved to a more universalist position, closer to Tutu's. One of the tragedies of his death is that we will never know.

The funeral was a huge occasion; some 30,000 people came from all over South Africa to honour him. Tutu had not known Steve Biko personally, but he did identify at a very deep level with the ideals for which Biko stood and his presence was warmly welcomed by Biko's friends like Justice Moloto and Dr Mamphela Ramphele.

In his oration Tutu emphasised one aspect of Biko's thinking especially near to his own:[16]

> Steve saw, more than most of us, how injustice and oppression can dehumanise and make us all, black and white, victim and perpetrator alike, less than God intended us to be. Now it has always sounded like sloganeering when people have said 'Oppression dehumanises the oppressor as well as the oppressed.' But have we not had an unbelievably shocking example of this, if he has been quoted correctly, in Mr Kruger's[17] heartless remark that Steve's death 'leaves him cold'? Of all human beings he is the most to be pitied. What has happened to him as a human being when the death of a fellow human being can leave him cold? And I bid you pray for the rulers of this land, for the police – especially the security police and those in the prison service – that they may realise that they are human beings too. I bid you pray for whites in South Africa.

While Steve Biko would have agreed with this sentiment, probably not everyone present felt like praying for their rulers at such a time. But it was typical of Tutu to make such a demand.

Tutu had not been in Lesotho for long before he noticed the number of women in the congregations – sometimes there would hardly be a man in the church. The reason was not hard to find. Over 100,000 Basotho men were in South Africa, working in the mines as migrant labourers.

The Nationalist government's declared aim was that Africans might only be in 'white' South Africa on a casual basis to sell their labour. They could own no land, have no political rights, they could not even bring their wives and children with them. As early as 1922 a government commission put it baldly: 'Natives should only be allowed to enter the urban areas to minister to the needs of the white man and should depart therefrom when he ceases so to minister.'[18] By 1970 the government still did not feel it had achieved its aims. The Minister of Bantu Education expressed his hopes thus: 'As far as I am concerned the ideal condition would be if we could succeed in due course in having all Bantu present in the white areas on a basis of migratory labour only.'[19]

So thousands of labourers, desperate for work, are herded together in conditions that would be condemned in many countries if they were inflicted on animals. For eleven months of the year up to 300 men live in dreary, barrack-like single-sex hostels, with as many as ten hostels in a compound. There is no heating, just one common room for entertaining and, as Helen Suzman told Parliament, 'an electronically controlled steel door that can be slid down to seal off any section of the building in case of riot or trouble . . . installed on the instructions of the former Commissioner of Police'.[20] There could be forty-eight people in a room, sleeping on concrete slabs just long enough and just wide enough to accommodate a man's body. Not much larger than a coffin. Once a year they go to the bantustan to which they had been allocated to see, for a few short weeks, their parents, wives and children, known in government-speak as 'superfluous appendages'.

Tutu, who regards any insult to people's dignity as, in the final analysis, an act of blasphemy, pointed out that while the system of migrant labour is not peculiar to South Africa, and cannot be abolished entirely 'while there are depressed areas contiguous with more prosperous and developed ones', for it to be standard practice, as it is for the South African labourer, is contrary to the Gospel. In 1968, while he was still teaching at the Federal Theological Seminary in Alice, he had written about the theology of migrant labour for *South African Outlook*. His argument was not concerned so much with the appalling conditions under which these men were forced to live as with the effect on family life. He adapted Shylock's lines from Shakespeare's *The Merchant of Venice* to emphasise that these men were of flesh and blood: 'Hath not an African eyes? hath not an African hands, organs, dimensions, senses, affections, passions? fed with the same food, hurt with the same weapons, subject to the same diseases, heal'd by the same means, warm'd and cool'd by the same winter and summer as a White man is?'[21] So why, in a country that observes Family Day as a national holiday, should the majority of its population be made to live in conditions where a healthy family life was impossible. Was it surprising if there was homosexuality, prostitution and illegitimacy?

He argues that, far from accepting the charge of interfering in matters that do not concern the Church, she cannot be true to her calling if she acquiesces in conditions that are subversive of a healthy family life. Further, the Dutch Reformed Church itself, not usually eager to disagree with the government, pleaded at a Synod in 1965 that the State should change, or at least adapt, a system which it admitted could have disastrous results for the Church in the republic.

The system also leads to specific problems for the priest. For instance, a migrant labourer, deprived of his wife for eleven months of the year, often takes a town wife; strictly speaking he is then excluded from Holy Communion. Should the priest risk offending members of his Church by giving such persons the Sacraments? On the other hand,[22]

> are we discharging our pastoral responsibilities to the victims of a callous system, since it means their exclusion from the Sacraments for virtually all their life, when by law they may not live with their families at or near a place of work? Is it realistic, let alone fair, to expect a married man to remain continent in the highly charged atmosphere of an urban township, when through no fault of his own, he has been separated from his wife and family?

Children whose fathers are constantly absent from home are known to have problems; Tutu points out that this absence can colour their ideas about God. Children base their conceptions of the fatherhood of God on their relationship with their earthly fathers. 'And can we blame the children of the migrant labourer when their conception of God is the heretical one of a deistic absentee landlord who visits his creation only occasionally?'[23]

Conscious that eventually the Basotho should have one of their own people as their spiritual leader, one of the first things Bishop Tutu did was to groom Philip Mokuku, whom he had appointed as his Dean, to succeed him. The previous Bishop, John Maund, had never allowed the clergy to travel, so Mokuku, who had grown up as a country boy in the mountains of Lesotho, had seen nothing of the world and had little idea of what a cathedral could be. Tutu asked the Department of Mission at the South African Council of Churches (SACC) to organise a world tour of cathedrals, to broaden Mokuku's horizons and expose him to what was going on in places like Singapore, Washington and Coventry.

Tutu had not expected to remain in Lesotho for more than five years, but he cannot have expected the next invitation to come quite so soon. After only a few months in his new diocese he was invited to become General Secretary of SACC. He consulted his fellow bishops, who not surprisingly, said he should not accept. After three months the person appointed to the post resigned; again Bishop Tutu was approached and again, uncertain of God's will in the matter, he placed himself in the hands of the Bishops. This time, to Tutu's surprise, the Episcopal Synod unanimously urged him to accept.

Though he had been in the diocese for such a short time it was not a hard decision. True, he had come to love the mountains and the people, but now he knew that his place was in South Africa: 'There was the uncomfortable feeling of being a renegade; of being away from South Africa where people were being hurt as they struggled for freedom.'[24] There were also personal reasons for leaving. The children did not affect the decision either way; Trevor was at King's College in London, Theresa was studying to be a doctor in Botswana and Naomi and Mpho were at school in Swaziland. But for Leah returning to the republic held many attractions. She was spending a week of every month working in Johannesburg, where she was National Director of the Domestic Workers and Employers Project, a body set up to try to ensure better working conditions and salaries for domestic workers, who are nearly all black. Living 300 miles from the office is hardly commuting distance and she was happy to return to Johannesburg.

Though there were many who were sad at Bishop Tutu leaving Lesotho, some who were angry and felt let down, even some who accused him of acting irresponsibly and of deserting his flock, most people who knew him well felt he was right to move on. 'Lesotho was too small for him,' said one. 'He couldn't have stood it much longer,' admitted another. Though he had been criticised for travelling too much, he had managed to spend a lot of time with the people, a man of the people mixing with them and earning their love in a way no white man could have done. He had infused the diocese with hope, he had let in a breath of fresh air – most of all, he had prepared Philip Mokuku to succeed him.

Father Aelred Stubbs, at the time in Lesotho himself, wrote to Tutu easing any doubts he may have had:[25]

> Some of us had been reconciled to the thought of your leaving Johannesburg by considering that a spell of five or six years as Diocesan here would fit you for Cape Town. But what *He* had in mind was that you should make it possible for a Mosotho of the Basotho to be made ready for the office and work of a Bishop in the Church of God here! So I hope you feel you can say Nunc Dimittis, as far as Lesotho is concerned, in great peace and thankfulness.

9

The Church wakes up

By returning to South Africa to be General Secretary of the South African Council of Churches, Bishop Tutu was to spearhead a body that had become a brave voice in the Churches' struggle against apartheid; it was a struggle they had been slow to join.

If the Christian conscience was pricked by apartheid's violation of human dignity it had not been very evident. There were a few notable exceptions like Archbishop Geoffrey Clayton, Bishop Ambrose Reeves, the Reverend Michael Scott, Father Trevor Huddleston and Dean Gonville ffrench-Beytagh among the Anglicans, the Roman Catholic Archbishop Denis Hurley, and Methodists such as C. K. Storey and the Reverend Douglas Thompson, but for years there were few signs of resistance within the Churches. This apathy was encouraged by the very success of apartheid. The ring of rough land that encircles each township, keeping it well out of sight of white eyes, is more than a symbol of separation; few of the privileged minority knew or cared how the majority lived or the extent of their humiliation and suffering.

Since first coming to South Africa in 1943, Father Huddleston had fought apartheid tirelessly; in 1954 his exasperation with the Church reached boiling point. In a powerful and prophetic article for the *Observer*, which he entitled 'The Church Sleeps On', he castigated the Churches' indifference, pleading: 'In God's name, cannot the Church bestir itself all over the world and act? Cannot Christians everywhere show their distress in practical ways by so isolating South Africa from contact with all civilised communities that she realises her position and feels some pain in it?'[1]

Trevor Huddleston was going to have to wait many years for the international community to become seriously involved, but six years later the tragic events of Sharpeville did at last stir the Christian community into action. In late 1960 the World Council of Churches convened the Cottesloe Consultation to discuss Christian responsibility in race relations. At the end of the week-long conference the WCC's eight South African member Churches – five English-speaking and three Afrikaans-speaking – issued a statement urging racial reforms. They demanded, for instance, that all racial groups should be regarded as indigenous, they called for freedom of worship on a multi-racial basis and encouraged consultation between the Churches.

Though it was a moderate statement, too moderate for many of the delegates, since it left the principles of separate development intact, it was not acceptable to the reactionary *Voortrekker* Church, the Nederduitse Hervormde Kerk (NHK), who rejected it outright. However, the marginally less conservative Dutch Reformed Church, who had in any case prepared the discussion documents, did agree to sign. But it reckoned without Prime Minister Verwoerd, who, like most of his government, was a member of the DRC. He called it to order, reminded it of the high purpose of apartheid and urged it to recant. The majority of the DRC delegates did as they were told. In fact they went further: the two DRC synods who had attended the Consultation withdrew from the World Council of Churches.

The Cottesloe Consultation had been a high point in the relations between the Afrikaans- and English-speaking Churches; the rejection of its concluding statement was a bitter disappointment. If the Afrikaans Churches were to continue to give support and biblical justification to apartheid, concerted action was necessary by those who were beginning to realise that they could not. A new initiative, independent of Church structures, must be taken.

The child of this marriage between need and defeat was the Christian Institute, founded by that charismatic man who had been one of the key figures in the DRC delegation at the Cottesloe Consultation, Beyers Naudé. The Institute was explicit in its determination not to be answerable to the Churches; it was a fellowship of individuals answerable only to itself. This independence, while it avoided the denominational problems encountered at Cottesloe, involved the 180 individuals concerned in anguishing decisions and great personal suffering. Prof. A. G. Geyser of the NHK was tried for heresy; most notably Beyers Naudé, who was in line to be Moderator of the General Synod of the DRC, a post second only to the Prime Minister in influence, was forced to choose between his Church and the Institute. At the time he was acting as Moderator, and in choosing the Christian Institute he was compelled to resign from that position, part from his congregation and leave the Broederbond[2] after twenty-two years of membership. His passport was withdrawn, he was harassed, vilified in the South African press, sent to gaol and finally subjected for seven years to a banning order.

Those who live in a free society would find it hard to fault the Christian Institute's aims. Firmly committed to peace and to non-violent change, it sought, through study groups and the Institute's journal *Pro Veritate*, to rediscover the original message of the Bible; it tried to identify with the poor and seek a redistribution of power; it encouraged a wider perspective by helping young clergy to study and travel overseas and by sponsoring visits to South Africa by eminent Church leaders and theologians.

But its activities infuriated the government. However much the government might wish it to be otherwise, theology and politics are not separately defined areas in South Africa; they are closely related, constantly interacting with each other. Nevertheless, given the government's need to justify apartheid biblically, the Institute was treading a dangerous path. Beyers Naudé's vision of forming a confessing Church movement, on the lines of that which arose in the 1930s in response to Hitler's Germany, made the parallels between apartheid and Nazism uncomfortably public; the Institute's encouragement of black initiatives like the Black Consciousness Movement was hardly likely to appeal to those who preferred to satisfy the demands of Afrikaner consciousness. Nor was the Institute's avowed aim to show Christians in South Africa that 'southern Africa is a sick society because of its alienation, and doomed to die unless it is healed'[3] likely to appeal to a government seeking to convince the world that separate development was for the good of all.

The Christian Institute did succeed in some of its aims. It not only helped to articulate an indigenous South African liberation theology, but, according to Peter Walshe, 'it functioned as a vital matrix for the dissemination of ideas at a time when African political organisations had been systematically repressed'.[4] It was also instrumental in forging bonds between the African Independent Churches (which have a total membership of about 3½ million) and in helping them relate to the wider Church. To this end it supported the establishment of the African Independent Churches Association.

The Institute was the subject of continual harassment by the government. In 1972, together with the National Union of South African Students (NUSAS), the University Christian Movement and the South African Institute of Race Relations, it was summoned to appear before the Schlebusch Commission. As a result of the Commission's findings the Institute was declared an 'affected organisation', which prevented it from receiving funds from overseas, thus effectively cutting off most of its financial support. This was not going to throttle these courageous people and shortly after the Soweto riots they defiantly published an account of political trials, detentions and bannings called *Is South Africa a Police State?*. The next year excerpts from another publication, *Torture in South Africa?*, reached both the local and the foreign press.

The end came on October 19th, 1977. The Christian Institute was declared illegal, *Pro Veritate* was ordered to cease publication and Beyers Naudé's banning order meant he was no longer allowed to speak in public, to be quoted in the press, to meet more than one person at a time or to travel beyond the magisterial area of Johannesburg. Many of the Institute's black workers were detained by the police, several of its senior staff like Theo Kotzé and Brian Brown went into exile. On that same day seventeen other groups were banned, including the Black People's Convention, Black Community Programme and the South African Students Organisation; so was the black newspaper *The World* and its editor Percy Qoboza; so was Donald Woods, the editor of the East London *Daily Dispatch*. It was one of the darkest days in the history of resistance to white domination in South Africa.

For the last nine years of its life the Christian Institute had been an active member of the South African Council of Churches, whose roots can be traced through the Christian Council back to the early years of the century with the founding, by both Dutch Reformed and English-speaking Churches, of the General Missionary Conference. In 1934 a visit from the American missionary Dr Mott inspired an attempt to form a stronger and more closely knit organisation, with the emphasis on the established Churches rather than on the missions, and in 1936 the Christian Council of South Africa (CCSA) was born.

The CCSA had an initial membership of twenty-nine Churches and missionary organisations, including the Cape and Transvaal Synods of the DRC. It was not long, however, before the inevitable conflict over racial policies, abetted by Afrikaner resistance to the use of English as the medium of communication, led to the DRC's withdrawal. Tentatively the CCSA began to speak against racial discrimination. In 1948, when the Nationalists came to power and began to institutionalise apartheid, the CCSA responded by, once again, searching the Bible. At a conference held in Rosettenville in 1949 it concluded that its work could not confine itself to the purely spiritual, it must extend to the search for unity. Further, in direct criticism of apartheid, it affirmed that the franchise should be accorded to all those capable of exercising it, that every child deserved the best available education and every man had the right to work to his highest ability.

In 1968, in keeping with the world-wide trend set in motion by the founding of the World Council of Churches, the Christian Council decided to become the South African Council of Churches, a change of name that not only reflected the end of its missionary phase, but the growing importance of the indigenous Churches. It also heralded a new phase in the Church's struggle against apartheid.

*   *   *

Within months the SACC was launched into the national headlines. It published and disseminated a six-page document, prepared in collaboration with the Christian Institute, called *Message to the People of South Africa*. Its thrust was simple. It declared apartheid and separate development to be contrary to the Gospel of Jesus Christ; it was 'a false faith, a novel Gospel, which holds out to men a security built not on Christ but on the theory of separation and the preservation of their racial identity.'[5] The Prime Minister, now John Vorster, reacted as violently as had his predecessor, Dr Verwoerd, to the Cottesloe Statement. He warned any clerics planning 'to do the kind of thing here in South Africa that Martin Luther King did in America' to 'cut it out, cut it out immediately, for the cloak you carry will not protect you if you try to do this in South Africa'.[6] An exchange of letters followed, in which the Church leaders assured the Prime Minister that 'as long as attempts are made to justify the policy of apartheid by appeal to God's word, we will persist in denying their validity'.[7] Vorster replied that it was 'with the utmost despisal [sic], however, that I reject the insolence you display in attacking my Church as you do.'[8] One message, two such different interpretations; it is hard to believe they shared the same Bible.

The *Message* ended with a challenge:[9]

> And so we wish to put to every Christian person in this country the question which we ourselves are bound to face each day, to whom, or to what, are you truly giving your first loyalty, your primary commitment? Is it to a subsection of mankind, an ethnic group, a human tradition, a political idea; or to Christ?

By now the Churches had taken the bit between their teeth. Far from being warned off, the Christian Institute and the SACC established SPRO-CAS – the Study Project on Christianity in Apartheid Society.

SPRO-CAS, the SACC's first venture into the socio-political scene, aimed, in the words of its Director Peter Randall, 'to help the church move from a mere denunciation of apartheid, no matter how eloquent and even passionate, to a more meaningful and concrete involvement in the hard issues facing those church members who opposed the policy.'[10] The project attracted a galaxy of talent – theologians, economists, lawyers and political thinkers. The novelist André Brink, Professor Fatima Meer, Chief Gatsha Buthelezi, Dr van Zyl Slabbert, Steve Biko and Desmond Tutu, at that time teaching at the Federal Theological Seminary at Alice, were all involved in its work.

The SPRO-CAS brief was to seek a social system in which racism would have no part and its first phase was directed towards finding viable alternatives to apartheid. SPRO-CAS II took the next and logical step: action. It sought, for instance, better wages and greater social security for black workers, to change white attitudes, to develop black awareness and black leadership. If the absence of a clear multi-racial attitude and the separation of black and white programmes seems curious today, it must be remembered that this was 1969, soon after the birth of black consciousness. SPRO-CAS was a child of its time, a time when the twin needs, to raise white awareness and to develop black community programmes, could best be served separately.

At the same time as SPRO-CAS was moving from theory to action, so too was the World Council of Churches. Founded, ironically, in 1948 (the year that the Nationalists came to power in South Africa) the WCC had for twenty years consistently opposed racism in resolutions, conferences and statements. In 1969 it felt impelled to move towards a more direct involvement with racism, wherever it might occur, and the Program to Combat Racism was established. The next year it announced that grants were to be made to anti-racist liberation movements such as the Patriotic Front in Rhodesia, Frelimo in Mozambique, Swapo in Namibia, the African National Congress and the Pan-Africanist Congress in South Africa.

The SACC, who had not been consulted by the WCC and who first heard this startling news through the daily newspapers, was caught unprepared for the threats that ricocheted back from Mr Vorster – the SACC must leave the World Council of Churches or face government action. The fact that the grants were made for humanitarian purposes and that the WCC was not commending violence, but only making it clear where its support lay – an important point of emphasis – was not conveyed to the South African public. Faced with a choice between its loyalty to the WCC and its own convictions, the SACC decided that while it supported most of the work done by the Program to Combat Racism, and while it would retain its membership of the WCC, it was committed to non-violence; on that issue it could not give its support.

It was not an easy decision. With hindsight it is easy to see that the WCC realised, ahead of the South African Church leadership, that the days when black hopes, aspirations and anger could be contained in non-violent protest were numbered; but at the time the SACC stood to be accused on the one hand of condoning violence by its continuing relationship with the WCC, on the other of failing to support the radical groups. Nor did its compromise decision please the government, who not only made it illegal for funds to be sent from South Africa to the WCC, but did its best to prevent anyone associated with the WCC from visiting South Africa. The SACC and the South African government were on a collision course.

In 1970 John Rees, a white Methodist layman, took over from Bishop Bill Burnett as General Secretary of the SACC. Under his leadership the Council grew rapidly – the staff quadrupled and the budget expanded. Raising money has special problems in South Africa, where the vast majority of Christians are black and poor, barely able to contribute to their own churches, let alone ecumenical organisations. Support from overseas churches and foundations was, and still is, essential; raising funds was something at which John Rees excelled.

During those early years the SACC grappled with many of the problems that were to tax Tutu in his years as General Secretary. Apart from the uproar which greeted the publication of the *Message* and the confusion following the WCC's decision to give grants to liberation movements, there were crucial questions concerning the Churches' attitude to issues like disinvestment and violence, which began to take on a significance that was eventually to lead to direct confrontation between Church and State.

One such issue was conscientious objection, which by 1974 was beginning to polarise opinion more sharply than ever before. Frelimo had recently won power in Mozambique, there was guerrilla warfare in Rhodesia and Namibia, civil war in Angola. In South Africa on the one hand young blacks were feeling that their time, too, might be at hand; on the other, the government was pouring money into military training and arms. The SACC needed to state its position on violence and military service.

At its annual national conference the delegates, some of whom had relatives in the militant arm of liberation movements, discussed the role of the Christian in war. While the Christian tradition regards the fighting of a 'just war' as acceptable, could it be right for a Christian to participate in a military force defending an unjust and discriminatory society? If the use of violence between Afrikaner and British in the Boer War was considered acceptable, why should the same not apply to the blacks, in their struggle for freedom? If violence is condemned when perpetrated by liberation movements, how can it be condoned when practised with the apparent respectability of government backing? Does military service become a duty simply because it is demanded by the State? Is not the Christian responsible to a higher authority?

After hours of heated debate, the resolution was finally passed. Its fifteen clauses included a refusal to accept that the Christian has an automatic duty to engage in war at the demand of the State; it pointed out that the primary violence was institutionalised apartheid and that the South African military forces were being prepared to defend this unjust system. It deplored the use of violence and requested that a task force should study methods of non-violent action for change and called on the member Churches who had chaplains in the armed forces to reconsider the basis on which they were appointed. In short it concluded that conscientious objection was a valid Christian option.

The resolution was supported by blacks and strengthened the standing of the SACC; predictably, it was also met by a barrage of criticism. Critics conveniently failed to notice that violence was explicitly deplored and the government introduced a Bill providing heavy penalties – up to ten years' imprisonment – for anyone trying to persuade another person to avoid military service. This Bill aroused so much opposition in Parliament that it was modified and, in fact, never invoked. The government also began a campaign of formal harassment of the SACC by funding the Christian League, a group headed by a Methodist minister, Fred Shaw, whose explicit purpose was to ward off the perceived threat of Communism and to persuade South African Churches to withdraw from the WCC.

One of John Rees's most significant contributions to the SACC was the determination with which he ousted apartheid from life in the office. Though blacks made up at least 80 per cent of the membership, when Rees took over as General Secretary authority was vested almost exclusively in whites and signs of 'petty apartheid' – different salaries, separate toilets – still belied the Council's stand on racial discrimination. Rees was not going to stand for that: 'We must increasingly make plans, not only within the Church structures, but also within the structure of the Council itself for the voice of our black brethren to be heard . . .'[11] He was as good as his word, paying black and white staff equal salaries for equal work, desegregating toilets, moving blacks into senior positions and giving every white administrator a black secretary and every black administrator a white secretary. At his first national conference a black President was elected.

Likewise in the matter of membership. As churches that had originated as missions were handed over to indigenous leadership, so they joined the Council. By 1971, with the added membership of the African Independent Churches' Association, hundreds of black-led churches were related to the SACC. In 1975 the admission of the Nederduitse Gereformeerde Kerk in Afrika (NGA), the black 'daughter' Church of the DRC (the DRC – the 'mother' Church – has three 'daughter' Churches, one each for blacks, 'coloureds' and Indians) was celebrated. By the time Tutu arrived in March 1978 the SACC was beginning to be a microcosm of a future, non-racial South Africa.

10

A parish without frontiers

On March 1st, 1978, when Bishop Tutu started work as the General Secretary of the South African Council of Churches, he was taking on a formidable task, demanding formidable qualities. The work was to involve him at many levels, in concentric circles of concern. Inside the Council itself there was the delicate matter of keeping a harmonious balance between the sixteen departments and judging the relative claims of long-range and short-term programmes; he would also have to involve himself in the often emotional relationships with the constituent Churches. At a national level he knew that there would be many people, from committed Christians to those with no claims to religious belief, who would question his integrity. Most crucially, there was the question of the increasing polarisation between Church and State and the harassment both the Council and Tutu personally were to endure from the government. Finally, he was soon to become an international spokesman for millions of black South Africans. What were the qualities that informed his actions in this exposed position? It is time to consider the nature of the man who for six years occupied a post known as 'the hottest ecclesiastical seat in the country'.

He immediately brought his own style to bear on the Council. Despite the tensions inherent in any such disparate body of people – there were over thirty different members and groups affiliated to the Council and the racial mix was accompanied by inevitable diversities of temperament – and despite the national issues that tend to pre-occupy South Africans, he insisted on seeing the Council's problems from a world perspective, resisting insularity, whether black or white. This global vision was one of the first things to impress his new colleagues, particularly the Methodist Minister Peter Storey, who was one of the two Vice-Presidents at the time: 'Here was a man who had been liberated from the paranoia and the almost psychotic obsessions that South Africa produces in us if we are concerned at all. He had experienced the broad vistas of human thought and behaviour across the world and he brought that global consciousness into our thinking.' Tutu's reports, whether at the national conferences or the quarterly executive meetings, were masterly surveys of contemporary world affairs. Peter Storey would tease him for taking them on 'Cook's Tours' as he castigated the puppet regime established in Afghanistan by the Russians or condemned United States support of the Contras in Nicaragua, spelt out the broad outlines of international debt, reacted to a recent change of government, lamented the unresolved strife in Ulster, or internecine war in the Middle East or urban terrorism in Italy. Smaller fish were caught in his net as he worried that Belgium might split up over the issue of language or wondered how the latest Springbok Rugby Tour was going to affect the meeting of Commonwealth Finance Ministers. He would welcome good news, praising the Peace Movement, rejoicing in the exchange of Ambassadors between Israel and Egypt or in the liberation of Zimbabwe from white minority rule and the extraordinary news that on Independence Night former Rhodesian soldiers paraded with former guerrillas.

Sometimes, undeterred by the limited value of such communications, Tutu's concern took the form of letters, statements and telegrams. In 1982, for instance, he cabled the Prime Minister of Israel, appealing to him to stop bombing Beirut: 'Be true to great Jewish tradition and don't let Jews be cause of untold suffering for others.' A simultaneous telegram to Mr Arafat called for 'greater realism about Israel's existence'. A third assured the people of Lebanon of 'our fervent prayers and God's strength in these horrible days'. On behalf of the SACC he wrote to the Prime Ministers of Zimbabwe, Lesotho and Swaziland and the Presidents of Botswana and Mozambique, thanking them for giving hospitality to South African refugees and appealing to them not to send any refugee back to South Africa against his or her will. Occasionally his intervention brought success; his appeal to the President of the Seychelles for the release of Martin Dolinschek, one of five South Africans who had been sentenced to death, brought him a grateful letter saying that he was the only person of stature to intercede – most of the letters sent to the President were appeals to save the turtles. And always Tutu remembered the international community in prayer, both private and public. Dr Margaret Nash, the ecumenical officer with the SACC, will never forget 'the sense in which he was, so to speak, taking the world in his hands and holding it up to God, place by place, situation by situation, person by person'. At the SACC he was a Bishop without a diocese, but now the world was his parish.

It was a parish with no boundaries, but it had a centre, a beating heart – the offices of the SACC. From the day he arrived his relationship with the staff was encapsulated in his response to the question greeting any new boss, 'What shall we call you?'. 'Father,' he replied and, apart from formal occasions when he was addressed as Bishop and a few close friends who called him Desmond, 'Father' or '*Baba*' (the African equivalent) he remained.

As the SACC is an ecumenical body, there were those from Nonconformist traditions who were not easy with this title, others who were resentful, feeling that addressing him as 'Father' prevented them being on equal terms. Yet the appellation suited his style and his temperament. Sophie Mazibuko, a colleague at the SACC and a close friend of Leah's, knows him in many roles: 'He can be a child, he can be an adult, he can be a father, he can be a strict husband, he can be a very good friend.' Versatile though he is, his instincts are paternal. Many of the staff tended to relate to him as a father and he encouraged them to do so; he seemed to think of them as 'his children' and would often address the younger members of his staff as 'My child'.

This paternal attitude was at its strongest in his relationship with his two secretaries, Thembi Segkaphane and Peter Storey's wife Elizabeth. Thembi is black and a Seventh-Day Adventist, Elizabeth white and a Methodist. Religious and racial barriers presented no problem and their friendship gave Tutu deep pleasure – it was how he wanted everyone to live. They were his daughters, one black, one white, each given appropriate duties but both part of his family, sharing each others' joys and sorrows. If they failed to greet him with a kiss on Monday morning, or kiss him goodbye on Friday afternoon there would be trouble. He could even be jealous of their husbands – in the office they were *his* family.

Thembi and Elizabeth were very sensitive to his moods, sometimes saying 'Now he's black' or 'Now he's white' and together working out the things peculiar to each culture. For instance, he is methodical, meticulous and punctual, something more easily understood by Elizabeth than by Thembi. On the other hand there were things from his culture that were foreign to Elizabeth. For instance if, in a European context, one is offered a biscuit, there is no offence in declining; Tutu (presumably on a day when he was black), would be furious, saying, 'You never say "no thank you" to food, it is food given to you and your family, so if you don't want it you take it home to your family.' To Elizabeth this would have felt hypocritical so eventually she plucked up her courage, stuck to her own culture and said 'No thank you'. His anger, considering how long he had spent in England, surprised even Elizabeth, who knows him so well.

Like any father, he could be strict. When a member of staff who had been on sabbatical leave failed to return in time for the national conference, as she had promised, she received a memo saying: 'I will have to come back and discuss this matter with you sternly, because this is not how I want to operate.' And even his greatest admirers were critical of him in his role of authoritarian Bishop; some were curious that he donned full episcopal regalia for the office Mass, others felt threatened by his insistence that they all went on yearly retreats, whether or not it was in their tradition.

He was loved, feared, respected, indulged, occasionally resented and to a great extent understood. They came to know his tastes – his love of 'fat cakes', samosas, dates, marshmallows and Yogi Sip, his passion for cricket and music, his habit of early-morning jogging and midday naps, his loathing of bad language. More importantly they learnt to cope with his sensitivity, to realise how very easily he could be hurt. This vulnerability is something he manages to conceal from the world at large, but it did not escape the notice of Elizabeth: 'He is very human and life isn't easy for him. He has great ups and great downs as well and sometimes they are very obvious. He can't cover things up, like his hurt – he gets tremendously hurt and he has this craving to be loved. He is a very ordinary person who has ordinary feelings.'

Tutu makes no secret of his wish to be loved, something he regards as 'a horrible weakness'; he is perhaps less aware of his vulnerability, which can cause trouble out of all proportion to the cause. Anyone failing to acknowledge an increment, or who is late for prayers and does not come up to his office to apologise, anyone who does not thank him, even for a small thing, risks giving him offence. Dan Vaughan, a senior and much respected colleague, once questioned the wisdom of one of his public statements. Tutu swung on him saying, 'I make my own decisions – no one is going to tell me what to say.' Though they were travelling together, it was not until the next day that a smile and a hand on the shoulder indicated that Dan was forgiven. Another colleague who had the temerity to disagree with him was told: 'You're a silly child. Get out of my office. I'm not going to talk to you again until you've come to your senses.' And for three weeks Tutu was as good as his word. While for the most part he shows the sensitivity to others that he would wish them to show to him, he can fall short of his own ideals. There was a period when he hurt Thembi because of her allegiance to the Seventh-Day Adventists. Ecumenist though he is, it took him some years to accept that one of his beloved children should belong to this particular sect.

Just as he is easily hurt, so both laughter and tears are as close as breathing. He is a man of passionate emotions, sometimes laughing when the only alternative would be to cry. He can make a joke even of such obscenities as the migrant labour system – 'This is the only country in the world where it is illegal to sleep with your own wife'; or of the white man's rape of his country – 'We had the land and they had the Bible. Then they said "Let us pray" and we closed our eyes. When we opened them again, they had the land and we had the Bible. Maybe we had the better of the deal.' His wit peppers every speech and sermon and his entry into a room is usually surrounded by an aura of good humour that is almost tangible. So, too, do his tears flow easily. Once, in the formal context of an executive meeting, he became so aware of white resistance to what he was saying that he burst out, 'Good people I am here to work with you, to serve the people of God. I am here as a brother and I love you so much', and burst into tears.

Like most honest people – and he is honest to a fault – he trusts his staff not only in their work, but in their integrity. In South Africa the possibility of informers is something that has always to be taken into account, but when there were convincing rumours that an informer was in their midst, on the staff of the SACC, he called a meeting, saying he could not and would not operate on a basis of suspicion, he would rather be deceived. It was eight years before he discovered that the rumours had been true. On another occasion he found that a junior secretary had for months been stashing away letters, cheques and receipts instead of posting or filing them. When he eventually became aware of what was going on he did not discipline her, he was not even angry; he said that his heart bled for her, that he could not 'throw her to the wolves' and simply moved her to another department. There were to be times when this refusal to be suspicious was to lead him into very deep waters indeed.

The essence of fatherhood, paternalism at its best, is found in the role of Pastor, the Shepherd of the Flock. It is in this sphere that Tutu feels most at home, most sure that he is doing God's will. His concept of priesthood demands faithfulness rather than success, a faithfulness that should be manifested in a disciplined rule of life with regular saying of the office, study of the Scriptures, prayer, meditation and – too often neglected – pastoral visiting. 'You can't love people and not visit them. You can't love them unless you know them, and you can't know them unless you visit them regularly. And the good shepherd knows his sheep by name.'[1] He values courteousness and humility in a priest as in a layman, and is eloquent in extolling the need for gentleness:[2]

> Let us watch our tongues. We can hurt, we can extinguish a weak flickering light by harsh words . . . It is easy to discourage, it is far too easy, all too easy to criticize, to complain, to rebuke. Let us try instead to be more quick to see even a small amount of good in a person and

concentrate on that. Let us be more quick to praise than to find fault. Let us be more quick to thank others than to complain – 'Thank you' and 'Please' are small words, but they are oh, so powerful. My dear Brothers, please be gentle with God's people.

Valuing priesthood so highly, rejoicing in his calling, it is no surprise that as soon as he had agreed to resign his see and take a secular job, he wrote to the Bishop of Johannesburg, Timothy Bavin, asking if he could help in a parish. Bishop Bavin suggested that until the demands on his time were known he should be content to work as a member of the relieving staff, so it was not until the beginning of 1981 that, in addition to his work at the SACC, Tutu became Rector of a church in Soweto – St Augustine's, Orlando West. It was in an area poor even by Soweto standards and the parish had been full of argument and quarrelling, but St Augustine's and Tutu gave each other life. He, far from finding yet more work the last straw after a busy week, was excited by the challenge. The parishioners were given a new dignity, a new peace. He persuaded them to paint the church, found a carpet to replace the worn old lino, took Bible Study classes and encouraged them to visit one another, street by street. Soon the children who came to Sunday school were getting scholarships to study and St Augustine's, from being a gossiping, defeated congregation, became a new living community. As their Rector became more and more widely known, so the television cameras came to film him preaching and the church became famous.

But his pastoral role is not confined to parish or congregation, its mantle embraces everyone he meets. His own need for affirmation is mirrored in his ability to affirm others; people feel better just for being with him. The tributes are endless: 'He has this amazing capacity to make people relax and help them to be freer.'[3] 'He really manages to bring God so close to you.'[4] 'I come away from quick and relatively casual meetings with a tremendous feeling of encouragement. My obedience is strengthened and I feel I am more of a Christian for being with him for three minutes.'[5] His conviction that every human being is made in the image of God, that we are all 'God-carriers', is so deep-rooted that he feels one should mentally genuflect to everyone one meets in the street. So when he meets a secretary at the British Council of Churches, he does not just smile and pass through to her boss's office, he spends ten minutes in animated conversation with her. And when she moves to another job, she receives a personal letter from him saying, 'I am devastated, you have forsaken me.' Sophie Mazibuko experienced his care in tragedy, when her son became a quadriplegic:

Fortunately Desmond was in the country then and I could phone him anytime and he would talk to me for fifteen or twenty minutes, trying to be a spiritual base. I dare not tell him if, for instance, I am trying to get my son into hospital in Cape Town because he would move the stars – so I don't tell him unless I have an insurmountable problem.

Nor is this sensitive attention only given when it is convenient. He was so determined to support the Anglican priest, David Russell, when he was on trial for breaking his banning order to attend a Synod, that he cancelled an important meeting and went back to Cape Town, from where, incidentally, he had just returned. Similarly he found time to be present for a few minutes at the funeral of a friend's father on, of all days, June 16th, 1976, the day of the Soweto killings. Neither is his care confined to those who are fond of him. He amazed an elderly man, who had made no secret of his dislike, by visiting him regularly while he was recovering from an operation. Similarly, he went to the funeral of a woman who had frankly hated him.

This concern for people, whether in matters great or small, also finds regular expression in his correspondence. Given the weight of his commitments he is prompt in answering his letters, at length if the occasion demands, nearly always with charity and gentleness.

Among the official letters, the stream of requests that he should recommend people for posts or vice versa, the requests to preach, speak at conferences, sit on commissions, attend ambassadorial functions, dine with businessmen, the occasional brush with authority – a traffic offence or an unpaid bill – his postbag reveals a glorious cross-section of humanity in all its richness. A browse through his files reveals, for instance, an invitation from the Kwazakhele Rugby Union to attend the opening of the Dan Qeqe Stadium, where he was to kick off the match, a letter asking him to speak at the Ikageng Women's Club, a card from a small boy, sick in bed, thanking him for the cartons of Pear Liqui Fruit. There are letters seeking help from people who see hope for all black South Africans in Bishop Tutu's own rise from location urchin to episcopal purple. To an ambitious correspondent who writes 'I would like to be world Bishop – I have passed Form Four', he suggests 'Shouldn't you pass Matric first and then study for ordination?' Equally practical advice is given to a fifty-one-year-old Principal of a primary school asking for financial assistance in his 'forlorn, FORLORN desire to learn music.' As he was a member of the Moravian Church, Tutu suggested he should ask his Church for help.

There are greetings from overseas admirers, like an Italian priest who has decided to make Tutu's name known in Europe: 'We never met, but it is almost the same for me as if I had. I feel I do know you as if I were your closest friend. I am not here to flatter you, but I feel today you are a real hope for the church in South Africa.' There is even a series of letters from a man for whom Tutu figured in visionary dreams: 'The Lord has laid it upon my heart to send the attached prophecies ... I saw the Prophet lying sick, suffering from severe poisoning. The prophet was a VIP ... Bishop Tutu was by the sea. There were two pillars named faith and prayer. Three times Jesus asked him "Desmond, do you love me?"'

Some people are filled with a generalised love for mankind; others are able to translate this love into practical care. Tutu belongs to the second category. His attention to the detail of people's lives is remarkable. The Mqotsis, African friends of the Tutus living in London, wanted one of the striped blazers worn at the University of the Witwatersrand. They had not been made for twelve years, Tutu told them, but would they like a Wits badge on a navy blue blazer? If so, he would bring it when he next came to England. He might write to the bank or the post office, commending a member of their staff who had been particularly courteous, send flowers to cheer a sick secretary or greet someone just released from prison. Often the morning starts with little notes being written to people he knows are going through a difficult time; when he is overseas, every member of the staff receives a postcard. He is meticulous in remembering birthdays and anniversaries, whether wedding, profession, or consecration. Perhaps this scrupulous attention owes something to the fact that he himself can be hurt if the dates significant in his own life are not remembered.

To the bereaved he writes with a sensitivity which must bring the recipient as near to hope as is possible at such a time:[6]

> I know that it may be true that it is easy on a full stomach to praise fasting and so for someone who has not been touched personally by a bereavement to speak about the consoling powers of God's Holy Spirit. I know that there is a void in your life which nothing and no one will be able to fill and that there are many moments when it seems like it is a dream or maybe a nightmare and that Tom will walk through the door with his pipe in his mouth. Or that you will hear his familiar tones as he tells a joke and chuckles away. But then it dawns on you that in fact, no, he won't physically, he is away. But in another sense he isn't. He has given you himself. He has helped to make you what you are just as much as you helped to make him what he was. And there are things that no one will ever be able to take away from you which you treasure. And then of course, we know, we believe, we belong to the resurrected body of our Lord Jesus Christ and that in Jesus we are always together.

That there is no separation. There is no farewell. There is no departure. There is only returning and finding one another.

From his first months at the SACC Tutu began to receive critical letters. When they were couched in reasonable, positive terms he would invite the writer to come and talk to him; when they were offensive – and they frequently were – he was capable of retaliating. A letter accusing him of 'bearing false witness' and ending 'look to your conscience if you have such a thing' received a stern reply: 'I expect a full apology forthwith for your scurrilous attack and if not given within a week I will place your letter in the hands of our solicitors.' (He duly received an apology.) Mostly, though, his reaction was to ignore them, taking St Paul's advice to 'rejoice, inasmuch as ye are partakers of Christ's sufferings'. Significantly, one of his favourite texts is, 'If God is for us, who can be against us?'

Any public figure attracts criticism, yet surely Tutu has had to endure more than his share? It is particularly painful for such a man, with so deep a need for love and affirmation, to know that he is not merely criticised, but is, for many, an object of hatred.

There are many possible reasons why Tutu should attract such venom; strong people evoke strong emotions. Though he has his critics amongst the black community – the radicals who find him too moderate, a few who, uncomfortable because they are not playing their part in working for justice and peace in their country, are irritated by his constant calls for change – those who dislike him are mostly white and politically conservative. Tutu not only threatens their way of life, but disturbs them; in their hearts they know that apartheid is abhorrent, that he is right to resist it. He also attracts a particular sort of racism, as Helen Suzman admits:

There's a natural antagonism among the majority of white South Africans at having to pay obeisance to a black man, be he a Bishop or not. And it is very hard for many of them who are not real, practising Christians but are Anglican members, or DRC or Roman Catholic or whatever, to get used to the idea of having a black man in command of a very important section of their lives. That, of course, is pure racist, but you can't ignore it in this country.

Tutu had experienced this attitude before he was a Bishop, when he preached at a white girls' school near Alice. After the service one of the girls said to the headmistress that it was one of the best sermons she had ever heard, adding: 'but I still think a black man should not come into our chapel'.

So from all sides the arrows flew. Within months of his return to

Johannesburg the *Sunday Express* was dismissing him as 'Tutu of the trendy specs and trendier hair-do, so sure that justice will be done'; headlines screamed 'BELT UP, TUTU'; a statement was greeted as 'the latest Tutu-muchism'; he was referred to as 'that insect in dark glasses' and accused of 'boring people with his particular mixture of syrupy promises and petty politicking'. Letters demanded 'Why, oh why do you spike Jesus' guns? Do you see what is wrong in our country more than Jesus does?'; asked 'Why do you promote Marxist goals? Many people grow sick of what you say'; informed him that 'One thing a Bishop should not suffer from is Foot in Mouth disease'. Death threats became commonplace and he has had to learn to live with constant physical fear. He was once walking through the concourse of Jan Smuts Airport when a white woman said, quite loud enough for him to hear, 'Isn't that that bastard Tutu – if I had a gun I would shoot him now.'

It is hard to believe that these angry people, many of whom did not even have the courage to sign their letters, are talking about the same man; the real person bears so little relation to the public image, as people who hear him for themselves find out. A young Afrikaner wrote to him in amazement after listening to him speak: 'How the newspapers must have distorted you – or how you must have changed! . . . it was the Spirit of Love, Patience and Reconciliation more than anything else that stirred my heart. Even more so because of the image I have of you which made me expect something quite different.'[7] Anyone who actually listens to what he is saying, anyone who talks to him face-to-face, has to revise their opinion. Even those opposed to him politically cannot but warm to him at a personal level. Peter Storey has found that 'time and again I have seen people introduced to Desmond with ice in their eyes and I have seen them melt as they discovered the real person'.

When the real Desmond Tutu is met he is loved, and one of the reasons he is loved is because of the love he feels – *really* feels, it is not just some priestly role he dons – for every man, woman and child; he sees and honours what the Quakers call 'that of God in every man'. He constantly reminds people, black and white alike, of their value as human beings, telling audiences they are 'princes and princesses' or 'masterpieces' – sometimes making hundreds of people say with him 'We are masterpieces'. Even his criticism is couched in these terms; talking to an audience which included the head of the Broederbond, ultra-conservative theologians and students he told them:[8]

I don't think many of you really believe that you are people of infinite worth. Because you don't realise this you tend to behave like bullies.

Bullies throw their weight about to make their mark. Whites amass
material wealth to prove their worth. But you have infinite worth because
God has created you in his image. If you would only believe it of
yourselves, you would believe it of others.

One of Tutu's great contributions to the SACC, something he gave
from the very centre of his being, was his emphasis on the spiritual
foundation of its work. On a formal level he introduced daily prayers,
insisting that the entire staff come together as a community from 8.30
to 9.30 a.m. every morning; once a month there was a Eucharist,
taken by the various denominations in rotation. During these periods
everything, from staff birthdays to the most recent national or international event, was considered in the light of the Gospel, prayed
about, placed before God. In keeping with Gospel teaching this
included a concern for people who might be considered enemies.
Despite continual pressure – even from fellow Christians – he steadfastly refuses to stop praying for P. W. Botha; when praying for friends
in prison he prays also for the jailors and the police 'because they are
God's children too'.

Sometimes he would recall with gratitude other people's prayers;
for him the concept of the world-wide Church community is rich in
meaning. He once wrote of this to an Australian priest who was
showing his support in prayer:[9]

> It is a great comfort to know that one need only throw oneself into this
> current and be borne by it and upheld by it . . . It is wonderful to belong
> to the Church of God and I know for myself that I would have collapsed
> long ago were it not for the fact that I know and experience myself as
> being upheld and buoyed by the sense of all those who love us and pray
> for us.

When the SACC staff felt despondent because of government harassment, 'so low we could crawl under a snake', he would be cheered by
remembering the prayers of a Lutheran Pastor from Alaska, or an
anchorite in Arizona who prayed for them at 3 a.m. every morning.
'What hope have the government got of defeating us when we are
being prayed for every day in Arizona?'

He also helped individual members of the staff with their prayer
life, not only insisting on the importance of regular prayer but encouraging them to relate to God as to a human being – to scold as well as
to petition, to express disappointment as well as reverence. Even, if
God seemed silent, to cry out 'What kind of God are you? Are you
God only for white people?' For many, brought up to a self-abasing
and penitential attitude to prayer, this brought profound relief. Sophie

Mazibuko is one of many who rejoiced in this approach: 'We were all brought up with the idea that God is the person with the big eye in the middle and that he is always looking at you. You never saw God as a friend, you never saw him as your creator and the best person to talk to when you are in trouble. Prayer is now something I can go along with.'

Extravert though Tutu is, he has also a deeply private, introvert side. Anyone who has spent even a short time alone with him will have sensed an indefinable quality, an undercurrent throbbing beneath the quick responses and easy jokes. Centredness? Peace? Communion with God? Whatever one calls it, there is no doubt that it is the fruit of his inner life. It is as if whatever he is doing, part of him, like a Russian *staretz*, prays without ceasing.

His life is shot through with prayer. He rises early in the morning, sometimes as early as 3.30, to be sure of a full hour's prayer before his daily jog; then, after a quick breakfast, he goes to Mass or, if it is not possible to go to church, he celebrates it at home, with Leah as his single congregant. During the working day every interview and meeting is preceded by a short prayer. However busy he is, whatever his current concerns, once a month he goes to a nearby convent for a 'quiet day' and occasionally he fasts and holds vigils; at least once a year he goes on a retreat of three days or longer. The importance of these longer periods of prayer and reflection in Tutu's life, especially before any crucial event or decision, can hardly be overemphasised. In that space he is strengthened, in that space he listens to what God is saying to him, finding answers to apparently insoluble problems. Peter Storey, whose first meeting with Tutu was waking one morning in a shared hotel room thinking he had seen a ghost – it was the small, sheet-covered figure of Desmond Tutu on hands and knees – found that when he came back from a retreat 'there was a new steel core to his resolution and a new initiative'. Dan Vaughan remembers one occasion when Tutu came into the office at a particularly tense time saying, 'I am going to fast for a week, this is what God has said to me.' So he spent all day in the chapel, his secretary brought him a cup of Milo at midday, and he went home at night.

His prayer life is not only disciplined and regular, it spills over into every activity – even driving the car. Regular passengers have learnt not to be surprised if he tells them to 'shut up' while he combines driving and praying; even so, Peter Storey remembers an occasion when he might have preferred prudence to prayer. They had driven together to Vendaland, where some Lutheran clergy were being ill-treated in prison. They went to the police station (Tutu with no passport – his way of showing that he does not recognise the 'homelands') saying they would like to pray with the prisoners. The police felt they needed to seek higher authority for this dangerous activity. The higher authority forbade it, adding that they were prohibited immigrants and would be deported. Escorted by two Land-Rovers, they were taken into the bush, where the police began to rough them up, threatening to kill them. Eventually they were released and drove thankfully away with Tutu at the wheel. As they crossed the border he joked about 'prisoners of Venda', saying, 'We could have been killed. We need to thank God for keeping us safe,' and as they sped along he firmly shut his eyes to pray.

This pattern of prayer evolved over many years, but during his time as Bishop of Lesotho another element was added when a Franciscan monk, Brother Geoffrey, came to his house in Maseru to hold a meeting about the Third Order of the Franciscans. Tutu was captivated, saying that this was what he had been searching for and asking if he might test his vocation as a Tertiary.

While the First Order of the Society of St Francis consists of men and women living an active life under the traditional vows of poverty, chastity and obedience and the Second Order of women leading an enclosed life of contemplative prayer, the Third Order is open to men and women, ordained and lay, married or single, who feel called to live out a Franciscan vocation in the world. Aspirants to this way of life undergo six months as postulants, followed by a novitiate of two years. Once professed, the intention is life-long adherence to the personal rule of life they will have drawn up with a spiritual counsellor, though to safeguard against merely nominal membership their vows are renewed annually.

Tutu's devotion to the Community of the Resurrection is such that one might have expected him to join *their* Third Order, rather than the Franciscans. What drew him away from his old family?

Perhaps the answer lies partially in the very closeness of this tie; the CR were his spiritual parents, their influence was, and still is, immeasurable. In taking this new step he needed to go forward rather than back, to be independent of these treasured parents. There is, too, much that is Franciscan in his spirituality. In the CR he found a toughness and a courage that appealed to him, he met men who were not sitting on the fence, but whose Christianity constrained them to join the fight for a just South Africa. This strengthened and inspired him, eventually encouraging and confirming his political commitment, but there was something else he needed. Bishop John Taylor suggests that 'He wanted his lightheartedness endorsed, that peculiar thing in Desmond that is carefree, a kind of troubadour fighter'. He found it with the Franciscans.

His counsellor used to hold him up as a model novice, meticulous in reporting every three months; since he was professed he has continued to renew his vows every year, though he rarely has the time to attend the Third Order meetings. The firm background given him by the Community of the Resurrection, combined with his own disciplined prayer life and the simplicity and joy of Franciscan spirituality, gave him an unassailable strength to tackle the problems ahead. In 1980 he wrote to a nun friend,[10]

> Recently I have been discovering again the tingling joy of the gospel that I have to do nothing to gain acceptance by God. That it is his acceptance of me which enables there to be me and for there to be acts and for there to be thoughts and words by me. One ought to have a semi-cartesian dictum, 'I am loved therefore I am'.

11

The hottest ecclesiastical seat

The South Africa to which Tutu returned in 1978 was as split as ever by the axe of apartheid; nothing much had changed in the two years he had been away. In fact apartheid was so successful that whites could still sip their exquisite wines, watch the sun set over the valley and thank their white racist God for so tranquil an existence. Though the more perceptive recognised 'a pall of despondency and helplessness hanging over South Africa,[1] there was a surface calm. Few whites knew (or if they suspected, they hastily repressed their suspicions) the conditions under which the majority of the population lived and the anger that seethed in the townships. Still fewer appreciated the extent to which the Black Consciousness Movement had restored black dignity; or that after the Soweto killings of 1976 a new generation of young blacks, fearless and determined, was emerging, young people who would not submit, as they felt their parents had, to the barbaric system of apartheid.

Though petty apartheid was slowly being abolished (some public parks were desegregated, blacks who could afford to were allowed to attend selected theatres and concerts, to eat in some of the same restaurants as whites and go into a few of the international hotels), the black community were still victims of an edifice of social engineering manifested in literally hundreds of laws and implemented with ruthless brutality. Forced removals were regular occurrences; during the preceding year nearly 300,000 people had been arrested under the Pass Laws; the murder of Steve Biko had been followed by the mysterious deaths of others held in police custody; people were still being reclassified under the Population Registration Act – blacks becoming 'coloured', 'coloured' becoming 'white' at the stroke of a pen. A tenuous peace was maintained by arresting, banning or killing any who dared oppose the system, but South Africans were living on top of a volcano.

Nor was the outward serenity of the National Party more than skin deep. 1978 was the year in which South Africa reeled from the political explosion caused by news breaking that a secret fund was being used by the South African Department of Information for clandestine counter-propaganda exercises. The 'Information Affair', as it came to be called, led to the resignation of Dr Connie Mulder, the Minister of Information, and many believe it played its part in the resignation of John Vorster himself. In September 1978 his place was taken by P. W. Botha.

The SACC, at least to all outward appearances, was riding high and Tutu was typically generous in his praise of John Rees. The new General Secretary felt he had inherited a very good team of colleagues and an impressive outfit: 'I could not possibly try to emulate my predecessor and so I can only do and be what I know best and that is to be myself. We have come to this job with considerable trepidation.'[2]

This trepidation was well-placed. He was taking on a job which would have been exacting and demanding at any time, never more so than at this period of South African history. With the banning of all the Black Consciousness organisations and several black newspapers in 1977, the SACC was one of the few organisations in the country able to articulate the aspirations of the oppressed majority. Tutu's wish was that the Council should play an effective part in the struggle for liberation by being the conscience of the community, pointing out how the apartheid system is inconsistent with the teaching of Jesus Christ. 'At the risk of sounding like a cliché-ridden creature, I hope that God will be able to use us as one of his instruments for justice and reconciliation; to be like those who demonstrated their solidarity with the poor and down-trodden and, as far as possible, to be a voice for the voiceless ones.'[3] Despite this overt commitment, from the very beginning he made it clear that the SACC was not a political body, but that everything it did was constrained by Christian imperatives. For instance in response to the Gospel demand to visit those in prison, he argued that while it was not the SACC's wish or intention to encourage subversive activities, it *was* its business to look after those who had been convicted of political crimes.

He had also taken on a huge and complicated administrative job. Though the Dutch Reformed Church was conspicuous by its absence and the Roman Catholics only had observer status, most of the other mainline Churches in South Africa, from the African Orthodox Church to the Student Christian Movement, from the Society of Friends to the Bantu Methodist Church, were members of the SACC. In terms of individual people, the number represented was around 12 million[4] and the annual budget about R4 million. The SACC ran sixteen divisions, each with its own Director, covering between them a huge spectrum of human concerns; it also published periodicals like *Ecunews* and *Kairos*.

But under the prosperous surface, all was not well. The SACC

Tutu inherited has been described as a huge circus tent, large and effective, but the whole edifice depending on the pole that had held it up – John Rees. With one young secretary, Rees had been responsible for all the administration and fund-raising, while finance came under the care of an outside agency. The other fifty-eight members of staff ran the sixteen divisions creatively and well, but less as a team than as a group of individuals, whose work programmes John Rees had little time to oversee. The Council had also become distanced from its thirty-odd member Churches, who felt so out of touch that they did not feel it necessary to pay their subscriptions; nor was payment even demanded. The Council had grown too big, too quickly.

Tutu had envisaged his role as that of a visionary, speaking up against evil and trying to exercise a prophetic ministry. In fact the first phase of his work was preoccupied with the need to scotch rumours of financial mismanagement that flew around once the surface of the administration had been scratched, then dealing with some extremely unpleasant irregularities that were uncovered. Far from carrying out a visionary role, the idealistic General Secretary found he was forced to wash his predecessor's dirty linen in public. Worse, he got much criticism and little thanks for his pains.

The fact that during John Rees's term of office financial control had been in the hands of an outside agency, the South African Council of Churches Accounting Services (SACCAS), was a cause of considerable tension. The firm was well-intentioned and tolerably efficient, though they were sometimes found to be slow in responding to requests, but its role in the Council's affairs was part of a deep and continually erupting resentment – why should financial control not lie in the heart of the Council? Resentment coupled with rumour hardly made for efficiency and in June 1980, with the approval of the Executive Committee, Tutu dismantled SACCAS and commissioned Tim Potter to investigate the SACC's affairs. In the light of the suspicions and distrust that were to follow it is worth pointing out that Tim Potter was a senior partner in a well-respected firm of chartered accountants and the immediate past-President of the Transvaal Society of Chartered Accountants. Tutu's worldly wisdom showed in his choice of so prestigious a man.

In August 1980 Tim Potter presented a preliminary report. Though he found the financial administration and record keeping between 1976 and 1978 'generally unsatisfactory', he had found no evidence of improper payments or self-enrichment in the Council. He gave it a clean bill of health.

However, Tutu asked Tim Potter to continue his investigations and, as layer after layer of the Council's affairs was uncovered, irregularities were disclosed. In the course of his investigations Tim Potter found that a junior member of staff had been cashing cheques intended to replenish the franking machine. While Tutu was able to dispose of this affair pastorally rather than through the courts, and the employee was simply dismissed as quietly as possible, another matter was more serious. Elphas Mbatha, the Chief Accountant of SACCAS, had, it seemed, taken advantage of the weakness in the controls of the company to embezzle substantial sums by falsifying invoices. As soon as he discovered this, Tim Potter prepared a separate report and placed it in the hands of the police. Mbatha was taken to trial, but was acquitted on the grounds that his guilt could not be established beyond reasonable doubt. The Magistrate suggested that the poor state of records at the SACC and SACCAS made adequate proof impossible and raised the possibility that 'the charges against the accused were laid in order to find a scapegoat and divert attention from the unsatisfactory state of the SACC's affairs'.[5]

Just as Mbatha's alleged fraud was uncovered by the SACC's determination to run a clean ship, in a similar way another offence was uncovered, this one more serious still. During 1978 it was found that St Ansgar's Mission, a property owned by the SACC and used as a theological school for Independent Church leaders, was being badly mismanaged, so a professional ombudsman, Eugene Roelofse, was appointed as Acting Manager to rescue the property. In the course of his duties he heard rumours of misdemeanours involving a senior member of the SACC, Bishop Isaac Mokoena, who was Chairman of the board of the South African Theological College for Independent Churches (SATCIC) and ran the college. Roelofse submitted reports to the General Secretary containing photographic evidence of forgeries committed by Mokoena in the signing of SATCIC cheques and at a meeting of the Praesidium of the SACC (which consisted of the President, the two Vice-Presidents and the General Secretary) Mokoena admitted to the forgeries already uncovered, confessed that there had been many more and offered to pay back what he had taken.

To Roelofse's dismay the SACC, partly because it recognised the sensitive situation that exists between the Independent Churches to which Mokoena belonged and the historic churches represented by the SACC, again decided not to prefer criminal charges but to deal with the matter pastorally; in fact, as Mokoena had already been dismissed, they even asked the ombudsman to discontinue his investigations. This was an offence to his professional pride and at his insistence enquiries were resumed. Further evidence was unearthed, Tutu was persuaded to lay charges and Mokoena was brought to trial. Despite his earlier confession in front of four people and the photographic evidence, he was, at two separate trials, found not guilty. Once again the state of the Council's books was blamed for the inability to prove fraud; once again the SACC was accused of trying to find a scapegoat – on this occasion being reprimanded for being 'slow to take protective steps in this matter'.[6]

The Mokoena affair hit Tutu where it hurt most poignantly: on several occasions and in several ways his integrity was questioned. For a man who claimed to be trying to be transparent in his dealings, who was doing his best to clean up the messy situation he had inherited, for someone to whom honesty and good repute were as natural as breathing, it was a deeply disturbing experience and one to which for months and months he continued to refer.

One of the first people to criticise him was Eugene Roelofse, who accused Tutu of having a blind eye in putting pastoral concerns before the clear issues of right and wrong. Just before Mokoena's second trial, in a confused and emotional interview held in Bishop Tutu's office at the SACC and attended by both human and electronic witnesses, the Bishop admitted to finding the whole situation intolerable. He could not understand why he and Peter Storey, to whom Mokoena had confessed, had not been called as witnesses; he needed to justify his wish to handle the matter pastorally; he wanted to know on what grounds he had been charged with using the case as a cover-up for the unsatisfactory state of SACC affairs; he urged Roelofse to explain why he had repeated a rumour that the General Secretary had shared Mokoena's ill-gotten gains; most of all he was concerned about the deteriorating relationship between himself and Roelofse.

This interview shows to an almost pathetic degree how deeply Tutu can be hurt and the innocent and almost childlike way in which he reacts to emotional pain. Time and again unguarded, emotional phrases burst out of him: 'I cannot accept to be thought of as having no integrity.' 'I will not accept being vilified even by innuendo.' 'I feel a deep hurt that you think I am trying to cover up.' 'I want to know what you think of me.'[7]

At Mokoena's second trial it was even worse as, in open court, the Magistrate accused Tutu of being 'vague, evasive and contradictory', of concealing evidence from the court, of wanting to place Mokoena in a bad light. Mokoena, who had been overheard saying 'I aim to smash the SACC, I'm going to grind them to dust' (or words to that effect), told the court that Tutu had offered him R1,500 'to skip the country' and that the SACC wanted to get rid of him 'because he knew too much'.[8] All this was of course reported in the press, with consequent humiliation and suffering for Tutu. A decade of exposure to jibes, innuendo and accusation has taught him to hide his feelings, but his reaction to this affair shows that underneath the mature, competent, assured man there is, as with half humanity, a vulnerable child.

Apart from dealing with these offences and clearing up the financial affairs of the Council, Tutu also found that structural changes had to be made: the weight of the tent had to be better distributed, the space inside it more equally shared. His determination that as a Council they should never forget the spiritual basis of their work provided the springboard; by talking with the senior staff and visiting the leaders of the member Churches he found the way. Soon a greater degree of consultation was established, given structural shape by the institution of monthly executive staff meetings at which the Directors thrashed out their problems together. They came to realise that they had been acting and thinking in too individualistic a way; under Tutu's leadership and with the help of structural devices, such as compartmentalising the divisions into three 'clusters', they began to work as a team.

Tutu's quick mind and skill as a delegator enabled these changes to happen surprisingly quickly and smoothly. If it seems curious that moves towards greater sharing, greater democracy, should have been initiated by one who is himself so very much a star, it should be remembered that one of Tutu's great gifts is his ability to create working conditions that are both efficient and happy; he is an individualist who thrives on working in a team. Dan Vaughan, who was at the time Director of the Division of Mission and Evangelism, feels that Tutu is 'not the grand planner, not the strategist, but he is intuitively brilliant. In a way he left us to do what we could do, supporting and encouraging us. Things happened because he was around.'

And despite these legal and administrative preoccupations, which must have seemed trivial and frustrating diversions from his real work, Tutu did indeed prove to be a catalyst, both in the support and encouragement he gave his staff and through his own creative initiative.

The heart of the Council's work is its programmes, run by the three 'clusters' known as *Church and Mission*, *Development and Service* and *Justice and Society*. The vitally important *Church and Mission* cluster dealt with the theological basis of the SACC's work and included the divisions of Theological Education, Mission and Evangelism, Ecumenical Resources and the smaller Choir Resources Project, which tried to encourage the use of indigenous music and instruments.

The *Development and Service* cluster was concerned to affirm that everyone, black and white, is made in the image of Christ and that the role of the Church is to help people towards a better society for all people. Its divisions included Inter-Church Aid, which tried to alleviate poverty, disease and unemployment by promoting self-help and self-reliance, a separate Unemployment Project and a Women's Desk, working mostly with the black domestic servants employed by white 'madams', women who not only have few facilities and little to do in their spare time, but who are very often unaware of their rights.

The cluster of *Justice and Society* provided most of the theological thinking on issues such as investments and violence, dealt with the bursary and scholarship programmes and included the Dependants' Conference, so-called because as well as providing legal aid for anyone in need of it, it looked after the dependants of those who had been found guilty of political crimes and were serving sentences in maximum security prisons like Robben Island. Many of its projects were financed by the Asingeni Relief Fund, a large fund in the control of the General Secretary.

One of Tutu's great virtues as a leader, and one of the ways in which he is able to cope with a vast workload, is his ability to delegate. He not only encouraged initiative in people running the various divisions, but once he had given a project his blessing he allowed them to develop it in their own way, sometimes so completely that, wanting to test out their ideas with him, they felt mildly neglected. This supportive trust earned him the gratitude of countless people, from senior members of staff like the wise and influential Dr Kistner, who had been Director of the Division of Justice and Reconciliation since before Tutu's arrival, to junior secretaries. Dr Margaret Nash, the ecumenical officer, feels it was Tutu's encouragement which launched her into a cycle of writing, both stretching and enriching her and leading to a significant contribution to the literature on forced removals and settlements.

He also showed imagination in projects he was responsible for initiating. One of the first things he did was to ask Sheena Duncan, at the time President of the Black Sash (the women's protest organis-ation and political pressure group started in 1955), to start advice centres. His idea was that volunteers should be trained to do in centres around the country what the Black Sash does in Johannesburg – namely, help black people find their way through the maze of pass laws, trying to ensure that they enjoy at least those few rights to which they are entitled. Mrs Duncan feels that this showed brilliant foresight, for though at first nobody was interested, now the centres cannot keep up with the demand. He also developed the Education Opportunities Council, whose objectives include encouraging South Africans to be educated overseas and to return and provide much-needed leadership in their own country.

His greatest single contribution to the programmes run by the SACC, the stand he took over forced removals, resulted directly from a conversation which seared into his imagination and which he resolved to repeat whenever the occasion offered. In June 1979 he visited Zweledinga, a resettlement camp near Queenstown. There he met a small girl coming out of a shack in which she lived with her widowed mother and sister. The Bishop spoke to her.

'Does your mother receive a pension or grant or something?'
'No,' she replied.
'Then what do you do for food?'
'We borrow food,' she answered.
'Have you ever returned any of the food you have borrowed?'
'No.'
'What do you do when you can't borrow food?'
'We drink water to fill our stomachs.'

This little family were among the three million Africans who, between 1960 and 1980, were forcibly removed to the so-called 'home-lands' for no other reason than that it suited the white minority. This policy has its roots in the 1913 Land Act, which forced Africans to settle in special 'reserves' to supply the mines with cheap and plentiful labour. The situation remained fairly static until the early 1950s, when legislation was introduced to set up the 'Bantustans' or 'Homelands', a massive social engineering project which segregated millions of Africans along strictly ethnic lines. In 1976 the Transkei was the first of the 'homelands' to become an independent national State, thus forcing its mostly unwilling inhabitants to give up any claim to South African citizenship and forswear any hope of political rights in the Republic. It was in order to implement this policy that black people living on land now allocated to white people were forcibly removed and 'resettled' in the 'homelands'.

These removals were perfectly legal, as the Prime Minister pointed out in response to a letter from Tutu on the subject, but legal and morally right are not the same thing. It was legal because a minority government had made it so in order to ensure that the whites lived separately on the best of the land, while enjoying the benefit of a large black workforce, prepared to settle for the poor pay and working conditions because they had no alternative employment. This ex-clusion of the black population from 'white' South Africa was quite deliberate and open. In 1976 the Minister of Bantu Administration and Development wrote:[9]

> All Bantu persons in the white areas, whether they were born there or not, remain members of their respective nations. In other words, the fact that they work here does not make them members of the white nation – they remain Zulu, Tswana, Venda and so on. The basis on which the Bantu is present in the white area is to sell their labour here and for nothing else . . .

The suffering endured by Africans uprooted from their homes and, in Tutu's words, 'dumped like a sack of potatoes' in remote, arid areas is incalculable. In a huge country, rich in resources, the vast majority (over 70 per cent) were allocated 13 per cent of the land, most of it too poor for extensive cultivation. For those who were not migrant labourers there was little work that did not involve lengthy journeys – it was not uncommon for six hours a day to be spent travelling. People were torn away from their homes, where sometimes they had lived for generations. 'What hurts is being driven like an animal out of your own home town. I was born in Johannesburg and proud of it. Now they tell me I'm a citizen of an up-country state called Qwa-Qwa – I've never ever seen the bloody place.'[10]

In the resettlement camps people were (and still are) starving. Tutu has seen this for himself:[11]

> They are starving not because of an accident or a misfortune. No, they are starving because of deliberate Government policy made in the name of White Christian civilisation . . . Many can't work, not because they won't work but because there is no work available . . . They are there as a reservoir, deliberately created, of cheap labour.

And they were starving to a point of serious malnutrition, which it was recognised could lead to irreversible brain damage. The *Financial Mail* admitted that 'humanitarian considerations apart, the present neglect is false economy which costs the country millions of pounds annually in hospitalisation'.[12]

Forced removals were not only a national scandal, they were a direct concern of the Church. Dr Margaret Nash points out that[13]

> Whole congregations have been dispossessed and dispersed; or removed and weakened in the process. Buildings representing the love, labour, sacrifice and devotion of two or three generations have been demolished or left as empty shells, to be ravaged by wind, weather and vandals. Clergy have been summoned by ethnic leaders and told quite bluntly what the religious policy of the new 'government' is to be. And

the message has been plain: if you do not like it, get out; because if you criticise or fail to conform, we shall not hesitate to act against you.

Tutu, however, was not going to be prevented from criticising; he declared he was prepared to give his life to be rid of this evil. He brought cases of threatened removals to the attention of Church leaders, involving himself in the plight of the residents of Driefontein, for instance, whose pleas to the Minister of Co-operation and Development were met with responses like 'only the terms under which the move will take place are negotiable'.[14] He also heightened the political cost of the removals policy by giving publicity to what was happening in statements and speeches, in specially made films and in pamphlets. While he recognised that in the long term the solution had to be political, he also operated through the normal channels of the SACC, who held its national conference the month after Tutu had been to Zwedelinga. Resolutions were passed to put the whole issue of forced removals and resettlement high on the agenda and a four-fold programme was worked out: to gather more information, to call the Church to a more effective ministry to people who were victims of the process, to give more financial assistance and to show solidarity with communities threatened with removal.

Tutu was so deeply shocked by the obscenity of forced removals that he was determined to show solidarity personally. In 1983 the people of Mogopa, a small village in the western Transvaal, were told they were to be moved from land they had tilled for generations and sent to the independent 'homeland' of Bophuthatswana. (Mogopa was on good land and the envy of white eyes, so it had been designated a 'black spot' – an area in which Africans own land, but which the apartheid regime has decided belongs to another group, usually white.) The lovingly built stone houses were demolished, bulldozers tore through the churches and schools, water pumps were taken away and the buses stopped. In the face of this brutal show of State strength the people refused to move: they simply began to rebuild their houses. Tutu telephoned other Church leaders and arranged an all-night vigil to protest against the removals. Dr Allan Boesak and Tutu were among those able to be present and it is easy to imagine what their presence meant to the villagers, whose community and way of life were threatened with destruction; equally, it is no surprise that their peaceful protest made not the smallest dent in the government's resolve. On February 14th, 1984, Mogopa was surrounded by armed police with dogs and loud-hailers. The villagers were informed that they were to be moved and the whole population was forcibly loaded on to lorries and buses and taken away, while white farmers bought up their livestock at a tenth of its value.

For the SACC to implement its programmes clearly involved considerable, potentially almost limitless, expense. Raising and spending money was one of the General Secretary's most pressing preoccupations.

Theoretically the member Churches were expected to contribute on a regular basis, but until 1984, when donations were regularised, this somehow did not happen. In his report to the executive committee in May 1980 Tutu appealed to them to step up their giving, pointing out that if 1,000 congregations gave as little as R50 a year it would amount to R50,000.[15] Yet by the following year nothing had changed. At the national conference an Indian delegate asked why the member Churches did not contribute more and how long ago had the minimum subscription of R50 a year been fixed? It turned out that no letter had ever been sent requesting the money and that such money as did come was entirely haphazard.

Nor did Tutu have much luck with the private sector. Some firms he approached did not even bother to answer, most sent their regrets. While he was grateful to the few businesses that did give funds, making a habit of telling them just how their money was spent, he also pointed out, with typical directness, that the private sector would be judged according to whether it assisted or sought to retard the liberation struggle.

Where Tutu, like John Rees, had phenomenal success was in raising funds from overseas donors. Though he was criticised for the amount of time he spent travelling, no one was less than grateful for the way these trips not only led to the building of strong links with overseas Church bodies, but filled the coffers of the SACC. As to the source of the funds, his approach, though strictly moral, was pragmatic. He did not mind, for instance, accepting money from institutions being boycotted by anti-apartheid groups overseas and would justify his stand. He felt that South Africans had to live with compromise (though he would never travel overseas with South African Airways, inside the country there was no alternative), so it was pointless to worry too much. This argument, coupled with the belief that the destination of the money and the urgent need for it justified its origins, did not have universal support.

Each division of the SACC drew up its own budgets to present to donors, who decided which projects they wished to finance; the allocation was then arranged through the finance committee under Matt Stevenson, whom Tutu had brought in to head the section.

The only discretionary money, and as such a cause of considerable controversy, was the Asingeni Fund.

The Asingeni Fund was set up after the Soweto killings, initially to help with the immediate needs of food, clothing and funeral expenses, later to help with bail and legal aid for people who were arrested. Feelings erupted soon after Tutu's arrival, when there were rumours that the finance department was considering tightening up on the General Secretary's discretion. Many of the staff, especially the blacks, were furious; it was openly pointed out that when the General Secretary was a white man he was given total discretion, so why should the goalposts be moved now that a black man was in charge? Although the balance of staff favoured blacks rather than whites, the power – and what is a more telling symbol of power than money? – was held mainly by whites. The overriding feeling in the Council was that Tutu should be firmly in control and seen to be so. When, therefore, finance was brought firmly into the Council, steps were also taken to ensure that Tutu retained his discretionary control over this large fund.

In practice nearly 80 per cent of the money went on legal expenses, only the remaining 20 per cent being used in a wholly discretionary way. The fact that there were some who criticised Tutu's use of the fund, suggesting that the bees drawn to his financial honey pot tended to include too many rice-Christian followers, underlines the difficulty of administering discretionary money. One man's discretion can so easily be another man's folly. A glance through the payments made from the Asingeni Fund tell much about the state of South Africa as well as reflecting something of Tutu's vision. There are frequent payments to help meet educational expenses and to relieve workers on strike; funds were made to the 'Release Mandela' campaign and for mourners to attend the funerals of Robert Sobukwe and Steve Biko; a substantial sum was spent on the making of a film about the SACC and there are sad entries which tell their own tale: 'Blankets for the needy', 'Crossroads rental arrears', 'Grant for working against eviction of Indians and Coloureds', 'Bill for food to Modderbee Prison'.

Virtually everyone who worked at the SACC during Tutu's time as General Secretary vouches for his qualities as a leader and praises the way he transformed the Council into a major institution on the South African political/religious scene. They stress the contribution he made through his insistence that the basis of the whole operation must be spiritual, finding great confidence in the way his words and actions clearly sprang from convictions so deeply rooted in a strong theology. He also contributed towards forming closer ties with the other Councils of Churches of Southern Africa – Swaziland,

Mozambique, Zambia, Zimbabwe, Angola, Namibia, Lesotho and Botswana.

But his influence extended beyond the Church. By raising the SACC's profile both nationally and internationally, by sharing in the distress of the people and by identifying with the struggle for liberation, he gave it greater credibility than it had ever had before. Though the Council had become larger and more bureaucratised, the black community were in no doubt whose side both it and its leader were on. This was due not only to the sense of direction he gave, but to his gifts as a spokesman and his courage in speaking and acting for human justice and against apartheid. The SACC's first black General Secretary had become the most articulate voice free to speak in South Africa.

12

Crying in the wilderness

From 1978, when Tutu returned to South Africa, he began to wear the lonely mantle of the prophet. The popular image of the prophet as one who foretells the future is only part of the biblical concept; the prophetic role is pre-eminently to communicate the word of God to the people, to act as God's spokesman. Prophets were messengers rather than soothsayers, or, as Tutu himself said in a lecture on the subject, 'forthtellers rather than foretellers'.

Though his detractors felt it inconceivable that Bishop Tutu was hearing the word of God and others found the prophetic role inappropriate to twentieth-century South Africa, he has been compared to the prophet Amos, whose message was delivered at a time when the few were accumulating wealth at the expense of the many. Amos recognised how much was wrong with the society in which he was living, how complacent were the leaders of that society. So strong were his indictments of Israel's social injustice that he was accused of sedition.

Tutu's stand on apartheid is unequivocal and, like the prophets, he speaks out courageously, with insight as much as with foresight; like the prophets, his utterances are disturbing to the advantaged, pleasing to the disadvantaged; like the prophets, he believes he is communicating the word of God and is adamant that he will speak as and when he sees fit and not as he is told, or even advised. He has declared that, whatever the cost to him, he will do all in his power to destroy apartheid; Leah, with typical wry humour, is sure that even if his tongue were cut off, he would not be prevented from speaking.

Since the publication of the *Message to the People of South Africa* in 1968 the SACC had been concerned with communication and by 1977 it had considerable expertise in the field; with the arrival of Bishop Tutu it had acquired a leader who excelled in the art. Not only is he fearless in speaking out, but his possession of that elusive gift, star quality, enables him to hold an audience spellbound – an American priest remarked that when he takes the podium 'everyone feels the electricity as if a 220 volt wire had suddenly been plugged in'. He is also able to handle tricky situations in a way that is little short of miraculous. He has what a colleague has called 'a good share of Holy Guile' and when uncertain what to do he simply plays the clown, frequently diffusing tense situations by scrapping his prepared text and amusing his audience until they are ready to hear what he has to say. On one such occasion, when he was Bishop of Lesotho, he strode on to the platform in an Afro-style shirt and mimicked Dorothy Lamour until the audience had relaxed into fits of laughter. But the quality that informs his every word and action rests deep in his spirituality. What he *is* shines through his words, whether they are serious or amusing, gentle or forceful. In him being and doing go hand-in-hand – the idea of Tutu being insincere or in any way untrue to himself is simply inconceivable.

Soon his voice was heard from Cape Town to Pietersburg, from Durban to Springbok. He spoke both personally and through the SACC. In addresses, sermons, press interviews and statements he said that the apartheid system, and all the suffering that follows in its wake, is not only unjust, but immoral and unChristian; that to claim that God created human beings to be separate and divided is totally alien to the traditional aim of an undivided Christendom. If, as members of the government sometimes claimed, apartheid was dead, then they 'would like to see the corpse first'.

Many of these statements were made in his role as General Secretary of the SACC, receiving its full support. For instance at the end of his first full year in office, in his report to the executive committee, Tutu warned that unless the attitude of whites changed significantly there could be a split in the Churches along racial lines. He went on to ask why there had been no public outcry at the recent eviction of 'coloured' and Indian families from their homes and to voice his disquiet at the way the press were being hammered by the government, while people like Dr Rhoodie and Dr Connie Mulder, key figures in the 'Information Scandal', were being treated so lightly.

In that same report the SACC expressed its concern at the increase of arrests under the pass laws (272,887 in 1978); it called on the West Rand Administration Board not to implement its 'black spots removal policy' by moving families from Alexandra township (at the time the only area in Johannesburg where blacks could still enjoy freehold rights) to live in single-sex hostels; it expressed alarm that thousands of children in Soweto had not been placed in schools; it called for a ceasefire in Namibia, 'in the name of God and of humanity'.

Speaking as it did, for God and humanity, there was no area of life that was not its concern, so in August 1981 the SACC's offices served as the venue for a meeting of black trades unions and representatives of the Azanian People's Organisation (AZAPO).[1] Black and multi-racial trades unions had been legalised only the previous year and new labour legislation was being debated in Parliament; as these measures would affect basic human rights the Council had no doubt that the Churches' involvement was justified.

At the meeting Tutu claimed that the government wished to control the trades unions as much as possible and that the Church should be in the forefront of those protesting at legislation directed against the workers. Further, the Church should play its part in the education of the black worker. The next month he wrote that the trades unions were the most significant force for reasonably peaceful change and that the government, recognising this, aimed to emasculate them.[2]

> The outside world is hoodwinked if it thinks that by recognising black trade unions, Government has begun to liberalise apartheid. It has done nothing of the sort. It realised that with the interest of multi-national corporations in the work situation it had to do something. Legislation will attempt to undermine the unions and curb them. The Black Unions have said that they will defy any laws that intend to turn them into toothless bulldogs and the SACC has said that it will want to be supportive.

While the SACC's involvement with the trades unions was not likely to please the government, an earlier resolution had worried it even more. During the 1979 national conference, where the theme was 'The Church and the Alternative Society', Dr Allan Boesak proposed that the Church, since the banning of most of the black organisations now more important than ever as a vehicle for the expression of black aspirations, should initiate and support programmes of civil disobedience on a massive scale. The proposal was enthusiastically received and a resolution was passed, saying:

> This Conference believes that the South African Churches are under an obligation to withdraw, as far as that is possible, from co-operation with the State in all those areas in the ordering of our society where the law violates the justice of God. We call upon all Christian people to examine their lives and to seek to identify the ways in which each one reinforces the policy and props up the system.

Tutu's backing of this proposal was untypically cautious, though soon after the conference he gave an example of civil disobedience on a BBC programme. He suggested that a white, coming into Soweto and wishing to accompany him to church, should flout the law demanding that he have a permit – from such small beginnings a process of disobeying unjust laws on a large scale could be built.

The conference did not suggest that acts of disobedience should be performed by the Council itself, nevertheless it was a significant move. The SACC had accepted the principle of civil disobedience, thus giving moral justification to any of its members who felt their cause could be furthered by refusing to co-operate with laws they considered unjust. This was significant enough for the *Cape Times* to report that 'A broadly representative gathering of South African Christians (excluding the DRC) have resolved that Christianity and apartheid cannot co-exist.'[3] The authorities were sufficiently frightened by the resolution to summon Bishop Tutu and warn the SACC and 'leftist ministers and spiritual leaders' to 'cease and desist from irresponsible action and encouraging people to break the law'.[4] Tutu's response was to challenge the government to take action against them.

Prophets tend to cause trouble, both for themselves and for those around them; Tutu was no exception. In September 1979, on a trip to Denmark, he was interviewed on Danish television. To the question 'Why is it that the Council is against foreign investment in South Africa?' he responded that the SACC was critical because it believed that foreign investment supported the system. Further, that efforts made by some businesses investing in South Africa to improve conditions for blacks only served 'to shift the furniture around the room, instead of changing the furniture'. When he was asked if he would advise Denmark to stop buying South African coal, the following exchange took place.

'Well,' said Tutu, 'I find it rather disgraceful that Denmark is buying South African coal and increasing a dependence on South Africa, whereas one would hope that we could get South Africa to having a weaker position in bargaining, so that we could get this change as soon as possible.' The interviewer replied, 'But if we do not buy coal, for instance, a lot of blacks are going to be unemployed.' Tutu responded, 'They would be unemployed and suffer temporarily. It would be a suffering with a purpose. We would not be doing what is happening now, where blacks are suffering and it seems to be a suffering that is going to go on and on and on.'[5]

He knew what he was doing. By simply speaking of the withdrawal of foreign investments he was risking prosecution under Section 6 of the Terrorism Act; he might also anger blacks whose jobs would be threatened by boycotts. He returned to South Africa to find the country split. On the one hand he was supported by prominent black spokesmen such as Dr Nthato Motlana, and by numerous letters to the black press; he was cheered to the echo when he told a meeting of the Soweto Civic Association: 'We want political participation, not petty dispensation. We want a completely integrated society'.[6] On the other hand his mandate to speak for black miners was questioned and he was greeted with fury and resentment by most of the white community. The government-controlled television and radio produced black leaders working within the system to refute his stand and he was called to Pretoria, reminded that his remarks were economic sabotage and told to retract his statement and apologise.

In view of his position at the SACC and the furore that had been generated by his remarks, a meeting was arranged between Tutu, the executive committee and leaders of several of the Churches. The subject: should the General Secretary be allowed to speak on his own behalf without reference to the Council? Tutu explained that he had been trying to make a sober contribution to his country's problems, arguing that it was essential to search for strategies of reasonably non-violent change and that these strategies must involve international economic pressure. Not everyone agreed with the statement he had made in Denmark, but they all supported his right to make it and resolved to stand by him. They noted that the significant constituency who agreed with him were inhibited by law from discussing the subject and unanimously agreed that for him to retract or apologise would be 'a denial of his prophetic calling'.

He had been given a green light. Had he previously felt any constraints on his freedom to speak, now he was licensed by his colleagues to follow his instinct. There was no holding him. At home and overseas, on radio and television, after dinners, at conferences, before audiences ranging from the United Nations Special Committee against Apartheid to groups of university students, he lived up to his own promise to do everything in his power to rid the country of the system he variously referred to as 'diabolical', 'this pernicious evil', 'one of the most vicious systems since Nazism'.

He constantly reminded his audiences that he was committed to black liberation because he was committed to white liberation and that whites could never be truly free until blacks were free. He urged them, in the name of morality and justice, to take sides, to express their commitment to a just redistribution of wealth and resources and to make friends with blacks before it was too late. A typical example was in 1980, when he ended a speech to the students at the University of the Witwatersrand with this rousing peroration:[7]

So join the liberation struggle. Throw off your lethargy and the apathy of affluence. Work for a better South Africa for yourselves and ourselves and for your children. Uproot all evil and oppression and injustice of which Blacks are victims and you whites are beneficiaries, so that you won't reap the whirlwind. Join the winning side. Oppression, injustice, exploitation – all these have lost, for God is on our side – on the side of Justice, of Peace, of Reconciliation, of Laughter and Joy, of Sharing and Compassion and Goodness and Righteousness.

So, too, he showed his support for those who were involved in the struggle. Shocked at the detention and banning of members of AZAPO within days of its formation, he issued a statement questioning the authorities' refusal to listen to the authentic spokesmen of the black community, criticising them for acting against the new group before it had even drawn up its constitution. He asked, as he asked so often in similar situations, why, if the activities of the detained men were illegal, they were not charged in a court of law? Was it perhaps that there was no evidence that could stand up to legal scrutiny? Similarly, when Dr Motlana, the Chairman of the Soweto Civic Association, was banned from speaking at public gatherings, Tutu again appealed to the authorities, not least in their own interests, to heed the voices of those the black community considered its leaders. He insisted that there could be no real peace or security until black views were taken seriously and that Dr Motlana was only articulating those views, not advocating violence or subversion.

Often he warned of what could happen if the present order did not change. If the government continued to treat the black community with contempt and brutality, if it continued to uproot people from their homes and dump them in some arid 'homeland', if it were determined to balkanise South Africa and to deprive blacks of citizenship, 'then there won't be a peaceful solution, then they are declaring war on us. What are Blacks then expected to do in such a situation. Fold our hands?'[8] He warned that, patient though blacks were, they could be provoked beyond endurance. The time might come when they would find it difficult to forgive the suffering that whites had inflicted on them. Quoting Alan Paton's fearful cry, 'Oh God help us that when the whites have turned to loving the blacks will not have turned to hating',[9] he warned of the bloodbath to which present policies could lead.

There is a thin line between a warning and a threat, but Tutu has been careful, often even explicit, in acknowledging the distinction. (In voicing these fears he was, in any case, in the company of such as Vorster, who warned of 'the alternative too ghastly to contemplate' and P. W. Botha, who urged his countrymen to 'adapt or die'.) In encouraging people to play their part in the liberation struggle Tutu frequently reminded them that a post-liberation South Africa will never forget who were their friends and who were not. 'Make no mistake about it, if you go over to the other side, then the day of reckoning will come. This is not a threat, it is just the plain truth. Blacks will never forget that you were traitors to the liberation struggle.'[10]

He warned his own people that liberation would be costly. In 1982, preaching at the funeral of Mlungiso Mxenge, a Durban lawyer believed to have been killed by agents of the authorities, he ended his oration, 'Many more will be detained. Many more will be banned. Many more will be deported and killed. Yes, it will be costly. But we shall be free. Nothing will stop us becoming free – no police bullets, dogs, tear-gas, prison, death, no, nothing will stop us because God is on our side.'[11]

And always he spoke with hope. He would quote from the book of Exodus, showing how God rescued the Israelites from slavery. He told a group of Anglican students that the Old Testament God did not just talk – he acted: 'He showed himself to be a doing God. Perhaps we might add another point about God – He takes sides. He is not a neutral God. He took the side of the slaves, the oppressed, the victims.' He assured his audience that God was still the same in twentieth-century South Africa: 'He does not sleep or go on holiday or take a day off. He is always there. So don't despair.'[12] Eager always to stress the good, he would marvel that the majority of blacks still wanted a non-racial South Africa, still wanted black and white to live and share together.

Later he was to be accused by those anxious to discredit him of making inflammatory speeches, of seldom expressing himself publicly 'on matters other than socio-political and economic issues',[13] so it is important to remember not only that most of his sermons were of a purely spiritual or theological nature, but that even his pronouncements against the system were desperate appeals for peace and justice, wherever possible couched in reconciliatory terms. Time and again he would declare that both he and the SACC were committed to finding and using peaceful means to bring about change. In lamenting the refusal of the Afrikaans Churches to attend a consultation on racism he asked their forgiveness for any way in which the SACC's attitude had hurt them. Often he agreed it was difficult for the whites to give up so much privilege, even admitting he would need a lot of grace to do it himself, were he in their position.

Whenever he could find reason to praise or show gratitude, he was keen to do so. He frequently commended P. W. Botha on his grasp of reality and his courage; he sent a telegram to Louis le Grange congratulating him for allowing political prisoners to do post-Matriculation studies; when calling for an end to the provocative use of army personnel he also pointed out that the police had a duty to maintain law and order and needed co-operation from the public; he commended Dr Koornhof for showing compassion to the people of

Crossroads and Alexandra. Are these the actions of a man seeking to inflame or to reconcile?

Tutu is adamant that he is not a politician. When accused of having political ambitions he frequently responds by saying that there are three very good reasons why religious leaders should not become politicians in the party political sense – the Ayatollah Khomeini, Bishop Muzerewa and Archbishop Makarios. Even when encouraged to consider himself a politician he declines. He once received a charming letter from a schoolboy headed 'Application for a share in your political experience' which said, 'As a political amateur, I wish to grow under your guidance'. Tutu's response was: 'I would like to explain to you that I really am not a politician as I work on the basis of the Christian Gospel.'

And that is the point. Tutu's politics spring directly and inevitably from his Christianity. He has often said that he is puzzled which Bible people read when they suggest that religion and politics don't mix. In Old Testament Israel no one would know what you meant if you tried to separate them, and, in any case, in South Africa *everything* is politics. The most innocent action – where you sit on a train, where you drink your morning coffee – can be interpreted as a political gesture. Tutu argues that a political conscience does not disappear with ordination and that Christians must always test political systems against the Gospel, asking if they are usurping the place of God. As a law-abiding citizen, he is in no doubt that the State should be obeyed when its authority is clearly legitimate, but if its laws conflict with the Gospel, then Christians not only have the right but the duty to agitate peacefully for their repeal. In a situation of injustice it is not possible to be neutral; not to oppose the system is in fact to support it.

He also points out that governments only object to clerics having political views when they criticise the status quo; those who uphold the system are applauded. It hardly befits the South African National Party, most of whose members belong to the DRC, who for many years sought to find biblical justification for apartheid, and one of whose Prime Ministers, D. F. Malan, was in fact a Dominee, to say that religion and politics do not mix.

So Tutu had no qualms about speaking against matters that could strictly be said to belong to the political arena. He refused to join the Buthelezi Commission on the constitutional and economic relations between Natal and KwaZulu 'Because of my total abhorrence of the Bantustan policy and my fear that this Commission could appear to give credibility to that policy.'[14] For the same reasons he opposed the Quail Commission on political options for the Ciskei: 'Such a

Commission should not have been allowed to happen. It assumes the premise that South Africa can be broken up, whereas we claim that until all the people of South Africa say "Yes" to such a proposition, South Africa must remain the unitary state that it is.'[15]

He pierced to the nerve centre of South African politics by predicting (in 1980) that there would be a black Prime Minister in South Africa within the next five to ten years. In the same week he called on parents to support a school boycott and warned the government that if it continued to detain and arrest protesters there could be a repetition of the 1976 riots. He told an audience of Stellenbosch students that the blacks did not want 'crumbs of concession from a generous master, they wanted to be at the table, planning the menu with him . . . the name of the game is political power-sharing'.

He did not hesitate to oppose government reforms that he, together with most of the black community, regarded as purely cosmetic or even dangerous. Most conspicuously he roundly condemned the report presented in May 1982 by the multi-racial President's Council, in which proposals were outlined for an electoral college consisting of white, 'coloured' and Indian members. Tutu conceded that the inclusion of non-white representatives on the council was a significant, indeed a revolutionary, departure from normal practice in South Africa, but drew attention to the report's fatal flaws. He pointed out that membership of the council was by nomination rather than by election; that, being only an advisory body, there was no guarantee that its suggestions would ever leave the realm of theory; third, and most seriously, that the African community was totally excluded, both from the council and from the proposed new constitution. The country was being encouraged to take the report seriously, to discuss and criticise it, but 'Why should we try to discuss its recommendations when we know we are not being listened to? Why shout into a void merely to hear your own echo?'[16] A few days later he told a meeting of the Natal Indian Congress why 'coloureds' and Indians were being co-opted into the system – because the whites could not defend the country on their own. If they joined the whites under the proposed new political dispensation the Africans would regard them as traitors in the liberation struggle and 'the day of reckoning would come'.

While the proposals were being debated in Parliament the following year, Tutu issued a statement in accordance with a resolution taken by the SACC. It drew attention to the fact that the new Bill not only permanently excluded 73 per cent of the population from sharing political power and legitimatised their exclusion, but that it also entrenched racial discrimination, ensured that the whites would retain their parliamentary majority and would make fundamental change by relatively peaceful means virtually impossible. He urged the member Churches to reject the proposed new constitution.

Tutu is by nature a reconciler; his wish is to build bridges rather than destroy them. In June 1980, during a period of sustained popular resistance, with school and university boycotts against apartheid education, bus boycotts, protests against rent increases, open support for the ANC and a campaign for the release of Nelson Mandela, he encouraged senior members of the SACC to seek a meeting with the Prime Minister to discuss the rapidly deteriorating situation.

It was not an easy decision to make. He was well aware of the danger of giving credibility to someone so distrusted in the eyes of the black community as P. W. Botha; he knew too how slim were the chances that he would be taken seriously. He admitted to the Pretoria Press Club that many whites regarded him as 'an irresponsible, radical fire-eater, who should have been locked up long ago'. He knew that others felt he was really a politician trying hard to be a Bishop, with 'horns under my funny bishop's hat, and my tail tucked away under my trailing cape'.[17] His conviction that the Gospel can change men's hearts and that as Christians they must try to communicate, even to deaf ears, was not shared by all his colleagues, but eventually they were persuaded and the letter requesting a meeting was sent.

Mr Botha prevaricated. He replied that he would grant the SACC delegation an interview on certain conditions: they must openly reject Communism for South Africa, guarantee not to undermine National Service, reject all organisations which supported violence and denounce the efforts of the ANC to overthrow orderly government. To this undignified sparring the SACC replied that, though it would have preferred to meet the Prime Minister unconditionally, it felt the need for dialogue was so great it would reiterate its standpoint on these issues. It wrote that it had never supported Communism, or indeed any other ideology, that though it insisted on the right of every citizen to conscientious objection it did not wish to undermine national service, it rejected violence to overthrow the system as much as it abhorred institutionalised violence and that as the SACC had never aligned itself with the ANC it was superfluous to dissociate itself from it.

So, on August 7th, 1980, Bishop Tutu, with representatives of the member Churches and the senior executives of the SACC, went to Pretoria to meet the Prime Minister, six Cabinet Ministers and two Deputy Ministers.

If ever a meeting demonstrated the differences between the two sides, it was this. The delegation was politely welcomed, the proceedings were civil, the name of Jesus Christ was invoked to guide the discussions; yet it was as if their words were no sooner uttered than they disappeared into the gulf between them. They quite simply could not hear each other.

The Prime Minister set the scene by saying that the State and the Church were two independent and autonomous bodies, who should not meddle in each other's affairs. Politics were not the function of the Church, nor was theology the affair of the State. In any case, with whom should he negotiate when the Church was itself divided? But as he aspired to rule by Christian principles, his door was open to Church leaders; he would give them two hours that morning, with the possibility of another meeting later in the year.

When it was Tutu's turn to speak he assured the Prime Minister that he had no political axe to grind, but that the Christian Gospel compelled him to reject apartheid. He urged the calling of a National Convention, to be attended by all the acknowledged leaders from every section of the population, including political leaders in prison or in detention. He then repeated his warning that though there was still much goodwill among the black community, patience was running out and anger and bitterness would continue to grow unless the government demonstrated clearly that it intended to bring about changes sufficiently fundamental to lead to political power-sharing. The nub of his presentation was a four-point prescription for change. First, that the government should commit itself to a common citizenship for all South Africans in an undivided South Africa; second, would it please abolish the pass laws; third, would it put an immediate stop to population removals; forth, it should set up a uniform education system. 'If these four things were done I would be the first to declare out loud "Please give the Government a chance, they seem in our view now to have embarked on the course of real change." I certainly would be one of the first to shout this out from the roof tops.'[18]

He might never have spoken. In his summing-up the Prime Minister made no reference to Tutu's suggestions, preferring to talk about fighting on the South African borders and to claim that South Africa's problem was a problem of minorities. He ended by saying he was prepared to lead his people on the road towards creating new dispensations, but he was not prepared to lead them on the road of a government of one man one vote. He warned the delegation that if they made 'provocative, negative statements' no further meeting would take place.

It was a historic meeting – never before had a black leader with no formal position inside the system talked with a white Prime Minister. Yet it did nothing to defuse the conflict, nor was Tutu's reputation as a negotiator enhanced. His approach was seen as politically naïve and soon afterwards leading South African theologians warned that further meetings could be met with resistance from radical black churchmen. Tutu could not share this view; his paradigms are biblical – Moses went to see Pharaoh not once, but several times. Whether or not Mr Botha, like Pharaoh, had hardened his heart, whether or not his actions received popular backing, Tutu would try again.

Though Desmond Tutu's instincts to negotiate rather than to confront, to reconcile rather than to attack, have received criticism, there has never been any doubting the courage of both his words and his actions, nor any wavering in his determination to stand with his people. From pinpricks like calling the Minister of Police 'an insufferable bore who needs a course in logic' for trying to depict the SACC as unpatriotic, to physically putting his own life in danger, he has shown the sort of courage that can only come from a deep sense of the rightness of his cause.

On one occasion in Soweto, seeing two large white policemen beating an elderly black man, he put his small frame between them, holding up his Bishop's cross until they stopped. On another he risked his life at a political funeral in the Ciskei by flinging himself across the body of a black security policeman being stoned by a large and angry mob. Thinking the crowd had desisted, he returned to the rostrum, his clothes soaked with the policeman's blood. They were, however, merely waiting for him to turn his back; later they dragged the policeman away and beat him to death. Though Tutu was prepared to protect this man in the government's employ, he was equally ready to attack the 'homeland' leaders working within the system: 'These leaders are largely corrupt men looking after their own interests, lining their pockets. South Africa consequently has a hold on them because they are almost without exception lacking integrity.'[19] Perhaps to make this statement needed even more courage.

There were numerous occasions when he spoke out in situations where many would have taken refuge in caution. On June 16th, 1982, he was taking a service in the Regina Mundi Church to commemorate the Soweto killings. In an effort to suppress press coverage of the event journalists were taken to the police station and the church was surrounded by hundreds of armed policemen. Inside the church Tutu was addressing 5,000 blacks in what Joseph Lelyveld, who later heard a tape recording, called 'an emotionally charged political litany'; '"Is there anyone here who doubts that apartheid is doomed to failure?" he cried. "No" the crowd shouted back. "Is there anyone who doubts we are going to be free?" "No" came the reply. Then Tutu made the crowd chant "We are going to be free!" [20] At the end of the service he went out to speak to the rioting crowd who were infuriated by the detention of the journalists, and persuaded them to stop throwing stones. It was on that occasion that he made the famous promise that on the day he was proved wrong about apartheid he would burn his Bible.

Several times he has spoken through peaceful protest. The first was in 1980 when he took part in a march organised by the General Secretary of the Congregationalists, the Reverend Joe Wing. Tutu, together with Leah, Bishop Timothy Bavin and fifty-one other church-men including the SACC Praesidium, marched to the Johannesburg police headquarters singing hymns and distributing pink and yellow pamphlets calling for the release of John Thorne, a Congregationalist minister whose attempts to diffuse a difficult situation arising from a schools boycott had led to his detention. The clergymen were stopped by policemen with automatic rifles and attack dogs, charged with contravening the Riotous Assemblies Act (carrying a maximum jail sentence of six months or a fine of R100) and held overnight in racially segregated cells. Tutu spent his first – and so far his only – night in jail praying, singing hymns and swapping stories with his fellow clerics. In 1981, in a show of passive resistance, he refused to celebrate the fortieth anniversary of South Africa becoming a Republic, asking what was there for blacks, second-class citizens in the land of their birth, to celebrate?

By the early 1980s Tutu had become an international figure; as early as 1979 his visits overseas were greeted with such publicity that he was finding it impossible to make a private visit. Honours were showered upon him: in 1978 he was elected a Fellow of his old college, King's College, London, accepting with pleasure but 'in a representative and corporate capacity'; by the end of the following year he had been awarded three Honorary Doctorates – from the General Theological Seminary in New York, from the universities of Kent in England and Harvard in the States. But while being honoured overseas, he was, for much of white South Africa, an object of hatred.

He was the recipient of a remorseless stream of death threats, obscene telephone calls and bomb scares. One evening he was speaking to 5,000 people at a meeting held by the South African Christian Leadership Assembly when the tyres of over 100 cars were deflated. Anonymous pamphlets, purporting to come from 'The United Trade Union Council' (a body which no one could trace) were distributed throughout the country to defame him, rumours and innuendoes about the financial administration of the SACC were encouraged to spread and the government-sponsored radio and television lost no opportunity to use the air-waves to stigmatise him. Puerile jokes were circulated – one even sank to the level of pointing out that in New Zealand a '*tutu*' is a poisonous plant. One day eight members of the National Front wearing crash helmets elbowed their way towards his office. They shouted abuse, then threw thirty pieces of silver into the outer office where his secretary was working, 'to pay you in the traditional way that all traitors are paid'.

There is something virtually unique about the vilification endured by Desmond Tutu. The hatred alone is bad enough; worse still was that much of it was organised by the government of the country to which, whether they would admit it or not, he belonged. Since 1974 the government had used a body called the Christian League as a front organisation to counter the influence of the World Council of Churches, infiltrate the SACC and break its influence. In the year 1979–80 it paid the Christian League R340,000 in return for its written undertaking to 'pursue an uninterrupted campaign against the SACC'.[21] At the very time that the Churches were, in good faith, holding talks with the government, that same government was doing its best to undermine the SACC.

So, simultaneously loved and hated, honoured and vilified, Tutu became a key figure in one of the most notorious confrontations between Church and State in the history of Christianity.

13

David and Goliath

The uniqueness of the confrontation between Church and State in South Africa, climaxing in the Eloff Commission, lay in the fact that it was not a case of an atheistic regime seeking to suppress Christianity, or even of a Christian government attacking a particular denomination. Here was a State, declared in its constitution to be Christian, taking on an ecumenical Christian body representing 12 million of its own people.

The government and the SACC had been on a collision course for years, in fact since 1949 when the Rosettenville Conference had opposed the government's new apartheid policies. A watershed was reached in 1968, with the publication of the *Message to the People of South Africa*; another in 1979, when Dr Allan Boesak challenged the Churches to adopt a programme of civil disobedience and actively to defy the apartheid laws. The government had been infuriated by the way the Church had spoken out on conscientious objection, on the South African Defence Force's raids into the frontline States and the unlawful occupation of Namibia, on bannings and detentions without trial; also by its support of the Free Mandela Campaign and by its boycott of the Republican Day festivals. In short the government were exasperated by the stance the Churches had taken against the whole apparatus of apartheid. The discord between Church and State is as easily defined as it has proved impossible to resolve. The Churches held a deep belief that the apartheid policy and its laws were evil, immoral and consequently unChristian; the government had passed those laws and intended to uphold them.

Against this backcloth of sustained disagreement, erupting into frequent open antagonism, appeared veiled threats and innuendoes directed against the SACC. There were rumours about past financial mismanagement, the press were probing, Christian right-wingers were pressing for an investigation. In 1981 the Prime Minister entered the fray personally, accusing the SACC of receiving more than R2½ million from abroad and channelling it into bodies and projects in order to further unrest. Tutu responded by saying that Mr Botha was lying and that he knew he was lying. Again, as he had after the resolution on civil disobedience in 1979, Tutu challenged the Prime Minister to charge the SACC in open court.

Mr Botha did not quite pick up the gauntlet which had been thrown down. Instead, on November 20th, 1981, he appointed a Commission of Enquiry to investigate the Council. The honourable Mr Justice C. F. Eloff, Judge of the Transvaal Provincial Division of the Supreme Court of South Africa, was the Chairman; his fellow commissioners, representing an entirely white perspective, were a chartered accountant, a Regional Court Magistrate, the Vice-Principal of the University of Pretoria and a senior civil servant. On March 1st of the following year the Commission began work and the SACC, still reeling from the report of the Steyn Commission on the press which had made a virulent attack on the World Council of Churches, the SACC and Bishop Tutu, was fighting for its life.

The government wanted to show that the SACC was subversive because its activities threatened the security of the State. Further that the Council's legitimate work, propagating the Gospel, had been abandoned in favour of matters beyond its competence. In its terms of reference the Commission was asked to enquire into the history and activities of the SACC and to report on all aspects of its finances and assets; there was also a catch-all clause covering 'any other matter pertaining to the SACC', including personnel, both past and present, so that a report could be made 'in the public interest'. As the limits of this phrase were determined by the government, clearly there were to be no inhibitions on the scope of the Commission's inquiries.

Behind these overt instructions there was little doubt that what the government hoped to do was to discredit both the SACC and Bishop Tutu. It was to attempt this on two fronts: on the one hand by trying to prove financial mismanagement; on the other by showing that the SACC was fomenting an unpatriotic revolution. Thus it could cause the Council to become an embarrassment to its member Churches and overseas donors, eroding support where it was most crucial. It also hoped to show that the Council was a microcosm of what it saw as an international conspiracy against the South African government. In the SACC the evils of internationalism – an aspect of the Council's work running counter to the insularity of Afrikanerdom and which had for years been an irritant – were encapsulated.

The Commission sat in a small rectangular room in a government building in Pretoria with the auspicious name 'Veritas'. Judge Eloff, flanked on each side by two commissioners, sat facing the witness and the two Counsels: the chief investigating officer Advocate K. S. P. O. von Lieres SC for the government and Sydney Kentridge SC, one of

South Africa's best-known advocates, who had represented the Biko family at the inquest into the death of Steve Biko, for the SACC. There were seats for a few visitors, and a handful of the press were usually present. It was, at least on the face of it, a quiet, civilised affair, with some special visitors being invited to take tea with Judge Eloff.

The SACC had decided to co-operate fully with the authorities; all the material they wanted was made available, nothing was concealed or ignored. Confident that it had nothing to hide, it wanted the world to know it. So every file requested was photocopied, catalogued and handed over. Extra help was brought in to trace the history of the Council, describe the developments of the various divisions and put all the papers together chronologically as a formal submission to the Commission. Dan Vaughan, in addition to his work as Planning Officer, was responsible for co-ordinating the preparation of the material. Not only did this cost the Council over R200,000, but its day-to-day work was constantly disrupted as staff were questioned and their papers searched.

The public hearings began in September with Tutu's evidence. Allistair Sparks was in the courtroom to hear what he suggested was probably 'the greatest sermon of the Bishop's life':[1]

> He sat bouncing and twisting in a carver chair, his hands shaping the outlines of his ideas with vivid gestures. It was like a mime show with voice accompaniment, when he spoke of the resurrection of the body, his arms folded around his own body in a hug.
>
> The voice was the other instrument in this concert performance. Sometimes it would be sonorous, playing with the cadences of his African accent, and sometimes it would break into a high-pitched chuckle as he would hit on some pertinent new insight. It would be sombre, joyful, impatient, humorous, reflective, switching rapidly in response to a quicksilver spirit.
>
> And all the while, the white Commissioners watched, expressionless.

Typically, Tutu began by expressing his appreciation to the officers of the Commission for examining the SACC's records in such a way as to dislocate its work as little as possible. Even more typically, he then went straight to the heart of the matter, stating that it was not the finances or any other activities of the SACC that were being investigated, but the Christian faith itself that was on trial. Quoting from an old leather-bound Bible, and showing that the SACC regarded the proceedings as a court case rather than an inquiry by resolutely addressing the Judge as 'My Lord', he demonstrated that all that the SACC did and said, indeed everything it was, was determined not by politics but by the Gospels, which not only licensed it to be actively involved with social justice but carried a divine obligation that it should be. The central issue was profoundly theological.

He argued that Jesus Christ was the Lord of *all* life, spiritual and secular. Though spirituality was central to the life of the Council, it knew that 'God does not permit us to dwell in a kind of spiritual ghetto, insulated from real life . . . He [Jesus] refused to remain on the Mount of Transfiguration, but descended to the valley beneath to be involved with healing the possessed boy.' Christ was on the side of the oppressed and his central work was to effect reconciliation between God and Man and between man and man. Apartheid is evil, he claimed, because it claims mankind was made for separateness, thus repudiating this central, reconciling truth of the Christian faith. Further, apartheid denies the unique value of each human being and its consequences are evil. In trying to defend it the government could only fail, 'for it is ranging itself on the side of evil, injustice and oppression'. It was also flying in the face of the recent declaration of the World Alliance of Reformed Churches (already rejected by the Afrikaner churches, whose membership of the Alliance had been suspended) that the theological justification of apartheid is a heresy.

Tutu was determined to show that the SACC and its member Churches were not 'a tuppenny halfpenny fly by night organisation' but they belonged to the Church of God, expressing their oneness in prayer, in giving and receiving and in suffering with one another. The only separation acknowledged by the Bible was the separation between believers on the one hand and unbelievers on the other.

He submitted 'with due respect' but with an impressive authority that no secular power, no Commission, had any competence whatsoever to determine the nature of the Gospel of Jesus Christ and that in trying to do so it was 'usurping divine prerogatives and the prerogatives of the church itself'. If the SACC had contravened the laws of the land, then there was an array of draconian measures at the disposal of the government. The Inquiry was 'totally superfluous' and the SACC had only agreed to appear before the Commission because it had nothing to hide. Nor did he fear the government:

> I want to say that there is nothing the government can do to me that will stop me from being involved in what I believe is what God wants me to do. I do not do it because I like doing it. I do it because I am under what I believe to be the influence of God's hand. I cannot help it. I cannot help it when I see injustice. I cannot keep quiet. I will not keep quiet, for, as Jeremiah says, when I try to keep quiet God's word

burns like a fire in my breast. But what is it that they can ultimately do? The most awful thing that they can do is to kill me, and death is not the worst thing that can happen to a Christian.

There were many milestones in the long journey of evidence and cross-examination that was the Eloff Commission. One was the suggestion of General Johan Coetzee, then Chief of the Security Police, that the SACC was the puppet of overseas organisations and that its financial help went to organisations that were in reality liberation movements. He said the SACC should be declared an affected organisation and subjected to the provisions of the Fund Raising Act. Such a step would cut off all overseas finance (96 per cent of its income) and bring such money as its member Churches could provide under direct government control and scrutiny. Another key moment was the appearance of Mr E. Cain, the Baptist editor of *Encounter*, an official mouthpiece of the government-sponsored Christian League and dedicated to the downfall of the SACC. He claimed that ministers of religion should have nothing to do with politics, except in the sense of attacking Communism and supporting the South African government; he even suggested that Jesus Christ had no concern for righting injustice. So ugly was the exchange, so nearly blasphemous, that the SACC defence stopped the cross-examination; even the Prosecuting Counsel felt unable to pursue it.

It is a curious fact that the Prosecution did not produce a right-wing theologian to support their case. Perhaps the experience of Mr Cain had discouraged them; perhaps it was the hesitancy of Afrikaner theologians, unaccustomed to being challenged, to go on record in justification of so dubious a cause. They might have hoped that the distinguished DRC theologian Professor David Bosch would have sided with them. In fact he only agreed to give evidence in order to introduce a slightly different perspective and was outstanding in his defence of the SACC's position. He gave it a strong theological legitimacy, addressing himself primarily to arguing that in attacking the SACC the Commission were attacking all the member Churches, who gave their total support to what the SACC was doing.

In November 1982, a year after the appointment of the Commission, came a turning point resulting from one of the most unpleasant episodes of the whole Inquiry. An anonymous letter, purporting to come from 'unhappy staff at the SACC', was sent to all its overseas donors and member Churches. It claimed that there was a rift between the SACC and its member Churches, alleged that the funds were disbursed for 'semi-political rather than evangelical or other strictly religious activities' and said they wished to express their 'distinct

unhappiness over the extent to which this organisation has disinte-
grated and deteriorated under the control of Bishop Desmond Tutu'.
The writers claimed to be sending the letter anonymously 'since we
face the very real possibility of retribution if we speak out openly
against the real situation in the SACC'. The letter (whose source was
never confirmed) was strongly repudiated by the staff, who expressed
their fullest trust and confidence in their General Secretary. In keeping
with his policy of total transparency, Tutu promptly forwarded a copy
of the letter to the Eloff Commission.

He also decided to invite the overseas donors to testify. The
authorities, anxious to show that they too were playing fair, allowed
entry visas to representatives from Norway, Denmark, Holland and
Germany, so the worldwide Church, already kept informed of the
situation by weekly telexes, was alerted to the gravity of the situation.
Significantly, the Archbishop of Canterbury, Dr Robert Runcie, took
the unusual step of showing the international support of the Anglican
Church by sending out a five-person delegation consisting of Terry
Waite, the lay assistant to the Archbishop of Canterbury on Anglican
communion affairs, the Primus of the Scottish Episcopal Church, a
member of the executive council of the Episcopal Church of the
United States, the Prolocutor of the General Synod of the Anglican
Church of Canada and the Primate of the Church of the Province of
New Zealand. The press, asking if the SACC had paid the fares, were
told by a delighted Bishop Tutu that they had not even paid the hotel
bills:[2]

> The South African government has not yet recovered from the shock
> administered to it by that ecumenical and worldwide presence and I will
> not be over-anxious to help them recover too soon. They had hoped
> that they would have succeeded in vilifying us and discrediting us to
> such an extent that our friends would not want to touch us with the
> proverbial bargepole. It seems that they have been hoisted by their own
> petard.

It was the first time Archbishop Runcie had done such a thing
(though he has done it twice since). 'It was to make the point that you
are not simply dealing with a domestic matter. If you touch Desmond
Tutu you touch a world family of Christians and there was a sense of
Anglican identity there, which was visible and effective and not just a
notional paper theory which crumbles when people see the autonomy
of provinces.' Though the Anglican Church in South Africa expresses
itself through its own culture and customs, it is historically tied
to Canterbury and Canterbury was proud to support it. For his
part Tutu's gratitude knew no bounds. This action by Runcie set

the seal on the admiration and affection the two men have for each other.

The evidence taken by the Commission ran to eighty-two volumes; its final report, submitted to the State President at the end of 1983, ran to 450 pages. In February 1984 the report was tabled and the findings published.

The Commission, heedless of the testimony of the SACC and its member Churches, concluded that the SACC had changed from being a body principally concerned with spiritual matters 'into one concerned with political, social and economic interests, and having specific objectives in these fields'. It had 'opted for a revolutionary rather than an evolutionary process' to effect change and had become increasingly identified with the struggle for liberation. To this end it had campaigned for civil disobedience and non-cooperation with the State, supported disinvestment and conscientious objection – none of which actions were, in the opinion of the Commission, in the national interest. It accused the SACC of trying to conceal the origin and disbursement of its funds and engaging in 'secret and covert operations'. Finally it criticised the Council's financial administration.

In its recommendations the Commission questioned the capability of the law to counter calls for disinvestment and urged that existing legislation be reconsidered; it suggested that the SACC should be brought under the discipline of the Fund-raising Act of 1978 (though this was in fact never done). However, it decided against declaring the Council an affected organisation – a curious *non-sequitur* in the light of the case being built up in those 450 pages. The Commission's explanation was that such action would be viewed as a restraint on religious freedom and that in any case it would not prevent the flow of funds from overseas. It had to admit that it had found no evidence of the SACC being manipulated by its overseas donors, but claimed that though 'the money spent by the SACC to help the needy and deserving can only be described as meagre compared to that used for political purposes, innocent people would suffer if the organisation were to be rendered largely ineffective.'

All that evidence, all those cross-examinations, all that paper, had achieved virtually nothing; none of the allegations had been made to stick, the Commission had certainly not succeeded in undermining the moral credibility of the Council. The publication of the Eloff Report was even described as 'an almost non-event'. Disappointed government officials took refuge in issuing warnings. Louis le Grange, the Minister of Law and Order, said that if the SACC continued its 'tendency towards confrontation' the State might be forced to act against it – it must remember it was not above the law: 'I warn him [Tutu] and the SACC that . . . I will not allow any wicked acts to be committed under the cloak of religion.'

Nevertheless, neither the SACC, nor its supporters and General Secretary, were going to let the accusations that had been levelled at them go unchallenged. Within hours the SACC Praesidium issued a strong statement denying that there had been a campaign of civil disobedience, rejecting the use of the word 'revolutionary' in relation to its work and stating, 'It is intolerable that the Church be denied the right to determine and interpret the Gospel mandate in terms of the challenges of its environment'. The Southern African Catholic Bishops' Conference commented on the inability of the Commission to find anything deserving legal action and stated, 'In the black milieu the topics referred to sound like very moderate Christian reactions to a situation of unbearable privation and frustration'.

Two Progressive Federal Party MPs also spoke out in their defence. Dr Alex Boraine said that while the SACC must accept the consequences if it defied the State, the Church had the right to be involved in political, social and economic issues. David Dalling said that his party believed the government had no business probing the SACC's financial affairs, that there was no doubting that the Commission was inspired by political motives and that the SACC was a private organisation, dealing with private money and comparable to the South African Bureau of Racial Affairs and the Institute of Racial Relations.

Of all the responses to the Commission's findings, none were so forceful as Tutu's. He could only find one point of agreement with the Commission – that they had little understanding of theology, so how could they be expected to make a fair judgment? 'It really was like asking (speaking respectfully) a group of blind men to judge the Chelsea Flower Show.' He repeated that no secular authority was entitled to tell the Church how to go about its work and that if the Council had contravened the law, then it should have been charged in open court. The Commission not only had no theological expertise, it had not included one black person. What did it know of the anguish and humiliation endured by the black community? How could it understand how blacks regarded the SACC?

Heeding the old adage that 'the essence of defence is offence', Tutu reminded the Commission of the high-powered delegations from all over the world that had shown their support for the SACC, and challenged it to 'point to any self-respecting overseas Church that supports the White Dutch Reformed Church?' He met accusations of fomenting unrest by pointing out occasions when he had acted as a mediator. He told it to stop trying to bribe the SACC staff to spy for them – if it wanted to know anything, it had only to ask. He warned that

> if they take on the SACC then they must know that they are taking on the Church of God and other tyrants before them have tried to destroy the Church – Nero, Amin, Hitler, Bokassa, etc. . . . Where are they today? They have bitten the dust ignominiously. I warn the South African government again – they are not Gods, they are mere mortals, who will end up as mere marks on the pages of history, part of its flotsam and jetsam. I am not afraid of them.

The one issue on which the SACC was vulnerable concerned its financial management. Though the Commission were never able to show that money was mishandled or used for purposes other than that for which it was given, there was still evidence of poor. accounting. This came as no surprise to the Council, which was the first to admit it; indeed, Tutu was well on the way towards bringing things under control before the Commission began to sit.

One reason for the poor book-keeping was the confidential nature of some of the donations, for instance when assistance was given to people who did not wish their names to be officially recorded. Another was that in trying to use their money as much as possible for the beneficiaries, the staff of the SACC kept their own salaries, from Bishop Tutu's downwards, as low as possible. The salary for a first-class accountant, qualified to handle its turnover of R4 million a year, would have been two or three times as high as that earned by the General Secretary. With hindsight it is clear that the Council's idealism led, in this respect, to an error of judgment.

The inadequacy of the accounting did, however, reveal a situation that was to cause much personal anguish inside the SACC. One of the State witnesses, Warrant-Officer A. J. Mills, found in the course of his investigations that the former General Secretary, John Rees, had deposited more than R250,000 from the Asingeni Fund in fifty-one bank accounts in his own name. The Council, knowing and admiring John Rees, were reluctant to prefer charges, but in the middle of their 1982 national conference news came that the former General Secretary had been arrested and charged with fraud. He was tried, found guilty and sentenced to ten years' imprisonment, suspended conditionally for five years. He was also fined R30,000.

This affair split the SACC. That John Rees's use of the money was unauthorised was not in question, but opinions were divided as to his motivation. Some felt he was playing Robin Hood, using the funds he had appropriated from the SACC to benefit the poor and needy; others saw his actions in various shades of grey, one person even suggesting he was 'a giant con-man buying power from the black community'. Nowhere was this division more personal or more painful than between Tutu and the SACC's distinguished President, Peter Storey.

Tutu, though unwilling to charge his predecessor and slow to believe in his guilt, was angry that the SACC should be brought into disrepute through events which had taken place before his time. He was also incensed by allegations that his reluctance to lay charges or to witness at the trial was due to John Rees having given him R14,000 towards buying a house – money which he had accepted, perhaps naïvely but certainly in good faith, as having been donated by a German Bishop but which turned out to have come from the funds misappropriated by the former General Secretary.[3] He felt, however, forced by the evidence to accept the guilty verdict.

Peter Storey's reactions were even more complicated. He was not only John Rees's friend, he was his pastor. His insistence on giving evidence in mitigation of John Rees was hard for Tutu to take, not least because of the ever-present suspicion of a racial dimension – was it a case of white supporting white (though too many blacks were devoted to John Rees for that charge to stick)? Eventually Peter Storey resigned as President of the SACC, an action which also lost Tutu Elizabeth, his devoted and able secretary who, as Peter Storey's wife, felt unable to work in the situation that had arisen between her husband and her boss. Peter Storey accepted that John Rees had been foolish, he had also to accept the verdict; but he felt he could not escape pastoral responsibility for a broken parishioner. Tutu, a pastor through and through himself, did not question this. What he *did* question was Peter Storey's refusal to admit John Rees's guilt. His final wistful comment on the matter was 'I only wish I had a friend like that'.

The John Rees affair, the one aspect of the Eloff Commission to hurt both the SACC and Tutu, emerged accidentally from the investigations. The Commission had not succeeded in proving any of its original accusations nor in discrediting the Council or its General Secretary. What had gone wrong for Pretoria?

They seem to have miscalculated the significance of the SACC on a number of levels. To start with they had not expected the Commission to become a world forum. The visible and vocal way in which the international community, particularly the Churches, rallied to the Council's support was a source of deep embarrassment. Impervious to world opinion though the South African government usually appears to be, it knew that to act against a body that had not been found guilty would be a judgment that could – and probably would – redound against it. Second, despite its own experience of Afrikaner unity under siege, it had not reckoned on the Council's capacity to draw closer against a common threat or taken account of the huge black membership of the SACC. Every assault against the Council, every accusation of involvement in the liberation struggle, was in fact a legitimatising of its role in the black community. With every attack the Council's credibility was increased rather than diminished.

Nor can the Commission have appreciated the extent to which it had entered the theological arena. This dimension proved to be its Achilles' heel, as a government claiming to be Christian could hardly be seen to behave, on so public a platform, in a way that was clearly unChristian. It was also caught out in a serious inconsistency. The Church was continually being told it must not be involved in politics (which meant the Church must not disagree with the government – those who agreed were not considered to be acting politically), yet the government had found itself involved in a debate that was, by its own implied admission, on the Church's territory. And in this matter it was a united Church; the State found that it was acting not just against a limb, but against the whole body. The Afrikaner Churches had been dismembered so long, had become so isolated from the body of the Christian Church, that memories of such unity were long forgotten. The Eloff Commission saw the ecumenical family at its best, taking one another's pain seriously, regarding a wound to one as a wound to all.

Most of all, it had reckoned without Desmond Tutu, in the whole affair the single most important person, both *ex officio* and through the charisma of his personality. Most Afrikaners are in thrall to an image of the black man as ignorant, slow, unsophisticated and gauche. The commissioners must have been perplexed to be faced with a profoundly spiritual man, who could run rings round them theologically and was at once widely travelled, witty and courteous, with a quicksilver mind and a disarming honesty.

As a result of some of the more damaging and vicious things that had been said and done in the course of the hearings, Tutu had elected to give evidence a second time. In this statement he not only illustrated the lives he and his countrymen led by giving a lengthy autobiographical sketch, he also drew attention to the way the police had 'sought to present a particular image of the SACC by a clever choice of words, by innuendo and by a kind of guilt by association' and, most relevantly, he brought the debate firmly back on to theological ground. As we have seen, Tutu's theology is, above all, incarnational. He is not much interested in the contemporary equivalent of medieval speculations as to how many angels could dance on the point of a needle; his theology is to do with the concerns of ordinary people in a particular place and time. So when the chief investigating officer asked him if the liberation struggle was part of the Church's role in South Africa, he responded by saying:

> You do not want biblical exegesis every time you ask me a question, but I think I have to indicate to you that liberation, setting free, is a key concept of the Bible. The paradigmatic event in the Bible is the Exodus, the setting free of a rabble of slaves . . . we are participating in God's glorious movement of setting his people free.

Nor should the light touch he brought to the proceedings be forgotten. For instance, when asked if he had indeed made a certain pronouncement about apartheid, he responded ruefully that they ought to have discovered by now 'that I sound like a cracked record, I am so repetitive'. On another occasion, for once slow to answer as he was engrossed in his written evidence, he apologised for not replying, explaining that 'I was reading. Sometimes I am surprised at the things I say.' His humour and honesty made him a powerful and persuasive witness. He was open to accusations made against his administration, willing to take the skeletons on board, a response foreign to government ethos and in contrast to the way the truth had to be dragged out, piece by piece, in the recent Information Affair.

His personal success was won in the face of the media's efforts to discredit him. His youthful tuberculosis has left him with an atrophied hand, which he has a habit of rubbing. During a particularly unpleasant piece of evidence the cameras of the South African Broadcasting Corporation would focus on his wringing hands, as if to indicate his discomfort and guilt. This was something that upset him deeply and to which he still refers. Again during the Eloff Commission, the press misleadingly ran a 'Fingers in the Till' headline next to a picture of Tutu.

The Eloff Commission was emotionally a most testing and frustrating time for both the SACC and Desmond Tutu. For months and months every aspect of his private and public life was laid bare, questioned, scrutinised, criticised and often condemned. His time and energy were consumed and his work crippled by the constant onslaught of the hearings, his administration came under fire, he was not even given credit for the work he had done in dealing with the administrative and financial problems he had inherited.

But there were pearls among the grit. Despite attempts to drive wedges between the staff, it was, said Peter Storey (whose rift with

Bishop Tutu over the John Rees affair was soon healed), 'A magnificent witness to our togetherness. Through it all ran a serene confidence in the righteousness of our cause, the knowledge that God would triumph.' The Council was forced to examine and re-evaluate itself, the solidarity of the world Church was reaffirmed. In Dan Vaughan's words, 'Eloff turned the Council around. Eloff was, under God, the best thing that could have happened.' There were, in a sense, no winners. The State had not been able to prove its case against the SACC; for the SACC the Inquiry had been costly and time-consuming and had led to the trial and conviction of John Rees, deeply distressing for the staff of the SACC, many of whom had known and admired him. But at last the SACC and Tutu were vindicated and free to continue their work. David's small stone of truth had prevailed against the Goliath of the State.

14

Voice of the voiceless

One reason behind the Eloff Commission's inability to discredit the SACC was the international standing of its General Secretary. Ironically, the publicity surrounding the Inquiry attracted more attention to both Tutu and the SACC, leading to yet more invitations to speak. By the time the Commission's findings were published Tutu had become an even wider-travelled spokesman for his people. All over the world he articulated the plight of the blacks of South Africa, becoming a voice for his voiceless people as he showed, with a passionate conviction which brooked no disagreement, that apartheid is evil, immoral and vicious and inconsistent with the Gospel of Jesus Christ. As he became known and respected, not only in the Church but in the United Nations, in universities and in government circles, and as his statements gained prominence in the press of every country he visited, so he became an increasing irritant to the South African government.

His emergence on to the international scene was gradual. He made countless friends during his student days at King's College, London, and yet more as he travelled to the countries of the Third World for the Theological Education Fund. While he was Dean of Johannesburg and Bishop of Lesotho he went overseas occasionally – for instance in 1976 acting as Theological Consultant at a meeting of the Anglican Consultative Council in Port of Spain, Trinidad, and the following year addressing a convocation at Saskatoon.

His first appearance before the world-wide Anglican community was when he attended the 1978 Lambeth Conference, where he was on the steering committee and where, as chairman of a section entitled 'What Is the Church For?', he was responsible for a document on social issues, including the potentially explosive subject of the ordination of women. It was a measured, irenic debate, opposing factions agreeing to disagree and declaring that the Church's unity as a family transcended their differences. The resulting document recognised that in some provinces the ordination of women was already an accomplished fact and urged sensitivity from those on all sides of the debate. Tutu, himself – after long deliberation – in favour of women priests, felt it was really 'a permissive resolution', enabling Churches who wished to ordain women to do so. In fact he felt able to respond to a letter from an English Deaconess by telling her that if she were to apply for ordination in five years' time, she might well be accepted. 'But I hope very much that you will not wear a dog-collar. Nothing puts me off women in the ministry more than that and I am sure they can find something more feminine and attractive!'[1] History has shown that this was an optimistic judgment, but at least he was among those refusing to sit on the fence on this controversial subject.

He also made a dramatic personal impact. The Ugandan Bishops present at the conference knew that President Idi Amin had sent spies after them and their understandable tension found great relief in a smiling, joking Desmond, coming in like a hurricane as he greeted old friends and made new ones. Suddenly he became the spokesman, the symbol, of the Church in Africa. He even enlivened the restrained Anglican worship by leading them, African-style, in singing, dancing and hand-clapping. 'How often your smiling face and bright eyes come to mind when reflecting on Lambeth,' wrote the Bishop of Nevada. 'Your presence, your joy, your faith, but above all you – was one of the great benefits of that gathering.'[2]

For Tutu it was 'the experience of a lifetime'. Deeply Anglican as he is, he was fascinated by this gathering of the leaders of the Anglican communion – 'fat bishops, lean bishops, white bishops, jogging bishops' – awed by experiencing the continuity of history as they met on the modern campus of the University of Kent overlooking Canterbury Cathedral. When he returned to South Africa he reflected on the strange phenomenon that is the Anglican community. Twenty-seven self-governing provinces consisting of nearly 400 dioceses stretching from the Arctic to Australia, from the South Pacific to the North Sea; a community embracing nearly 70 million people of all tongues, complexions and cultures yet having no central authority but reaching their decisions through a process of consultation:[3]

> It really has no reason to exist in a world that is so fissiparous, yet it continues . . . The Anglican Communion continues to baffle all outsiders, because it is a family with all the tensions and differences, loves and hates, squabbles and agreements that characterize a family. Yes, we have the peculiar Anglican genius for accommodating all kinds of views in this extraordinary attribute called our comprehensiveness.

While he was in England Tutu gave an address to the Royal Commonwealth Society in which he said many of the things he was to repeat again and again all over the world. He urged the international community to apply diplomatic and economic pressures on South

Africa to avert the impending holocaust. He assured them that the blacks were on the winning side and that there was a new breed of young blacks who feared neither the police nor death. There was no doubt that the oppressed people were going to be free and when that day came the black community would remember who their friends were. The blacks had no wish to drive white South Africans into the sea, but if they were frustrated for too long, then white fears could become self-fulfilling prophecies. He said he feared that only a miracle could avert 'the alternative too ghastly to contemplate' but if the international community were alive to the situation and took action there was still time to effect a reasonably peaceful change. If these words have a familiar ring today, it must be remembered that this was 1978, only two years after the Soweto disturbances and long before the role of the international community in South African affairs had become something the newspaper reading public took in with their morning coffee.

In May 1979, Desmond and Leah visited the United States at the invitation of Bishop Jack Spong, one of the Bishops who had assisted at Desmond's own consecration. For a month Tutu worked as assistant Bishop in the Diocese of Newark, sharing in the pastoral work that he loves, taking confirmations and preaching, happy in an ethnically mixed diocese whose permanent staff included Koreans and Japanese priests and where Bishops from the Third World were encouraged to come and share their insights and experience. Inevitably he found himself asked to speak about the political situation in South Africa and though he would raise the question of the apartheid system being upheld by foreign investment, he refrained from calling explicitly for sanctions, knowing that such a call could have brought a charge of economic sabotage and the possibility of a five-year prison sentence. Similarly, in Boston, though he spoke on migrant labour and deplored the way the South African economy was built on the destruction of black family life, he was careful to avoid openly advocating disinvestment, simply telling his audience the consequences of apartheid policy. It was, however, later that year that he visited Copenhagen, where he made the much publicised remark about his disappointment that Denmark was still importing South African coal. Early in 1980 his passport was withdrawn.

The convoluted story of Tutu's passport, with its overtones of the school playground and the 'ya-boo' element of a child taking away his playmate's football, reflects poorly on the way the South African government has sought to control its turbulent priest. The government holds that it does not have to give reasons for issuing or refusing a passport – it is a privilege, not a right. Tutu, by making public statements that were, in South African law, only just on the right side of treason, had forsworn that privilege.

The first time his passport was seized was on March 4th, 1980. He was about to begin a service of thanksgiving for Robert Mugabe's election as Prime Minister of Zimbabwe, when two men, one a security policeman, arrived with an order withdrawing his passport. The reaction was immediate and world-wide. In seeking to silence Tutu the government had only succeeded in giving him yet more publicity. It even ran the risk of turning him into a martyr. Black leaders, in the company of the United Nations, condemned the action; messages of support came from American Church leaders and politicians; children from St James's Church in Madison Avenue sent 'passports of love'; the Archbishop of Canterbury, Dr Robert Runcie, led twenty-four Anglican Primates from all round the world in a statement deploring the action. It even caused comment in the South African House of Assembly, where Helen Suzman asked, 'Why infuriate blacks throughout South Africa by confiscating Bishop Tutu's passport? That was a petty, spiteful action and it did the government no good with thinking people in South Africa and with democratically minded people overseas.'[4]

She was right. It did not do the government much good with anyone, nor did it daunt Tutu. He pointed out that his speeches at home were so widely reported in the foreign press that his physical absence overseas would not silence his voice. Perhaps, he suggested, the government's real purpose was to test the measure of overseas reaction?

He has never feared authority. In 1978, when his passport was taken away at Maseru Bridge and he found his name was on the police files, he wrote to the security police demanding to know why he was on that blacklist, since at the time he travelled through other border posts in southern Africa without difficulty. He also protested at the discourteous way he was treated by a police constable who had said to him in Afrikaans: 'Desmond, *is jy stout?*' (Desmond, are you naughty?):[5]

> I am a Bishop of the Church and a leader of the churches in this country and would expect that every member of the public would be treated courteously by civil servants whatever his status. I want to point out that unless I get a satisfactory response from you on both these counts that I am going to take this matter up at the highest level in the Government.

It would have been interesting to see the expression on the faces of the police as they read these commanding words from someone they were accustomed to consider as merely 'a cheeky Kaffir'. His reaction to the seizure of his passport was equally dignified. He informed the authorities that he would be going on with the work God had given him and if they were trying to intimidate him they were wasting their time.

Clearly, however, it was extremely frustrating. The intermittent withdrawals of his passport, the refusals of his applications for its renewal, forced Tutu to turn down countless invitations to overseas conferences, synods and assemblies. It also prevented him from receiving personally the awards that were beginning to be heaped upon him.

The first was from his old college, King's College, London, which elected him an Honorary Fellow in March 1978. Honorary doctorates from the General Theological Seminary of New York and the University of Kent in England followed swiftly. Whether or not he could receive these awards personally depended, in each case, on the whim of the South African government. One of the highlights of his 1979 visit to the United States was when he was able to receive an Hon. LL.D from Harvard University, who recognised him as 'a Churchman of great faith and courage willing to risk his life on behalf of freedom and dignity for all people in South Africa'.[6] He found the occasion both touching – he was given a standing ovation by the 20,000 people present – and awesome, the ten others being honoured including the conductor Sir George Solti, Jean Jacques Cousteau ('who does funny things under water'),[7] the Nobel Prize-winning economist Milton Friedman and Helmut Schmidt, who was guarded by a phalanx from the secret service. On the other hand, though he had hoped to receive his honorary doctorate from Aberdeen University in person – indeed he had wired cheerfully 'Have passport, can travel' – his telegram had barely reached Scotland before he was once again without a passport. He was the first person ever to be awarded an honorary doctorate by the Ruhr University in West Germany, but again he could not be there; nor – most notably – could he attend the commencement exercises at Columbia University, where he was to have been awarded an honorary doctorate of Sacred Theology in May 1982.

In a moving address the university's President, Michael I. Sovern, explained that the empty chair on the platform would be left vacant until Tutu could fill it. Their absent guest was 'a beacon of hope and decency in a dark land and we want to help keep that light burning. We want him to know that we care. We want the government of South Africa to know that the world is watching. And we want to reaffirm our own humanity by presuming to claim that he and we are brothers.' Columbia University does not award degrees *in absentia*, so, for only the third time in its 228-year history (the other two people thus honoured were Abraham Lincoln, whose movements were restricted by the Civil War and a Judge of the Supreme Court, unable to travel through ill-health), they decided to award the degree off campus: 'To express our respect, with the highest honour in the gift of the University, we would go to the ends of the earth.'

So Dr Sovern and a small group of his colleagues applied for visas to South Africa, openly stating that their reason for visiting the country was 'to confer an award on Bishop Tutu'. They arranged to borrow the great hall of the University of the Witwatersrand, packed their academic caps and gowns and flew to Johannesburg. The hall was filled to overflowing when, on August 3rd, 1982, in a ceremony combining European academic splendour with African music from his favourite trio[8] (who sang in Xhosa a song which included the words 'How long, dear God, are we going to slave? How long this enslavement, this oppression?'), Bishop Tutu was awarded his fifth honorary doctorate.

Despite the restrictions on his movements overseas, whenever Tutu was granted the 'privilege' of a passport he used it well; apart from Pope John Paul II, he must be the most travelled churchman of his time. Of the numerous trips he made while he was General Secretary of the South African Council of Churches, three deserve special mention.

First there was the extensive tour of cities in Europe and America he made in 1981. In January of that year, when for ten months he had been unable to leave South Africa, his passport was returned and he was in a position to consider some of the invitations he had been forced to refuse. Peter Storey, at the time President of the SACC, encouraged him not just to respond to requests, but to set up a major itinerary across the world. Though in many ways the staff of the SACC had been relieved to have their General Secretary in one place for a while, there was a need for him to re-establish face-to-face contacts with their overseas partners. Equally both Tutu and the Council wanted to alert leaders in Church and State to the deteriorating situation in their country and to enlist their support in persuading the South African government to negotiate a settlement of the national crisis.

He left South Africa on March 4th, going first to Switzerland, where, in an hour long meeting at the Foreign Ministry, he stressed the need for the international community to apply political, diplomatic and above all economic pressures to bring the South African government to the negotiating table. He also suggested that the Swiss government show its disapproval of apartheid by demanding visas from South African nationals entering Switzerland, a suggestion that led to a long discussion of the meaning of neutrality and the inability of a neutral country to involve itself directly in the affairs of another State. He spent several days each in West Germany, Sweden, Norway and Denmark, and by March 20th he was in America, where he had a long meeting with Dr Waldheim, the Secretary-General of the United Nations, met Mrs Jeane Kirkpatrick, the United States Ambassador to the United Nations, and addressed the United Nations Special Committee Against Apartheid. At this meeting he is reported to have described the racial society of South Africa as 'one of the most vicious systems since Nazism' and to have again appealed for international economic pressure on the South African government on behalf of his 'voiceless' black compatriots. On to London, where he met the Lord Privy Seal, Sir Ian Gilmour, was interviewed by BBC Television's *Panorama* and, in a sermon in Westminster Abbey, accused certain Western countries and big business of 'a conspiracy to keep South African blacks in bondage'. He also admitted, in a public address, that he had 'decreased enthusiasm for another meeting between the SACC and the government because the government has not shown itself ready to move from its intransigence'. On his way back to South Africa he stopped off in Rome, where he met the Pope for the first time. Though on this occasion he just had a privileged place at a general audience in St Peter's Square, in 1983 he had a private audience, when he was able to discuss personally with the Pope the current situation in South Africa. In those days, before he had become accustomed to moving amongst eminent luminaries, he would come out of such meetings amazed that they had taken place, saying 'Pinch me, is it true?' Dan Vaughan, who was with him in Rome, remembers that Tutu was untypically nervous, delighted at the medals given to commemorate the occasion and highly amused that Dan, a Baptist, should meet the Supreme Pontiff.

On April 9th, 1981, Tutu arrived back in South Africa to a hero's welcome. Among the joyful crowd welcoming him was Peter Storey, who sensed that having met world statesmen and held his own had given him a new confidence. He also appreciated the 'weight on those very little shoulders' and the knowledge that as they walked out of the airport, through the jostling crowd, there could so easily be someone who wished him dead. 'One also sensed on that return that here was someone who knew – perhaps he had always known – that he came back as someone with destiny on his shoulders. A sense of having to be the instrument of his people's liberation, to be their spokesman.'

Prime Minister P. W. Botha must have had the same feeling. In a political rally in the Orange Free State he repeated his conviction that a passport was 'a favour from the State' and that Tutu had exploited it. 'As far as I am concerned, when he returns, his passport will be taken away.' It was. This came as no surprise to Tutu, who had thought it probable that he would also be banned or put under house arrest. The day after his return, on the eve of Good Friday, his passport was withdrawn for the second time in just over a year. It was as well he had used it with so much energy and courage.

One September afternoon in 1982, this time after nearly eighteen months without a passport, Tutu was attending the afternoon session of the Eloff Commission hearings in Pretoria when the proceedings were interrupted by officials bearing a limited 'travel document' for himself and Leah. It was more a letter of identity than a passport, it did not say where he had been born and opposite 'Nationality' it bore the offensive words 'Undeterminable at present', but at least it allowed him to attend the Triennial Convention of the Episcopal Church, USA, in New Orleans. Before the week was out the Tutus were on their way to the States.

Many people had been working for the return of Tutu's passport, this partial success being eventually achieved by none less than George Bush, the Vice-President of the United States and himself, along with many members of the United States government, an Episcopalian and one of the speakers at the 1982 Convention.

On this trip Tutu refrained from calling for economic pressure against Pretoria, but in no other way did he appear to be inhibited by fear of reprisal. He assured his audience that though South Africa's white rulers were powerful, they were scared, so busy protecting their privileged position that they could no longer enjoy it; that apartheid was not being dismantled, in fact in trying to co-opt the so-called 'coloureds' into Parliament the government was trying to reduce the proportional strength held by the Africans. Yet 'the people who are perpetrators of injury in our land are not sprouting horns or tails. They're just ordinary people like you and me. We are talking about ordinary people who are scared. Wouldn't you be scared if you were outnumbered five to one?'[9]

He made his audience laugh, suggesting that the Almighty himself must laugh at man's wilful, wayward behaviour – in South Africa an eighteen-year-old pimply white policeman, barely able to read or write, could, by virtue of his colour, exercise a vote while he, over fifty years old, a Bishop of the Church of God and the recipient of numerous academic degrees, could not. Among those present was

John Walker, the Bishop of Washington, who admits that at first the laughter was uncomfortable; soon, however, the audience realised that humour was being used to make a very real point about the problems of blacks in South Africa. Once Tutu knew they were on his side he became serious. 'He is *par excellence* a dramatist when he's speaking,' says Bishop Walker, 'and when he gets serious he takes you to the top of the mountain and you weep with him. He plays every emotional chord there is in the human body.'

The convention was electrified. They laughed, wept, clapped and roared their approval, constantly interrupting his address with bouts of spontaneous applause. When, after a fifteen-minute standing ovation, he left the hall, they could talk of nothing but this remarkable South African. For his part Tutu knew that the Episcopal Church of the United States was firmly on his side; he could say anything, do anything, and they would support him.

The travel document allowed the Tutus to be out of the country for nineteen days, so when the convention had ended they went to Kentucky to spend the weekend with their daughter Naomi and her American husband; it was not, however, an entirely domestic weekend. In a widely syndicated press interview Tutu said that apartheid in South Africa was far worse now than five years ago, when Steve Biko had died in jail. He feared that the authorities were resisting peaceful change, citing signs such as the recent death of two government opponents in jail and the limitations imposed on black activists by the extension of banning orders. Once again he deplored the provocative exclusion of the black majority from the limited power-sharing proposed for Asians and 'coloureds'. He feared that 'unless something happens quickly, we may be faced with Armageddon'. Before he returned to South Africa he met Dr Chester Crocker, the Assistant Secretary of State for African Affairs, and gave a major news conference. He loves America and the American people, but he has frequently criticised the Reagan administration. On this occasion he reminded the press that though the administration might have won him travel papers, its policy of 'constructive engagement' had not stopped banning orders or detention without trial. He also repeated his criticism of the proposed (but eventually withdrawn) Orderly Movement and Settlement of Black Persons Bill. He said it was the National Party's final solution for blacks, rather as the Nazis had a final solution for Jews.

Every time Tutu wanted to travel during the early 1980s he had to apply to the Department of Internal Affairs for permission, each case being 'considered on its merits' and most of them refused. He was, for instance, unable to accept an invitation to preach at St Paul's Cathedral. Even a formal protest to the South African Ambassador in London by the Dean of St Paul's, together with the Principal, Vice-Principal and Dean of King's College and seventeen of its Fellows, was met with a further refusal. But suddenly, while Tutu was in hospital having minor surgery on his nose, he received permission to attend the Sixth Assembly of the World Council of Churches in Vancouver. The Assembly had already begun, so Tutu took the next plane to Vancouver, where he was met by the Archbishop of Canterbury.

The Sixth Assembly was a huge affair. A thousand delegates from all over the world celebrated both their unity and their diversity as they sang Orthodox *Kyrie Eleisons* and Zimbabwean *Hallelujah's* in the great yellow-and-white striped tent that was the focus of the conference and met in groups, formulating the World Council of Churches' policy for the next seven years. Bishop Tutu arrived on the evening of the Feast of the Transfiguration, during a vigil for peace and justice linked with the anniversary of the dropping of the atomic bomb on Hiroshima and to which the whole of Vancouver had been invited. After a few hours' sleep he addressed the assembly. It was one of those events which no one present will ever forget.

It was five minutes to midnight. For nearly six hours there had been singing and dancing and worship. The procession, holding balloons and pigeons, had arrived at the tent, where they had held a solemn service of dedication and commitment to peace. They knew of the problems the delegate from the South African Council of Churches had been facing; they knew he had suddenly been given permission to come. There was, as Martin Conway, one of the British delegates, found, 'a tremendous sense of expectation and hero worship. You can just imagine the lionising we were all ready for.' It was a delicate moment to handle, in fact there were those who wondered whether the organisers had made the right decision in putting one of the delegates in this critical and exposed position. They need not have feared. 'I really cannot exaggerate how astonishingly right it was,' Martin Conway remembers:

> Every touch in it was simply marvellous. It was brief, people were tired and if he'd gone on even a few minutes longer it would have been too much after that long day. It was absolutely right in terms of this world-wide assembly. It was deeply prayerful. It was completely aware both of South Africa and of the rest of the world. I recall that as a moment of the most deeply winning Christian charm, of which no one else in the world would have been capable.

It was Desmond Tutu at his best. Sensing the mood of his audience and responding to it, humorous (even in that setting he drew a laugh by referring to the 'few local problems' they had had in South Africa), God-centred, fully aware of dramatic effect and, as so often, grateful. He reminded his audience of Zachariah speaking about Yahweh as a wall of fire around Jerusalem: 'It's been almost like a physical sensation, sometimes, when the powers of evil seem to be on the rampage, then we have experienced Yahweh in your prayers, like a wall of fire, keeping away the evil.' He ended by repeating the word 'Amen' until it was so soft that you could have heard an angel pass.

When Tutu first came to the States in the early 1970s he was an unknown black South African Bishop, relieved to be given a break from the claustrophobic atmosphere of his own country, hoping to raise money from wealthy and generous bodies such as the Ford Foundation and the National Council of Churches; if not exactly 'cap-in-hand' (he has too much dignity for that epithet ever to fit), he was certainly petitioner rather than petitioned. He stayed with the Rockwells in their New York apartment, sleeping in the room their young daughter Martha was happy to vacate for him. Háys Rockwell noticed how, after the award of the Harvard honorary doctorate, his friend became increasingly in demand; by the time of the commencement day ceremonies at Columbia University and the symbolic empty chair, he was a well-known figure receiving regular press coverage.

Typically of this small man, whose heart and mind span so vast a spectrum of human characteristics, the effect he has on Americans ranges from awed reverence to accusations of demagoguery. What is the nature of this impact? How much did he change American perceptions of the South African situation?

In America, as everywhere, Bishop Tutu is first and foremost a preacher and a pastor. Not only because he was initially invited as a churchman, carrying the credibility of the institution before he made his personal reputation, but because he is so infused by his priesthood that the man and the role cannot be disentangled. America's glittering, voracious variety is reflected in the three New York churches with which he is most closely connected. There is the suburban parish of St Simon's with its congregation of upper middle-class black professionals; then the wealthy, white parish of St James's in Madison Avenue, whose Rector, Hays Rockwell, had met Tutu in 1976; and thirdly the Church of the Intercession, a huge parish adjacent to a mixed-race community in upper Harlem. Here the congregation is almost entirely black, two-thirds speaking English and a third Spanish;

they also host a Marthoma community – about 300 Tamil-speaking Indians under the protection of the Bishop of New York. Tutu is equally at home in all three parishes.

Much of the impact he has on the macrocosm of the country can be seen in his effect on the microcosm of these parishes. Their congregations responded eagerly to his enthusiastic, rousing sermons, to the eucharistic nature of his ministry, to his insistence that Christians are 'prisoners of hope'. 'He is transparently a vehicle of God's grace,' says Canon Williams of Intercession Church. 'Our people see that and they respond to his authenticity and his integrity.' Joan Campbell, a priest in the Church of the Disciples of Christ, goes even further: 'Bishop Tutu helps me to understand what a saint is, if you believe that a saint is someone that the light shines through, even for a brief period. He illumines the truth for us.' So, too, his pastoral attention is constantly appreciated – from remembering someone's heavy cold four months earlier to sharing a friend's grief at the death of her elderly mother. Hays Rockwell is still touched at the memory of Bishop Tutu telephoning him after he had stood, unsuccessfully, for election as Bishop. 'In some part of you there is disappointment and I am calling to speak to that little part.'

His wider role in America was as a vehicle of information. Though America was waking up to the situation in South Africa and though organisations like Trans-Africa played an important part in this slow process, Tutu's contribution is significant enough to earn the praise of those in sympathy with him and infuriate some of those who are not. In America's complex society a distinction must be made between his effect on the black and the white community.

Of course white Americans had heard of apartheid, but South Africa is a long way from the United States and conditions there seemed very remote; in any case, unlike the English, Americans have no blood ties with South Africa. There was too, a certain resistance to the issue; their own civil rights movement was too recent, guilt over their involvement in slavery too pervasive.

Many Americans tended to equate their own civil rights movement with black South Africans' struggle against apartheid. They did not all realise that in South Africa it is the law itself which is against the majority of its citizens. Tutu, speaking to an American audience, expressed the difference:[10]

> Ours is of course not a civil rights movement. You here were claiming what was guaranteed to you under your Constitution. The law was at least theoretically on your side. At home we are struggling for fundamen-

tal human rights and we are excluded by the Constitution from any meaningful participation in decision making. The law of the land is against us.

There was also ignorance of a kind bound to affect their reaction to any black coming from South Africa. Most Americans believed, as they were encouraged by Pretoria to believe, that blacks in opposition to white government were terrorists; they knew nothing of Oliver Tambo and only a few had heard of Nelson Mandela. Through Desmond Tutu they saw black opposition in a different light. He was able to make apartheid real, to bring home to them just how black South Africans live, how long they have suffered and what patience they have showed. 'He was just extraordinary,' says Caroline Macomber, a member of St James's congregation. 'None of us had had any contact with this issue. It was a revelation – he was the ideal spokesman. Not everyone believed him at first, but slowly and surely they were converted.' They were not only converted, they were proud, especially the Church leaders. A Methodist minister admits that 'For once a Christian was at the face front, not just sucked in and following'. American Christians had found a spokesman who could address them on one of the most crucial issues of the day.

Tutu has his critics in the United States, though few of them know the Bishop personally and most are unwilling to go on record as to the exact reason for their criticisms. The largest contingent is among fundamentalist Christians, many of whom are suspicious of a priest who seeks to change the social order, fearful that their theological beliefs will be subverted by his radical stand, threatened by his role as a leader both in and outside the Church. Slinging his arrows with the greatest venom was the television evangelist Jerry Falwell, the leader of the so-called Moral Majority; his accusations that the Bishop is 'a phoney' were widely criticised and Falwell himself somewhat discredited by making them. Tutu has a predictable and more formidable critic in the South African Ambassador, Herbert Beukes. Ambassador Beukes claims that the South African government is willing to negotiate and that Tutu knows very well that it is. In the company of other white leaders, he criticises Tutu for not condemning the exiled African National Congress and complains that 'he has caused greater division than healing'.[11] A few feel that he is facilitating a takeover by radical blacks; others complain at his temperance, urging him to endorse the revolution. His oratorical skill and his ability to sway the emotions of his audience opens him to accusations of demagoguery, notably from Elliot Abrams, an Under-Secretary in the State Department, and Patrick Buchanan, President Reagan's chief media adviser, who charged that 'whatever his moral splendour, the Bishop is a political ignoramus'.[12]

Though Tutu's stand on sanctions attracts criticism from white American businessmen, who consider his statements irresponsible and say that the consequences of what he is advocating would be the destruction of the country, few black leaders of any significance disagree with him. Even those not in total agreement with him remain convinced that he has the welfare of his people at heart and that he would not recommend economic measures if he could see any alternative. He is also considered a valuable counterweight to the Sullivan Principles, whose admirable concern for providing better working conditions for black South Africans does little to overthrow the actual structures of apartheid; in fact Leon Sullivan himself (who has since given up on 'Constructive Engagement'and backed the call for United States withdrawal from South Africa) is said to have a high personal regard for him. While extravagant claims have been made for Tutu's contribution to the sanctions debate in America – there have been suggestions, for instance, that he has done more than any other single person to influence the American people, and thus Congress, to favour sanctions – it is hard to overestimate his influence. The decision of the labour unions to back sanctions was more weighty, more crucial, but the eminent black Washington lawyer Vernon Jordan is probably right in saying that though Tutu alone has not swayed the American people, it could not have been done without him.

The black American community does not accept uncritically those who speak for it or for black people overseas. According to Dr William Howard, the Executive Director of the Black Council of the Reformed Church in America:

> The black community sits in constant evaluation and judgment of people like Desmond who emerge. They have seen leaders emerge and be overtaken by events and they constantly review, because for them leaders are not static. They have a sense that the outcome of the South African situation is directly related to their own destiny, so Desmond is one of their champions, because he is advancing a cause of which they are an integral part.

American blacks, better informed about apartheid and identifying with South African blacks in a way impossible for American whites, look back at their own long history of oppression, back to slavery, back to their struggle for civil rights, and they are in solidarity with Tutu. 'We recognise the cadences of oppression, he strikes a responsive chord because we recognise him as one of our own. He has incarnated the South African struggle for us, so that it has become our struggle,' says Canon Williams. Further, the Church is the strongest organised base of black Americans, automatically giving its spokesmen stature. But Tutu's high standing in the black community was earned, not given.

It was earned by the way he personalised the South African situation in a way equalled only by Dr Allan Boesak, through his ability to speak with theological authority and challenge apartheid as morally indefensible. It was earned by his ability to transcend all divisions and reach the broader community. Most of all it was earned by his determination to seek justice through peaceful means and his courage in speaking out in full knowledge of the risks. To Vernon Jordan he is 'A voice of conscience, a voice of reason, a voice of moderation, a voice of daring, fearlessly fighting against the oppressive system of apartheid and willing to put his life on the line to save other lives.'

To his own embarrassment and to the irritation of many of his friends (who see it as irrelevant), Tutu finds himself being likened to the civil rights leader Martin Luther King. Though King was a Baptist, Tutu an Anglican, though King's reserve is in contrast to Tutu's sparkle and wit, with both men being black ministers, both speaking out of a sense of moral outrage, both passionately affirming the humanity of every individual person, both advocates of non-violence – the comparison is inevitable. The minister and politician Jesse Jackson, who feels Desmond Tutu's stature is such that he should be seen in the prophetic tradition with Jesus Christ and Mahatma Gandhi, came back from a visit to South Africa in 1979 claiming to have met 'the Martin Luther King of South Africa ... his manner, his steadfastness, his blend of the infrastructure of the Church on the one hand and his calling beyond the Church on the other' recalling the civil rights leader. The journalist Allistair Sparks pointed out that both men were Christians with a mission, rather than politicians with a strategy, both have a streak of militancy within their moderation, both have a way with words, though Tutu's 'in a style with more of a cutting edge than King's rolling rhetoric'.[13] Dr Howard feels that Tutu has Martin Luther King's ability 'to hew a stone of hope from a mountain of despair'.

It is Tutu's outspoken remarks about apartheid and his calls for support from the international community that bring him into the headlines, but his role as a fund-raiser, though less visible, is a constant undercurrent to his trips. His charisma acts as a magnet to money; it is drawn from every source – individuals, churches, foundations – sometimes even before he asks. Hays Rockwell was one of the first to form a bond between his rich parish and the poor diocese of Lesotho (of which Tutu was then Bishop) when he became

Rector of St James's Church, so twice Tutu was the beneficiary of a portion (about one-third) of the annual spring festival, an event which brings in as much as $60,000 dollars a year. Smaller amounts come in from the most surprising sources. Mary Barbour is a retired and very poor seamstress who used to make costumes for the Dance Theatre of Harlem and attends Intercession Church. Though her hands are stiff and painful with rheumatoid arthritis, she took small sewing jobs, talked to her friends and eventually told her priest, Canon Williams, that she had collected some money. He suggested that she should come to a party being given for the Bishop and present the money to him herself. Timidly, she eventually agreed and, with the words 'So that our people can be free', she handed him an envelope. To everyone's amazement it contained $1,000. Then, feeling around in her pocket and saying 'I don't think that's enough for all the fine work you've done', she handed him a second envelope, containing another $1,000.

Some members of the professional funding community feel that Tutu oversimplifies the sanctions issue and that he is an unsubtle analyst of power structures; they notice too, that his name is too often used to underwrite projects, sometimes even without his knowledge. However, these reservations do not affect their willingness to finance him, though they do influence the causes to which they are prepared to give money. In fund-raising the proof of the pudding is in the eating, and the amount he has raised (in one way or another he was responsible for raising the entire SACC budget, which rose to R4 million in 1984) shows what success he had. William Carmichael of the Ford Foundation found him not only articulate, engaging and endearingly grateful, but a good correspondent, who keeps in touch and knows how to respond to queries. And if his reports are sometimes late, they are by no means the latest.

Desmond Tutu's trips to America resulted in funds for numerous projects to help his people and led to millions of people knowing something about the reality of the conditions under which South Africans were living. With every trip his friends grew more numerous and his fame increased. Soon he was to become a household name.

15

A kind of sacrament

At nine o'clock on October 15th, 1984, a limousine pulled up at the General Theological Seminary on New York's Ninth Avenue and the Norwegian Ambassador to the United Nations emerged carrying a huge bunch of yellow lilies, blue irises and red zinnias. He was shown up to the Tutus' flat, where he told the nervously awaiting couple that Desmond Tutu had been awarded the Nobel Peace Prize.

It did not come as a complete surprise. It was widely known that Tutu had, for the third time, been nominated for the prestigious award and the world's press had been gathering on Ninth Avenue since six o'clock; indeed, the night before the Ambassador had telephoned the Dean, James Fenhagen, to ensure that the Bishop would be free to see him. Dean Fenhagen had had the pleasurable task of giving the Tutus the news, at the same time alerting everyone at the seminary, who had been praying that the Ambassador's call really meant that their visiting lecturer (he was in the middle of a three-month sabbatical, taking a course in Contemporary Ecclesiology) had indeed been chosen. Within minutes of their hopes being confirmed the chapel bells were pealing and the entire staff – students and lecturers, cooks and maintenance men, along with various friends and neighbours – had assembled in the chapel. The campus was deserted and silent as the Dean, the Ambassador and the Tutus walked across to join them. After the thunderous applause which greeted their arrival there was a joyful rendition of 'Now Thank We All Our God', prayers of gratitude and a short address from the emotional and overcome Bishop.

Then the seminary gates were opened, the press poured in and Desmond Tutu became the property of the world. He was interviewed and photographed, he was on television morning, noon and night, he received telephone calls, telegrams and letters by the hundred, he was fêted daily, recognised wherever he went. The seminary had never seen anything like it. Calls came from all over the world as Prime Ministers, Kings and film stars, old friends and colleagues, rang to send their congratulations until the overworked switchboard broke down; a student was assigned to help with the mail but it soon became clear that a full-time secretary was needed. The staff tried to protect the man at the centre of it all, but he seemed tireless as, with shy delight and a humility and gratitude that was universally recognised as genuine, he responded to the endless demands.

His own reaction was to stress the corporate nature of the award. He saw it as a recognition of the patient suffering of his people, a tribute to the significance of the Church's contribution to their struggle, an affirmation of the justness of their case, a 'tremendous political statement', and 'a kind of sacrament, a wonderful symbol'. He knew that the award was a tremendous boost to the morale of the South African blacks. 'Hey, we are winning,' he declared. 'Justice is going to win.' And he knew that his place at this time was with his own people. After two hectic days in New York he and Leah, together with Naomi and Mpho, who were both in the United States at the time, flew to Johannesburg.

At Heathrow, where they stopped to change planes, they were greeted by the Archbishop of Canterbury and a group of distinguished churchmen. Terry Waite caused much amusement by welcoming the passengers disembarking from the British Airways Concorde with, 'The Archbishop greets all passengers, it's part of the deal', until eventually the Tutus, last off the plane, could accept the welcome themselves. There was just time for embraces, laughter and a vivacious news conference – at which he said most of the £160,000 prize money would go into a trust to help young blacks to study, but he and his family might enjoy a little of it themselves – and he was on the next plane.

A security police officer at Jan Smuts Airport had tried to prevent the waiting crowd from singing – singing was not allowed in the hall, he declared – but as soon as the Tutus appeared the jubilant crowd ignored his instructions and exploded into a rapturous welcome. Several hundred people, members of the South African Council of Churches, fellow clergymen, familiar friends and unknown supporters, surged round him, waving banners saying 'Welcome Baba' and 'Apartheid Goodbye', cheering, singing, dancing. Every time the police managed to quieten one section of the crowd another simply took up the refrain; in despair one policeman said to Dan Vaughan, at the time Acting General Secretary of the SACC, that if the crowd did not disperse immediately they would set the dogs on them. At which Dan, secure in the knowledge that the television cameras would let the whole world see if such a thing were done, laughed and said, 'Please feel free!' Order was only imposed when the crowd wished it, as everyone stood still, Desmond and Leah with heads bowed, to sing *'Nkosi Sikele' iAfrika'*. It took the travellers almost an hour to make their way out of the airport; then the Tutus were taken to a hotel to have a rest before the celebratory lunch at the South African Council of Churches.

At Khotso House, the heart of Desmond Tutu's work, there was more embracing, laughing and singing as a gyrating, ululating human chain danced through the SACC's corridors and offices. Allan Boesak, who had flown up from Cape Town for the occasion, spoke about the great honour that had been bestowed on the General Secretary and on all the people of South Africa who had struggled so long against racism. The courageous Afrikaner Beyers Naudé, his voice breaking and on the edge of tears, said, 'I pray the day may come when my own people will understand something of the message you bring to black and white.'

There was an expectant hush when it came to Tutu's turn to speak, but typically he started singing a hymn in the Sotho language, 'Let Us All Give Praise To The Lord'. Only after giving thanks did he speak, and then it was to thank again: 'What does one say on an occasion such as this, except feebly, inadequately, thank you.' He went on to say how the award was for those 'whose noses are rubbed in the dust every day', the banned, the exiled, the detained; the mothers trying to support their families, the fathers living in single-sex hostels, the 3½ million people who had been forcibly resettled – 'uprooted and dumped as if they were rubbish', the children who refuse an education designed to make them inferior, for all who seek to change the evil system of apartheid peacefully.[1]

There were many celebrations in those few days. One especially near to his heart was a Thanksgiving service held at St Augustine's Church in Orlando West. A reporter for the *Sowetan* newspaper noted that as the Bishop warned 'Even if our enemies seek to destroy us, God will give us victory in the end', 'the heavens were ripped apart by a loud thunderclap, releasing a shower of rain. Elderly women wept. The heavens themselves were blessing Bishop Tutu as he stood at the altar thanking God for the award he had received.'[2] Then there was a feast, with a beast killed and the Sowetan choir Imilonji ka Ntu singing Xhosa and Sotho songs so movingly that Tutu removed the garland round his neck and placed it on the conductor, George Mxadana.

In choosing to celebrate the award with his own people Tutu had also to face a cruel barrage of criticism. The tragic divide between blacks (with a handful of whites) and the vast majority of white South Africa, was starkly revealed.

Amid all the rejoicing in the black community there was a deafening silence from Pretoria, just as there had been twenty-four years earlier when Chief Albert Luthuli won the prize. Whenever possible the government did not return calls from journalists; if caught on the telephone, for the most part they refused to make any official comment. President P. W. Botha and Foreign Minister 'Pik' Botha remained resolutely silent; the leader of the Conservative Party, Dr Andries Treurnicht, accused the Bishop of having threatened violence if government policy was not changed; the Minister of Internal Affairs, Mr F. W. de Klerk, pointed out that as Bishop Tutu had no passport he would have to apply for a travel document 'in the normal way' to receive the award in Norway. The South African Broadcasting Corporation (showing a curious news sense in view of the world-wide publicity) omitted all reference to the award in its afternoon news radio broadcast, but in the following *News Focus* programme subjected the Bishop to a ten-minute diatribe. It was suggested that the exuberant reaction to the award 'throws suspicion on the event' and that the Peace Prize had 'degenerated into an international political instrument'. Earlier awards to Albert Luthuli and Lech Wałesa were cited in a manner intended to throw doubt on the selection committee and Tutu's recent plea to a London audience, 'Do not abandon us, even – perhaps especially – if our struggle becomes violent', was used to show that his contribution to peace 'is neither remarkable nor consistent'.

The television news did cover the story; in the early evening it was placed sixth and given fifteen seconds, later it rose to fourth place and one minute's coverage. Needless to say there was no mention of the world-wide congratulations, no sight of the jubilant celebrations. The Afrikaans television service, attempting to show that while speaking of peaceful change, the Bishop in fact encouraged and promoted violence, showed footage of Tutu talking with his characteristic gesticulations, but soundless and apparently aggressive under the commentator's voice, until a phrase about a possible bloodbath was heard, out of context (a fate to which he has had to become accustomed) and shorn of the qualifying words with which he always surrounds such a statement.

Though some of the Afrikaans papers condemned the government's childish refusal to offer Tutu formal congratulations (notably *Die Vaderland*, whose editorial asserted that the Bishop was indeed advocating non-violent means for change), there were some vicious comments. *Beeld* referred to Tutu as 'the strangest recipient yet' and accused him of standing for anything but peace; *Die Transvaler* said Alfred Nobel could never have intended the prize to go to a man who, 'under the banner of the church, moves among the world's radicals and revolutionaries, and advocates violence as an option for our country's problems'.[3]

There were unenthusiastic, if predictable, reactions from people like the Reverend Fred Shaw, chairman of the Christian League, and from the conservative group, United Christian Action, who organised a protest and translated it into seven languages for world-wide distribution. Most surprising was an open letter in the *Sunday Times*, written by none other than Alan Paton, the author of *Cry the Beloved Country*, respected critic of apartheid and supporter of white protest. He objected to the award as a sign of world interference and criticised Tutu's views on sanctions, saying his morality was 'confused just as was the morality of the church in the Inquisition, or the morality of Dr Verwoerd in his utopian dreams'. With an extraordinary failure to understand Tutu's love and concern for his fellow blacks, he wrote: 'I do not understand how you can put a man out of work for a high moral principle.'[4] The following week Professor Charles Villa-Vicencio sprang to Tutu's defence, justifying the case for disinvestment as a strategy for reform and politely accusing Paton of being simplistic.[5]

The mixed reactions buffeted Tutu up and down, as he sought to maintain his equilibrium on a see-saw of venom and jubilation, assumed indifference and enthusiastic pride, resentment and delight. As at the General Seminary, the SACC's telex machine and switchboard worked overtime to keep up with the endless messages, even the local post office reeled under the weight of mail. Congratulations came from unexpected quarters – from a senior security policeman, a teenager living in a Pretoria suburb and the Coca-Cola company; also from university Professors, Ambassadors, Church leaders and heads of State; from Chief Gatsha Buthelezi and Oliver Tambo; from Dr Frederik van Zyl Slabbert and Mrs Helen Suzman; from Pope John Paul II, the Archbishop of Cape Town and a pastor of a small Winburg parish; from Lech Wałesa and Coretta Scott King; from Breyten Breytenbach and Nadine Gordimer; from Ronald Reagan, Walter Mondale, Neil Kinnock, Willy Brandt, Bob Hawke and Indira Gandhi. It was heady stuff.

The churlish critics were right in one thing, the Nobel Committee was indeed making a political statement – it made no bones about it. The text stated clearly that

> It is the Committee's wish that the Peace Prize now awarded to Desmond Tutu should be regarded not only as a gesture of support to him and to the South African Council of Churches of which he is leader, but

also to all individuals and groups in South Africa who, with their concern for human dignity, fraternity and democracy, incite the admiration of the world.

Later, when asked whether the choice of Bishop Tutu was meant to effect change in South Africa, the chairman of the committee agreed that it was. The argument against the award – shorn of bitterness and lies – was that political activism should not qualify for a peace prize. But the question went deeper. The Nobel Committee regarded apartheid itself as a threat to peace and argued that Tutu's continual resistance to racial oppression and his determination to oppose it peacefully unquestionably qualified him to receive the award.

Four of Tutu's pronouncements, considered unwise even by some of his supporters, had particularly fuelled white protest in South Africa: his references to economic pressures and disinvestment; his comparison of the apartheid system with the Nazi regime; his statement that the Russians would be welcome as liberators if they came to South Africa (made on the assumption that anything would be better than what the blacks were enduring); and his warning that a bloodbath was awaiting South Africa. He was criticised in particular for making these statements overseas, though, as he continually reminds his critics, he has said nothing abroad that he does not say at home. Whatever the rights and wrongs of his colourful way of speaking, he had succeeded in both stimulating and inspiring initiatives against apartheid and enraging the white community, who found the endorsement of his words and actions in so distinguished and public a way more than they could bear. Beyers Naudé, writing about the award, remarked that 'For the first time it seems as if a concerted action of disinvestment may get under way overseas and this creates a wave of uncertainty in the hearts of many whites who are concerned above all to hold on to their wealth, their privilege, and their power to the very last.'[6]

The significance of the award is immeasurable – the critics would not have been so vocal were it not so. It acknowledged both Tutu's role as a living symbol of the fight against apartheid and his success in communicating, with such passion and conviction, the agony, the humiliation and the aspirations of millions of his oppressed countrymen. Through the media exposure surrounding the award his message reached an even larger audience, focusing attention as never before on the problems of South Africa. The unacceptability of the new South African constitution, the inhumanity of forced removals, the indignity of the pass laws and the deep anger seething beneath the township unrest were brought to the attention of the world. Tutu was confirmed as a man of peace and his credibility increased, especially among his own people. Now he was an international figure, with access to heads of Church and State all over the world. It became harder for the government to harass or arrest him, virtually impossible for them to ignore him. It also placed an even greater responsibility on his small shoulders.

Desmond and Leah returned to America exhausted and content, but hurt by the official silence with which they had been greeted in South Africa. Tutu longed for the whites to 'stop treating me like an ogre'. His reception was, he said, 'as if I had raped a white woman'. But he does not easily harbour grudges and his first concern was to use the numerous opportunities he now had to spread awareness of the South African situation. Though he had hoped to find a little quiet during his three months on sabbatical at the General Seminary, the remainder of his time there was a whirlwind of interviews, addresses and meetings, not to mention his duties at the seminary which still had to be fulfilled. Dean Fenhagen was deeply impressed that through it all, even when in November his mother died and he and Leah had to return to South Africa for another short visit, he never missed a class or a seminary function.

That Tutu should have been in the United States when the award was made was a gift to the American media. His friend Frank Ferrari, the Senior Vice-President of the African–American Institute, remembers how 'He saturated the news. He got more space, more coverage, more copy than anything to do with South Africa ever had in the States. Whether Americans liked him or not, they saw him when they got up on the morning talk shows, they saw him on the evening talk shows and they went to bed with him on the late evening news.' Trans-Africa, a black-led anti-apartheid group that had come into being shortly after the Soweto killings in 1976, sprang into new life with a long series of picketings before the South African Embassy and daily demonstrations at which people put themselves forward for arrest. Jesse Jackson pointed out how the timing of the award, coming as it did just before the second Reagan–Mondale debate in the American election campaign, ensured that apartheid would be on the political agenda, just as the civil rights movement had come to the fore twenty years before, when Martin Luther King won the award. America was on the move, a growing majority of its people determined to make their government act against apartheid.

Two events stand out in this short and hectic period, the first being an invitation to Desmond Tutu to address the United Nations Security Council. Anyone seeking to use this address to prove their accusations against Tutu would have a hard time. It was gentle and reasoned, seeking to inform rather than inflame. He told them of an old lady he had met in one of the townships who looked after her grandchildren and the children of neighbours who were at work. One day her daughter burst in to the kitchen, calling for her. 'A grandson had fallen just inside the door, dead. The police had shot him in the back. He was six years old.' He commended President Botha for his courage in declaring that the future of South Africa could no longer be determined by whites only, but pointed out the inherent racism in the new constitutional proposals – that the first qualification for membership was racial and that this 'instrument in the politics of exclusion' was overwhelmingly rejected not only by the Africans who were denied a place (73 per cent of the population) but by a huge majority of the so-called 'coloureds' and Indians, who recognised it as perpetuating minority rule. He acknowledged the non-aggression treaty with Mozambique, the Nkomati Accord, but asked, 'Why is détente by the South African government only for export? Why is State aggression reserved for the black civilian population?' His statement contained no call for economic pressure, simply saying,[7]

> We ask you, please help us; urge the South African authorities to go to the conference table with the authentic sections of our community . . . Help us, that this freedom comes for all of us in South Africa, black and white, but that it comes with the least possible violence, that it comes peacefully, that it comes soon.

Since 1981, when Frank Ferrari introduced him to Senator Mark Hatfield, Tutu had been meeting Senators and Congressmen and had good contacts with the Congressional Black Caucus and the Africa Sub-Committee in the House and the Senate. In December, every door now open to him, Tutu found himself in the White House, politely disagreeing with the most powerful man in the world. Only three days earlier he had received a standing ovation from members of the House of Representatives Foreign Affairs Sub-Committee on Africa for the passion with which he had castigated the Reagan administration. However, on this occasion (which he referred to as friendly, but leaving them as far apart as ever), he restricted himself to telling the President that the situation was worsening. In support of this claim he quoted a recent report accusing the South African security forces of violence against civilians and asked the administration to act more forcefully to protest against South African policies. The President knew better. At a news conference after the meeting he claimed that those who criticised American companies for doing business in South Africa were ignorant: 'The simple truth is that most black tribal leaders there have openly expressed their support in American business investment there.' Nor did he agree that the situation had worsened: 'It has not. We have made sizeable progress there in expressing our repugnance for apartheid and in persuading the South African government to make changes. And we're going to continue with that policy.'[8] It was not surprising his position had remained unchanged: he would not listen to his own Congress; he was not likely to listen to a black Bishop.

The day after this meeting Desmond Tutu was on his way to Norway to receive the Nobel Peace Prize and enjoy four more days of feasting and celebration with the people of Oslo. Many friends were with him: Tom Manthata, Dan Vaughan, Joe Seremane and the trio of singers were among the dozen representing the SACC; the Rockwells, the Fenhagens and the Ferraris came from America; and the British group included Terry Waite, representing the Archbishop of Canterbury. The central event, the presentation of the award, was accompanied by a cornucopia of happenings. There was a magnificent torchlight parade of thousands of students; the labour unions – the first time they had ever done such a thing – organised a great celebration of folk music with the churches in the Trade Union Hall; there was a formal state dinner with music from the Norway Symphony Orchestra; the SACC contingent addressed meetings all over Norway.

The actual award took place in the aula of the University of Oslo on December 10th, when he was presented with the Gold Medal and Diploma (the cheque was given to him informally). But controversy is never far from Tutu. Half way through the dinner someone went up to the King's table and whispered in his ear – there was a bomb scare. With slow dignity the King left, followed by the orchestra; then everyone else was told to leave. They all clustered together on the steps of the university as Tutu led them in singing 'We Shall Overcome' and the security policy checked the hall. An hour later it was declared safe and the King returned, followed by most of the guests. However, the orchestra had other ideas and was never seen again, so the SACC group, joined by ex-patriate South Africans living in Norway, went on the stage to take their place. The evening continued with South African songs, including '*Nkosi Sikele' iAfrika*', instead of Greig.

In a sermon in Oslo cathedral Tutu gave thanks for the demonstrations against apartheid that were mushrooming in the United States; in the traditional Nobel Lecture he was careful to refrain from any provocative utterances. It was, in the words of the *New York Times* reporter, 'more an invitation to believe than an incitement to action'.[9]

His account of the effects of apartheid was restrained, calls for pressure on the South African government giving way to observing that the injustice to be found in his country was a microcosm of conditions found, in different degrees, all over the world. Peace and justice are inseparable, so 'If we want peace . . . let us work for justice. Let us beat our swords into ploughshares.'

It was Desmond Tutu's humility and gratitude that most impressed those who shared this great experience with him. It is an honest humility, that enables him to recognise his strengths as well as his weaknesses and which allowed him to take huge pride in receiving the award, at the same time never forgetting that he was doing so on behalf of his people. His manner was best expressed by Frank Ferrari: 'Desmond is a walking example to me of gratitude. He was so grateful that the gratitude that emanated from Desmond Tutu was all over Oslo.'

16

'Everybody's Bishop'

The award of the Nobel Peace Prize kept Tutu's name in both international and domestic news headlines for weeks; in fact since that day in October he has rarely been far from the limelight. On November 13th, in the middle of the hectic period between the announcement of the award and the celebrations in Oslo, fuel was added to the media flames by his election as Bishop of Johannesburg. It was the first time that a black man had occupied this post, after the archbishopric of Cape Town the most influential position in the Anglican Church in South Africa.

His appointment was surrounded by controversy. Together with several others, including the Reverend Peter Lee, Bishop Michael Nuttall of Natal and Bishop Bruce Evans of Port Elizabeth, he had been nominated in August, when it was announced that the present Bishop of Johannesburg, Timothy Bavin, was to return to England. On October 23rd the electoral assembly of the Johannesburg diocese (214 delegates consisting of all the clergy and one layman from each congregation) tried for two days to reach a decision. Although these proceedings are always held in secret, the *Sowetan* reported that after several rounds of voting Tutu was supported by 89 delegates, Peter Lee by 60, the remaining votes going to other candidates. Whether or not these figures were accurate, there is no doubt that the assembly could not reach the necessary two-thirds majority and that it was deadlocked.

Nobody doubted Tutu's ability to fill the post, few questioned his qualities as a Christian leader, but his supporters had to fight his case against fierce arguments from his opponents. There were suggestions that his international responsibilities would lead to his spending more time outside the diocese than in it, accusations of ambition, hints that he only wanted to be Bishop of Johannesburg as a stepping stone to the top job, Archbishop of Cape Town. Among the whites there was resentment at the thought of appointing a black Bishop in a diocese where, though 60 per cent of the diocese were black, the financial brunt was born by the remaining (and of course infinitely wealthier) 40 per cent; doubts from many who disapproved of Tutu's 'political' statements and, conversely, others who feared that occupying such a high ecclesiastical post would have a muzzling effect on him. Most of all there was concern that his appointment would divide the diocese. The assembly felt that the Church was in an invidious position. 'If it appoints Bishop Tutu as Bishop of Johannesburg, this will be seen as a political appointment,' said one clergyman. 'If it doesn't appoint him, it will be seen as a political disappointment.'[1]

It was largely a racial divide, with conservative, mostly white, priests blocking Tutu, while an equal weight of black priests prevented a white candidate from being chosen. So, amid a general feeling that Tutu would not be elected and that a compromise candidate would be chosen, and with the press reporting that the election had thrust the Church to the brink of its greatest crisis in years, the matter was referred to the synod of Bishops. It was these twenty-three men who, three weeks later, took the courageous decision to promote the controversial Bishop.

The appointment received, predictably, a mixed reaction. The black clergy were jubilant – the Johannesburg diocese was now, with its Suffragan Bishops Simeon Nkoane, based in KwaThema, and Sigisbert Ndwande on the West Rand, entirely run by Africans. Was the era of black Church leadership in the Christian community in sight? The Archdeacon of Johannesburg West, the Reverend David Nkwe, said that Tutu's appointment was the 'greatest thing to happen to the Church of God. In Desmond we have a caring pastor, a reconciler, who is always clear in what he wants to say and the direction he will guide the church into.'[2] The Roman Catholic Church and the Methodists welcomed the appointment and the Reverend T. M. Swart, General Secretary of the Baptist Union, said, 'This new posting can only be for the ultimate good of the Church as there are so few black church leaders in this country.'[3]

Opinions were not entirely divided by race. Many whites supported Tutu, including the outgoing Bishop Bavin, his fellow nominee Peter Lee, the Most Reverend Philip Russell, Archbishop of Cape Town, and Dan Vaughan, who, despite losing him as General Secretary of the South African Council of Churches, said he was 'a true man of God ... definitely the right man for the position'.[4] The Reverend Dr Francis Cull expressed himself as 'three times delighted'. Surprisingly, some conservative congregations, like Turffontein and Nigel, were happy with the decision, though other parishes reported phone calls from disgruntled parishioners. On the other hand Chief Lennon Sebe, President of the Ciskei, said Tutu did not speak on behalf of blacks and asked 'how this man, preaching blood and starvation, can call himself a Bishop in the Christian Church?'[5]

Once again the white press was less than enthusiastic; once again there were harsh statements from right-wing religious organisations. United Christian Action declared that Tutu's appointment was a potential cause of further division and criticised the Bishops for succumbing to world pressure; Father Arthur Lewis of the Rhodesia Christian Group forecast that in a few years the Bishop would be 'no more than a forgotten demagogue';[6] the Gospel Defence League stated that Tutu gave 'open support for those who are involved in violence, promotion of the anti-biblical liberation theology and blasphemous statements concerning Jesus Christ'.[7] There were also letters to the press from angry Anglicans. One, who signed himself 'Toti Anglican' (it is interesting how seldom Tutu's critics are prepared to be named), asked what he had done for peace in South Africa? 'His only remarks and sentiments have been vicious, appallingly ill chosen, bitter, resentful and anything but peaceful.'[8]

The ability of the electoral assembly to reach a consensus and the referral to the synod of Bishops was distressing and mildly humiliating for Tutu. He was further hurt by the official silence and by the lack of any formal welcome from the City Council – a hurt that was to persist throughout his time in Johannesburg and beyond. However, he had for some time wanted to return to the pastoral ministry and his ebullient nature rose to the occasion as he welcomed the challenge of the new post and rejoiced at the honour of following in the footsteps of previous Bishops of Johannesburg, great Christians such as Geoffrey Clayton, Ambrose Reeves, Lesley Stradling and his immediate predecessor Timothy Bavin.

In his charge, delivered at his enthronement on February 3rd, 1985, he sympathised with those who felt he had been 'foisted on an unwilling diocese' and admitted he would have loved to have been chosen by the elective assembly. He allowed himself to indulge in a little self-justification, citing occasions where he had initiated moves towards reconciliation or congratulated government Ministers when he felt they deserved credit. Keen to allay worries exacerbated by the debate surrounding his election, he affirmed that in order that his new flock could get to know him better he had turned down virtually all invitations that would take him away from the diocese – perhaps he might turn out to be 'not quite such a horrid ogre as they thought'. He also assured them that unless it became abundantly clear that God had other ideas for him, he hoped to end his active ministry in Johannesburg. He went on to gratify his critics by calling for apartheid to be dismantled – remarking on the obscenity of the police van, frequently parked outside the cathedral ready to pick up worshippers without correct passes – and by promising to call for punitive economic sanctions (something he had so far stopped short of doing) if there were not signs that this was being done within eighteen to twenty-four months. He would do this whatever the legal consequences for him might be.

For the most part, however, his charge was a theological dissertation on the nature of the Church and of his intentions for the diocese. He questioned whether the Church was a cosy club, a mystical ivory tower, a spiritual ghetto or a centre of good works. No, it existed primarily for the worship of God. In the Old Testament language he is fond of using, he declared:

> The Church is the fellowship whence adoration, worship and praise ascend to the heavenly throne and in company with the angels and archangels and with the whole host of heaven we sing as did the cherubic choir in Isaiah's vision and as we shall soon be bidden to do in his glorious service: 'Holy, Holy, Holy, Lord God of Hosts, Heaven and earth are full of thy glory.'

In order to enrich the diocesan life of worship and to ensure the centrality of the spiritual, he made various suggestions. He urged the daily celebration of the Eucharist, encouraged penitence and intercession and the offering to God not only of time and talent, but of money. He would like the diocese to tithe its income to help in development programmes at home and abroad and he set a target of an Endowment Fund of R5 million. He expressed his hope that the diocese would become more and more non-racial, to this end promising more non-racial appointments, encouraging people to learn one another's languages and suggesting that it might be important to have white priests in black townships 'to dispel any erroneous notions which people may have picked up in having unfortunate dealings only with the police, the army and a phalanx of bureaucrats who have the unenviable task of applying evil and unChristian policies'. Finally he assured them that he loved them deeply and asked for a chance to show his love. Even if they did not give him that chance he would still love them.

Johannesburg is a large, cumbersome diocese, stretching 400 miles from Christiana to the Swaziland border, taking in a vast swathe of the southern Transvaal. It is the home of nearly a third of South Africa's Anglicans, including many of extreme right-wing political persuasion. Like most South African dioceses, it is rarely without some financial embarrassment, though there was one gratifying problem: so many men were applying for the priesthood that there was never enough money or enough places in the theological colleges to train them.

The eighteen months Desmond Tutu spent as Bishop of Johannesburg were not enough for him to see the wishes he expressed in his charge fulfilled or to make any structural changes, though he made a start. Previous Bishops had tried to make non-racial appointments and he already had two African Suffragan Bishops and a 'coloured' Dean, Mervyn Castle; he asked his old friend Godfrey Pitje to become Deputy Registrar of the diocese and a black woman, Connie Nkosi, to be Deputy Bursar. Soon after he took office he appointed two white Fathers from the Community of the Resurrection to Holy Cross Church in Soweto's Orlando district, but his efforts to make black appointments in white parishes, and vice versa, met with resistance from both sides. He inherited a white secretary, Margaret Davies, and brought Thembi Sekgaphane, who had been one of his secretaries at the SACC, as his personal assistant. Painfully aware that he had not been chosen by the electoral assembly and that there were many who resented his appointment, he made a point of visiting the white parishes as soon as he could, hoping that his image, so distorted by the media, could be balanced against the reality. Most of them soon came to realise he was not the political revolutionary they had been led to expect, though there was always the hard core whose resistance went too deep for change. Some white parents would not let him confirm their children – the thought of his black hands being laid on their white heads was too much for them.

As they have climbed the clerical ladder, the Tutus have had to endure many taunts about personal extravagance. In fact becoming a Bishop did not mean an increase in salary, far from it: Tutu took a considerable drop, though of course there was an allowance for official duties. Previous white Bishops had their own furniture, while what little the Tutus owned was to remain in their Soweto house (they were determined to keep a base in the townships), so the diocese had to cover the expenses involved in furnishing and redecorating the Bishop's official residence at Westcliff. However, the man who should know best, the Diocesan Secretary, considered that Tutu was not extravagant and had not cost the diocese very much. Though the Tutus like to live comfortably and perhaps feel a certain duty towards the black community to prove that blacks can succeed and be seen to succeed, and while they have a certain casualness in their attitude to money, they give as freely as they receive and many who know them well will vouch for their generosity in matters great and small. After trips overseas Tutu would, for instance, give small presents to all fifteen members of the diocesan office; once they were all given orchids on St Valentine's day. He would constantly give money to people in need, or send flowers to celebrate a special occasion. As far as Africans are concerned money is a commodity to be used; it should be circulated, not hoarded.

The way he dealt with the diocesan financial problems is typical of this abundance of nature. There were some white parishes who withdrew their diocesan quota in protest at his appointment and this, in addition to the ongoing financial hardship of the diocese, led to fears of bankruptcy. In fact it was a small, if vociferous, minority who acted in this way and Tutu actually left the Johannesburg diocese considerably better off than he found it, not by financial caution – in fact staff accustomed to thrifty Bishops were at first alarmed by his easy spending – but because he himself brought in so much money from his overseas travels. Questions were continually being asked about who paid his travelling expenses, questions which were easily answered – it was those who invited him who bore the cost. On these trips he would raise huge sums of money (R50,000 resulted from one visit to California) for black education, clergy training, or his own discretionary fund. He was thus able to insist, for instance, that a plan to reduce clergy stipends (they only got R532 a month in any case) was not implemented – he gave money from his discretionary fund to make up the difference. During his episcopate money moved freely; he both spent more and brought more into the diocese.

He is an exceptional administrator, able to place his trust in those to whom he has delegated responsibility. He also has an astonishing memory for detail. His successor Bishop Buchanan, who says Tutu was one of the most remarkable Bishops he has ever come across, once acted as his Vicar-General while he was abroad and remembers his briefing:

> For an hour and a half, without one note, he gave me a run down on every parish and every priest in the diocese. He knew their names, where they were, what their good points and their bad points were; he knew most of their family situations, though probably not all the children. He knew the wives and their problems, he knew the parishes themselves, very frequently he was also able to name the church wardens.

At the time there were, incidentally, 102 parishes.

It was not only an astonishing memory that made this feat possible, it is a reflection of his concern as 'pastor of pastors'. His informal style of leadership, continually accompanied by laughter, gave the clergy a sense of being loved and cared for in a deeply personal way. Though a few people complained that he was not sufficiently accessible, they were a minority. Father Sipho Masemola felt Tutu had more time for his priests than any other Bishop he had worked under and was impressed that he never had to wait more than a week for an interview. (Tutu tried to keep every Wednesday as an open day for clergy.) And if calls on his time prevented him from seeing them personally, he had what Bishop Bavin calls 'a great ministry on the telephone'. Stories abound of his loving attention to people, even to those who did not count themselves among his admirers. Like one sick priest, openly against his new Bishop, who was astonished that Tutu rang him every day for the two weeks he was in hospital. A less attractive side of Tutu's personality was revealed by another priest, who recalled an occasion when the Bishop was visiting him in hospital and was not recognised by the nurses. Tutu was so affronted that he complained audibly.

One very public example of his attitude to his priests was when Mervyn Castle, the Dean, was arrested on a charge of public indecency. Tutu wrote in *The Watchman* (the Diocesan newspaper) pleading that the Dean should be surrounded by love and care while he was passing through this traumatic time. He pointed out that the prosecutor had refused to accept the Dean's admission-of-guilt fine and noted how the newspapers had been tipped off three days before the court appearance, clearly indicating that someone was keen to extract the maximum benefit from the adverse publicity attracted by the case to the Anglican Church. He assured his readers that he would not think any less highly of the Dean, whatever the outcome of the case: 'The Dean is a greatly loved Pastor who has endeared himself to many by his quiet strength and compassionate caring . . . we in the Church must demonstrate that we belong to the forgiving Koinonia of the forgiven and the reconciling fellowship of the reconciled.'[9]

It is part of a Bishop's job to give direction and focus to the people in his charge. Duncan Buchanan, whom Tutu had appointed Dean after Mervyn Castle's resignation, found Bishop Tutu was giving the diocese

> an air of freshness which stood the diocese on its head. He cut through a lot of encrustation, going right to the heart of things. Going into committees you discovered that people were thinking differently as a result of his being involved. That their eyes had been opened, their perceptions and vision were bigger than they were before.

While giving a special boost to the morale of the black people, he somehow managed to belong to everybody. When he visited a parish, every denomination claimed him as its own, recognising him as a Christian, rather than simply an Anglican, leader. It was that quality which led Bishop Jim Thompson, the Bishop of Stepney, to dub him 'Everybody's Bishop'.

Tutu tried to live up to his promise to cut down on overseas travel; indeed he was, by his own peripatetic standards, restrained. There were official visits in his ecclesiastical role which attracted no criticism. He attended the planning session for the 1988 Lambeth Conference in England and he accepted invitations from the Welsh Council of Churches, the World Council of Churches, the Churches of China and Japan and the Church of the West Indies. Although he did succumb to pressure from the United States, the American trips during his time as Bishop of Johannesburg only took him out of the country for a total of four weeks. His presence is so visible that he somehow gives the impression of travelling even more than he does.

However, of all his meetings with national and international figures, the one which was to have the most significant repercussions, which indeed was regarded by Tutu as a watershed, took place in his own country in January 1985, just a month before he was enthroned as Bishop of Johannesburg. It was the visit of Senator Edward Kennedy.

The Kennedy family had been concerned with South Africa for a long time. They had known a number of young, mostly white, anti-apartheid activists associated with the National Union of South African Students and Robert Kennedy had visited the country in 1966. Throughout his twenty-five years in the Senate, Edward Kennedy has focused on abuses of human rights wherever they have occurred and in October 1984, distressed that American policy towards South Africa had played so little part in the presidential campaign, he tried to organise a forum to draw attention to the subject. An important debate on nuclear arms control forced the cancellation of this meeting, but it so happened that both Tutu and Dr Allan Boesak, the President of the World Alliance of Reformed Churches, were in the United States at the time and on October 4th a lunch was organised with the two South Africans, Senator Kennedy, Frank Ferrari and Gregory Craig, Senator Kennedy's National Security Advisor.

Both Tutu and Boesak spoke powerfully about the suffering of the blacks and about how the level of deprivation was increasing both politically and economically. At the end of the lunch, when Senator Kennedy asked what he could do to help, they asked him to come to South Africa. He had never been there before, he wanted to be able to speak in the Senate from experience and he was keen to see South Africa through the eyes of black people, to witness for himself the conditions under which black South Africans lived rather than to rely on Pretoria's promises of reform. He accepted.

The invitation was, by pure chance, well timed. Only days later the Nobel Peace Prize was announced and the whole of America learned something of what Senator Kennedy had been told. Soon after Gregory Craig went to the South African Embassy to file applications for visas the first demonstration outside the Embassy, organised by Randall Robinson and the Free South Africa Movement, began. So the Kennedy trip was conceived in the early days of the wave of American revulsion to apartheid.

It was an invitation extended and accepted in goodwill. However, a section of black South Africans, including members of the Azanian People's Organisation, thought otherwise. When Senator Kennedy and his entourage arrived at Jan Smuts Airport on January 5th, they were welcomed by Bishop Tutu, Dr Allan Boesak and the Reverend Beyers Naudé, but jeered by some forty AZAPO demonstrators. On his way to Brandfort to see Winnie Mandela, Kennedy passed graffiti bearing the words 'Kennedy go home – and take Tutu with you'. As he flew to Durban to see Archbishop Hurley, there were demonstrators from AZAPO at the airport. Nevertheless, though there were conflicting reports about Kennedy's handling of the delicate situations with which he was faced, much of the visit was, at least in the opinion of his aides, a spectacular success. It included a candle-lit reception from 500 chanting Soweto residents, where he defied the Group Areas Act by spending the night with the Tutus, challenging speeches in Cape Town and Johannesburg and a visit to a resettlement camp in the Orange Free State. He received a rousing welcome at Crossroads and courageously reprimanded Chief Buthelezi for his attacks on Tutu and Boesak. Most telling of all was a letter from Winnie Mandela assuring him of the good wishes of 30 million of her people:[10]

> The memory of your visit to Brandfort, your profound concern about the tragic suffering inflicted upon the oppressed people of my country and your enduring campaign against the crime of apartheid *inter alia* has given me strength to carry on when the cross was at times too heavy for my tired shoulders . . . We attribute the escalation of the campaign from the American public against apartheid directly to your visit.

This letter must have afforded the Senator much comfort, for his visit ended in chaos, when, on his last day, he was due to make a major speech at Regina Mundi Cathedral in Soweto. It was to have been the climax of his visit and up to 4,000 people were assembled to hear him. However, among the crowds were about 100 AZAPO supporters, bearing placards saying 'SOCIALIST AZAPO VS CAPITALIST KENNEDY' and 'AWAY WITH CIA, KENNEDY, OPPRESSION AND CAPITALISM'. They marched towards the altar shouting, 'No more Kennedy', creating such disturbance that a distressed Bishop Tutu had to intervene. He told the crowds that Senator Kennedy was his guest, that he had invited him to the country not as a liberator, but to help expose the evil system of apartheid. He warned them too, that 'the system knows how to turn us against ourselves'. (Senator Kennedy's aides are in no doubt that the government helped AZAPO create division by telling them where Kennedy was going to be, even helping to transport them to places on his schedule.) When Tutu asked the audience if they wanted Senator Kennedy to address the meeting, there was a great cry of 'Yes' from well over 3,000 people, challenged by 'No' from the vociferous minority of AZAPO supporters. It was clear that the overwhelming majority wished to hear what the Senator had to say, but the situation was tense and armed riot police and troops were only a few hundred yards away. The risk of a serious confrontation was great and eventually, on Tutu's recommendation, the Kennedy aides decided that the visit must be cancelled. The text of his prepared speech was issued and Senator Kennedy's motorcade, waiting some way from the cathedral while a decision was made, turned round and took him to the airport.

Tutu was humiliated and angry. He had not foreseen the political implications of the invitation and his hopes of bringing people together had ended in disaster. From its beginning he had supported AZAPO, publicly registering a protest when two AZAPO men were detained within days of its foundation. In 1983 he had been invited to the launch of the National Forum, a heterogeneous umbrella group bringing together AZAPO, ex-PAC members and other Black Consciousness groups, none of whom subscribed to the Freedom Charter. Two months later, despite its disagreements with AZAPO, he had become a patron of the non racial United Democratic Front (UDF). He had tried to avoid identifying too much with any political ideology, to hold on to a vision of peace and justice above man-made divisions. This incident underlined the differences he had sought to reconcile; there was a complete breakdown of communication between Tutu and AZAPO.

AZAPO had taken its stand against Kennedy before it knew of Tutu and Dr Boesak's involvement. Its members opposed, to the depths of their being, America's role in Cuba, Vietnam, Nicaragua and Granada and, however unjustly, regarded the Senator, who at the time was standing for President, as a symbol of United States imperialism. Further, they were convinced that he was using South Africa's suffering to help his election chances. Even though he represented the Democrats, to them he was part of the system; they felt it was impossible that a Kennedy could be welcomed by black people.

Though AZAPO says it was prepared to meet the Senator privately, it was unable to accept the high profile he was being given. The fact that it had not been consulted over his invitation to South Africa compounded the situation. South African blacks are among the most democratic people in the world, acutely aware of whether or not anyone is mandated to speak on their behalf. That Tutu should have invited Kennedy to visit South Africa without reference to them was, in the eyes of many adherents to Black Consciousness, intolerable. Tutu could not be a voice in isolation; he only carried weight to the extent that he was supported by the community. AZAPO considered that by acting in this unilateral fashion he was placing himself above the people.

The UDF had mixed feelings. It understood Tutu's reasons for wishing Senator Kennedy to visit the country and was prepared to listen to him; in fact, many of its members felt the Bishop's role in the affair was not inconsistent with his spiritual calling. Though some were critical of Tutu for failing to consult them, any resentment they felt was overridden by their personal loyalty to him.

AZAPO's stand against Tutu proved to be ill-advised tactically; it had underestimated the support he had amongst the mass of the people. Though efforts at reconciliation were made, relations between AZAPO and Tutu have never quite recovered and from that time Tutu began to distance himself from the Black Consciousness movement and identify more with the UDF.

Desmond Tutu has never sought a position of leadership in the secular world, insisting that he is only 'a leader by default', due to the actions taken by the government against black leaders like Nelson Mandela. Still less does he seek a political role. Nevertheless, in August 1985 a poll declared that 24 per cent of the black population considered him the best potential President of South Africa and he is never out of the political limelight, his every word and deed acquiring political overtones.

His short time as Bishop of Johannesburg was crammed with examples of his defiance and courage. Often these took place in a firmly ecclesiastical context, as in April 1985, a month after the police massacre of nineteen blacks in Uitenhage had shocked South Africa and the world, when he defended the Rector of Sharpeville, the Reverend Geoff Moselane. This shining Anglican priest had been detained for six months, a period which, in Tutu's estimation, was ample time for the authorities to have preferred charges against him. He decided to demonstrate his abhorrence of detention without trial and his support of this particular priest in a public act of witness. In full episcopal regalia and with his two Suffragan Bishops, Simeon Nkoane and Sigisbert Ndwande, he led a march of about forty clergymen from the Anglican Cathedral in Johannesburg to the local police headquarters at John Vorster Square. They presented a petition demanding Moselane's release, then held a short prayer service. Afterwards they were told by the head of the security police, Colonel Hennie Muller, and the Acting Divisional Commissioner, Brigadier Dries van den Heever, that the case was now with the Attorney-General and that the matter was no longer in police hands.

Though the names and addresses of everyone present, including journalists, were taken, there were no arrests. This came as a surprise to several of the clergy, who had feared the protest would be seen as a provocative act. Indeed the Diocesan Secretary was so sure it would lead to trouble that he had withdrawn R10,000 as bail for arrested clergy. On this occasion Tutu showed respect and tact in his dealings with the other clergy, many of whom had tried to persuade him not to go. He compromised by leaving the decision to individual judgment; he made it clear that he was determined to march, even if he had to march alone, but that those who chose not to accompany him would not be judged.

By 1985 there was virtually a state of war between the police and the people. In the first nine months of the year an estimated total of 700 were killed in township unrest; there were mysterious and unexplained deaths in detention. Children were now in the front line, venting their feelings by boycotting school, with the slogan 'Liberation now, education later'. In their frustration and anger the blacks, provoked by a mysterious force thought to be instigated by the government, began to turn on one another, inflicting on those they regarded as collaborators with the government the horrific 'necklace' killings (a rubber tyre placed round the neck of the victim, drenched with petrol and set on fire). One of the clergy's constant and tragic duties was to conduct the funerals of those who had died, funerals which became occasions not only of mourning, but of political demonstration. They also became occasions where Tutu made some of his most outspoken and publicised statements and where his courage took the form of risking his life.

One such was in Duduza, a township on Johannesburg's East Rand. Duduza is scarred by ruined houses – the homes of black policemen and community councillors burned by blacks who regard them as collaborators, the homes of activists allegedly burnt by the police. As in many townships, corrugated iron shacks are attached to houses to provide scant accommodation for homeless friends and relatives. Children urinate on the dirt-track roads, there is no sewage disposal, no running water (just stand pipes every ten houses or so), no recreational facilities save for one barren sports field, few shops, no gardens. Nothing alive, nothing beautiful or even pleasant to look at except its 40,000 inhabitants, who somehow manage to emerge fresh and clean from their squalid dwellings. Duduza had become a centre of dissent and in that week of July 1985 ten blacks had been shot dead by police.

During the funeral of four young men who had died in an explosion, Tutu had urged the mourners to forgo violence and to change apartheid by peaceful means. The young men were barely in their graves when the crowd turned on a black onlooker, accusing him of being a police spy. Crying 'Let the dog die', enraged youths attacked the man, overturned his car and set it alight 'to provide his funeral pyre'. Tutu tried arguing with them. 'Why don't we use methods of which we will be proud when our liberation is attained? This undermines the struggle.' 'No, it encourages the struggle,' was the unheeding reply. Words were no use. Bishop Simeon Nkoane and Bishop Kenneth Oram, a senior white Anglican cleric, somehow created a diversion and Tutu dragged the terrified, bleeding man into a car.

The wish for peaceful reconciliation had met, head-on, the passionate anger and frustration of the blacks, one of whom asked Tutu, 'Why don't you allow us to deal with these dogs in the same fashion that they treat us?' Tutu argued that no one should kill another person, whatever the provocation, and asked the questioner if he accepted the Bishops present as their leaders. He received grudging assent and managed to persuade the crowd to disperse quietly.

Only ten days later Duduza was the scene of one of South Africa's most horrific killings. Maki Shosana, a young woman living with her mother and five-year-old son, was suspected of collaborating with the police. At another funeral, in full view of the television cameras, a screaming crowd turned on her shouting, 'Informer'. David Beresford was there.[11]

They chased her across the veld, they beat her, they stoned her, they tore her clothes off, they set her on fire, they put a huge rock on her so that she couldn't get up and they rammed a broken bottle into her vagina. Her mother was crying uncontrollably. The two black clergymen with me couldn't take any more and one of them lumbered to his feet and said 'Let us pray'. And so we stood there with heads bowed, around a plain kitchen table in the township of Duduza in the middle of the Transvaal. And her mother wept on and there were tears in all our eyes: tears for Maki, tears for the beloved country.

A few days later Tutu was conducting yet another funeral, attended by the Bishop of Lichfield, the Right Reverend Keith Sutton, who had been sent by the Archbishop of Canterbury to represent the Anglican Church and support both Bishop Tutu and Bishop Nkoane, who had been receiving death threats and whose house had twice been attacked. Addressing a crowd of 30,000 people in the sports stadium of KwaThema township, Tutu denounced violence and brutality, whether it came from the government or the black people; he implored the mourners to avoid bloodshed. His small purple figure stood high above his audience, arms and voice striving to express his feelings about the death of Maki Shosana:[12]

> If you do that kind of thing again I will find it difficult to speak for the cause of liberation. If the violence continues, I will pack my bags, collect my family and leave this beautiful country that I love so passionately . . . I say to you that I condemn in the strongest possible terms what happened in Duduza. Our cause is just and noble. That is why it will prevail and bring victory to us. You cannot use methods to attain the goal of liberation that our enemy will use against us.

Though a few taunted him for his moderation, most of the crowd supported him. The meeting ended with Tutu leading them in singing 'We dedicate ourselves to the freedom struggle, for all of us black and white. We shall be free.'

There may have been a certain arrogance in his assumption that his threat of leaving the country could influence the passionate rage with which black anger was turning against itself, indeed within hours he had qualified his statement, admitting that he spoke under extreme emotional pressure and hoping that he would not be put to the test. But no one there doubted his courage in standing so firmly against violence, nor the risks he was running in alienating both the government – by his insistence that theirs was the primary violence – and the militant blacks, too oppressed for too long, no longer able to hear the message of peace.

On July 20th, 1985 – just ten days after Tutu had rescued the police informer in Duduza and on the same day that Maki Shosana was so brutally murdered – the government declared a state of emergency in thirty-six magisterial districts. It was a serious move, the first time such a thing had been done since 1960, when a state of emergency was declared in the wake of the Sharpeville massacre. The authorities were empowered to detain any person, without warrant and indefinitely; they could use force, 'including force resulting in death', if anyone refused to heed instructions; they could use these powers in the knowledge that, by means of an indemnity clause, they had complete freedom, while the victims had no legal redress – indeed they could only consult a lawyer with ministerial permission. Further, restrictions on press coverage enabled the police and the army to operate as they wished, uninhibited by the presence of reporters or camera crews. (Though the state of emergency was suspended after nine months, its reimposition on June 12th, 1986, brought even tighter controls.)

Tutu, along with many others, was surprised that the government felt it necessary to add to its already draconian powers; he warned that any calm to which it might lead would only be a surface calm and that there could be 'an almighty explosion'. Within days restrictions were imposed on funerals of 'unrest victims' in areas where the state of emergency was in force. Only one person could be buried at a time, only ordained ministers of religion could speak and they could not 'defend, attack, criticise, propagate or discuss any form of government, any principle or policy of government'.[13] Nor could they comment on the state of emergency or the actions of the security forces. Mourners could not travel on foot, use loudspeakers or display banners and their route would be designated by the local police commander.

All eyes were on Tutu. How would he react to this latest crackdown? There should not have been much doubt. During a funeral service at Tumahole (which was not one of the thirty-six districts under the state of emergency), he called on the Minister of Law and Order to reconsider these regulations and announced that he would defy them, saying, 'I will not be told by any secular authorities what gospel I must preach.' (He was to take a similar line the following June, when he defied the ban on meetings to commemorate the Soweto killings by instructing the clergy to organise services and himself led prayers for justice and peace.)

He seldom missed an opportunity to let the outside world know what was happening in South Africa. When he was in London in October 1985 to discuss the forthcoming Lambeth Conference, he had a fruitless, if civilised, meeting with the intransigent Margaret Thatcher; he was one of the key people to talk to the Eminent Persons Group, though his refusal to see Geoffrey Howe was yet another blow to the British Foreign Secretary's ill-fated mission to South Africa; he was among those who met the British trades union delegation when it visited South Africa. In a talk to the International Press Institute in Vienna he reminded his audience that the South African media were constantly serving sectional interests and that the South African Broadcasting Corporation was 'really an extension of the Nationalist Party'. They had an 'Esau complex', he said; they had 'sold their birthright for a mess of potage'. He frequently castigated President

Reagan, Margaret Thatcher and Chancellor Helmut Kohl for doing so little to bring about reform in South Africa.

He even entered the arena of financial affairs. On October 22nd, 1985, he, the Reverend Beyers Naudé and Allan Boesak wrote to South Africa's creditor banks, asking them to make the rescheduling of South Africa's debt 'conditional on the resignation of the present regime and its replacement by an interim government responsive to the needs of all South Africa's people'. News that South Africa had reached agreement with its major foreign creditors led to an angry Desmond Tutu appearing on ITV's Channel 4, saying that South African blacks would see this as 'whites clubbing together against them' and that the West was 'good at rhetoric but develops cold feet when it comes to translating it into action'.

His outspoken defiance overseas reached a climax when he went to the United States for two weeks in January 1986 under the auspices of the Adelphia Foundation and Mrs Lia Belli. Even by his standards it was a hectic trip. He made as many as four or five speeches a day, covering twelve cities including New York, Washington, Baltimore, Detroit and Atlanta, where he received the Martin Luther King Peace Prize. Its organisation left much to be desired. He was constantly late – on one occasion the Mayor of Philadelphia had to wait two hours for him to arrive – and many criticised his judgment in allowing himself to be whisked across the country in sleek black limousines. However, from his point of view the trip was a resounding success. His purpose was to thank the Americans for their support, to raise funds and, in the light of the press clampdown, to keep the world informed of the state of affairs in South Africa. Apart from the fact that he also received four more honorary degrees, three gold medallions and the freedom of the city of Baltimore, he was ecstatically received by capacity crowds, eminent people queued up to meet him and he was entertained at endless prayer breakfasts, civic functions, small private meetings and huge formal banquets. His fund-raising for political prisoners, refugees and the Anglican Church was rewarded by donations and pledges amounting to R1 million. But predictably his statements about living under an apartheid society incurred the wrath of white South Africa.

The South African press covered these remarks widely, selectively and largely out of context. They reported that Tutu had warned that black servants could poison their employers' coffee, that the blacks might start picking up stones and fighting, that white school buses might be attacked; that he had predicted that the government would use nuclear weapons against the blacks in a 'scorched earth' policy; that he had again promised to call for sanctions unless reforms were started by the end of March; that he had said that under certain circumstances violence could be justified and that he had, most provocatively of all, called on Western governments to support the banned African National Congress.

On his return home Tutu was met by a chaotic reception of journalists, plainclothed and uniformed police and placards reading 'Tutu – no jobs, no food' and 'Tutu – down with the ANC'. He was ashamed of nothing and made no denials, but such had been the attacks on him in his absence that he called a press conference in which he stood by everything he had said. Unrepentant, he wished the 'lickspittle sycophants' of the South African press and television would prepare whites for the inevitable, as the country was not going to be run by a minority for ever. He repeated his determination to call for sanctions if there was no significant change before the end of March and reaffirmed his support for the ANC and his wish that Western leaders would side with them. He pointed out that his remarks on this matter had been directed to the US Vice-President, George Bush, who was on the platform at the time, and that he was questioning a foreign policy that could back the Contra guerrillas against the Sandinistas in Nicaragua, yet refuse to support the ANC against the South African government. Why was it justifiable to back one guerrilla movement seeking to overthrow a government by force and not another? He reminded the press that the Church teaches that there can be times when it is justifiable to overthrow an unjust government by violence, though that situation had not yet been reached. He challenged the government to show that he had been lying when he said that fourteen-year-olds had been in detention for five months, that children 'die by deliberate government policy', when they were dumped in places where the government knew there was no food.

While many doubted the wisdom of his remarks about 'soft targets', such as the possibility of black servants poisoning their employers' coffee, in fact such ideas had been in circulation in South Africa for years. In mentioning such things he was trying to avert them, not commend them; he was issuing warnings, not threats. As he said at his news conference, 'You tell people, "Look at that pile of cups on the edge, it is going to fall". You are warning them and the pile of cups falls and you are blamed for letting it fall.'

The following Sunday many white Anglicans stayed away from church in protest, threatening to withdraw their financial support. The Dean of Cape Town, the Reverend E. L. King, admitted that the Church was involved in 'the biggest and broadest controversy that's faced us to date', but he rejoiced in prophetic voices like

Desmond Tutu's making challenging and uncomfortable statements, adding with typical courage: 'The more people take their money out, the better the church – the kind of religion they're paying for is going off the market.'[14] The Bishop found support, too, in the liberal wing of the Progressive Federal Party, though the party was split and he was denounced by some Transvaal MPs. A Cabinet Minister declared his American speeches 'unworthy of a man of the cloth' and the right-wing conservatives went further, arguing that he should be prosecuted under the Internal Security Act for supporting a banned organisation. However, the government was apparently delighted that he was antagonising white liberals. Certainly it took no action against him, even when, on April 2nd, 1986, in a symbolic action courting arrest, he fulfilled his promise and called for immediate punitive sanctions against South Africa.

At the national level Bishop Tutu attempted, frequently and in vain, to relate to the State President, P. W. Botha. His reaction to the state of emergency was not only to condemn it and to defy its unreasonable restrictions, but to try to bring about some sort of reconciliation, so he offered himself as a broker to start negotiations with the President. The two men had not met since the unsatisfactory interview in 1980, just before the Eloff Commission was appointed. Nevertheless, Tutu made it clear that he would not be prejudiced by past events, though the talks must address the subject of the dismantling of apartheid. On July 29th, with the state of emergency just over a week old, with eighteen blacks killed and over 1,000 people arrested, he sent a telegram to Mr Botha asking for an urgent meeting to discuss the situation. The President's private secretary said he would arrange a meeting at the President's earliest possible convenience; but, in what the London *Times* called 'a calculated snub', Tutu received a telephone call informing him that President Botha refused to see him: he would not meet anyone who did not denounce violence (which Bishop Tutu had repeatedly done) and renounce civil disobedience (which he had not). The Bishop was told that President Botha had agreed to see Archbishop Russell and a small delegation on August 19th, but that his schedule made a separate meeting with Bishop Tutu quite impossible.

It is hard to justify this rebuff. The President found time that week to fit in a delegation of businessmen – his schedule seemed to be flexible when he wished it to be. A mediator was urgently needed and many people, including distinguished academics like Professor Adam Small, regarded the Bishop as the best person to fill the role. Tutu had risked his credibility among the blacks in requesting an interview;

Mr Botha had nothing to lose by extending a reconciling hand.

The refusal left Tutu with a difficult decision to make: should he join the other churchmen on August 19th? The Archbishop had said he would be welcome, a spokesman from the President's office had said it was possible he could be included. But to join this separate delegation might jeopardise the chances of the one-to-one meeting that Tutu felt would be more valuable; in any case he was not prepared to renounce civil disobedience. At the last minute, exposing himself to accusations of pique, he decided to pull out. This earned him a fresh stream of criticism, but in the event he had not missed much. The delegation had made four demands in a written memorandum. They asked that the government should announce its intention to dismantle apartheid, that a National Convention should be called, that the black people should have the right to select their own leaders for negotiation and that the state of emergency should be lifted. The nine clerics told a press conference that the President had addressed none of these issues.

Eventually, nearly a year later, Tutu and President Botha did meet. They had talks on June 13th, just after the reimposition of the state of emergency and again in July. Both meetings hurt Tutu politically and neither achieved very much. The first he described as 'frank and cordial' and of the second, which lasted for two hours, all the Bishop could say was 'We agreed that we are both Christians'.

Desmond Tutu is thought by some people to give too much time and attention to his national and international contacts at the expense of involvement at grassroots level. This accusation is not borne out by the facts. Though high office removed him, to some extent, from day-to-day contact with his fellow blacks, by keeping his house in Soweto he remained close to the feelings of the community. He sympathised with the rent boycott, part protest against apartheid in general, part a refusal to confer financial authority on the community councils imposed on the townships by the Botha government; he even showed his support by himself withholding his rent. He played an active, if controversial, part in the school boycott, taking a significant lead in the Soweto Parents Crisis Committee. He was also one of the most articulate voices in the Conference on Education held at the University of the Witwatersrand, when black educationalists agreed that if certain conditions were not met they would support the children boycotting school. He tried to reconcile warring factions at Crossroads – indeed he was among those who helped to bring about a ceasefire. Most conspicuously, he tried to diffuse an explosive situation in Alexandra.

Alexandra is one of the oldest townships on the Witwatersrand, its grimy square mile of shacks and potholed streets, home to 100,000 blacks, provocatively close to the fresh white municipality of Sandton. Mark Mathabane, who was born there in 1960, remembers living in constant fear, both of the police and of deportation to the tribal reserves: 'It meant hate, bitterness, hunger, pain, terror, violence, fear, dashed hopes and dreams . . . In the ghettos black children fight for survival from the moment they are born. They take to hating and fearing the police, soldiers and authorities as a baby takes to its mother's breast.'[15]

In February 1986 feelings were running high and the township was seeing its worst rioting in months. Shops were petrol-bombed, the streets were scarred with barricades and burnt-out cars, scores of people had been injured and twenty-two killed, sixteen of them by the police (other reports put the figure much higher). On February 18th, during an executive meeting of the SACC at which Tutu was present, news came that a large crowd had assembled in the football stadium. A group of senior churchmen, including the Reverend Beyers Naudé and Dr Boesak, went to Alexandra and tried to pass through the road blocks to speak to the people. At first they were refused entry, but Tutu, after arguing for more than an hour with heavily armed soldiers (an encounter filmed by courageous television crews, who were detained for breaking the new restrictions forbidding cameras or notebooks to be carried 'within telephone range' of the township), was eventually allowed through to the stadium.

He managed to diffuse the tension and bring some calm to the enraged residents. He told them not to discredit their cause by violent behaviour and promised that God saw what was happening to them. 'God will free you from oppression. There is no way in which you can be for ever oppressed. God says you are going to be free.' He undertook to put three of their demands to the local police chief: that the security forces should be withdrawn, that township residents should be released from detention and that the state of emergency should be lifted. The crowd dispersed and Tutu went to see the local Brigadier.

He did more. He and a small delegation of churchmen representing several denominations travelled to Cape Town to see P. W. Botha. Though once again he was snubbed by the State President, he was given an interview with Adriaan Vlok, the Deputy Minister of Law, Order and Defence. Tutu refused to tell the press what had passed between them. First he had to report back to Alexandra.

The expectant crowd gathered, over 40,000 of them; the public-address system was fixed. In a forty-minute address in Xhosa he told the residents that the government had granted none of their requests, only promised to 'look into them'. The crowd was sullen and angry, some of the younger people taunting and booing, others arguing with him and refusing to let him leave. He pleaded with them to be patient, to stop confronting the police. 'A man does not go up to a lion and say "Hullo lion" and jump into its mouth. We have to work at other ways of catching the lion.' But he could not communicate to the angry and disappointed crowd. They shouted that they were not going to put up with police harassment any longer and that they would not be prevented from responding in their own way. Eventually, sadly with head bowed, he managed to leave, admitting to Peter Storey, who was with him, 'They are not going to listen to me much longer.'

17

'Tutu can't swim'

Mention Desmond Tutu's name anywhere in South Africa and the odds are that the response will be a story – for instance, how President Botha gave up chess because he did not know how to move the black bishop. Tutu gleefully tells some of these legends himself, perhaps starting an address with 'Have you heard of Tutu fried chicken? It's got two left wings and a parson's nose!' Or he might recall the occasion on a flight from Durban when the stewardess asked if he would autograph a book for a group of of passengers. 'I was trying to look suitably modest, when she went on to say, "You are Bishop Muzerewa, aren't you?"' If he has more time to spare he will tell the story of how he died and took his turn in the queue at the pearly gates. Two men were in front of him. To the first St Peter said, 'For your sins you will be incarcerated with this lady', introducing him to a wizened old crone; to the second he said the same, but the lady was even more wrinkled, more bent. When Tutu's turn came St Peter produced Brigitte Bardot, saying to her, 'For *your* sins you will spend eternity with this little man.'

But the most frequently repeated Tutu story tells of an occasion when the Bishop and the President come together for talks, in search of privacy meeting in a small boat on Zoo Lake in northern Johannesburg. However, the ever-vigilant press hear of it and assemble round the lake armed with binoculars, telephoto lenses and radio microphones to record the historic event. As the two men talk the wind blows the President's hat into the water, so with a confident 'Don't worry', the Bishop gets out of the boat and walks across the water, retrieves the hat and returns it to the President. The next day the headlines read: 'Tutu kan nie swem nie' ('Tutu can't swim').

This story, whose archetypal nature is emphasised by its different locations (it is placed variously on the Vaal dam or in Cape Town harbour, with the press keeping watch from Table Mountain, as well as on Zoo Lake), illustrates how, whatever he does, Tutu attracts criticism from someone. He is on a tightrope, in his own words 'a marginal man between two forces'. It is time to disentangle the strands of this rope and discover how it is that he has not yet lost his balance.

Not only has fate placed Desmond Tutu in one of the most polarised situations of recent times, he has also had to come to terms with contradictions in his own temperament. His extravert nature conceals a private, introvert side that needs space and regular periods of quiet; his jocularity runs alongside a deep seriousness; his occasional bursts of apparent arrogance mask a genuine humility before God and his fellow men. He is a true son of Africa who can move easily in European and American circles, a man of the people who enjoys ritual and episcopal splendour, a member of an established Church, in some ways a traditionalist, who takes a radical, provocative and fearless stand against authority if he sees it to be unjust. It is usually the most spiritual who can rejoice in all created things and Tutu has no problem in reconciling the sacred and the secular, but critics note a conflict between his socialist ideology and his desire to live comfortably, dress well and lead a life that, while unexceptional in Europe or America, is considered affluent, tainted with capitalism, in the eyes of the deprived black community of South Africa.

His success and personal fame have led to other tensions, tensions which would have torn apart any but the most centred. He has to ride the see-saw of acclamation overseas, castigation at home. Even in the relative privacy of his office he might be reading a letter from a devoted admirer when the telephone rings, the see-saw tips, and he has to listen to tirades of abuse, even to hear threats on his life. (He lets the caller finish, blesses him and hangs up.) He loves the Americans but feels impelled to denounce Reagan's South African policies.

The sustained vilification and abuse by the South African media, the organised campaigns against him, often originating in the government itself, have ensured that the public image has no relation to the reality. When press and people indulge in 'Tutu-bashing' (one of South Africa's favourite sports) it is that public image they are abusing. It is an impressive fact that, apart from the conditioned and prejudiced, those who attack Tutu are invariably those who have not met him. Those who know the real man may fault him, but the feelings they have for him are deep affection, respect and – overwhelmingly – love.

It is in his passionate desire for reconciliation that Tutu finds himself so precariously balanced. He is, in the words of Professor Charles Villa-Vicencio, both 'the prophet who confronts the status quo on behalf of the people and at the same time the person who seeks to reconcile church and state. So he gets criticised from both sides.' In a country whose people are separated by law, whose aspirations are mutually exclusive, who are divided into oppressors and oppressed and where even members of the same Church are on opposite sides of the struggle, Desmond Tutu is a man of peace. And the peace he longs for is more than the absence of war; it is, to quote Professor Villa-Vicencio again, 'the active, positive exaltation of justice and social harmony, which Bishop Tutu has come to symbolize'.[1]

While it would be easy for him to keep quiet, time and again he speaks up and offers himself as a mediator between opposing forces. In initiating dialogue with the government, in insisting that 'Botha is my brother' and in refusing to believe that God's grace cannot operate on the President, by pleading with the Dutch Reformed Churches to join the SACC and to help find a solution to the country's problems, in his public speeches at universities and schools, in his contacts with the African National Congress, in his refusal to accept violence from anyone, black or white, he continually places himself in the firing line. His loving, reconciliatory approach even incurs disapproval from some of his black colleagues. One Roman Catholic priest has openly said that 'Bishop Tutu should learn to hate a little'.

Tutu's vision for South Africa was concisely expressed in 1979:[2]

> Basically I long and work for a South Africa that is more open and more just; where people count and where they will have equal access to the good things of life, with equal opportunity to live, work and learn. I long for a South Africa where there will be equal and untrammelled access to the courts of the land, where detention without trial will be a thing of the hoary past, where bannings and such arbitrary acts will no longer be even so much as mentioned, and where the rule of law will hold sway in the fullest sense. In addition, all adults will participate fully in political decision making, and in other decisions which affect their lives. Consequently they will have the vote and be eligible for election to all public offices. This South Africa will have integrity of territory with a common citizenship, and all the rights and privileges that go with such a citizenship, belonging to all its inhabitants.

This may read as no more than a claim for ordinary human rights, but for South African blacks it has a Utopian ring, while for the whites it poses an intolerable threat.

Tutu has sometimes caught glimpses of this vision and loves to recall them. For instance at a funeral in Uitenhage, when he saw two young women embracing each other – one white, one black. Or at another potentially explosive funeral, to which a young white couple came with their two-year-old child; the black people made way for the little family, patting the child on the head and smiling delightedly. He often recalls his young American friend, Martha Rockwell, who would regale him by the hour with stories of her wonderful teacher, Miss Morgan. Then one day all three met at a party. Eight-year-old Martha rushed up to the Bishop, saying, 'Bishop, Bishop, she's here, my teacher's here.' And he saw that Miss Morgan was black, something so unimportant to Martha that she had not thought to mention it.

Most vividly, most movingly, was the funeral of Molly Blackburn, that courageous white woman who campaigned fearlessly against apartheid. Ninety per cent of the 20,000 people there were black, people who, as Tutu said,[3]

> you would have thought by this time would be saying 'To hell with all white people'. They say 'Ah-ah, we don't hate white people, we hate apartheid, we hate injustice, we hate oppression and we are for goodness, for justice and for peace ... We are going to stride into this great future, this new South Africa, this non-racial South Africa where people will count not because of the colour of their skins, but where people count because they have been made in the image of God.'

While Desmond Tutu long ago resolved any conflict in combining a political role with his Christian calling, summarising his attitude by expressing his wonder at which Bible people are reading when they suggest that religion and politics do not mix, inside the maze of South African politics his conciliatory role faces him with daunting problems. While some people are impressed at his skill in surviving at all in such a political minefield, even many of his admirers consider that he is a bad politician; that he is too good a Christian, too ready to believe in people's inherent goodness, too ready to prefer honesty to expediency and too politically naïve to indulge in the necessary tactical manoeuvring.

It is in his position between the militant blacks, who criticise him for being too moderate, and most of the whites, who consider him a supporter of radical black nationalists, even referring to him as a terrorist, that Tutu's position is at its most perilous. But there are many cleavages in South African politics apart from the racial separation; there are divisions inside both black and white communities, tensions between individuals, problems caused by the physical separation of those at home and those, like the ANC, forced into exile. Tutu relates to them all.

He does so in a dual role of infinite complexity, speaking both as a Bishop, where his duty to interpret the Gospel clearly does not stem from the democratic process, and as a political leader expressing the wishes of his people. Though he has no political ambition and steadfastly refuses to align himself exclusively with any particular political grouping, Tutu seems most at home with the United Democratic Front, an umbrella grouping of 600–700 grassroots organisations which, while not an explicit political party, embraces the broad demands of over 1 million people. In its aim to be a unifying force for national aspirations, in its adherence to the principles of the

Freedom Charter and in its desire for a non-racial South Africa achieved through non-violent means, it is totally in accord with Tutu's philosophy.

For its part the UDF appreciates his role. It recognises that as a priest he is first and foremost accountable to God and that it is quite proper for him to play a reconciliatory role, and understands that his refusal to take up an identifiable political position frees him to speak out and to fulfil his prophetic function. But while it sees the need for a negotiator, it is doubtful about his doctrine of reconciliation. His inclination is to equate political conflict with quarrels between individuals, capable of reconciliation by a change of heart, whereas the UDF feels that experience in other parts of the world shows that major changes have to be made to political structures before reconciliation can take place. In any case it has found that irenic moves from the black people are undermined by the violence of the State.

The various Black Consciousness organisations, which formed themselves into the National Forum Committee (NFC), are smaller and more sectarian. They represent an ultra-left political position, rejecting the Freedom Charter and talking in terms of the class struggle. While their position is pro-black rather than anti-white, they make a distinction between their racial attitude before and after liberation. They see no part for white people in the reshaping of South Africa, but are prepared to join hands in a post-apartheid society, whereas the UDF feels that a non-racial attitude should be part of the birth of a new South Africa.

Tutu, determined to talk to everybody and initially comfortable with the Black Consciousness Movement, was an executive member of the NFC, helping to prepare for its inauguration in 1983, even reading papers himself. He is a patron of the UDF, though he was not present at the Cape Town launch. This attempt to unify the forces against apartheid led to amazement – there would be laughter when he admitted at meetings 'I am a member of the NFC and a patron of the UDF'. In fact his dual commitment could not be maintained. After Senator Kennedy's visit was brought to its knees by the behaviour of AZAPO there was an attempt at reconciliation, when the UDF hosted a rally at Soweto to celebrate Tutu winning the Nobel Peace Prize, but it did not work. UDF and AZAPO went their separate ways and AZAPO, which valued his support even though it found his stance too moderate, was disappointed at Tutu's increasing sympathy with the UDF. It was inevitable and predictable. Many people felt that black consciousness had done its work in giving the black man back his dignity and that AZAPO's exclusion of whites was no longer necessary or even good strategy. Bishop Tutu's present stance implies that he is among those who feel that AZAPO's time is over.

Tutu's desire to unite the forces against apartheid is shared by the banned African National Congress, which appreciates the contribution the black consciousness movements have made to the struggle and has sought to relate to them and encourage them. However, like Tutu, it is worried by the racial element in their ideology. (As far back as 1973 the ANC had declared that 'the assertion of the national identity of the oppressed black peoples . . . is not an end in itself'.)[4] The ANC represents the views of the mass of the South African people and is seen to do so by most of the international community; it enjoys observer status at the United Nations and the Organisation of African Unity. Though membership of the ANC is forbidden in South Africa, even the possession of its literature being a treasonable offence, Tutu has never hidden his support. Whenever he is overseas he makes a point of meeting the Congress leaders and he frequently says that he agrees with their objectives of a non-racial, democratic and just society, but disagrees with their methods, particularly the use of violence by the armed wing, Umkhonto we Sizwe. They admire and respect him, amicably agreeing to differ on some matters and accepting what, in their eyes, are his limitations; in fact, Oliver Tambo, who once considered being a priest, has said that Tutu is doing exactly what he would have done, had he followed that early calling.

In his controversial trip to America in January 1986 Tutu moved even closer to the ANC, when he was publicly quoted as saying he hoped that the leaders of the Western world would side with the ANC, 'which sought to change an unjust system peacefully, non-violently and were only sent into the arms of the struggle through violence because the West abandoned us'.[5] He went on to express his inability to understand the logic of the United States government, which offered help to Unita in Angola and the Contras in Nicaragua, but would not support the ANC. This open siding with the ANC, who had welcomed the advent of the UDF and whose views coincided so closely with the UDF's, was too much for AZAPO. It claimed that the Bishop had destroyed his role as a neutral peacemaker in black politics and that his words would indirectly fan the flames of discord between AZAPO and the UDF.

Tutu's political ideology is, once again, in the centre. If pressed for a label he describes himself as a socialist, as someone looking for a sharing society. He abhors capitalism, which he regards as an ideology of the survival of the fittest, based on man's lowest instincts; he considers that Communism is too materialistic and atheistic an ideology to satisfy the deep spiritual aspirations of Africans. Predictably, he is denounced by whites as being a tool of the Communists and, though in fact he has read quite widely on the subject, criticised by radicals for having an ill-informed and unprogressive attitude to Communism and Marxism. But despite the ANC's long association with the South African Communist Party, his own attitude is quite unequivocal. After provoking howls of indignation when, preaching in England, he declared that most South Africans would welcome even the Russians as liberators, he justified the remark by saying: 'I hate communism with every fibre of my body, as I believe most blacks do – but when you are in a dungeon and a hand is stretched out to free you, you do not ask the pedigree of its owner.'[6]

For the trades unions Tutu's ability to unite people is his greatest strength. They find that his passionate pleas that radical elements should not destroy the struggle or lend credence to the theory that blacks cannot govern does succeed in having a calming effect; his insistence on the justice and dignity of their cause does inject a certain confidence. Though they wish the Church as an institution would provide stronger leadership, though they wish it could contribute more – for instance in giving more assistance during strikes by mobilising their communities at local level and by lending church facilities for community gatherings (the ecclesiastical authorities tend to bow to State pressure, such as the levies put on church buildings used for these purposes) – the feeling is that Tutu himself makes a significant contribution, though he could do more. A representative of the Council of the Unions of South Africa (CUSA) considers that 'He has this magnificent power and magnetism. If it was more coherently used, more logically used, it could take the struggle on to a whole new phase.'

In the opinion of those who have worked with Tutu at a political level his greatest weakness is that he tends to act without first consulting other concerned bodies. His solitary role, unidentified with any political grouping, coupled with his spontaneous temperament, lead him to draw his own conclusions and act on them unilaterally. 1985 saw two instances of this, both of which made him the object of much criticism.

The first was when he called for a day of prayer on October 9th. From the point of view of the unions this was ill-considered and impractical. October 10th was a public holiday, the 11th was a Friday, a day off for many workers; in effect it would mean three days without pay. The date also coincided with school examinations and the careers of thousands of pupils would be put in jeopardy.

In fact his call was not quite so high-handed as it appeared. The idea originated at a National Initiative for Reconciliation, organised by the evangelical organisation African Enterprise under the chairmanship of Michael Cassidy. Four hundred Christians from forty-seven denominations met in an effort to bring peace to a land increasingly torn by riots and bloodshed and at this meeting the delegates voted overwhelmingly to declare October 9th a day of prayer, fasting and mourning for 'those sinful aspects of our national life which have led us to this present crisis'.[7] It was a purely Church initiative, a stay-away rather than a strike, and Tutu, though it was his idea (in fact he originally wanted a full week's stay-away), was just one voice at the meeting, though it was his voice that was remembered, his call that featured in the press, he who spoke at a press conference, appealing to organisations not to hijack the day of prayer and explaining that it was called by the Churches and not trades unions or political organisations.

Nevertheless, there does seem to have been a lack of communication. Though letters were sent to industry and commerce and Barclays closed its banks countrywide, allowing employees to take leave if they wished to pray for the whole day, no one contacted the trades unions. At the least it was tactless, though it is unclear why it was Tutu who had to shoulder the entire blame.

The second instance concerned education, something that has deeply concerned Tutu since he decided to give up teaching rather than contribute to the humiliating system of Bantu education introduced by the government in 1955. Using one of the few weapons available to them to demonstrate against apartheid, students had been boycotting classes for a year when, on December 29th, a conference on the crisis in black education was convened by the Soweto Parents Crisis Committee in the Great Hall of the University of the Witwatersrand.

In his address to the 600-strong audience, Bishop Tutu praised the students for their uncompromising opposition to apartheid and the inferior education they were offered, but warned against an uneducated generation who would not be able to occupy skilled posts in a post-liberation South Africa. He then not only brought forward his deadline for sanctions, but called for a general strike of students, teachers, lecturers and Church leaders if their demands were not met by March 30th, 1986. His recommendations were unanimously adopted and there was no argument in the black community over the demands: that there should be freely elected student representative councils, that the Congress of South African Students should be unbanned, that student leaders in detention should be released, and that arrangements should be made for pupils to catch up with their lost studies. However, Tutu's call for a general strike without reference to the trades unions brought him such tirades of criticism that the occasion served as a turning point for him as he began to realise the necessity of proper consultation. Since then he has, on a number of occasions, acted in conjunction with someone like Allan Boesak when previously he might have gone ahead on his own; a month later when he attempted to negotiate with the government on behalf of the people of Alexandra, he went with their full knowledge and was careful to report back before he made any public statements. Even if it was over-optimistic to the point of naïveté, the fact that it ended in failure was no fault of his.

But actions such as this unmandated call for a general strike endanger his credibility. Ian Linden, the General Secretary of the Catholic Institute for International Relations, has said that:

> The degree to which he is able to act in a much more consensus fashion, with much more of a sense of participation in a popular movement, will be the degree to which his acceptability continues. The degree to which he speaks out off the top of his head will be the degree to which people reject him. Without any doubt.

It is curious that a man of such sensitivity and intelligence should have been so slow to realise that with a people as democratic as black South Africans he cannot act on his own. There have been suggestions that it is his background as an Anglican Bishop that distances him and leads him to act in this fashion, but there is a more profound explanation. He may disturb some colleagues by not talking things through with them sufficiently (though Bishop Buchanan is one of many who found he not only asked advice, but took it), but there is one person he consults regularly and humbly every day of his life, and that is God. There is something reminiscent of Moses – and deeply moving – in the image of Tutu going to the mountain top, seeking God's advice in prayer, then descending to tell the people what God has said to him. There is admittedly a contradiction between this prophetic model, implicitly announcing 'Thus saith the Lord', and the democratic process, which must always question whether the prophet truly represents the cry of the people; but it is neither arrogance nor insensitivity that leads him to these unilateral actions – it is an unshakeable conviction that he is doing the will of God.

Though his independence and his tendency to speak on behalf of the people without consulting other leaders land him in trouble with groups who have a political mandate, Tutu's ability to endear himself to virtually everyone who actually meets him – as opposed to those who absorb the media image – enables him to maintain affectionate relationships with individuals on a personal basis. There are of course exceptions – few members of the Nationalist government offer him more than the most superficial respect, black leaders co-operating with the system see him as a threat to their authenticity, Bishop Mokoena never misses an opportunity to sling stones in his direction – but by those working for a free South Africa he is accorded at the least grudging admiration, at the most something akin to reverence. Despite the government's attempt to create rifts between them, he and Allan Boesak have a good working relationship and his personal friends include people from all walks of life: the Church, the arts, the political world, the diplomatic corps. The one person with whom there are problems is Chief Gatsha Buthelezi.

Buthelezi, who now prefers to be known as Mangosuthu rather than Gatsha, is the Chief Minister of ZwaZulu, a self-governing, though not 'independent' 'homeland' in Natal, and founder of Inkatha, a Zulu cultural association which has become a political party boasting 1 million card-carrying members. His opposition to economic sanctions and his readiness to deal with Pretoria have led to his being portrayed by the media, both inside and outside South Africa, as the moderate man of peaceful change and many whites speak of him in glowing terms; but to the mass of the black people, including the ANC, the UDF and AZAPO, he is a 'Pretoria puppet' and Inkatha a Zulu version of Afrikaner nationalism. Further, he gives credibility to the government by enabling it to cite him as someone who opposes apartheid and yet has not accepted independence, which proves, it argues, that those who have accepted independence have done so freely.

Despite their real differences of strategy, Tutu would like to have amicable relations with Buthelezi. In fact, when the Tutus were living at the Federal Seminary in Alice and Buthelezi was a member of the college council, he was sometimes a guest in their house. The split in their personal relationship dates from 1978 and the funeral of the great Robert Sobukwe.

It took place in the rugby stadium at Graaf Reinet in Cape Province. Though it was well before the big funerals of the mid-1980s, it was at one level a political event and Chief Buthelezi's determination to be on the platform was not welcomed by thousands of the blacks who were present. In fact he was not just unwelcome, his presence was deeply resented and the atmosphere became more and more tense. Archdeacon David Nkwe still bears the scars from the kicks he received when he became part of the human wall that tried to protect the Chief from the increasingly violent young people. Eventually some of the priests persuaded Buthelezi that his life was in danger and that he must bow to these strong feelings. Led by Bishop Tutu, they managed to take him away to safety.

Since this humiliation Buthelezi has constantly attacked Tutu, whose refusal to respond must add salt to the wound. Though there have been many attempts to reconcile the two men, apart from one appearance on the same platform in 1982 and Buthelezi's formal congratulations on, for instance, the Nobel Peace Prize, the best that can be said of the relationship is that it has ceased to exist.

Of all the issues with which Tutu, along with all South Africans, has to grapple, the most crucial and the most complex are those of economic sanctions and the use of violence. Though no economist and unlettered in the detailed implications of economic measures, Tutu has long been in favour of sanctions, which he sees as the only peaceful option in the face of an intransigent government. Granted that there is no guarantee of their effectiveness, they are the last non-violent option left, the only alternative to taking up arms.

He argues that there are three ways in which change can be effected in a social dispensation: by the exercise of a democratic vote, something not available to blacks in South Africa; by violence, an option he rejects; or through the intervention of the international community. History shows that no one gives up power voluntarily and that pressure can be effective: the sports boycott led to some multi-racial sport in South Africa, the disinvestment campaign at least brought the Sullivan and EEC codes into being. And governments seem quite content to use sanctions when it suits them; for instance, America has acted against Poland and Nicaragua, and the United Kingdom, with arguable effect, against Rhodesia.

In taking this stand Tutu is speaking for the great majority of blacks. The ANC, recognising the extent to which apartheid is buttressed by overseas links, first called for sanctions twenty-five years ago. A poll taken in August 1985 showed that 77 per cent of urban blacks agreed with their imposition. They receive overwhelming support from the trades unions. Allan Boesak goes even further, suggesting that 99 per cent of the blacks feel Tutu is right on sanctions. Overseas members of the pro-sanctions lobby include Rajiv Gandhi, Kenneth Kaunda, Robert Mugabe, Bob Hawke, Sonny Ramphal and the British Labour Party. What, then, are the arguments against sanctions and why has Tutu's advocacy of economic pressure made him the object of such hatred? Why are there so many, notably Helen Suzman and Chief Buthelezi inside the country, and the American, United Kingdom and West German governments overseas, who vehemently oppose sanctions?

It is an infinitely complex subject and pitfalls of over-simplification yawn at the feet of every commentator, but there is no dodging the element of pure self-interest. White South Africans clearly have much to lose, as have a few blacks with a stake in the system; trading partners, such as Britain, with billions of pounds invested in the country, would not only be putting their financial interests in jeopardy, but have to consider the knock-on effects on jobs at home. There is, too, the obvious risk to all concerned of severe long-term damage to the South African economy and the certainty that, unless sanctions are comprehensively imposed, there will be sanction-busting from some opportunistic regime. Most tenuous, even hypocritical, is the argument that those who will be most hurt are the black South Africans themselves. Tutu has no problem dealing with this. In America he met the point by saying 'Blacks retort "When did you suddenly become so altruistic? Did you not benefit from black cheap and black migratory labour? Did you ever protest against these and other causes of black suffering?"'[8] In his own country, when accused by a government Minister of being indifferent to the suffering sanctions would bring to black people, he retorted 'His new found altruism is quite galling, when you realise that he is a member of a government whose policies have inflicted quite deliberately and of set purpose unnecessary and unacceptable suffering on our people . . . The Minister should spare us his crocodile tears.'[9]

The majority of blacks take a philosophical view on the harm sanctions would inflict on them. Representatives of the British Churches, visiting South Africa in 1985, found that the blacks felt that 'their present suffering was intolerable and they were prepared to accept whatever more the ending of apartheid would entail. "There is a difference," we were told, "between suffering in hope and suffering in hopelessness".'[10]

In his numerous statements on the subject, delivered all over the world in every available forum, Tutu has drawn a fine line between advocating diplomatic and economic pressure and calling for punitive sanctions; time and again he has skated close to making treasonable statements. Some think him wrong, some find his views naïve and ill-informed, but even those who do not agree with his thinking on the subject cannot but admire his courage when, on April 2nd, 1985, he fulfilled his promise and called for punitive economic sanctions. In doing this he not only faced the taunts of those who accuse him of commending fasting while himself enjoying a full stomach, but risked the real possibility of being charged with treason. Only his international fame has kept him out of prison.

Tutu's support of sanctions is a reflection of his abhorrence of violence, since 1984 endemic in the townships and certain to become worse if apartheid is not dismantled. (It must not be forgotten that the occasional periods of apparent calm are the result of brutal State suppression; true peace is a stranger in South Africa.) He has frequently said that he rejects all forms of violence, whether the primary violence of a repressive system or the violence of those who try to overthrow it. But, he usually adds, he is a peace-lover, not a pacifist.

The Church has traditionally defined the 'just war' by giving certain criteria which must be met by Christians before participating in an armed struggle: the cause must be worthy; the intention should be the advancement of good; the war must be waged by 'proper means'; there must be a reasonable chance of success; the good to be gained must be greater than the harm inflicted; all other methods of resolving the situation should have been attempted. How do these criteria apply in South Africa?

Apart from the right-wing minority there can be few people who do not appreciate the justice of the cause, nor can anyone who has studied the history of the ANC, or followed the fruitless attempts at peaceful protest made by opponents of apartheid, doubt that the blacks have not only shown extraordinary patience but are, as Tutu often says, 'peace-loving to a fault'. All methods of achieving a peaceful solution have been tried and failed. If exasperation has spilled over into unworthy means, such as the horrific 'necklace' killings, they have been repeatedly condemned, not only by Tutu, but by the majority of the people. The question of what might follow armed insurrection is obviously hypothetical, but Tutu is in no doubt of what his attitude would be if a black government came to power; if it perpetrated the same atrocities that are being perpetrated today he would be just as outspoken as he is in the face of the current white political dispensation. The hardest of these criteria for black Christians to meet is the question of the probable success of taking up arms. Given the huge power exercised by the whites – they proudly announce that they have not yet unleashed a fraction of their power – the chances are, to say the least of it, not high. The blacks have virtually no weapons to take up; all they have on their side are their numbers and the justice of their cause.

Tutu's tightrope is at its tautest and most precarious in his efforts to maintain a non-violent position in a situation of such hopelessness. To support violence is foreign to everything he stands for, yet the pressure to do so is overwhelming, both in terms of his own wish for justice and in his personal credibility, particularly with young blacks impatient of his moderation. Though he has never deviated from his wish for a non-violent solution, he argues that non-violence demands a certain minimum morality from the government if it is to be effective. As that is absent, he is increasingly expressing his sympathy with those for whom a violent response to a violent regime is the only answer, frequently saying, 'there may be a time when we have to take up arms and defend ourselves'. In June 1986 he went even further, saying at a rally in Toronto that if sanctions failed to persuade Pretoria to dismantle apartheid, 'The Church would have no alternative but to say it would be justifiable to use violence and force to overthrow an unjust regime'.[11]

There is an uncomfortable contradiction between, on the one hand, Tutu's condemnation of violence, on the other his readiness to admit that the Church itself teaches that there are times when it is justifiable to resort to arms. Though he has clarified his position on sanctions, on the even more crucial matter of violence his position is more ambivalent. While radical blacks think not only that he should come down on the side of the armed struggle, but that he will, Tutu insists that violence is evil, even when conditions make it justifiable. Most people agree that the conditions of the just war theory have been fulfilled in South Africa in the 1980s as surely as they were in Europe in 1914 and 1939. Many are aware that those who denounce blacks fighting for their freedom did not have any problems when countries defended themselves in two world wars. But the furthest Tutu will go is to say that the time is approaching when violence may be seen as a lesser evil than the continued oppression of the people. Even then, he says that people must decide for themselves – he could not pick up a gun and fight. It is hard to blame him.

Another strand of the tightrope Tutu walks, not least in the dilemma he faces over the issue of violence, is theological. He is firmly in the Anglican episcopal tradition, a custodian of a deposit of faith handed down through many generations, yet he lives in a country which is developing a strong modern contextual theology, rooted in the experience of people in South Africa and talking in terms of the oppressor and the oppressed. The problems for anyone living this duality were highlighted by the publication of one of the most significant theological statements to emerge from the crisis in South Africa, the *Kairos Document*.[12]

The *Kairos Document* (*Kairos* – the moment of truth), was released in September 1985 under the signatures of 151 South African theologians who had been meeting regularly to discuss the crisis into which South Africa has been plunged. It is a theological comment, not an official statement of the Church; a part of the on-going debate about the Christian response to the South African situation, not a final document. In pursuit of its goal – to articulate the experience of faith for the majority of South Africans – the document offers an analysis of how the Church, with its ill-matched bedfellows of both oppressor and oppressed, should respond to the situation in the country. It was intended to stimulate discussion and prayer and to lead to action.

It outspokenly condemns what it calls the 'State Theology' used to justify apartheid, saying it is not only heretical, but blasphemous; it is critical of 'Church theology', the response of the so-called 'English' Churches, saying it 'tends to make use of abstract principles like reconciliation, negotiation, non-violence and peaceful solutions and applies them indiscriminately and uncritically to all situations'. The authors insist that politics and political strategies cannot be bypassed and call for a 'prophetic theology'. The conflict, they state, is between the oppressor and the oppressed, between 'two irreconcilable causes or interests in which the one is just and the other unjust'. Reflecting on the question of whether the South African government should properly be termed tyrannical, they point out that a tyrant has tradition- ally been defined as an enemy of the common good and there is no doubt that the majority of people in South Africa think that apartheid is indeed that. If the State is tyrannical then 'the most loving thing we can do for both the oppressed and for our enemies who are oppressors is to eliminate the oppression'. God is undoubtedly on the side of the oppressed.

It ends with a message of hope and a challenge to action. The Church must take sides unequivocally, never doing anything that might appear 'to give legitimacy to a morally illegitimate regime'; further it must be prepared to be involved in civil disobedience, as 'a Church that takes its responsibilities seriously in these circumstances will sometimes have to confront and to disobey the State in order to obey God'.

Many senior churchmen of all denominations were disturbed by the *Kairos Document* and there has been much speculation as to why Bishop Tutu's name did not appear amongst the signatories to the document. Did it indicate his disapproval? Was he erring on the side of caution? Could he have been offended at the suggestion that it was aimed at people like him, who by virtue of their office represent the established Church? Had he perhaps not even been asked? The truth is simpler. The Kairos theologians were not campaigning for signatures; the document was signed only by those who had partici- pated in the discussions and Tutu had not been amongst them. They did, however, keep him informed and made sure he had a copy of the draft, not least to prepare him for the inevitable questions from the press. The issue, in reality, was not whether he signed, but the nature of his reaction.

So part of the reason that he did not sign the document was that he had not been involved in it and had been too busy to read it closely.

But in the event he was glad he had not signed as, though he supported its broad outlines, he had reservations, which, had he been present at the discussions, he would have raised. He was distressed by 'the kind of blanket condemnation of what you would call white Church leadership', citing people like the Most Reverend Philip Russell, then Archbishop of Cape Town, and Peter Storey, then president of the Methodist Church of Southern Africa, who had risked so much in the struggle for freedom. He also felt the Kairos theologians had come close to justifying violence, something he simply could not do. He sympathised with its angry tone, reflecting that 'Prophets, I suppose, were not noted for their delicate language';[13] but, most crucially, he had real and deep-rooted problems over the question of reconciliation.

The Kairos theologians are adamant that repentance must precede reconciliation. They argue that there are conflicts – and South Africa's is one –

> where one side is a fully armed and violent oppressor while the other side is defenceless and oppressed. There are conflicts which can only be described as the struggle between justice and injustice, good and evil, God and the devil. To speak of reconciling these two is not only a mistaken application of the Christian idea of reconciliation, it is a total betrayal of all that Christian faith has ever meant.

While Tutu may, intellectually, be persuaded by the logic of this argument, though there is no question whose side he is on, for him to stop seeking reconciliation goes directly against the grain of both his Christianity and his temperament; for him reconciliation is about people, not positions. As in the case of violence, he does not think less of those who are persuaded by such an argument; it is simply that he, in his heart, is not.

In the constantly changing situation in South Africa, Desmond Tutu holds determinedly to a central position. The things he says and does are radical, courageous and provocative, thus offending those with less determination to change the system; yet he comes over as a moderate man, too ready to negotiate to satisfy militant demands. So he is criticised from all sides, often by people who cannot hear what he is actually saying. It is not a comfortable position. He has to remember also that, in the words of Frank Chikane, 'There is no guarantee that because a group of people are oppressed they are saying what God is saying'. Though he listens ever more acutely to the voice of the community and is increasingly sensitive to the groundswell of popular feeling, he is an independent man, with ultimately one guide and counsellor, the God with whom he daily spends long hours in prayer.

18

Archbishop of Cape Town

In November 1985, when Philip Russell announced that he intended
to retire as Archbishop of Cape Town the following August, speculation as to who his successor would be began to mount. Tutu,
nominated when elections were last held in 1981, was an obvious
front-runner for the post, but there were predictable objections.

The months preceding the Elective Assembly had seen Tutu polar-
ising opinion even more than he had for the past decade. He was
constantly in the eye of the storm, reviled and loved, castigated and
admired, buffeted from every direction. Should so controversial a man
occupy the highest position in the Anglican Church in South Africa?
There were plenty of people who thought he should not. Though his
acts of courage in saving lives and his condemnation of violence,
whether from the police, the army, the ANC or the black community
themselves, had gained him some support in white eyes, it was
outweighed by his controversial American tour in January, in particular
by his call that the West should support the ANC. The balance tipped
further against him when, the shock-waves of that particular episode
still reverberating, he demanded punitive international sanctions
against South Africa. Among blacks he was, as ever, loved as a man
and honoured both as a religious leader and as a symbol of black
achievement, but some of his actions – his meetings with the President,
his threat to leave the country if the 'black-on-black' violence did
not stop, the confusion over his call for a day of prayer and his doomed
effort to negotiate with the government on behalf of the people of
Alexandra – had lessened his influence, particularly over the young
people, and diminished his credibility. He himself tells of a youth who
asked him what his efforts at reconciliation had actually achieved; he
even admitted, 'If I were a young black I wouldn't listen to Tutu any
more.' Poised on the threshold of high achievement in the Church,
as a political leader he was, according to a leading black journalist,
still a useful spokesman, 'but people will not follow him as they follow
the United Democratic Front or Cosatu' (the Congress of South
African Trade Unions.)[1]

He himself did not want the job. He has never denied being

ambitious – indeed when he was at the SACC he told a reporter with disarming candour that one day he would like to be Archbishop – but since becoming Bishop of Johannesburg he had assured the diocese that he was happy to retire in that job; indeed, after so short a time in the post, had he any right to subject the diocese of Johannesburg to another change? Also he knew that Leah, her considerable energy and talents harnessed to her work with the Domestic Workers Employment Project and with many friends in Johannesburg, was adamantly opposed to moving to Cape Town.

But this was not something to be decided by the country at large, it was a matter for the Anglican Church. Whatever his political standing, whether the graph of his credibility was moving up or down, there was no question in the minds of the majority of the clerics and lay people concerned that when they met to make their choice Bishop Tutu's name should be included among the nominees. Against his will and in spite of his wife's strong reservations, he was persuaded to stand. If it were God's will that he should stay in Johannesburg, he argued (as he had done a decade earlier before he became Bishop of Lesotho), then he would not be elected.

So on April 14th the Advisory Committee duly submitted the nominations and the 500-strong Elective Assembly, consisting of all the clergy of Cape Town Province, the elected lay representatives and one priest and one layman from every other diocese of the Province, met in Cape Town to consider each nominee in turn, put the arguments and vote for their choice. (The Bishops of the Province are present at the discussions but do not vote.) They were prepared to sit for many days, expecting the proceedings to run to the statutory maximum of five or six ballots before they could reach the necessary two-thirds majority; they might even reach deadlock and be forced to refer the decision to the Bishops, for it was a decision with far-reaching implications and a fierce battle was anticipated.

Though there were several strong contenders, notably the Right Reverend Michael Nuttall, Bishop of Natal, attention was concentrated on Bishop Tutu and there is a sense in which the questions the Assembly had to consider were the very same issues which had bedevilled Tutu for so long. What would be the effect of Tutu's appointment be on the already worsening relations between Church and State? Though recent holders of the post – Archbishops Robert Selby-Taylor, Bill Burnett and Philip Russell – were all resolutely opposed to the government, none were so controversial, none so vociferous, none had so high a profile. If they chose Tutu would there be white defections from the Church, with all the resulting financial as well as spiritual consequences? Might there even be a split in the

Anglican Church? The choice of Bishop Tutu would most certainly indicate the Churches' support for his stand on sanctions, already the subject of a resolution by the SACC. And as always there was the racial issue, stirring up the same contradictory feelings as before he became Bishop of Johannesburg. This dilemma was summed up by Peter Collins, senior lecturer in political studies at the University of Cape Town: 'If Bishop Tutu is elected many whites will think the church has sold out to radicals. If he isn't elected many blacks will think the church is hypocritical in its commitment to non-racialism.'[2]

The very next day the press blazed out the news: TUTU CHOSEN. TUTU TO LEAD ANGLICANS. CHOICE OF TUTU IS HAILED. ELECTION OF TUTU WON'T PLEASE ALL. TUTU: 'CHOICE WILL RENEW CONTROVERSY'. Far from being a battle, the delegates had reached their conclusion in a matter of hours rather than days. Proceedings are held behind locked doors and are confidential, but it is widely thought that only two or three ballots were necessary; certainly they had achieved a clear two-thirds majority and the choice was unanimously approved by the Bishops.

The speed and unanimity of the decision baffled and, at least temporarily, muted his critics. Though the initial reaction among local white Anglicans was cool, a surprisingly large section of the press welcomed his appointment, recognising that it marked a historic moment in the history of the Anglican Church. They acknowledged the daunting task ahead of the Archbishop-Elect, asserting that he was 'an invaluable bridge across the racial gulf',[3] referring to him as 'a man of godliness and great courage'[4] and welcoming the even greater spiritual authority he would now have. The *Cape Times* even voiced the vain hope that perhaps there might be some mark of official recognition and goodwill.

The SACC expressed 'deep joy', the clergy of Cape Town were delighted, congratulations came from the Progressive Federal Party and the Azanian Students' Organisation, the Archbishop of Canterbury Dr Robert Runcie and Chief Buthelezi, from the DRC Minister Dr Nico Smit and Dr Alex Boraine, from Dr Allan Boesak, Bishop Michael Nuttall, the Dean of Cape Town, the Very Reverend E. L. King, Mary Burton of the Black Sash and many more. The black community rejoiced, as they had rejoiced when Tutu received the Nobel Peace Prize, feeling the election of a black man was a victory for all victims of apartheid.

Tutu's critics in the press mostly restrained themselves to admonishment, hoping that the new Archbishop would 'learn humility and greater understanding';[5] that he 'would moderate his political activities and viewpoints'[6] and that the responsibilities of high office would 'temper his impetuosity'.[7] The *Daily News*, in similar vein but with a lighter touch, hoped that his new responsibilities would have a restraining effect, reminding its readers of the Afrikaans proverb '*Maak die wolf die skaapwagter*' (Make the wolf the shepherd) and hoped that the new Archbishop would 'nurse his flock with tender care, not set fire to the pasturage'.[8] The *Daily Dispatch* used the occasion to point out that the apartheid system had been shown to be 'no barrier to his progress'.[9]

Many individual voices were raised in opposition to his election, in tones ranging from the tentative to the downright hostile. Alan Paton expressed his wish that Tutu would do well, but admitted that he would rather have seen the Bishop of Natal elected; the Deputy Minister of Information, Louis Nel, showing a curious ignorance of the Archbishop's views, urged him to reject violence as a means of change and to try to reconcile the different communities in the country; President Botha declined to comment. The rage of the right-wing knew no bounds. Dr Treurnicht, the leader of the Conservative Party, said that the election of Bishop Tutu did not bode well, as he had distinguished himself more as a political agitator than as a Church leader, and Louis Stofberg, the General Secretary of the Herstigste Nasionale Party, described the election as shocking, adding that it would further efforts to achieve a revolution in South Africa. Professor Ben Engelbrecht, head of the Department of Divinity at the University of the Witwatersrand, was the most hostile, calling the Bishop a 'theological impostor' and 'a prophet on a band-wagon'. 'Were it not for apartheid,' he wrote, 'it is almost certain that the name of "Tutu" would have remained in obscurity.'[10]

The man at the centre of it all had been nervous during the Assembly. He may not have wanted the job, but neither did he savour the idea of rejection, or even a repeat of the Johannesburg experience, when the inability of the delegates to agree caused the decision to be referred to the Bishops. He was so overcome by the news of his election that Moira Henderson, with whom he was staying, said, 'He was terribly subdued – all the bounce had gone out of him'. His first thought was to telephone Leah in Johannesburg; not expecting the decision for several days, she had gone out for the evening and he did not want her to hear from the press. He then celebrated with some of his future colleagues and – untypically – slept late the next morning.

Though Leah took a while to come to terms with yet another move, the shy delight on Tutu's face in the press photographs show that his doubts and misgivings had been dispelled by the unhesitating decision. 'I'm tongue-tied,' he told reporters; 'and some people hope it's permanent.' 'It's all like a dream. I am quite overcome by the awesomeness of it all, and of the tremendous responsibility that has been placed on my shoulders.' At a special thanksgiving Eucharist in the Chapel of Diocesan College, the Cape Town boys' school where the election proceedings had been held, his critics began turning into fans. The same boys who had been asking 'Why has a black wog been appointed Archbishop?' were, by the end of the service, queueing up to meet him. He had delighted them, not least by telling them that the reason the election was over so soon was that the delegates did not like the portable toilets that had been imported for the occasion and could not be done with it soon enough.

But he knew that not everyone would be won over so easily. In countless press interviews he asked people to remember that he would not be a one-man band, but would work with his fellow bishops. If people were angry over his appointment, 'they must not be angry with God and pull out of the Church. They must rather try to change my views.' He stressed that the Church has a mandate to speak out against oppression and that his intention was to show that the Church was one family, black and white together, and that it would continue to work for justice, peace and reconciliation. He was vindicated by the certainty of the decision, convinced that by changing from white leadership, with its traditional control of money and power, the Church 'was sending out a signal to the rest of the world and to the authorities here'. Refusing to apologise for his style of leadership, he asserted: 'I am me! I operate in the way Desmond Tutu operates. I don't sit down and work out strategies. I operate almost instinctively as I believe the Gospel demands.'

The five months between Tutu's election as Archbishop of Cape Town and his enthronement in September saw the situation in South Africa deteriorate yet further. There was not only the second state of emergency, with its ever-increasing expansion of police power and even fiercer restrictions on press freedom, but the accompanying detentions and the continual harassment and torture of blacks reached horrific proportions. The political divide widened even further with the upsurge of the right-wing, as Eugene Terre Blanche's followers, complete with Swastika-type flags and Nazi salutes, gained hysterical momentum; black despair reached a pitch which caused Oliver Tambo to call on South African blacks to 'steel themselves for war'. The government were losing control and death was a part of daily life.

Tutu was involved at every level, defiant and outspoken, constantly reacting. He greeted seemingly significant changes to apartheid, such as the dropping of the pass laws, with a warm welcome, but warned of the sting in the tail: 'One has to be very careful that they are not going to find another way of harassing blacks through "orderly urbanisation" or other means.'[11] (He was right. Though blacks were no longer liable to immediate arrest if found in white areas, there were still rigid controls over where they could live and work.) He repeated that he was not interested in incremental change – Franken-stein cannot be reformed, only destroyed; the name of the game was political power-sharing. He encouraged whites to be more involved in peaceful demonstrations and again urged Christians to be prepared to disobey unjust laws non-violently. He unequivocally condemned the recent spate of bomb attacks, praised the End Conscription Campaign as a sign of hope, expressed his admiration of people who boycotted the 1986 Olympics in their desire for sanctions against South Africa and his disappointment at the stubbornness of Margaret Thatcher. And he continued to say that there was still hope for South Africa – if the international community helped.

It was also during this period that his reaction to President Reagan's speech on July 22nd, 1986 caused people all over the world, even his admirers, to wonder if this time the Bishop had not gone too far. In this speech Reagan had, once again, declared his outright opposition to sanctions against South Africa and Tutu had responded by saying that the President, along with Britain's Margaret Thatcher and West Germany's Chancellor Helmut Kohl, were in effect saying to blacks 'You are utterly dispensable'. Reagan's speech he found 'nauseating', it was 'the pits' and for his part 'America and the West can go to hell'. Should a Bishop, even an admittedly angry Bishop, consign fellow human beings to hell?

He received so much flak for this remark that he did concede that his anger was unnecessary, because he should have known not to expect any better from President Reagan; and yes, perhaps he could have used 'less salty language'. But for the most part he was unapolo-getic. It was good for people to know how deeply blacks feel, he claimed, good for them to be reminded that South Africans were not just engaged in academic discussions. In any case, in speaking out so strongly he was following a distinguished biblical tradition:

> What do they make of what Our Lord said to the Pharisees? 'Generation of vipers' 'You whited sepulchres. You walk around looking smart outside when you are rotten bones inside.' And what about Paul? I mean, Paul says, 'I consign you to the devil.' He also said, 'He who Jesus says is not Lord, let him be accursed.' Well, saying the West can go to hell is no worse than that!

It was a good argument.

As so often, it was not so much the sentiment that outraged people, but its expression. Peter Storey has observed that

> He often says 'If you don't do such and such, then South Africa is for the birds' and the press always pick it up. If he had said 'South Africa will advance into deepening darkness', there would have been no problem. But this phrase 'for the birds' is the kind of thing that gets under whites' skins, they can't stand it.

Similarly, had he responded to Reagan's speech with a more considered phrase like 'We shall carry on our struggle without regard to America or the West' it would have annoyed fewer people, but equally it would probably have gone unnoticed. If his manner irritates, so does it draw attention to the enormity of the black predicament in South Africa. There are many such phrases in Tutu's verbal armoury. As when he said, again of Reagan, 'Your name is mud', or his tart response on being told that business companies were trying to improve working conditions for blacks – 'Baloney'. His remarks about the possibility of domestic workers poisoning their employers' coffee, which were intended as a warning, not a threat, or that the Russians would be received with open arms, struck many as flippant and irresponsible. How people respond depends partly on whether they enjoy his sense of humour, but even more on how well they understand the man and appreciate the sentiment behind the expression.

At the end of July, Tutu bade his formal farewell to the diocese of Johannesburg. (An occasion dubbed by one newspaper as 'Ta-ta for Tutu' – only one degree better than a cartoon captioned 'It Takes Tutu Tambo'. Such is the penalty of fame coupled with an unusual name.) Despite his rather equivocal election twenty months earlier, he had in fact succeeded in winning over a vast proportion of the community and, in the face of rumours of financial embarrassment, diocesan giving had actually gone up by 17 per cent in 1985. Suggestions that he had been appointed to Cape Town to remove him from Johannesburg were palpably untrue, not least because only two representatives of the Johannesburg diocese took part in the Elective Assembly.

So the farewell ceremony was an emotional occasion, as 2,000 members of the community gathered at the Ellis Park tennis stadium in a service for unity and peace. Tutu took the Christian family and the importance of sharing as his themes. Using one of his favourite sayings, 'A person is a person through other persons', he reminded his audience that Christians could not find salvation in isolation and that freedom was not something any person or group of people could have on their own. 'Freedom has to be shared, otherwise those who have it have no time to enjoy their separate freedom – they are too busy guarding it with guns and guard dogs and states of emergency. We all share in each other's glory – and equally in each other's shame.' Defying the government's ban on naming people in detention and warning once again that all that was legal was not necessarily moral, he urged people not to be intimidated, but to pray regularly for detainees by name. He also suggested that they devote one day a week to prayer and fasting for justice and peace and that they ring the church bells every day at noon until the state of emergency was lifted. By using the ways of the Church in the service of man, he had demonstrated yet again the close interrelation between religion and politics.

The parting words, delivered by Mr Henry Bennett, a lay member of the community, must have compensated for some of the hurt he had received as Bishop of his home city. After thanking Tutu for the 'outrageously long hours he worked and for listening to us with care', Mr Bennett said 'We admire you; we respect you; and we would like to emulate your steadfastness of purpose.'

Less personal, yet more poignant, was his last sermon in Soweto as Bishop of Johannesburg. During the previous week twenty-one people had been killed in riots in the White City area and Tutu had visited a mother who had lost a son in the shootings. All his optimism seemed drained out of him as, in a low anguished voice, he whispered,

> What do you say to these people? How do you tell them about the love of God? We suffer in a land that claims to be Christian and we suffer at the hands of those who say they are Christians. The price we have paid already is a heavy price. We will go on, paying yet more in lives.

In this service the pathos of South Africa's tragic divide was encapsulated. Not far away more than 100 police in armoured cars were preventing reporters from attending the funeral of a victim of the violence; inside the church hundreds of whites from northern Johannesburg, without the protection of permits, moved around the church in a multi-racial chain of worship carrying flowers and chanting 'Peace, Peace'.

As September 7th, the day of Tutu's enthronement as Archbishop of Cape Town, drew near, so did controversy mount. There were conflicting reports about disgruntled white conservatives leaving the Anglican Church. The Church of England in South Africa, from which the Church of the Province of South Africa had split in 1870, claimed that it was opening up new churches as defectors from the Church of the Province joined it; another breakaway Church, the Christian Fellowship, also boasted of growing congregations. A church in Natal found that so many supporters had withdrawn in the wake of Tutu's appointment to Cape Town that it was unable to pay its assessment to the diocese; conservative farming communities reported that their churches were 'virtually empty'. Yet most Anglican priests considered it was the casual attenders, not the regular churchgoers, who were leaving and the Very Reverend E. L. King, the Anglican Dean of Cape Town, felt that in Cape Town congregations had, if anything, increased. Bishop John Carter, the Anglican Church's provincial liaison officer, refused to be either surprised or concerned. He felt that black attendance could well be increasing and that more young people were joining the Church. 'We are just weathering the storm and are not depressed about it . . . The church will be here long after all this is over.'[12]

One issue that, however improbably, commanded international headlines was Tutu's guest list. Should he have invited members of the government? Should he be allowed to invite anyone he wished? Should so many leading black American entertainers and politicians have been included? Did he really know all these people, or was he merely trying to impress – and at the same time taunt the government?

The star-studded guest list, considered as Tutu's latest challenge to the government, even as a slap in the face for Pretoria, was published well in advance of the enthronement. The 165 invitations were issued to churchmen from all over the world, to politicians including Senator Edward Kennedy, Gary Hart and Congressman William Gray and to entertainers such as Harry Belafonte, Lionel Ritchie and Stevie Wonder. The former United Nations Ambassador Andrew Young was invited, as was the tennis star Arthur Ashe, the United Nations Secretary-General Javier Perez de Cuellar, Coretta Scott King, the widow of Martin Luther King and the Irish writer and fellow Nobel Peace Prize-winner Sean McBride.

Tutu asked the government for an assurance that his guests – who were in fact all personally known to him – would be granted visas, a request they predictably refused. The normal demands on the time of busy people saved them some embarrassment, as did the unwillingness of some of the more controversial figures to give the government the gratification of refusing them entry. Nevertheless, the sixty requests for visas that were received placed the authorities in an awkward predicament. Could they refuse visas to such distinguished guests? On the other hand how could they give their blessing to a major gathering of anti-apartheid campaigners? Political observers forecast that visas for churchmen and less controversial figures would be approved, while action on most requests would be delayed until after the ceremony. In fact, even some churchmen had difficulty obtaining entry. Some, like Bishop Ding, President of the China Christian Council, were refused visas. (When he rang Cape Town to express his disappointment Tutu said, 'It's outrageous, but let's pray for these people.') Some of the African Bishops were turned away at Jan Smuts Airport and some kept waiting for hours.

The day before the enthronement Cape Town's airport was throbbing with pressmen as the Tutus arrived to meet the Archbishop of Canterbury, Dr Robert Runcie, and his personal assistant Terry Waite. Even in the face of the government's restrictions many foreign dignitaries were in Cape Town that night. Among the Anglican primates were the Archbishops of Central Africa, Kampala, the Indian Ocean, Japan, Australia and New Zealand; Bishop John Walker of Washington and Bishop Edmond Browning, the Presiding Bishop of the Episcopal Church, had come from America, Bishop Amos Waiaru from the Solomon Isles. The Methodists, the Lutherans, the Baptists, the Churches of Norway and Sweden, the Roman Catholics, the Greek Orthodox Church, the Union Theological Seminary and the World Council of Churches were represented. Lay people included Mrs Coretta Scott King, the Mayor of Detroit, University Chancellors and Professors, a Congressman and a former Ambassador to the United Nations. From all over South Africa priests, colleagues and friends, including Winnie Mandela and Dr Ntatho Motlana, Dr Allan Boesak and Dr Beyers Naudé, Helen Joseph, Percy Qoboza and Allistair Sparks, were gathering.

While the Tutus' guests and friends were assembling in Cape Town, so too were their family. They were all there: the elder children – Trevor with his wife Zanele and daughter Palesa, a heavily pregnant Theresa and her husband Mthunzi – came from Johannesburg with Desmond's sister Gloria and Leah's blind mother; the Tutus' two younger daughters Naomi and Mpho flew over from the United States. They spent much of the time together at the home of Moira Henderson, where Desmond and Leah were staying, and Mrs Henderson remarked, as so many have done, on the closeness of the family and the way they welcome others into their circle: 'You all become Tutus, they absorb you into their family.' On the Saturday, with Helen Suzman, Martin Kenyon and various relations, they all went for a picnic; a few hours privacy before the next day's ceremonials.

* * *

On Sunday morning Tutu was up early, praying. For hours he prayed, then he had a glass of orange juice and he and Leah left for the cathedral.

Cape Town had known controversial Archbishops, indeed Tutu was inheriting a mantle worn by uncompromising critics of apartheid such as Geoffrey Clayton, Joost de Blank and Robert Selby Taylor, all thorns in the flesh of the various governments of their time. Politics and religion, symbolically close in the proximity of St George's Cathedral to the House of Assembly, were to be drawn even closer in the person of the Eleventh Archbishop of Cape Town; even with this heritage the enthronement of the provocative Bishop Tutu was an event that was creating world-wide interest. There were claims that 200 million people would be watching on television, even that as a television event it would come a close second to the recent royal wedding in Great Britain. The South African authorities ensured that this would not be so by forbidding any live transmission of the ceremony and barring all film crews, save a small independent production company, from the cathedral; the event was completely ignored in the South African Broadcasting Corporation's morning radio broadcasts. So, although press coverage the following day was lavish, with full pages of colour pictures, immediate appreciation of the event was limited to those fortunate enough to be present at the cathedral.

At this, the highest moment of Tutu's ecclesiastical career, the polarised reactions he provokes were in evidence on the very steps of St George's Cathedral. As he prepared to strike the great west door three times with his silver crook, a scuffle broke out: his supporters were trying to remove a wreath of white and purple flowers laid provocatively in his path by a white woman in black mourning dress acting in the name of United Christian Action and intended to mark 'the death of the Anglican Church'. The Gospel Defence League was distributing anti-Tutu tracts, in which his sayings (often inaccurately recorded) were set against quotations from the Bible. Another elderly white Anglican woman was standing with a placard bearing the legend 'TUTU STATEMENTS UN-CHRISTIAN. TUTU SANTIONS [*sic*] AGAINST BLACKS'.

Just as the ceremony took place in a context of conflicting praise and protest, so, inside the cathedral, some 1,700 people, including 150 Bishops, were gathered for a service which, in a curiously unerring way, reflected the rich diversity of the Archbishop's nature. It was both formal and informal, dignified and intimate. Deeply Anglican, it held African elements in an easy embrace; deeply spiritual, it was imbued with a spirit of festivity. Its high seriousness did not exclude humour.

It was a glittering affair, with the Tutu family in the front row, gaily dressed in bold African prints, the chancel a sea of priests wearing embroidered vestments in red, green, gold, silver, purple and white and the cathedral burnished and garlanded with flowers. The key points of the ancient ritual, from the three knocks on the door to the presentation of the diamond-studded Kimberley Cross and the shout of the people 'We welcome you in the name of the Lord', were firmly in the Anglican tradition, but an Anglican church has seldom resounded to such an uninhibited shout of 'VIVA TUTU'. No music could echo Anglican sentiments more truly than Sir Hubert Parry's 'I was glad when they said unto me', the hymn 'Praise to the holiest in the heights' or, by special request of Archbishop Tutu, 'Jesu Joy of Man's Desiring'. Yet for many people the musical high point was the singing of the eighty-strong group from Soweto, Imilonji ka Ntu, the black choir taking their turn with the cathedral choir. They had composed a traditional African praise-song for him, something that was a surprise to the Archbishop himself. 'Sing, here comes the msimbithi stick', it began, 'Sing, here comes the redemption stick'. In a glorious ten minutes of singing and ululating and interjections from Africans in the congregation, the praise-song traced the Archbishop's life from its roots 'in barren soil . . . it was weak as it grew' through overseas travel and international honours to that day: 'Go on mysterious stick, collect your sheep and lead them . . . Take them from the kraals of oppression . . . Lead them to spiritual pastures where they'll feed with no considerations of colour. Then the msimbithi stick will become the stick of redemption.'

Archbishop Tutu's charge ranged over God and Man, religion and politics, the spiritual and the secular, the humorous and the profoundly serious, while remaining rooted securely in its central unifying depths. He began by quoting a sermon given by Trevor Huddleston which started 'In the beginning, God' and finished 'In the end, God'; then, speaking in English, Sotho and Afrikaans, he spent some time in welcomes and thanks. More in the fashion of a good after-dinner speaker than a preacher, he amused his audience by greeting his 'brother . . . er . . . primates . . . a somewhat unfortunate name, that', his valued friend the Archbishop of Canterbury and 'the utterly inconspicuous Terry Waite'. He mentioned literally scores of people by name, ending with thanking his mother-in-law for providing Leah for him.

The central part of his address was vintage Tutu. Though it contained little that keen Tutu-watchers had not heard before, it was as complete a summary of his views as he has ever given at one hearing. In stressing the centrality of the spiritual he offered praise 'to God that our God is such a God' – a God for whom no one is a nonentity and whose existence makes all life religious. He compared the family of the Church with the human family, where disagreement does not destroy unity and whose members receive in relation to their need, not their contribution. Members of a family care for one another.

> How I pray that Our Lord would open our eyes so that we would see the real, the true identity of each one of us, that this is not a so-called 'coloured', or white, or black or Indian, but a brother, a sister – and treat each other as such. Would you let your brother live an unnatural life as a migrant worker in a single-sex hostel?

He reflected sadly that 'the fundamental attitude that "blacks are human, but . . ." has not changed' and that God wants to enlist us as his agents of transformation.

Typically, the sharp reminders of man's cruelty to man were followed by gratitude for the welling up of goodness. He praised the women of the Black Sash and the young people working with the End Conscription Campaign; he rejoiced that blacks could still forgive. Like a priest who, as he was being tortured, thought 'These are God's children and they are behaving like animals. They need us to help them recover the humanity they have lost'; and a former colleague who, after 230 days in solitary confinement and nearly a year in detention said on his release, 'Let us not be consumed by bitterness.'

While he offered the traditional prayers for President P. W. Botha 'and all in authority under him', he could not resist making a point that he knew would reach the absent government – but this time there was a difference. He said that he did not want sanctions and that if the government would lift the state of emergency, remove the troops from the townships, release political prisoners and detainees, unban political organisations and negotiate with the authentic representatives of the community for one undivided South Africa, 'then, for what it is worth, I would say to the world "put your sanction plans on hold". The onus must be on those who say no to sanctions – provide us with a viable non-violent strategy to force the dismantling of apartheid.'

As Archbishop Tutu left the cathedral to the tolling of bells, blessing the people and the city, the day was far from over: 10,000 people were already assembling at the Goodwood Stadium for a Eucharist, one of the largest ever held in South Africa. There were greetings to the new Archbishop from the UDF and, through Dr Allan Boesak, from forty-five heads of state and the exiled ANC President Oliver Tambo. There were massed choirs and marimba bands, the singing of Anglican and African hymns, including of course '*Nkosi Sikele' iAfrika*'. The Archbishop of Canterbury gave a brave and impressive sermon, setting the tone of his call for peace with the sombre words, 'As I stand here, on the tip of Africa, I cannot escape the sense of history unfolding – the sense that here on what was once the Dark Continent, there is the threat of greater darkness still.' But even in the midst of this great celebration of unity, there were stirrings of unrest. Not from the police, who kept a discreet distance, but from young members of the UDF, wanting to use this vast gathering as a platform for their political views. So great was their excitement at seeing Winnie Mandela that she took the generous course and turned back, rather than let the service become a demonstration. Seeking another outlet, they started running rhythmically round the congregation – was this a good-humoured contribution to the proceedings or did it bode trouble? After a quick consultation it was agreed that Dr Allan Boesak and Mrs Albertina Sisulu, the wife of Walter Sisulu, in prison with Nelson Mandela, should take their turn amongst those speaking from the altar. Their words diffused the situation, though many were upset that a religious ceremony had come so close to becoming a political rally.

Tutu has never forgotten the way his election as Bishop of Johannesburg was ignored by that city, so the evening celebrations, when the Mayor of Cape Town hosted a reception in his honour in the Banqueting Hall, were balm to his soul. Though as he entered the City Hall he had to pass white youths bearing placards saying 'TUTU PREACHES SANCTIONS NOT THE GOSPEL' and 'OUR CHILDREN STARVE WHILE TUTUS EAT', once inside, he was among friends, not only those who had travelled to be with him for his enthronement, but his new friends in Cape Town. At last he had received an official welcome and, as he moved among the guests, at one stage climbing on to the stage to dance with the group who had come from Soweto, his delight shone from him.

It had been a great day, a day heralding a new era in the history of Christianity in South Africa. What lay ahead? The Dean of Cape Town, the Very Reverend E. L. King, summarised many people's feelings of excitement and apprehension as he said to the parish council at their first meeting after the enthronement, 'Hold on to your seat belts and enjoy the ride.'

Epilogue

After just two years as Archbishop of Cape Town there were already clear indications as to the direction in which Tutu sought to steer the province.

His first wish was, as always, for reconciliation. 'I would think that I had been used effectively if the Anglican Church in South Africa were to recognise ourselves as family, if we were to recognise ourselves not as black, white, coloured, Indian and so forth but that we were family. And that therefore we wanted to hold on to each other, despite all the centrifugal forces that are trying to pull us apart.' So he started in his immediate domain, remembering the clergy in every dimension of their lives. His office buzzed with life, acting as a centre for information and care for the sick, a listening ear for anyone with problems; special care was taken to include retired clergy and clergy widows in diocesan functions and the entire staff trooped to the funerals of clergy they thought long dead. He continued his generous practice of sending flowers to colleagues on their wedding anniversaries or their wives' birthdays, continued to issue reprimands to clergy who didn't send him photographs of themselves and their families. ('How can I pray for you if I can't *see* you?') He and Leah both wanted Bishopscourt to be a home for the diocese and one of the first things they did was to encourage the township children to come and swim and picnic in the extensive grounds. It was a microcosm of hope of things to come, as hundreds of black children enjoyed the benefits of what had hitherto been an exclusively white suburb, and where the Tutus lived illegally, if officially.

He wanted the province to be enterprising, visionary and characterised by generosity. Rather than fostering a penny-pinching approach, automatically fearing resources would not be available, he encouraged people around him to dream, then to see what money was needed and try to raise it. The province was not poor and Tutu felt it should be giving, not seeking assistance from overseas. 'If only we could manage somehow to respond to the divine generosity by an answering generosity on our part.'

But behind the sense of family, the hopes and visions, his passionate wish to affirm the centrality of the spiritual ran like a golden thread. To this end he appointed Dr Francis Cull [1] as Director of Spirituality, but the effect of Tutu's personal charisma and his own faith is incalculable. Edward King, then Dean of Cape Town, wrote that 'He just can't understand why so-called Christians cannot be aghast with "wonder, love and praise" as he is', and was deeply impressed by the simple fervour with which the Archbishop preached to a huge gathering of all the rectors and church wardens in the diocese. 'It was just the outpouring of a man amazed at God's goodness . . . he spreads a spiritual contagion and you *know* he believes what he says.' [2]

This spiritual contagion touched his fellow bishops and archbishops in July 1988, when he played an important role in the Lambeth Conference. His contribution both to the planning committee and as a conscientious vice-chairman of the section on Christianity and the Social Order was greatly appreciated; his part in the controversial debates on women in the ordained ministry and on the resolution on the appropriate and inappropriate use of violence was received with the respect that he increasingly commands throughout the Anglican Communion. But most of all the Conference was grateful to him for never forgetting the spiritual nature of the exercise; especially they were deeply moved by the meditations he led at the opening vigil and at the conclusion of the Conference. In the words of the secretary of the conference, the Reverend Canon Sam van Culin, 'He gave himself with a glad and generous heart.'

The year 1987 saw little change for the better in South Africa. A glimmering of hope might be seen in the DRC's admission that its theology over apartheid was in error, but the admission soon led to a split in the DRC church and the formation of the dissident Afrikaanse Protestantse Kerk, an exclusive right-wing church for white Afrikaners. Spirits were temporarily raised in November, with the release of the ANC leader Govan Mbeki after twenty-three years, only to be dashed shortly as a restriction order was placed on him. He was not allowed to leave the magisterial district of Port Elizabeth without permission, to give interviews or to write for any publication. Overall Tutu sees the situation as 'infinitely worse'. After the white elections in May, which saw the National Party strengthened and the Progressive Federal Party ousted by the right-wing Conservative Party as the official opposition, Tutu's reaction was unequivocal. He warned that South Africa was entering 'the dark ages of the history of this country' and that the stage was now set for further polarisation. On the one hand he foresaw 'an escalation in the intransigence of this government, an escalation in oppression and intolerance of any dissent'; on the other hand he felt 'the despondency in the air will deepen and so will the anger of the black community, where, even up to now, an amazing degree of goodwill still existed'.

As Archbishop, Tutu continued to speak out, enraging some, delighting others. Immediately after the election he was in Brazil, calling for all nations to break diplomatic relations with South Africa; the following month he joined radicals protesting against the government by urging Anglicans to wear black armbands and toll bells on the first anniversary of the state of emergency; on the eve of the Commonwealth Conference in Vancouver he renewed his call for sanctions; in December 1986, with an estimated 1,300 to 1,800 children held in detention, he called for their release, asking, 'What country detains eleven-year-olds because they are a threat to the security of the State?' With that informal directness which infuriates his critics, he said that the state of emergency had achieved nothing and warned the government that 'if you do not deal with the basic problems you are playing marbles'. And at a graduation ceremony at the University of the Western Cape he told the students, 'If Christ returned to South Africa today he would almost certainly be detained under the present security laws, because of his concern for the poor, the hungry and the oppressed.'

Though like all South Africans, he was muzzled by press restrictions and though what has become known as 'sanctions fatigue' resulted in statements receiving less coverage than in the first half of the decade, in both words and actions Tutu continued to defy Pretoria. He refused to attend the State Opening of Parliament, he led a group of religious leaders in talks with the ANC, he urged the government to return District Six to the coloured community and once again criticised them for 'moving people around like sacks of potatoes', he attacked the international banks for extending credit to South Africa without guarantees that apartheid would be eliminated. Most deliberately he held a service for detainees in St George's Cathedral. In doing this he was one of many clergymen putting to the test the latest government restrictions which made it illegal to sign petitions, to protest, to wear T-shirts calling for the release of detainees or even – until the public outcry forced the government to back down – to pray publicly for detainees. (The government figures put the number of people detained between June 1986 and February 1987 at 13,244, but that figures excludes those held for less than thirty days. Other estimates put the figure as high as 25,000.)

Approval of these actions was shown in ways varying from the American jazz trumpeter Miles Davis naming his new album 'Tu Tu' to readers of the *Sowetan* newspaper placing him after Nelson Mandela and Oliver Tambo in their own poll for the leader of a post-apartheid government. He also, in the first ten months of 1987, received three more honorary doctorates, The Freedom of the City of Durham, two awards from Brazil, and the 'Pacem in Terris' award from Cleveland, Ohio. As usual criticism came from all quarters, perhaps most dramatically from an Australian who referred to him as 'a modern-day witch-doctor dressed up in the garb of a clergyman'. And the misquotations continued. A pastoral visit to Mozambique became a political event as he was accused of saying, 'The time for violence has come.' What he had in fact said was, 'I will tell you the day I believe we must tell the world that we have now reached a point where we must use violence to overthrow an unjust system. I do not believe we are there yet.'

In his first year as Archbishop, Tutu kept a relatively low political profile: 1988 was to see this change dramatically. The catalyst came on February 24th with President Botha's decision to prohibit the UDF, AZAPO and fifteen other anti-apartheid bodies from 'any activity whatsoever' for which prior permission had not been granted by Adriaan Vlok, the Minister for Law and Order. In effect these groups were prevented from any activities other than keeping their books and paying the bills.

Not only were these prohibitions condemned world-wide but they also had, at least temporarily, precisely the opposite effect to that intended by the government. Once again South Africa was on the international agenda, new life was breathed into the dormant sanctions campaign, the ANC warned that the crack-down would boost recruits to the armed struggle. Most specifically, the churches, now one of the main extra-parliamentary groupings able to function at all, stepped decisively into the political vacuum. They openly identified with the restricted organisations and challenged the government in a series of statements and actions that faced Pretoria with a church-led civil campaign. The churches had taken on the anti-apartheid struggle, and Church and State, more than ever before, were in head-on collision.

The church leaders acted immediately. The day after the restrictions were announced, they met in Johannesburg and issued a defiant statement saying they would continue to call for the release of detainees and for the unbanning of political organisations; they would continue to press for negotiations with 'the true leaders of our country', declaring, 'Our mandate for these activities comes from God, and no man and no government will stop us.' The next Sunday, at 3 p.m., churches throughout the country held services of protest.

This was only a prelude to what was to come. On February 29th, after a short, though packed, service at St George's Cathedral, Cape Town, Tutu and other church leaders, including the Roman Catholic Archbishop of Cape Town, Stephen Naidoo, the president of the Methodist Church, the Reverend Khoza Mgojo, Dr Allan Boesak and Frank Chikane, General Secretary of the South African Council of Churches, attempted to lead a march to the Parliament buildings bearing a petition protesting against the crack-down on anti-apartheid groups. As participants in the dignified procession, walking slowly with arms linked, reached Parliament Street, they were met by squads of riot police, who ordered them by loudhailer to disperse. (The procession infringed a security law prohibiting demonstrations near Parliament.) When the priests at the head of the procession refused to disperse, merely kneeling down to pray, they were seized by security police, bundled into cars and taken to police headquarters for questioning. Water cannon were then turned on the other marchers, 150 or so clerics, nuns, diplomatic observers, journalists and others who had disregarded the orders. Drenched to the skin, they too were taken off in police vans.

Though the clergy were released quickly – indeed, they were back at St George's Cathedral within an hour – the procession, which if left alone might have passed off quietly, became world news. Not only was police behaviour seen in marked contrast to the tolerance shown to thousands of armed men belonging to the Afrikaner Resistance Movement (AWB) who only a few days earlier had marched through the streets of Pretoria, but also statements made by the clergy at the press conference following their release, leaving no doubt about the churches' stand, reached an international audience. 'The government can kill the dreamer, but not the dream,' said Archbishop Naidoo. 'This is an illegitimate government that deserves no authority and does not have it,' declared Dr Boesak. It gave Tutu the chance to gesture to the others who had been detained and say, 'At least they can't say it was just those rabble-rousers Tutu and Boesak.' Later he told the *New Statesman* that the procession was just and that it was part of a process. 'As long as apartheid is around and as long as the authorities react the way they have done, so the people will have to respond. The initiative is not with the authorities, the initiative is with us. They can't ban us – what we are doing is what the community wants. To stop us they would have to ban the whole population.'[3] Not only had they been undeterred by the police warning that if they went ahead with the march they would be arrested; they were prepared to risk arrest again. Tutu felt they had proved that 'it is still possible to take direct non-violent action and not just speak about it.'[4]

He continued to take non-violent action. He protested to President Botha over the detention of the Methodist leader, the Reverend Stanley Mogoba; he called on Western governments to act now to stop another Lebanon in South Africa. Together with other senior clerics he announced a new group, the 'Committee for the Defence of Democracy', which was to respect 'part of the people's response from those committed to working towards a non-racial democratic society'. Ten days later the new committee was banned and the planned meeting

– to commemorate National Detainees Day – prohibited. So a service was held at St George's Cathedral, at which Boesak told a congregation of 2,000 people of all races and denominations: 'No government can challenge the word of God and survive,' and Tutu said defiantly, 'We refuse to be treated as the doormat for the government to wipe its jackboots on.'

Though in most of these actions the initiative was taken by a large group of church leaders, it was on Tutu and Boesak that the resulting rage and hate was concentrated. Death threats against both men became even more commonplace, and they were the subject of a strong attack from the largest of the three Dutch Reformed Churches. The General Synodical Commission of the DRC issued a statement saying that Tutu and Boesak had come into conflict with the Scriptures and with the State: 'They cannot therefore regard the actions of the State against them as actions against the "Church" or a "challenge to God" . . . The GSC makes an urgent call to Archbishop Tutu and Dr Boesak to abandon this wicked path and to discuss their problems frankly and open-heartedly with the [Cabinet] Minister and even with the State President, who are both confessing Christians.'

The now open conflict between Church and State, embodied in the persons of the State President and the head of the Anglican Church in South Africa, found expression in an astonishing exchange of letters and an angry meeting. The petition, failing to reach its destination when carried on the ill-fated march, was eventually delivered by more conventional means, and on March 16th, in a letter distributed to members of Parliament and the media, Botha wrote to Archbishop Tutu asking if the march on Parliament was necessary and doubting whether Tutu's assertion that there were 'virtually no other and effective and peaceful means' of 'witnessing effectively' was true. Was it not planned as a 'calculated public relations exercise'? He sought to associate Tutu with the ANC and the South African Communist Party, suggesting that the Archbishop was 'no doubt aware that the expressed intention of the ANC/SACP alliance is ultimately to transform South Africa into an atheistic Marxist state.' He argued that Tutu's understanding of evil was at issue. 'Is atheistic Marxism the evil, or does your view of evil include the struggle on behalf of Christianity, the Christian faith, and freedom of faith and worship, against the forces of godlessness and Marxism? . . . The question must be posed whether you are acting on behalf of the kingdom of God, or the kingdom promised by the ANC and the SACP? If it is the latter, say so, but do not then hide behind the structures and cloth of the Christian church, because Christianity and Marxism are irreconcilable opposites.'[5]

On March 16th Tutu went to see Botha, primarily to plead for the lives

Epilogue

of the so-called 'Sharpeville Six' who, despite international appeals, had
been condemned to death for being part of a crowd present at a murder,
though not one person was able to witness to their direct involvement.
(The prosecution were, for the first time in a security trial, making use of
the doctrine of 'common purpose', the principle being that an accessory
to a crime is liable to the same extent as the person who commits it.)
Botha said he was not prepared to intervene, claiming that it was up to
the Supreme Court. (The following day a four-week stay of execution
was granted fifteen hours before they were due to hang. On July 12th the
Sharpeville Six were granted an indefinite stay of execution.) He further
harangued Tutu for leading the February 29th march and accused him
of preaching 'under a flag depicting a hammer and sickle'.

Tutu took both the letter and the meeting very seriously and responded
with a 2,000-word letter justifying his involvement in politics with
numerous biblical references. Following Botha's example, he made the
letter available to the press, suggesting that 'as you are a fair-minded
person, I am sure that you will ensure that my reply receives the same
publicity accorded to your letter to me.' It was his most forthright attack
yet on the government's policies. He charged Botha with 'contravening
basic ethical tenets' by implementing 'vicious policies' such as forced
population removals, and reminded him of the Nationalist Party's
attitude to World War Two – 'Many Afrikaners being pro Nazi at
the time refused to support the war effort, and many who wore the
uniform of the Union Defence Force used to be turned away from NGK
(DRC) church services.' He stated categorically that he stood by all that
he had done and said in the past concerning 'the application of the Gospel
of Jesus Christ to the situation of injustice and oppression which are of
the very essence of apartheid' and affirmed again that he supported the
ANC in its objectives but not its methods; he further reminded Botha
that it was a matter of public record that on his visits to Lusaka in 1987
he had tried to persuade the ANC to suspend the armed struggle. The
letter ended: 'I work for God's Kingdom. For whose kingdom do you
work? I pray for you, as I do for your ministerial colleagues, every day
by name. God bless you.'[6]

Though it was Tutu who led protests and attacks on the government,
and Tutu the one most quoted and vilified, now more than ever he was
acting with his colleagues. And increasingly they made their support for
him visible. Towards the end of March 1988, amid fears that the South
African government were doing their best to isolate Tutu and to prepare
the way for taking action against him, even that South Africa right-wing
groups might try to assassinate him, the bishops of the Church of the
Province of South Africa, with the then Bishop of Lichfield, Keith
Sutton, bringing the backing of Dr Runcie, met to show their support.

They issued a statement offering their loyalty and saying 'Archbishop Desmond is our father in God, who belongs to us as we belong to him. When you touch our father in God, you touch the children of God. We shall not allow the government to isolate him.' Dr Runcie also sent a letter to the Anglican Primates throughout the world saying that the South African struggle had reached a new phase and that the Churches' responsibility for the rights of the people were greater than ever. It was generally seen as a warning to Pretoria to stop making personal attacks on Archbishop Tutu.

However comforted he was by this public support, the thought of Tutu relaxing his stand against the injustice of apartheid was unimaginable. He continued the struggle in any peaceful way he could find. He was the main speaker at a two-day 'emergency convocation' which met in Johannesburg to discuss the ways in which civil disobedience might be used to put pressure on the South African government. On June 10th he issued a statement condemning the renewal of the two-year state of emergency. At the end of the month he led a call to all anti-apartheid leaders to boycott the forthcoming municipal elections, a violation of the emergency regulations carrying a maximum prison sentence of ten years. As he had promised, he had no intention of going quietly.

So much in the tragic situation in South Africa remained the same, it was not surprising that Tutu's responses did not, on the surface, seem to have changed. But, while he still felt it necessary to isolate South Africa through economic sanctions, he was also thinking towards that apparently ever-receding horizon of a post-apartheid society. Painfully aware that South Africans have never really belonged to their own continent, he was convinced of the need for a wider vision. For too long apartheid had driven black South Africans into isolation, forced them into introspective agony on the one hand and reliance on America and the West on the other. One of Tutu's dearest wishes was that they should be identifying with their own continent, their own people.

This stance was not only part of Tutu's own development but was required by his role as Metropolitan of Southern Africa, a huge area including not only South African itself, but Mozambique, Namibia, Lesotho, Swaziland, St Helena and Tristan da Cunha. Now his official duties were taking him to these countries he had first-hand knowledge of what was going on and an ever more prestigious platform from which to speak. His concern for South Africa's relationship to the continent, and his colleague's welcome of that concern, was demonstrated by his election in September as President of the All-Africa Conference of Churches.

As businessmen and academics went to Lusaka to talk to the ANC, as the British and American governments swallowed their prejudices and talked to Oliver Tambo, regent political leaders like Archbishop Tutu considered returning to the wings and leaving the centre stage to the politicians. Brian Brown, then working at the British Council of Churches, saw Tutu's willingness to accept this role as 'an endorsement of the integrity of his person. His strength is that the ultimate liberation of his people is more important than his prestige and power. It is like Moses reaching the mountain top and seeing the promised land, but saying, "I am not here to do the leading, but to share the vision".' Once there is a commitment to justice the role of the prophet changes; demands for justice are replaced by demands for reconciliation. It needs just as much courage to say 'Pardon our enemies' as to say 'Let my people go'. What his role would be once South Africa was free he could not know; he just continued to stand uncompromisingly for justice.

In a sermon in September 1987 Tutu said suffering was unavoidable, especially for the Christian who witnessed for Christ in a situation of injustice, oppression and exploitation. 'When we make the so-called preferential option for the poor, when we become the voice of the voiceless ones; when we stand in solidarity with the hungry and the homeless, the uprooted ones, the down-trodden, those that are marginalised, we must not be surprised that the world will hate us, and yet, another part of the world will love us.'[7]

He was speaking at a service to commemorate the tenth anniversary of the death of Phakamile Mabija in detention. He could have been speaking of himself.

Postlude

Archbishop Tutu always considered himself an interim leader, happy to become, as he put it, 'just a nice bishop' once his country was free of apartheid. Now, with the African National Council in power, he has been as good as his word and tries to keep a low profile. Last year, 1995, however, on a brief visit to Britain, he talked to Colin Morris about the new South Africa and his hopes for its future.

Desmond Tutu Last year we prohibited all our ordained personnel in the Anglican Church from being card-carrying members of any political party, because we say it was quite crucial that people realized that we were being evenhanded. We would be deeply political but not party politically aligned. And we were heavily criticised by some of our young clergy, but it was a deliberate act, and perhaps you would say that more recently we have tried to demonstrate that while we have a solidarity, it is a critical solidarity with our friends; I mean you know we criticised them for the so-called 'Gravy Train'; we are criticising them over the arms trade. It isn't easy, I can assure you. It isn't easy to condemn people we are very, very fond of, and people who have been, as it were, comrades-in-arms.

Colin Morris Do they listen to you?

D.T. Well, they've certainly done something about the whole question of their salaries. They responded to that. And the President, we had a spat with him, I mean he clobbered me in public and I clobbered back, which was good for democracy. They do . . . yes, I think, they do.

C.M. The dynamics of this situation are absolutely fascinating; you know that there was, obviously, this row between Mandela and de Klerk. The miracle is that there aren't a dozen of those rows every week. Where has this extraordinary magnanimity and forgiveness come from – on the black side?

D.T. One of the younger leading lights of the ANC, who is now Premier of the Orange Free State, came to speak to a meeting of our senior bishops, and you know he said, 'Aren't you surprised that so many, certainly in the ANC, speak the language of reconciliation, if you are surprised, then you have forgotten the role of the Church.' That is one – that the influence of Christianity has been pervasive. Nelson does not make any bones about acknowledging his debt to the Church and to Christianity, but before that, something called *ubuntu* – the essence of being human – which places a great premium on solidarity, on social harmony. Anything that undermines that is bad, and anger and resentment, and desire for revenge, eat away the vitals. What they really want is for someone to say I am sorry for what we did, and then when somebody says that they are ready to stretch out a hand of fellowship in forgiveness and say yes, now we can close the door on that past, because we've dealt with it. And let us now move together into this glorious future that opens up in front of us.

C.M. You need to bottle that magic elixir and send it to Bosnia, and about a dozen other places throughout the world of conflict, don't you?

D.T. One of the reasons why I believe we have succeeded as particularly as we have done, is I believe precisely because God is saying, 'These are such an unlikely lot; who could ever have thought that these would be held up as a paradigm,' and here we are, in order to give hope to situations that seem so utterly hopeless, because we can point to our situation and say, 'If it can happen in South Africa, given the antecedents there, it will happen here in Bosnia, it will happen in Northern Ireland, it will happen in the Middle East.'

C.M. So it's been a wonderful start, but obviously there is still an enormous gap; there are still the have-nots, there are still the homeless in great numbers. I mean, do you think the gap between faith and reality can be bridged?

D.T. Yes, that is why we have faith, why we are dreaming; we're dreaming that this tremendous country . . . the day we stop dreaming, the day we stop having faith, we're for the birds. It's going to happen. It must happen. It must be that this vote must be translated into something tangible, it must become a new hope, a job, a school, a clinic, lights, clean water. If that doesn't happen, then the whole thing is going to explode in our faces.

C.M. Now you've been at the centre of great events in South Africa for a very long time, I mean all the drama of it, all the excitement of it; if there is normality in the future in South Africa, are you going to find yourself, as it were, marginalised, would you find it very difficult just being an Archbishop in normal circumstances?

D.T. (With much laughter) Wonderfully, I mean, one had said, long ago, 'I am an interim leader, I am around because our leaders are either in gaol or in exile,' and as soon as the political process is normalised, then I will adopt a more reasonable, lower profile.

C.M. Do you think, temperamentally, that's possible for you?

D.T. (More laughter) Yes. I mean, we are there to do the kind of thing that the Church must be doing, to help in the process of reconciliation and healing. We must be there to participate in the reconstruction and development. But we must be there constantly to be saying 'Thus saith the Lord', when the Government strays from the straight and narrow.

C.M. But once you get a figure as dominant as you have been, how easy it is going to be for the Church to draw other figures who will be, if you like, prophets?

D.T. There are very many people around already, and mercifully I am retiring in 1996.

C.M. You really are!

D.T. Really, I'm much looking forward to this.

C.M. You've always given the impression of absolute certainty, of knowing exactly where you're going, where the Church should be going, where the nation should be going. But privately have you had doubts, do you wonder whether you got it wrong?

D.T. Some of the things have been quite clear. When you have a policy of injustice, it is quite clear what God's will must be, that that must be ended. It's quite clear when people are poor and homeless, I mean you know which way you've got to go; you've got to work to provide new homes for them. And it's been fairly straightforward, it's got nothing to do with my own particular native smartness, it's just been that the Gospel is available to all of us, and I belong to this glorious thing, the Church of God.

Broadcast on February 5th 1995 on Radio 4's *Sunday* programme and reproduced with the kind permission of Colin Morris and the BBC.

Curriculum Vitae

The Most Revd Desmond Mpilo Tutu Archbishop of Cape Town

Born	7 October 1931 in Klerksdorp, Transvaal
Parents	Father a school teacher. Mother relatively uneducated.
Married	Leah Nomalizo (née Shenxane)
Children	Trevor Thamsanqa, Theresa Thandeka, Naomi Nontombi, Mpho Andrea

1945–50	High School Education – Johannesburg Bantu High School, Western Native Township up to Matric
1951–53	Teacher's Diploma at Pretoria Bantu Normal College
1954–	B.A. (University of South Africa)
1954–	Teacher at Johannesburg Bantu High School
1955–58	Teacher at Munsieville High School, Krugersdorp
1958–60	St Peter's Theological College, Rosettenville, Johannesburg Ordination Training – Licentiate in Theology
1960	Ordained Deacon – served title in Benoni Location
1961	Ordained Priest
1962–65	Part-time Curate at St Alban's; lived at Golders Green, London
1965	B.D. Hons (King's College, London)
1966	Part-time Curate at St Mary's, Bletchingley, Surrey
1966	M.Th. (King's College, London)
1967–69	Federal Theological Seminary, Alice, Cape – member of staff; Chaplain: University of Fort Hare
1970–72	UBLS Roma, Lesotho: lecturer – Department of Theology
1972–75	Associate Director: Theological Education Fund of the World Council of Churches based in Bromley, Kent. Lived in Grove Park, London, and was honory curate of St Augustine's.
1975–76	Dean of Johannesburg
1976–78	Bishop of Lesotho
1978–85	General Secretary, South African Council of Churches
1985–86	Bishop of Johannesburg
Sept 1986	Archbishop of Cape Town

HONORARY DEGREES

Aberdeen University, UK: Hon. Doctor of Divinity 1984

Australian National University, Canberra, Australia: Hon. Doctor of Laws 1994

Brown University, Rhode Island, USA: Hon. Doctor 1990

Central University Durham, NC, USA: Hon. Doctor of Humane Letters 1986

Chicago Theological Seminary, USA: Hon. Doctor of Divinity 1986

Claremont Graduate School, USA: Hon. Doctor of Law 1984

Clarke University, Atlanta, USA: Hon. Doctor 1991

Columbia University, USA: Hon. Doctor of Sacred Theology 1982

Dickinson College, USA: Hon. Doctor of Sacred Theology 1984

Emory University, Atlanta, USA: Hon. Doctor of Divinity 1988

General Theological Seminary, NY, USA: Hon. Doctor of Divinity 1978

Harvard University, USA: Hon. Doctor of Laws 1979

Howard University, USA: Hon. Doctor of Humane Letters 1984

Hunter College, University of New York, USA: Hon. Doctor of Humane Letters 1986

Kent University, Canterbury, UK: Hon. Doctor of Civil Law 1978

Kings College London, UK: Fellow 1978

Kirchliche Hochschule, Berlin, Germany: Hon. Doctor of Theology and other Sciences 1993

L'Universite Nationale du Benin, Benin: Docteur Honoris Causa 1990

Lincoln University, Pennysylvania, USA: Hon. Doctor of Divinity 1990

Morehouse College, Atlanta, GA, USA: Hon. Doctor of Humane Letters 1986

Morehouse School of Medicine, Atlanta, GA, USA: Hon. Doctor of Humane Letters 1993

Mount Allison University, Sackville, Canada: Hon. Doctor of Laws 1988

North Eastern University, Boston, USA: Hon. Doctor of Laws 1988

Oberlin College, Davenport, Iowa, USA: Hon. Doctor of Divinity 1986

Oxford University, UK: Hon. Doctor of Divinity 1990

Quinnipiac College, Hamden, Connecticut, USA: Hon. Doctor of Humane Letters 1994

Ramapho College of New Jersey, USA: Hon. Doctor of Humane Letters 1993

Ruhr University, Bochum, Germany: Hon. Doctor of Theology 1981

Schippenburg University, Pennysylvania, USA: Hon. Doctor 1991

Seton Hall Univ, New Jersey, USA: Hon. Doctor of Laws 1990

South Bank University, London, UK: Hon. Doctor of Laws 1994

St Paul's College, Lawrenceville, USA: Hon. Doctor of Humane Letters 1984

Stetson Univ, Florida, USA: Hon. Doctor of Laws 1990

Temple University, Philadelphia, USA: Hon. Doctor of Laws 1985/86

The Selly Oak Colleges, Birmingham, UK: Hon. Fellowship 1989

Trinity College, Hartford, USA: Hon. Doctor of Divinity 1986

Trinity Lutheran Seminary, Columbus, Ohio, USA: Hon. Doctor of Divinity 1985

University of Cape Town, RSA: Hon. Doctor of Laws 1993

University of Missouri, Kansas City, USA: Hon. Doctor 1990

University of New Rochelle, NY, USA: Hon. Doctor of Humane Letters 1990

University of Natal, South Africa: Hon. Doctor of Laws 1995

University of Puerto Rico, Puerto Rico: Hon. Doctor 1990

University of Rio, Brazil: Hon. Doctor 1986

University of South Africa, Pretoria, RSA: Hon. Doctor of Theology 1994

University of South Carolina, USA: Hon. Doctor 1991

University of Strasbourg, France: Hon. Doctor 1988

University of the South, Sewanee, USA: Hon. Doctor of Divinity 1988

University of the West Indies, Trinidad: Hon. Doctor of Divinity 1986

University of the Witwatersrand, Johannesburg, RSA: Hon. Doctor of Laws 1993

University of Tromsö, Norway 1994

Wesleyan University, Connecticut, USA: Hon. Doctor of Divinity 1990

Wilberforce University, Ohio, USA: Hon. Doctor of Humanities 1994/95

CITY HONOURS
Durham, UK: Freedom of the City 1987

Florence, Italy: Freedom of the City 1985

Hull, UK: Freedom of the City 1989

Kinshasa, Uganda: Freedom of the City 1990

Lewisham, UK: Freedom of the Borough 1990

Methyr Tydfil, UK: Freedom of the City 1986

AWARDS
Bishop John T Walker Distinguished Humanitarian Service Award 1992

Joint recipient: Third World Prize 1989

USA: Martin Luther King Jr Humanitarian Award 1984

Norway: Nobel Peace Prize 1984
Brazil: Order of Merit of Brasilia 1987
Brazil: Order of the Southern Cross 1987
The Family of Man Gold Medal Award 1983
Atlanta, USA: Martin Luther King Jr Peace Award 1986
Claremont Graduate School. CA, USA: President's Medal 1990
Emmanuel College, Boston, MA, USA: Albert Schweitzer Humanitarian Award '88
Glassboro State College, NJ, USA: USA President's Award 1986
John-Roger Foundation, Los Angeles, USA: International Integrity Award 1986
Leonard Fox Foundation, Johannesburg: Community Service Award 1992
Memphis, USA: National Civil Rights Museum Freedom Award 1992
Nuclear Age Peace Foundation: Distinguished Peace Leadership Award 1990
Onassis Foundation: Prix d'Athene 1980
Pacem in Terris Foundation, Cleveland, Ohio, USA: Pacem in Terris Peace & Freedom Award from the Quad Cities 1987
San Rafael CA, USA: World Public Forum Award 1986

ROLES
Archbishop of Cape Town; Church of the Province of Southern Africa: 1986
Chancellor; University of the Western Cape: 1988
President; All Africa Conference of Churches: 1987, re-elected 1992

PATRON
Action from Ireland (AFrI): 1994
Beacon Millennium, UK: 1994
Bonhoeffer Congress: 1994
Caen Memorial International Meetings: 1994
Cape Town Olympic Bid Committee, RSA: 1993
District Six Museum Foundation, SA: 1989
East Timor Ireland Solidarity Campaign, Ireland: 1994
Global Co-operation for a Better World, UK: 1988
Global Co-operation for a Better World, London
Happening Ministries: 1989
Harmony Child Foundation, USA: 1995
Hillbrow Social Centre and Theatre Project: 1995
Hospice Association of Southern Africa: 1995
Link Africa: 1994
Living Stones Trust, UK: 1993

Operation Peace: 1994
Our Kind of Cape Town: 1994
Pan-African Book Foundation: 1991
Peace Visions, Cape Town, RSA
Renaissance Maritime Charitable Trust: 1995
SACLA Health Project
The Cambodia Trust Patron: 1992
The Cambodia Trust Patron: 1995
Tools for Self Reliance: 1995
Umtapo Centre, Durban
Wilberforce Council, Hull, UK: 1989
World Campaign against Military and Nuclear Collaboration with South
    Africa: 1994
World Council of Global Cooperation, Canada: 1987
World Trust/ World Orchestra, USA: 1988

PUBLICATIONS
Collections of sermons and speeches:
Crying in the Wilderness, RSA: 1982
Hope and Suffering, RSA: 1983
The Rainbow People of God, UK/USA: 1994
An African Prayer Book, London, Hodder & Stoughton: 1995
(also many forewords and other contributions to books and journals)

TRUSTEE
African European Insitute: Chairman of the Board of Trustees
Children's Trust: SA
Desmond Tutu Education Trust, RSA
Educational Opportunities Council, RSA: Chair of Exec Committee
Equal Opportunity Foundation
Kagiso Trust, RSA
Phelps Stokes Fund, USA
Project Vote: Chairman of the Board of Trustees
SACHED Trust, RSA
Tshezi Trust
University of the Western Cape: Community Law Centre

OTHER ROLES
African Academy of Sciences, Nairobi, Kenya: Fellow 1991
Afro Pentecost (Winterthur, Switzerland): Member of Honorary Com-
    mittee 1994 and 1995
Beyond War Foundation: Award Selection Committee Member 1990
Campaigns for Human Rights: Director

Carnegie Commission on Preventing the Deadliest Conflicts: Member of Distinguished Advisory Council 1994

Cathedral of St John, NY, USA: Member of Honorary Committee for UN50 Anniversary 1995

Center for Attitudinal Healing: Member of Advisory Council 1994

Center for Politics and Economics at Claremont Graduate: Member, Board of Visitors 1993

Center for the Study of Conflict: Member of International Advisory Board 1994

Center for Politics & Economics, Claremont University Centre, CA, USA: Member of Board of Visitors

Children of War: Honorary Chairman of Advisory Board 1991

CIT, TecAfrica: Sponsor 1994

Civicus; World Alliance for Citizen Participation: Member 1995

Civilian-based Defence Association: Member of Advisory Committee 1989

Claremont University Center, California, USA: Member of Board of Visitors

Conference on International Social Welfare in a Changing World: Member of Advisory Committee 1994

Conflict Resolution Program: The Carter Center of Emory University: 1994

Earth Council, Costa Rica: Honorary Member 1993

Forum of Democratic Leaders in the Asia-Pacific Region: Honorary Senior Advisor

Fund for Education in South Africa: NY, USA: Member of Disbursements Committee 1988

Gleitsman Foundation: Member of Board of Judges for International Activist Award

Global Education Associates, NY: Project Global 2000, USA: Charter Member of the Religion Council 1994

Harry S Truman Research Institute for the Advancement of Peace: Member of International Nominating Panel 1990

HSRC Humanitas Award, RSA: Member of Selection Committee

Hunger Project, NY: Member of Honorary Committee: Africa Prize for Leadership for the Sustainable End to Hunger

Independent Board of Enquiry: Board Member

Institute for Education in Democracy, Nairobi, Kenya: Member of Int'l Advisory Board 1994

Interfaith Encounter: Universidad de Alcala de Henares, Madrid, Spain: Member of the Honour Committee, Interfaith Encounter 1994

International Alert: Vice-Chairman 1986

International Forgiveness Institute, USA: Member of Board of Directors 1995

International Human Rights Law Group's 1994 Awards: Member of Host Committee 1994

International Institute for Human Rights and Democracy in Africa: Member 1991

International Negotiation Network: Council Member

International Peace Policy Research Institute, USA: Member of International Advisory Board

International Social Prospects Academy: Designated Member 1983

Laureates in support of the initiative to stop child exploitation: Signatory 1999

Manifesto against Conscription and the Military System: Signatory 1994

Memorial to Imre Nagy and companions: Hungarian Human Rights League, Hungary: Member of Committee of Honour 1988

MESAB Annual Dinner 1994: Member of Honorary Committee 1994

National Association for Advancement of Coloured People: Life Member 1985

National Peace Campaign Forum: Member 1994

Nuclear Age Peace Foundation, USA: Member of Advisory Council

On the Cutting Edge (a publication dedicated to redefining rights, obligations and dignity in the post-nuclear age): Advisor to the Editorial Board

Panel of Religious Leaders for Electoral Justice: Member 1994

Peace International Group (PIG), Australia: Honorary Member 1994

Presidential Inauguration, RSA: National Inauguration Committee Member 1994

Reconte Inter-Africaine, 9–16 Aug 1994: Member of Committee of honour 1992

Revelation and Environment (95–1995 AD): Member of Honorary Committee 1995

Robert F Kennedy Memorial Human Rights Award, USA: Member of International Advisory Committee 1988

Schomberg Center for Research in Black Culture, USA: Member

Special Fund for Health in Africa, USA: Member of Honorary Committee 1990

St Bernadette Institue of Sacred Art: Honorary Board Member 1994

The 12th November Association (East Timor): Honorary Member 1994

The Project on Religion and Human Rights: Honorary Chairman 1994

The Youth Action Foundation International, Los Angeles: Member of Advisory Board 1994

UN50 Advisory Group for the 50th Anniversary of the UN: Member

University of Fort Hare: Member of Council

University of the Witwatersrand, Centre for Applied Legal Studies: Member of Board of Control

University of the Witwatersrand, Centre for Continuing Education: Member of Board of Control

USAID South Africa, SA: Human Rights and Democracy Division 1994

WEMFA, Lagos, Nigeria: Member of the Advisory Board 1994

WHO Special Fund for Health in Africa, Brazzaville, Congo: Member of Honorary Committee 1990

World Conference on Religion and Peace (WCRP): Honorary President

World Constitution & Parliament Association, USA: Honorary Sponsor

World Council of Panafrican Organisations (PANAFRICA): Honorary President 1984

World Organisation against Torture, Geneva, Switzerland: Member of Executive Council 1999

World Public Forum: Declaration of Human Unity: Signatory

Notes

1 'HERTZOG IS MY SHEPHERD'

1 Umteteli Wa Bantu, '"Civilized" labour policy' October 29th, 1932: quoted in Tim Couzens and Essop Patel, eds, *The Return of the Amasi Bird*.
2 'A Vision for Humanity', Address given on the award of the Martin Luther King Peace Prize, January 1986.
3 Ibid.
4 Ibid.
5 Evidence to the Eloff Commission, *Ecunews*, June 1983.
6 Ibid.
7 *New York Review of Books*, September 26th, 1985.
8 Letter from Desmond Tutu to Mrs Florence Blaxall, March 5th, 1979.
9 Stanley Motjuwadi in *Drum*, December 1984.
10 Ibid.
11 Ibid.
12 Ibid.
13 Evidence to the Eloff Commission, loc. cit.
14 Ibid.
15 Ibid.

2 FORBIDDEN PASTURES

1 Figures from Mary Benson, *The Struggle for a Birthright*.
2 I. B. Tabatha, *Education for Barbarism*.
3 M. B. Yengwa, source unknown.
4 Evidence to the Eloff Commission, *Ecunews*, June 1983.
5 Trevor Huddleston, *Naught For Your Comfort*.
6 Desmond Tutu, *Crying in the Wilderness*.
7 Trevor Huddleston, op. cit.
8 Albert Luthuli, *Let My People Go*.
9 Ibid.
10 *Hansard*, V, 11, 1945.
11 Ibid.
12 Ibid.
13 Ibid., V, 11, 1953.
14 I. B. Tabatha, op. cit.

15 Desmond Tutu, Nineteenth Feetham Lecture, Witwatersrand University, 1985.

3 GROWING INTO PRIESTHOOD

1 Interview with Shirley Moulder, *South African Outlook*, February 1982.
2 Evidence to the Eloff Commission, *Ecunews*, June 1983.
3 *South African Outlook*, February 1982.
4 Evidence to the Eloff Commission, loc. cit.
5 Anthony Sampson, *Drum*.
6 Jan van Riebeeck, the first government official at the Cape, is seen as the founding father of the nation by white South Africans.
7 Mary Benson, *The Struggle For a Birthright*.
8 Anthony Sampson, op. cit.
9 *Fair Lady*, May 1st, 1985.
10 *South African Outlook*, February 1982.
11 Ibid.
12 'Address to Deacons Lesotho, 1977', *Hope and Suffering*.

4 NO PASSBOOK REQUIRED

1 Letter from Desmond Tutu to the Dean of King's College, London, October 16th, 1961.
2 Ibid., February 1st, 1962.
3 Ibid., November 19th, 1962.
4 Evidence to the Eloff Commission, *Ecunews*, June 1983.
5 Comment, *King's College Newsletter*, December 1984.
6 Ibid.
7 Evidence to the Eloff Commission, loc. cit.
8 Ibid.
9 Comment, *King's College Newsletter*, December 1984.
10 Ibid.
11 Letter from Desmond Tutu to the Dean of King's College, October 27th, 1964.
12 Ibid., July 29th, 1964.
13 Evidence to the Eloff Commission, loc. cit.
14 Letter from Desmond Tutu to the Dean of King's College, August 23rd, 1965.
15 Walter Makhulu, later Bishop of Central Africa, was a curate in Battersea while Tutu was in England.
16 *Daily Mail*, October 7th, 1985.

5 AN OASIS IN THE EASTERN CAPE

1 Desmond Tutu to Martin Kenyon, December 19th, 1966.
2 Ibid., January 1st, 1967.
3 Leah Tutu to Mrs F. Brownrigg, March 9th, 1967.
4 Desmond Tutu to Martin Kenyon, February 24th, 1967.
5 Ibid.

6   Leah Tutu to Mrs F. Brownrigg, March 9th, 1967.
7   William Shakespeare, *Twelfth Night*, Act II, Scene V, 158.
8   Interview with Shirley Moulder, *South African Outlook*, February 1982.
9   Nelson Mandela, *The Struggle Is My Life*.
10 Steve Biko, *I Write What I Like*.
11 Desmond Tutu to Martin Kenyon, March 5th, 1968.
12 Ibid., February 24th, 1967.
13 Steve Biko, op. cit.

6   OUT OF SOUTH AFRICA

1   Evidence to the Eloff Commission, *Ecunews*, June 1983.
2   *Hope and Suffering*.
3   Ibid.
4   Ibid.
5   Kofi Appiah-Kubi and Sergio Torres, eds, *African Theology en route*.
6   Ibid.
7   *Hope and Suffering*.
8   Kofi Appiah-Kubi and Sergio Torres, op. cit.
9   *Hope and Suffering*.
10 St Luke, 4:18.
11 *Hope and Suffering*.
12 *Crying in the Wilderness*.
13 Charles Villa-Vicencio and John W. de Gruchy, eds, *Resistance and Hope: South African Essays in Honour of Beyers Naudé*.
14 Kofi Appiah-Kubi and Sergio Torres, op. cit.
15 Letter from Canon Sydney Evans to Dr Shoki Coe, August 25th, 1971.
16 Letter from Dr Shoki Coe to Canon Sydney Evans, August 5th, 1971.
17 *South African Outlook*, February 1982.
18 *Concord Weekly*, October 26th–November 2nd, 1984.
19 Evidence to the Eloff Commission, loc. cit.
20 Letter from the Reverend Charles Cartwright to the author, July 21st, 1986.
21 From a taped talk given when Desmond Tutu was at the Theological Education Fund.

7   DEAN OF JOHANNESBURG

1   Christmas letter from Dean Tutu to friends, November 22nd, 1975.
2   *Hope and Suffering*.
3   *Concord Weekly*, October 26th–November 2nd, 1984.
4   Ibid.
5   *Pro Veritate*, 1975.
6   'Politics and Religion – The Seamless Garment', *Hope and Suffering*.
7   John W. de Gruchy, *The Church Struggle in South Africa*.
8   'Politics and Religion – The Seamless Garment'.
9   Circular letter to friends, September 16th, 1975.

10 *Race Relations News*, January 1976.
11 Ibid.
12 Ibid.
13 Open letter to Mr John Vorster, quoted in *Hope and Suffering*.
14 Ibid.
15 Ibid.
16 Ibid.

8 THE MOUNTAIN KINGDOM

1   *South African Outlook*, February 1982.
2   The Federal Theological Seminary moved to Pietermaritzburg in the mid-1970s.
3   Bishop Tutu to the Reverend Professor Hanson, November 14th, 1978.
4   Basotho: the people of Lesotho; Mosotho: singular.
5   Bishop Tutu to the Reverend Professor Hanson, op. cit.
6   Circular letter from Bishop Tutu to friends, December 3rd, 1976.
7   Bishop Tutu to the Reverend Professor Hanson, op. cit.
8   *South African Outlook*, February 1982.
9   Bishop Tutu to Bishop Walter Makhulu, February 21st, 1979.
10 Ting: corn meal made sour, like sour cream porridge.
11 The Inaugural Desmond Tutu Peace Lecture, September 1985. (This was to be held in Soweto, but was never delivered as the police banned the meeting.)
12 Nelson Mandela, *The Struggle is My Life*.
13 'An African Views American Black Theology', *Worldview*, vol. 17, no. 8, August 1974.
14 'Black Theology/African Theology – Soul Mates or Antagonists?', *Journal of Religious Thought*, 32, no. 2, Fall–Winter 1975.
15 Evidence to the Eloff Commission, *Ecunews*, June 1983.
16 Desmond Tutu, *Crying in the Wilderness*.
17 Mr Kruger was Minister of Justice at the time.
18 *Apartheid: The Facts*, International Defence and Aid Fund, 1983.
19 Allen Cook, *South Africa: The Imprisoned Society*.
20 Ibid.
21 'The Theology of Migrant Labour', *South African Outlook*, December 1968.
22 Ibid.
23 Ibid.
24 *South African Outlook*, February 1982.
25 Father Aelred Stubbs to Bishop Tutu, February 16th, 1978.

9 THE CHURCH WAKES UP

1   *Observer*, October 10th, 1954.
2   A secret Afrikaner society founded in 1918.

3 Marjorie Hope and James Young, *The South African Churches in a Revolutionary Situation*.
4 John de Gruchy, *The Church Struggle in South Africa*.
5 John de Gruchy and Charles Villa-Vicencio, eds, *Apartheid Is a Heresy*.
6 Councils in the Ecumenical Movement: South Africa 1904–1975 (Johannesburg: SACC, 1979), quoted in Hope and Young, op. cit.
7 'Pseudo-Gospels in South Africa', a report published in Johannesburg 1968, quoted in John de Gruchy, op. cit.
8 Ibid.
9 John de Gruchy and Charles Villa-Vicencio, op. cit.
10 John de Gruchy and Charles Villa-Vicencio, eds, *Resistance and Hope*.
11 Report of the Commission of Enquiry into the SACC (Republic of South Africa, 1983).

10 A PARISH WITHOUT FRONTIERS

1 *Hope and Suffering*.
2 Ibid.
3 Professor Francis Wilson in conversation with the author.
4 Helen Joseph in conversation with the author.
5 Martin Conway in conversation with the author.
6 Bishop Tutu to Mrs Campbell, November 5th, 1979.
7 David Botha to Bishop Tutu, June 29th, 1979.
8 *Argus*, March 5th, 1981.
9 Bishop Tutu to the Reverend V. Roberts, October 11th, 1982.
10 Bishop Tutu to Sister Pauline OHP, January 30th, 1980.

11 THE HOTTEST ECCLESIASTICAL SEAT

1 *Crucible*, July–September 1978.
2 Letter from Bishop Tutu to the Suffragan Bishop of Oregon, April 26th, 1978.
3 *South African Outlook*, February 1982.
4 Estimate based on 1970 statistics in the SACC report.
5 Report of the Commission of Enquiry into the SACC, 1983.
6 Ibid.
7 Transcript of taped interview between Bishop Tutu and Mr Eugene Roelofse, February 4th, 1980.
8 *Encounter*, April 1980.
9 *Apartheid: The Facts*, op. cit.
10 Ibid.
11 *Hope and Suffering*.
12 *Financial Mail*, March 1980.
13 Margaret Nash, *Black Uprooting from 'White' South Africa*.
14 Letter from the Minister of Co-Operation and Development to Mr Saul Mhkize, who was later shot dead by police during a removals protest.

15 At the time the South African Rand was equivalent to about 53p. sterling or 44 US cents.

12 CRYING IN THE WILDERNESS

1 'Azania' is a name used for South Africa by sections of the black consciousness movement. AZAPO was founded in the tradition of Black Consciousness after the banning of the black activist organisiations in 1977.
2 Report of the Commission of Inquiry into the SACC, 1983.
3 *Cape Times*, July 30th, 1979.
4 Marjorie Hope and James Young, *The South African Churches in a Revolutionary Situation.*
5 Report of the Commission of Inquiry into the SACC.
6 Hope and Young, op. cit.
7 Report of the Commission of Inquiry into the SACC.
8 Ibid.
9 Alan Paton, *Cry the Beloved Country.*
10 Report of the Commission of Inquiry into the SACC.
11 Ibid.
12 *Hope and Suffering.*
13 Report of the Commission of Enquiry into the SACC.
14 Letter from Bishop Tutu to A. J. Ardington, April 28th, 1981.
15 Letter from Bishop Tutu to R. Proctor Sims, July 19th, 1980.
16 *Star*, May 20th, 1982.
17 *Hope and Suffering.*
18 Transcript of the meeting between members of the SACC and P. W. Botha, August 27th, 1980.
19 *Citizen*, June 30th, 1982.
20 *New York Times*, June 17th, 1982.
21 *Ecunews*, vol. 9, 1979.

13 DAVID AND GOLIATH

1 *Observer*, September 5th, 1982.
2 The Drawbridge Lecture, November 19th, 1984, published by the Christian Institute Trustees.
3 On learning the true source of the money Bishop Tutu immediately refunded it.
    All other quotations in this chapter are from documents appertaining to the Eloff Commission in the possession of the SACC.

14 VOICE OF THE VOICELESS

1 Bishop Tutu to Deaconess Cooke, August 17th, 1978.
2 The Right Reverend Wesley Frensdorff to Bishop Tutu, October 17th, 1978.
3 *Parishioner*, September 1978.

4 *Rand Daily Mail*, April 17th, 1980.
5 Bishop Tutu to the Officer-in-Charge, December 22nd, 1978.
6 *Harvard Gazette*, June 7th, 1979.
7 Bishop Tutu to Betty Ward, July 17th, 1979.
8 Thembi Sekgaphane, Mary Mxadana and Lenki Khanyile from the SACC.
9 *Rand Daily Mail*, September 7th, 1982.
10 'A Vision for Humanity', Address on the award of the Martin Luther King Peace Prize, January 1986.
11 *Washington Post*, February 16th, 1986.
12 *Penthouse*, June 1986.
13 *Observer*, August 8th, 1982.

15 A KIND OF SACRAMENT

1 A longer section of this speech is quoted in the Prologue to this book.
2 *Sowetan*, October 22nd, 1984.
3 Quoted in the *Church of England Newspaper*, November 16th, 1984.
4 *Sunday Times*, October 21st, 1984.
5 Ibid., October 28th, 1984.
6 *Christianity and Crisis*, February 4th, 1985.
7 *Africa Report*, January–February 1985.
8 *New York Times*, December 8th, 1984.
9 Ibid., December 12th, 1984.

16 'EVERYBODY'S BISHOP'

1 *Sunday Times*, October 28th, 1984.
2 *Ecunews*, December 1984.
3 *Citizen*, November 15th, 1984.
4 Ibid.
5 *Sunday Star*, November 25th, 1984.
6 *Evening Post*, November 15th, 1984.
7 Ibid.
8 *South Coast Sun*, November 30th, 1984.
9 *Watchman*, November 1985.
10 Letter from Winnie Mandela to Senator Kennedy, January 24th, 1986.
11 *Guardian*, July 26th, 1985.
12 *Time*, August 5th, 1985.
13 *Guardian*, August 1st, 1985.
14 *Weekend Argus*, February 1st, 1986.
15 Mark Mathabane, *Kaffir Boy*.

17 'TUTU CAN'T SWIM'

1 Buti Tlhagale and Itumeleng Mosala, eds, *Hammering Swords Into Ploughshares*.

2   *Crying in the Wilderness.*
3   'Words for Penn', *Almanac*, March 4th, 1986.
4   *Second National Consultative Conference of the ANC* (ANC, 1985).
5   *Sunday Star*, January 26th, 1986.
6   Peter Godwin, *Sunday Times*, 1985.
7   *Seek*, October 1985.
8   Speech given in America 1986.
9   Press statement, August 1986.
10 'Whose Rubicon?', BCC and CIIR, 1986.
11 *Cape Times*, June 2nd, 1986.
12 Published by the Kairos Theologians, PO Box 3207, Braamfontein 2017; and in the UK by the Catholic Institute for International Relations and the British Council of Churches.
13 *Washington Post*, October 2nd, 1985.

18   ARCHBISHOP OF CAPE TOWN

1   *Observer*, September 7th, 1986.
2   *Weekend Argus*, April 12th, 1986.
3   *Star City*, May 15th, 1986.
4   *Natal Witness*, April 16th, 1986.
5   *Pretoria News*, April 15th, 1986.
6   *Citizen*, April 17th, 1986.
7   *Eastern Province Herald*, April 17th, 1986.
8   *Daily News*, April 15th, 1986.
9   *Daily Dispatch*, April 16th, 1986.
10 *Sunday Star*, April 20th, 1986.
11 *Cape Times*, April 19th, 1986.
12 *Star*, August 31st, 1986.

EPILOGUE

1   Dr Francis Cull remains the Archbishop's confessor and spiritual director, though he ceased to be Director of the Institute of Christian Spirituality at the end of 1994.
2   Letter to the author, September 29th, 1987.
3   *New Statesman*, March 18th, 1988.
4   *Daily Telegraph*, March 2nd, 1988
5   Letter from P.W. Botha to Archbishop Desmond Tutu, March 16th, 1988.
6   Letter from Archbishop Tutu to P.W. Botha, April 8th, 1988.
7   *Seek*, September 1987.

Quotations used in the text and not listed above are from interviews with the author.

Select bibliography

Appiah-Kubi, Kofi, and Torres, Sergio, eds, *African Theology en route*, Orbis Books, 1983.

Austin, Dennis, *South Africa 1984*, Routledge & Kegan Paul, 1985.

Benson, Mary, *The Struggle for a Birthright*, International Defence and Aid Fund, 1985.

Benson, Mary, *Nelson Mandela*, Penguin Books, 1986.

Biko, Steve, *I Write What I Like*, The Bowerdean Press, 1978.

Boesak, Allan, *Black and Reformed*, Orbis Books, 1984.

British Council of Churches, *Whose Rubicon?*, 1986.

BCC & CIIR, *The Kairos Document*, 1986.

Calvocoressi, Peter, *Independent Africa & the World*, Longman, 1985.

Catholic Institute of International Relations, *South Africa in the 1980s*, CIIR, 1986.

CIIR, *Treason Against Apartheid*, CIIR, 1985.

Church Information Office, *The Report of the Lambeth Conference, 1978*, CIO Publishing, 1978.

Cole, Ernest, *House of Bondage*, Allen Lane/Penguin, 1968.

Commonwealth Report, *Mission to South Africa*, Penguin Books, 1986.

Cook, Allen, *South Africa: the Imprisoned Society*, IDAF, 1974.

Couzens, Tim, and Patel, Essop, eds, *The Return of the Amasi Bird*, Ravan Press, 1982.

Davidson, Basil, *Southern Africa, Progress or Disaster?*, IDAF, 1984.

Davies, J. G., *Christian Politics and Violent Revolution*, Orbis Books, 1976.

Davies, O'Meara and Dlamini, *The Struggle for South Africa*: Vols 1 and 2, Zed Books, 1984.

Desmond, Cosmas, *The Discarded People*, Christian Institute of South Africa, 1970.

Dube, David, *The Rise of Azania*, Daystar Publications Ltd, 1983.

Feinberg, Barry, ed., *Poets to the People*, George Allen & Unwin, 1974.

Fugard, Athol, *Tsotsi*, Penguin Books, 1980.

Gastrow, Shelagh, *Who's Who in South African Politics*, Ravan Press, 1985.

de Gruchy, John, *The Church Struggle in South Africa*, Eerdmans Publishing Co., 1979.

de Gruchy, John, *Cry Justice*, Collins, 1986.

de Gruchy John and Villa-Vicencio, Charles, eds, *Apartheid is a Heresy*, David Philip, 1983.

de Gruchy John and Villa-Vicencio, Charles, eds, *Resistance and Hope*, David Philip, 1985.

le Guma, Alex, *Apartheid – a collection of writings on SA Racism by South Africans*, Lawrence & Wishart, 1972.

Harrison, David, *The White Tribe of Africa*, Ariel/BBC, 1981.

Hinchcliff, Peter, *The Church in South Africa*, SPCK, 1968.

Hope, Marjorie, and Young, James, *The South African Churches in a Revolutionary Situation*, Orbis Books, 1981.

Huddleston, Trevor, *Naught For Your Comfort*, Collins, 1956.

International Defence and Aid Fund, *Apartheid: The Facts*, IDAF, 1983.

Joseph, Helen, *Side by Side*, Zed Books, 1986.

Kuzwayo, Ellen, *Call me Woman*, The Women's Press, 1985.

Leach, Graham, *South Africa*, Routledge & Kegan Paul, 1986.

Lelyveld, Joseph, *Move Your Shadow*, Michael Joseph, 1986.

Luthuli, Albert, *Let My People Go*, Fount Paperbacks, 1982.

Mandela, Nelson, *The Struggle Is My Life*, IDAF, 1978.

Mandela, Winnie, *Part of my Soul*, Penguin Books, 1985.

Mathabane, Mark, *Kaffir Boy*, Macmillan, 1986.

McConkey, E., *The Failure of Bantu Education*, Progressive Federal Party, South Africa, 1970.

Moore, Basil, *Black Theology*, C. Hurst & Co., 1973.

Mphalele, Ezekiel, *The African Image*, Faber & Faber, 1962.

Nash, Margaret, *Black Uprooting*, SACC, 1980.

Omond, Roger, *The Apartheid Handbook*, Penguin Books, 1985.

— Vols One and Two, Zed Books 1985.

Parsons, Neil, *A New History of Southern Africa*, Macmillan, 1982.

Paton, Alan, *Apartheid and the Archbishop*, David Philip, 1973.

Paton, Alan, *Cry the Beloved Country*, Penguin Books, 1958.

Paton, Alan, *Federation or Desolation*, South African Institute of Race Relations, 1985.

Pityana, Barney, *From South Africa to England*, Christian Concern for South Africa.

Sampson, Anthony, *Drum*, Hodder & Stoughton, 1956.

Sampson, Anthony, *Black and Gold*, Hodder & Stoughton, 1987.

SACC, *Relocations: The Churches' Report on Forced Removals in South Africa*, SACC, 1984.

Stanton, Hannah, *Go Well, Stay Well*, Hodder & Stoughton, 1961.

Tabatha, I. B., *Education for Barbarism*, Prometheus Durban, 1959.

Thlagale, Buti and Mosala, Itumeleng, eds, *Hammering Swords into Ploughshares*, Skotaville Publishers, 1986.

Tutu, Desmond, *Crying in the Wilderness*, Mowbray, 1982.

Tutu, Desmond, *Hope and Suffering*, Collins, 1983.

Uhlig, Mark, ed., *Apartheid in Crisis*, Penguin Books, 1986.

Villa-Vicencio, Charles, 'Southern Africa Today', *Journal of Theology for Southern Africa*, December 1984.

Woods, Donald, *Biko*, Penguin Books, 1978.

Ziemer, Gregor, *Education for Death*, Constable, 1942.

Index

Adams College, 68
Africa Report, 205 *n*7
African-American Institute, 204
African Independent Churches, 122, 127
African Methodist Episcopal Church, 28, 29
African National Congress (ANC), 34, 47, 125, 164, 268; ban on, 51; Buthelezi, view of, 238; Mbeki, 260; sanctions, 239; Tutu's support for, 224, 234, 235; Tutu condemns violence, 247; talks with, 261
African Orthodox Church, 143
African theology, 113–14
African Theology en route, 53 *nn*5,6; 84 *n*8
'African time', 112
'Africans', 32
Alexandra township, 156, 226–8, 237, 247
Alice (Eastern Cape), 67–9, 72, 78, 80, 112, 238
Almanac, 232 *n*3
ANC *see* African National Congress
Anglican Students Federation, 75
Apartheid, 25; American view of, 193–5; Bantu Education, 41–2; beaches, on, 98; laws, 31–3; Nazi comparison, 203; ordination candidates, 44; 'petty', 127; Reagan on, 205–6; removals, forced, 149–2; SACC, 120–3, 124; successful, 142
Apartheid is a Heresy, 124 *nn*5,7,8
Apartheid: the Facts, 116 *n*18, 150 *n*9
Appiah-Kubi, Kofi and Torres, Sergio, *see African Theology en route*
Argus, 139–40 *n*8
Asingeni Relief Fund, 148, 153
Awards to Tutu, 186–7, 261 *see also* 272–4
Azanian People's Organisation (AZAPO), 156, 160, 216–18, 235–6, 240

Azanian Students' Organisation, 247
'Bantu', 31
Bantu Administration and Development, 150
Bantu Affairs, Dept. of, 32
Bantu Authorities Act 1951, 33
Bantu Methodist Church, 143
Bantu Normal College, The, 34
bantustans, *see* homelands
Barbour, Mary, 197
Barth, Karl, 71
Basotho, the, 110; as migrant labourers, 116–17, 118
Basuto National Party, 81
Bavin, Bishop Timothy, 92, 97, 104, 106, 107, 133, 218, 219
Beeld, 201
Bennett, Henry, 252
Benoni, 52–4, 55
Benson, Mary, 31 *n*1, 48 *n*7
Beresford, David, 220
Bergquist, Jim, 86, 87, 90
Beukes, Herbert, 194
Beyers Naudé, Rev. Dr C. F. *see* Naudé, Rev. Dr C. F.,
Biko, Steve, 68, 74 *n*10, 100–1; funeral, 115–16, 153; ideology, 74–7; Kentridge, Sydney, 170; murder of, 142, 190; SPRO-CAS, 124
Blackburn, Molly, 232
Black Community Programme, 123
Black Consciousness Movement: history, 73–5; Tutu's reservations, 78; Biko, 100–1; hope in, 102; SPRO-CAS II, 125; 142–3, 217, 233
Black People's Convention, 115, 123
Black Sash, 148, 247, 257
'Black Theology', 82–5, 99
Black Uprooting from 'White' South Africa, 150–1 *n*13
Blakall, Rev. Arthur, 23
Blaxall, Florence, 23, 24
Bletchingley, 61–4, 80, 96
Boesak, Dr Allen, 151, 157, 169,

196, 200; relationship with Tutu, 238; sanctions, 239; USA, 216
Bophuthatswana, 33, 151
Boraine, Dr Alex, 176, 247
Botha, 'Pik', 103, 201
Botha, P. W., 138, 143, 160; commended by Tutu, 161; Eloff Enquiry, 169–70; meets Tutu, 164–6, 228; passports, 189; rebuffs Tutu, 225–6, 227
Botswana, Lesotho and Swaziland, University of, 78
Brandt, Willy, 202
Bretenbach, Breyten, 202
Brink, André, 124
British Broadcasting Corporation (BBC), 157, 188
Broadcasting Corporation, South African *see* South African Broadcasting Corporation
Broederbond, the, 121, 137
Bromley, Kent, 86, 90
Brown, Brian, 123, 267
Brownrigg, Frankie, 93
Brownrigg, Canon Ronald, 59, 62, 65
Buchanan, Dean Duncan (later Bishop), 214, 237
Burnett, Bishop Bill, 126, 246
Bush, George, 189, 224
Buthelezi Commission, 162
Buthelezi, Chief Mangosuthu (Gatsha), 68, 124, 202, 216, 238–9, 247

Cain, Mr E, 173
Canada, *see* Vancouver
Carmichael, Canon Michael, 70, 93
Carmichael, William, 197
Cartwright, Rev. Charles, 90–1
Cason, Dr Walter, 86
Castle, Dean Mervyn, 212, 214
Catholic Church, *see* Roman Catholic Church
Catholic Institute for International Relations (CIIR), 237
Charles, Brother, 72
Chikane, Frank, 244
Chou, Ivy, 87, 89
Christ the King, Church of, 29
Christian Council of South Africa (CCSA), 123

Christian Institute, 121–4
Christian League, 127, 168, 173, 202
Christianity and Crisis, 203 *n*6
Church and Mission (SACC), 147
Church of England Newspaper, 201–2 *n*3
Church Struggle in South Africa, The, 100 *n*7, 122 *n*4, 124 *n*7
Ciskei, the, 162, 166, 209
Citizen, 166 *n*19, 209 *nn*34, 247 *n*6
civil disobedience, 157–8, 169, 170, 226
classification, racial, 31–3
Clayton, Archbishop Geoffrey, 120, 255
Coe, Dr Shoki, 86, 87, 89, 93
Coetzee, Johan, 173
Coggins, Richard, 58–9
Colfe's Grammar School, 90
Collins, Peter, 247
Communism, 164, 173, 234, 235
Community of the Resurrection, 27, 36, 44, 46, 55, 57, 68, 70, 140, 142, 212; Fraternity of, 62
Concord Weekly, 92 *n*18, 98 *nn*3,4
confrontation between Church and State, 125–9, 157, 168, 169
Congress of South African Trade Unions, *see* Cosatu
conscientious objection, 126–7, 164
'contextualisation', 88–9
Contextual Theology, Institute of, 88
Conway, Martin, 133 *n*5, 191–2
Co-operation and Development, Minister of, 151
Cosatu (Congress of South African Trade Unions), 245
Cottesloe Consultation, 120–2, 124
Craig, Gregory, 215–16
Crocker, Dr Chester, 190
Crowther, Bishop, 75–6
Crucible, 142*n*1
Crying in the Wilderness, 36*n*6, 85*n*12, 116*n*16, 231*n*2
Cry the Beloved Country (Paton), 160*n*9, 202
Cull, Rev. Dr Francis, 209
Czechoslovakia, human rights in, 78

Daily Dispatch, 123, 248
Daily Mail, 66 *n*16

Daily News, 248 *n*8
Danish television, *see* Denmark
Davies, Margaret, 212
Dean of King's College, London, *see* Evans, Rev. Sydney
Defiance Campaign 1952, 47–9
de Gruchy, Professor John W., *see* Gruchy, Professor John W. de
de Klerk, F. W., *see* Klerk, F. W. de
Denmark, 158, 184
Dependents' Conference, 148
Development and Service (SACC), 147–8
de Wet, J. J. *see* Wet, J. J. de
Die transvaler, 201
Die Vaderland, 201
disinvestment, *see* foreign investments
Dolinschek, Martin, 129
Domestic Workers and Employers Project, 119
Douglas-Home, Sir Alec and Lady, 75
Driefontein, 151
Drum, 25, 47
Duduza, 219–21
Duncan, Sheena, 148
Dutch Reformed Church (DRC), 35, 61, 117–19, 121, 123, 127, 143, 162, 176, 231, 260

Eastern Province Herald, 248 *n*7
economic sanctions, *see* sanctions
ecumenism, 68–70, 115, 169, 174, 179 *see also* Tutu, ecumenism
Ecunews, 46 *n*2, 115 *n*15, 143, 168 *n*21, 209 *n*2
Edendale School, 40
Education: Bantu Education Act 1955, 39–42, 43, 49, 68; Bantu Education Department, 68; Bantu education schools, burning of, 51; Deputy Minister of, 76, 117–18; *Education for Barbarism*, 33 *n*2; Opportunities Council, 149
Eiselen Commission 1949, 41
Eloff Commission, the, 169–82, 89, 225; evidence to, 21 *n*5, 22 *n*6, 34 *n*4, 46 *n*2, 56 *n*4, 57 *nn*7,8, 61–2 *n*13, 90 *n*19, 115 *n*15
Eloff Report, *see* Eloff Commission

emergency, state of, 51, 221–2, 225, 257, 261
Encounter, 146 *n*8, 173
End Conscription Campaign, 250, 257
England, Tutu in, *see* Bletchingley, Bromley, Golders Green, Grove Park
Enquiry into SACC, 170–81
Episcopal Church of the USA, 189–90
Ethiopia, 88
Ethiopian Church of South Africa, 28
Evans, Bishop Bruce, 208
Evans, Rev. Sydney, 55, 58–9, 60, 62
Ewington, John, 63, 65
Ezenzeleni Blind School, 23, 24

Falwell, Jerry, 194
Federal Theological Seminary (Fedsem), 67–70, 78, 107, 124
Fenhagen, Dean James, 198, 204, 206
Ferrari, Frank, 204, 205, 206, 207
ffrench-Beytagh, Gonville, 96, 97, 106, 120
finance, *see* South African Council of Churches; Tutu, attitude to
Financial Mail, 150
Ford Foundation, 197
foreign investments, 158 *see also* sanctions, economic, 190, 205
Fort Hare University, 50, 68, 70, 72, 75; strike at, 76–7, 99
Franciscans, 140
Freedom Charter 1955, 49, 50, 233
Freedom Day (June 26th), 48
Frelimo, 125, 126
Fund Raising Act, 173, 175
funerals, restrictions on, 222, 252

Gandhi, Indira, 202
General Missionary Conference, 123
General Theological Seminary, New York, 198, 204
Ghetto Act 1950, *see* Group Areas Act 1950
Goad, Sarah and Tim, 65
Golders Green, 55, 61, 63
Gordimer, Nadine, 202

Gospel Defence League, 210
Gqubule, Simon, 69
Group Areas Act 1950, 32, 53, 94;
    defied by Edward Kennedy, 216
Gruchy, Professor John de, 85
Guardian, 220 *n*11, 222 *n*13

Hail Stick of Redemption (praise-
    song), 12–13, 256
Halsey, Rev. John, 61
*Hammering Swords into
    Ploughshares*, 231 *n*1
Hanson, Rev. Professor, 108
    *nn*3,5; 110 *n*7
Harare (Salisbury), 88
harassment campaigns: Alexandra,
    228; hate and threats, 167–8;
    ignoring Nobel Prize, 199–202;
    official silence, 210; SACC by
    government, 127; SACC and Tutu,
    128, 231, 250, 257; *see also* South
    African Broadcasting Corporation
Harvard Gazette, 186 *n*6
hate campaigns; *see* harassment
Hawke, Bob, 202
Hawthorn's School, 64
Hertzog, General, 19
Holy Cross Church, Soweto, 212
Holy Land, The, 71
Home, Lord, *see* Douglas-Home,
    Sir Alec
homelands (bantustans), 33, 103,
    117, 149, 151, 162
Hope and Suffering (Tutu's Address
    to Deacons), 54 *n*2, 82 *nn*2,3 83
    *n*4, 84 *n*7, 96 *n*2, 99 *n*6, 101 *n*8,
    103–4 *nn*13–16, 132 *nn*1,2, 150
    *n*11, 161 *n*12, 164 *n*17, 275
horseback travelling in Lesotho, 109
Howard, Dr William, 195, 196
Huddleston, Archbishop Trevor,
    24, 27, 28, 35, 37, 40, 43, 49, 95,
    120, 256
Hurley, Archbishop Denis, 120

Ikageng Women's Club, 134
Immortality Act, 31
Independent African Church, 29
Indian Council, South African, *see*
    South African Indian Council
indigenisation, *see* contextualisation

'Information Affair, The', 143,
    156, 180
Information, South African
    Department of, *see* South African
    Department of Information
Inkatha, 238 *see also* Buthelezi,
    Mangosuthu (Gatsha)
Inter-Church Aid, 148
International Press Institute,
    Vienna, 222
Islam, Tutu's study of, 60–1, 71, 72
I Write What I Like (Biko), 74
    *n*10, 76, *n*13

Jabavu, Professor, 80
Jackson, Jesse, 196, 204
Johannesburg, 15, 48, 52, 55, 56,
    67, 152; Rivonia, 73, 92–105;
    Alexandra, 156
Johannesburg, Bishops of, *see* Bavin,
    Timothy; Reeves, Ambrose;
    Stradling, Leslie; Desmond Tutu
Johannesburg, Deans of, *see* Bavin,
    Timothy; Buchanan, Duncan;
    Castle, Mervyn; ffrench-Beytagh,
    Gonville; Tutu, Desmond
John Paul II, Pope, 187–8
Jonathan, Chief Leabua, 81, 107
Joost de Blank, Archbishop, 61, 255
Jordan, Vernon, 195, 196
Joseph, Helen, 50, 97, 98, 133
    *n*4, 254
Journal of Religious Thought, see
    Religious Thought, J. of
Justice and Society, 147–8

Kaffir Boy (Mathabane), 227 *n*15
Kairos, 143
Kairos Document, the, 242–4
Kennedy, Senator Edward, 215–18,
    233, 253
Kentridge, Sydney, 170–1
Kenyon, Martin, 57, 62, 67, 70 *n*4,
    75 *n*11, 76 *n*12
'Kernel of Apartheid', *see* Group
    Areas Act 1950, 32
Killarney Golf Course,
    Johannesburg, 25
King, Coretta Scott, 202, 253
King, Very Rev. E. L., 247, 253,
    259, 260

King, Martin Luther, 124, 196, 223
King's College, London, 55, 58–61, 71, 86, 167
King's College Newsletter, 56 n5, 58 n9
Kinnock, Neil, 202
Klerk, F. W. de, 201, 268
Klerksdorp, 20
Kliptown, 49, 50
Koornhof, Dr, 161
Kotzé, Theo, 123
Krugersdorp, 24, 35, 43
Kwazakhele Rugby Union, 134

Lambert, Melanie, 62, 64
Lambert, Uvedale, 62–3
Lambeth Conference 1978, 182–3; Planning session for 1988, 215, 222
Land Act 1913, 149
Langa township, 51
Language as an issue, 37–8
Law and Order, Minister of, *see* le Grange, Louis
Lee, Rev. Peter, 208, 209
le Grange, Louis, 161, 175
Lelyveld, Joseph, 166
le Roux, J. N., 41
Lesotho, 105, 106–19
Lesotho, University of, *see* Botswana, Lesotho and Swaziland University
Let My People Go (Luthuli), 40 n8
liberation, 159–61, 179, 180, 221, 267; *see also* liberation theology
liberation theology, 82, 85, 98, 122, 180; Latin American, 90, 99; *see also* African theology; Black theology
Lieres, Advocate K. S. P. O. von, 170
'Liturgy' 75, 96
Lovedale College, 68
Lundie, Ruth, 70, 81
Luthuli, Chief Albert, 40, 48, 50, 68, 201
Lydbury North, 57

Mabija, Phakamile, 267
Macmillan, Harold, 51
Macomber, Caroline, 194
Madibane, Mr, 26, 30

'Madibane High' School (Western High), 35
Makhene, Pastor, 29, 43
Makhulu, Walter, 63, 111
Mamohato Queen of Lesotho, 107
Mandela Nelson, 68, 73, 113, 153, 164, 218, 261, 268
Mandela, Winnie, 216, 254, 258
Masemola, Fr. Sipho, 46, 213
Maseru, 107, 109, 140, 185
Mathabane, Mark, *see Kaffir Boy*
Matlhare, Kuku, 20, 25
Matthews, Professor Z. K., 50, 68
Maund, Bishop John, 118
Mazibuko, Sophie, 130, 133–4, 38–9
Mbatha, Elphas, 145–6
Mbiti, John, 113
media campaigns, 115; *see also* South African Broadcasting Corporation
Meer, Professor Fatima, 124
Merchant of Venice, The (Shakespeare), 117
Message to the People of South Africa (SACC), 124, 155, 169
Mhkize, Saul, 151 n14
migrant labour, 116–17
Mills, Warrant-Officer A. J., 177
mission education, 40
Mixed Marriages Act, Prohibition of, *see* Prohibition of Mixed Marriages Act
Mogopa, 151–2
Mohutsioa, Zakes, 43, 71, 111
Mokoatla, Canon, 52, 53, 54
Mokoena, Bishop Isaac, 145–7, 238
Mokuku, Philip, 118, 119
Moloto, Justice, 75, 76, 77, 116
Mondale, Walter, 202
Moroka, Dr James, 48, 68
Morris, Colin, 268–70
Moselane, Rev. Geoffrey, 218
Moshoeshoe II, King of Lesotho, 107
Mosley, Nicholas, 57
Motjuwadi, Stanley, 25 n9, 26 n10, 27 nn11,12, 37
Motlana, Dr Ntatho, 101, 158, 160, 254
Motlana, Sally, 30
Moulder, Shirley, 46 n1, 72 n8
Mozambique, *see* Frelimo; Nkomati Accord, the

Mphahlele, Ezekiel, 30
Mqotsi, Mr and Mrs, 135
Mugabe, Robert, 185
Mulder, Dr Connie, 143, 156
Munsieville, 24, 27, 29, 30, 36
Munsieville High School, 37–9, 43, 44
Mxenge, Mlungiso, 161

Nash, Dr Margaret, 29, 148, 150
Natal Witness, 247 *n*4
National Action Council of the Congress of the People, 49
National Front, the, 168
National Party, 31, 34, 39, 123, 142, 190; 1987 Election, 260
National service, 164
National Union of South African Students (NUSAS), 122
Native Affairs, Department of, 41, 42, 44
Native Laws Amendment Bill, 44
Naudé, Rev. C. F. Beyers, 121, 122, 123, 200, 203, 216, 223, 227, 254
Naught for Your Comfort, (Huddleston), 35 *n*5, 40 *n*7
Nazism, comparison with: apartheid, 122, 188, 190, 203; segregation, 22; Dr Verwoerd a sympathiser, 41; Terre Blanche, Eugene, 49
Ndwande, Bishop Sigisbert, 209, 219
'necklace' killings, 219, 241
Nederduitse Gereformeerde Kerk in Afrika (NGA), 127
Nederduitse Hervormde Kerk (NHK), 121
Nestor, Donald, 110
newspapers, Afrikaans, 201; *see also* under individual names: *Die Vaderland, Beeld, Die Transvaler*
newspapers, South African, 94; *see also* under individual names
New York Review of Books, 23 *n*7
New York Times, 166–7 *n*201, 206
Nkoane, Bishop Simeon, 209, 219, 220, 221
Nkomati Accord, the, 205
Nkosi, Connie, 212
Nkwe, Archbishop David, 46, 47, 94, 209, 238
Nobel Peace Prize, 15, 198–207, 239

Nuttall, Bishop Michael, 208, 246

Observer, 120, 171 *n*1, 196 *n*13, 245 *n*1
Oram, Bishop Kenneth, 220
Ordination of women, 183

Pan-Africanist Congress, 36, 51, 73, 125; Poqo, 73
Parishioner, 183 *n*3
Parrinder, Professor Geoffrey, 58
'passbook' document, 22, 56, 67
Pass Laws, 142, 148, 156, 165, 203
Paton, Alan, 160, 202
Patriotic Front (Zimbabwe), 125
Pawson, Fr Godfrey, 44
Penthouse, 194–5 *n*12
Pitje, Godfrey, 43, 52, 53, 212
Pityana, Barney, 75–7, 112
Plural Affairs, Department of *see* Bantu Affairs, Department of
police, 51, 73, 77, 88, 115; deaths in custody, 142; duty, 161; Eloff evidence, 179; 'God's children', 138; Jan Smuts Airport, 199; Johannesburg, 219–2; Kennedy visit, 217; Maseru Bridge, 185; Mogopa, 151–2; Soweto funeral, 252; Tutu defends black, 166; prays for, 116; Vendaland, 139–40
Pope John Paul II, *see* John Paul II, Pope
Population Registration Act 1950, 33, 34, 142
Poqo, *see* Pan-Africanist Congress
Potter, Tim, 144–5
President's Council Report, May 1982, 163
Press, *see* newspapers
Pretoria (government), 159, 165, 170, 194, 238, 242, 253, 261; *see also* National Party
Pretoria News, 249n
Pretoria Press Club, 164
Progressive Federal Party, 225, 247, 260
Prohibition of Mixed Marriages Act, 31
Pro Veritate, 98–9 *n*3, 121, 123

Qoboza, Percy, 123, 254

Quail Commission, 162

Race Relations, Institute of South
    African, *see* South African
    Institute of Race Relations
Race Relations News, 102 *nn*10,11,12
racism, religious, 44, 96, 138
Radcliffe (blind, deaf and dumb),
    23–4
radio and television, South African,
    see South African Broadcasting
    Corporation
Rakale, Fr Leo, 92, 93
Ramphele, Mamphela, 100, 116
Randall, Dr Peter, 124
Rand Daily Mail, 185 *n*4, 189 *n*9
Ransom, Charles, 86
Ravensbourne School for Girls, 90
Reagan, Ronald, 190, 202, 205–6,
    230, 250, 251
reconciliation, 47, 160, 161, 233, 268,
    270; National Initiative for, 235–6;
    see also Tutu as reconciler
Rees, John, 126, 127, 143, 144, 152;
    Eloff Commission, 177–8
Reeves, Bishop Ambrose, 52, 53, 57,
    120, 210
Regina Mundi Church, Soweto, 106,
    166, 216
Religious Thought, Journal of,
    113–4 *n*14
'reserves', *see* homelands
resettlement camps, 151–2
*Resistance and Hope: South African
    Essays in Honour of Beyers
    Naudé?*, 85 *n*13, 124 *n*10
Resurrection, Community of, *see*
    Community of the Resurrection
Return of the Amasi Bird, 19–201
Rhodesia, *see* Zimbabwe
Rhodesia Christian Group, 210
Rhoodie, Dr, 156
Rietfontein Hospital, 28
Riotous Assemblies Act, 167
'Rivonia Trial', 73
Robben Island, 44, 73, 148
Rockwell, Rev. Hays, 191, 196, 206
Roelofse, Eugene, 145–6
Roma, 78, 79–86
Roman Catholic Church, 143,
    189, 209

Roodeport, 23, 29
Rosettenville Conference, 169
Royal Commonwealth Society, 183–4
Runcie, Dr Robert (Archbishop of
    Canterbury), 174–5, 185, 199, 247,
    254, 257–9
Russell, Rev. David, 134

St Alban's Church, Benoni, 52
St Alban's Curch, Golders Green,
    55, 61
St Ansgar's Mission, 145
St Augustine's Church, Bromley,
    90–1
St Augustine's, Soweto, 133, 200
St Bede's, Umtata, 69, 70
St Benedict's House, 52
St James's Cathedral, Maseru, 109
St Mary the Virgin, Bletchingley, 65
St Mary's Cathedral, Johannesburg,
    54, 96–9, 109
St Paul's College, Grahamstown, 45,
    71
St Peter's College, Rosettenville,
    40, 44, 45, 46, 50; moved to
    Alice, 67–71
Salisbury (Rhodesia), *see* Harare
    (Zimbabwe)
Sampson, Anthony, 47–8 *nn*5,8
sanctions; diplomatic, 261; economic,
    188, 195, 197, 202, 239–40, 257
Sapsezian, Aharon, 87, 90
Schlebusch Commission, 122
Scott, Rev. Michael, 120
Scouts, Boy, 25; *see also* Mohutsioa,
    Zakes
Sebe, Chief Lennon, 209
*Second National Consultative
    Conference of the ANC*, 234 *n*4
security forces, South African;
    see police
segregation, 149–50
Seek, 236*n*7, 267*n*7
Sekgaphane, Fr, 29–30, 43
Sekgaphane, Thembi, 130, 131, 212
Seremane, Joe, 39, 44, 206
Setiloane, Professor Gabriel, 112
Sharpeville, 51–2, 73, 120, 218–19
Shaw, Rev. Fred, 127, 202
Shenxane, Leah, *see* Tutu, Leah
Shosana, Maki, 220–1

Sibiya, Joe, 25, 26–7, 30
Simon, Professor Ulrich, 58
Sirkassian, Archbishop, 94
Sisulu, Albertina, 258
Slabbert, Dr van Zyl, 124, 202
Small, Professor Adam, 225
Sobukwe, Robert Mangaliso, 36, 68, 153, 238
Society of Friends, 143
Sophiatown, 24, 25, 26, 27, 28, 34, 46
South African Broadcasting Corporation, 16, 57, 159, 168, 180, 201, 222, 255
South African Christian Assembly, 167
South African Council of Churches (SACC), 120–32, 136, 138, 143–54; Eloff Commission of Enquiry, 69–81; Tutu as General Secretary, 156–68
South African Council of Churches Accounting Services (SACCAS), 144–5
South African Indian Council, 47
South African Department of Information, 142–3
South African Institute of Race Relations, 102, 122
South African Students Organisation (SASO), 74, 115, 123
South African Theological College for Independent Churches (SATCIC), 145
South Coast Sun, 210*n*8
South Park, Bletchingley, 62
Sovern, Dr Michael I., 186–7
Sowetan newspaper, 200, 208
Soweto, 16, 84, 94–5, 97, 101; massacre, 104–5; St Augustine's, 134–5; Tutu defends man, 166; Regina Mundi, 166, 216, 224, 226, 236, 252, 256, 253
Soweto Civic Association, 158, 160
Sparks, Allistair, 171, 196, 258
Spear of the Nation, the, *see* Umkhonto we Sizwe
Spong, Bishop Jack, 184
Stanton, Fr Timothy, 47
Star, 163 *n*16, 253 *n*12
Star City, 247 *n*3

Stellenbosch, University of, 163
Stevenson, Matt, 152
Steyn Commission on the press, 170
Storey, C. K., 120
Storey, Elizabeth, 130, 131, 178
Storey, Peter, 128, 137, 139, 146, 178, 180–1, 187, 188, 228, 251
Stradling, Bishop Leslie, 92, 210
??????, Lesley, 210
Struggle for a Birthright, The, 31 *n*1, 48 *n*7
Struggle is My Life, The (Mandela), 73 *n*9, 113 *n*12
Strydom, Captain, 41
Stubbs, Fr Aelred, 45, 53, 55, 57, 59, 60, 69, 71, 72, 73, 77, 88, 92, 100, 107, 119
Student Christian Movement, 143
Study Project on Christianity in Apartheid Society (SPRO-CAS), 124–5
Stutterheim, 73
Sullivan Principles, the, 195, 239
Sunday Express, 137
Sunday Star, 209 *n*5, 234 *n*5, 248 *n*10
Sunday Times, 202, 209 *n*1, 235 *n*6
Suppression of Communism Act, 48
Sutton, Rt Rev. Keith, 221
Suzman, Helen, 117, 136, 185, 202, 239, 254
Swart, C. R., 41
Swart, Rev. T. M., 209
Switzerland, 187–8

Tabatha, I. B., 33 *n*2
Tambo, Oliver, 57, 68, 202, 257, 261, 267
television and radio, South African, *see* South African Broadcasting Corporation
Terrorism Act, 158
Thatcher, Margaret, 222, 250
'Theological Education by Extension', 90
Theological Education Fund, 68, 88–93; mandates, 89–90, 95, 101
Theology, 44, 45, 55, 59, 68, 71; contextual, 88–9; in Eloff Commission, 172, 173, 176, 179; and politics, 122; *see also* African theology; Black theology; *Church*

Index

and Mission; Kairos Document, the; Liberation theology
Thokoza, 53
Thompson, Rev. Douglas, 120
Thompson, Bishop Jim (Stepney), 215
Thorne, John, 167
Tillich, Paul, 71
Time, 221 n12
trades unions, 156–7, 235
Trans-Africa group, 204
Transkei, 149
'Treason Trials', 50
Trueman, Fr, 55
Treurnicht, Dr Andries, 201
Tsebe, Canon John, 35, 43
Tumahole, funeral at, 222
Tutu, Aletha Matlhare, 20, 24, 25, 30, 204
Tutu, Desmond Mpilo: family background, 20; birth, 20; childhood and schools, 21–7; Matriculation, 30; tuberculosis, 27–30; teacher training, 34; BA, 35; teaching, 35, 37–9, 41–2; marriage, 36–7; priesthood training, 43–7; deacon, 47, 52–3; children, 52–3; curate, 52; King's College, 55; B. D. degree, 59; Master's degree, 66; curate at Golders Green, 55–6; Bletchingley, 61–6; theologian at St Peter's College, Alice, 67; Roma, Lesotho, 79–85; TEF Asst. Director, 86–91; Dean of Johannesburg, 92–105; Bishop of Lesotho, 106–19; Gen. Sec SACC, 118–97; Third Order St Francis, 140–1; first meeting P. W. Botha, 164–6; Eloff Commission, 170–81; Nobel Peace Prize, 198, 207; Bishop of Johannesburg, 208–44; Archbishop Cape Town, 245–62; President All-Africa Conference Churches, 266
Characteristics: bitterness, lack of, 58, 67, 89, 204, 257; courage (especially moral), 27, 93, 154; (especially physical), 38, 77, 166, 218–21, 227, 240, 245; ecumenism, 29, 65, 115, 133; food preferences,

26, 131; generosity, 64, 88, 212, 259; global view, 97, 113, 128–9, 138; humility, 45, 132, 180, 207; humour, 27, 63, 98, 131–2, 156, 189–90, 192, 229, 251; leadership, 30, 93, 100, 147, 148, 153, 155, 208, 213, 218, 245; 'star quality', 147, 155; 'ubuntu', 112; vulnerability, 131–2, 136, 146, 214
As administrator, 88, 147, 213; apartheid, effect on his personality, 89; effect on residence, 94–5; prophecies concerning, 155–8; P. W. Botha, 165; views on (Eloff), 172; is evil, 182; in Oslo, 206–7; as Archbishop Cape Town, 257, 260; as 'boss', 89, 130–2; effect on others; 70–1, 77, 96, 133–7, 190, 237–8; see also Bletchingley; as family man: 79–80; finance, attitude to: pocket money, 25, 60; SACC, 144–7, 152–3, 158, 177, house-buying, 175; as fund-raiser, 196, Endowment Fund, 211; personal, 212; diocesan, 213; foreign creditors, 223; see also Eloff Commission; as negotiator: 165–6, 233; pastimes; boxing, 30; cricket 57; music, 131; jogging, 131, 139; pastoral care; 54, 72, 78, 90, 108–11, 118, 132–7, 192–3; of clergy, 213–14; as Archbishop, 259; as politician: 99–101; tightrope, 99, 230–1, 241, 242; initiative, 102–4, 114–16, 137, 162, 218, 232; weakness, 235–6; power, problem of, 110–11; as prophet: 155, 159, 184–5, 224, 237, 260; prayer: 46, 91, 93, 139–40; intercession book, 110; for police, 116; international 291; SACC, 138; and driving, 139–40, WCC Assembly, 191–2; as reconciler, 98–9, 143, 160, 161, 164, 166, 214, 220, 230, 231, 233, 244, 245, 259; spirituality, 46, 91, 93; African, 112; 154, 179; centrality of, 211; as teacher, 37–9, 42, 43; as theologian: on African and Black theology, 113; of migrant labour, 117; in Eloff Commission Enquiry,

176, 179–80, Kairos Document, 242–4; *as traveller*, 187–97, 215, 223; violence, views on, 240–2, 245; youth, concern for, 101, 199

Tutu, Gloria Lindiwe, 20, 24, 36, 254

Tutu Leah, 36, 37, 52–3, 56, 63, 64, 70, 71, 90, 92, 106, 107, 119, 155, 167, 199, 246, 254

Tutu, Mpho, 60, 63, 70, 80, 90, 92, 99, 199, 254

Tutu, Nontomdi Naomi, 53, 56, 63, 80, 90, 92, 199, 254

Tutu, Sylvia Funeka, 20, 37

Tutu, Thandeka Theresa, 52, 56, 63, 80, 90, 92, 119, 254

Tutu, Trevor Thamsanqua, 52, 56, 63, 64, 80, 90, 93, 254

Tutu, Zachariah, 20, 22, 24, 25, 28

Tweedy, Fr Mark, 70–1

Twelfth Night (Shakespeare), 72 *n*7

Twenty-third Psalm, parody of, 19

'ubuntu', 112, 269

Uganda, 88, 183

Uitenhage massacre, 218

Umkhonto we Sizwe (Spear of the Nation), 73

United Christian Action, 210, 255

United Democratic Front (UDF), 217, 218, 232–4, 238, 245, 258

United Nations, 31, 185, 188; Security Council, 204

United States of America, 184, 198, 189–90, 192, 223

University Christian Movement, 73, 122

Urban Areas Act, 68

Vancouver, 191–2

Vaughan, Dan, 131, 139, 171, 181, 188, 199, 206, 219

Ventersdorp, 21, 28, 30

Verwoerd, Dr, 23, 41, 121

Villa-Vicencio, Professor Charles, 202, 230, 231

'Vision for Humanity, A' (Address), 20–1 *n*2

Vlok, Adriaan, 227

Voortrekker Church, *see*

Nederduitse Hervormde Kerk

Vorster, John, 102–4, 124, 125, 143, 160

Waite, Terry, 174, 199, 206, 254, 256

Walesa, Lech, 201, 202

Walker, Bishop John, 190, 254

Walshe, Peter, 122

Ward, Betty, 86, 186 *n*7

Washington Post, 194 *n*11, 244 *n*13

Watchman, The, 214

Weekend Argus, 225 *n*16, 247 *n*2

Western Cape, University of, 261–3

Western High School, Sophiatown, 275

Westminster Abbey, Tutu's sermon in, 188

West Rand Administration Board, 156

Wet, J. J. de, 76

Williams, Canon, 195–6, 197

Wilson, Professor Francis, 133 *n*3

Wilson, Professor Monica, 61

Wing, Rev. Joseph (Joe), 167

Witwatersrand, University of, 30, 34, 36, 42; blazer, 135; Columbia doctorate at, 187; Conference on Education at, 226, 236; Tutu's 1980 peroration at, 159–60

Woking, retreat in, 93

Women, ordination of, *see* ordination of women

Woods, Donald, 123

World, The, 123

World Council of Churches (WCC), 55, 120, 125–7, 170, 191

Worldview, 113 *n*13

Xuma, Dr, 34

Yengwa, M. B., 33 *n*3

Zaire, 88

Zimbabwe, 88, 125, 126, 129, 185

Zulu, Bishop Alpheus, 43, 92

Zulu, Fr Laurence, 45

Zweledinga resettlement camp, 149–51